Creative Strategy in Advertising

Fifth Edition

Titles of Interest from the
Wadsworth Series in Journalism and Mass Communications

Advertising and Marketing to the New Majority: A Case Study Approach
Gail Baker Woods

Communications Media in the Information Society
Joseph Straubhaar and Robert LaRose

Communications Research: Strategies and Sources, 3rd edition
Rebecca B. Rubin, Alan M. Rubin, and Linda J. Piele

Creative Editing for Print Media
Dorothy A. Bowles, Diane L. Borden, and William Rivers

Design Principles for Desktop Publishing, 2nd edition
Tom Lichty

The Interplay of Influence: News, Advertising, Politics, and the Mass Media, 3rd edition
Kathleen Hall Jamieson and Karlyn Kohrs Campbell

Introduction to Photography, 4th edition
Marvin J. Rosen and Dave DeVries

Mass Media Research: An Introduction, 4th edition
Roger D. Wimmer and Joseph R. Dominick

Media/Impact: An Introduction to Mass Media, Updated 2nd edition
Shirley Biagi

Mediamerica/Mediaworld: Form, Content, and Consequence of Mass Communication, 5th edition
Edward Jay Whetmore

Public Relations Cases, 3rd edition
Jerry A. Hendrix

Public Relations Writing: Form and Style, 4th edition
Doug Newsom and Bob Carrell

The Search: Information Gathering for the Mass Media
Lauren Kessler and Duncan McDonald

This Is PR: The Realities of Public Relations, 5th edition
Doug Newsom, Alan Scott, and Judy VanSlyke Turk

Visual Communication: Images with Messages
Paul Martin Lester

When Words Collide: A Media Writer's Guide to Grammar and Style, 3rd edition
Lauren Kessler and Duncan McDonald

Women and the Media: Content, Careers, and Criticism
Cynthia M. Lont

Creative Strategy in Advertising

Fifth Edition

A. Jerome Jewler
College of Journalism and Mass Communications
University of South Carolina

Wadsworth Publishing Company
I(T)P™ An International Thomson Publishing Company

Belmont ♦ Albany ♦ Bonn ♦ Boston ♦ Cincinnati ♦ Detroit ♦ London ♦ Madrid ♦ Melbourne ♦
Mexico City ♦ New York ♦ Paris ♦ San Francisco ♦ Singapore ♦ Tokyo ♦ Toronto ♦ Washington

Communications Editor: Todd R. Armstrong
Editorial Assistant: Laura Murray
Production Services Coordinator: Debby Kramer
Production: Tina Samaha
Print Buyer: Karen Hunt
Permissions Editor: Bob Kauser
Designer: Ellen Pettengell
Copy Editor: Tina Samaha
Cover Designer: Kathleen Heafey/Bay Graphics Design
Compositor: G&S Typesetters, Inc.
Printer: Quebecor Printing Book Group/Hawkins
Cover Printer: Phoenix Color Corporation

Printed in the United States of America
1 2 3 4 5 6 7 8 9 10—01 00 99 98 97 96 95

For more information, contact Wadsworth Publishing Company:

Wadsworth Publishing Company
10 Davis Drive
Belmont, California 94002, USA

International Thomson Publishing Europe
Berkshire House 168-173
High Holborn
London, WC1V 7AA, England

Thomas Nelson Australia
102 Dodds Street
South Melbourne 3205
Victoria, Australia

Nelson Canada
1120 Birchmount Road
Scarborough, Ontario
Canada M1K 5G4

International Thomson Editores
Campos Eliseos 385, Piso 7
Col. Polanco
11560 México D.F. México

International Thomson Publishing GmbH
Königswinterer Strasse 418
53227 Bonn, Germany

International Thomson Publishing Asia
221 Henderson Road
#05-10 Henderson Building
Singapore 0315

International Thomson Publishing Japan
Hirakawacho Kyowa Building, 3F
2-2-1 Hirakawacho
Chiyoda-ku, Tokyo 102, Japan

Library of Congress Cataloging-in-Publication Data

Jewler, A. Jerome.
Creative strategy in advertising / A. Jerome Jewler. — 5th ed.
p. cm.
Includes bibliographical references and index.
ISBN 0-534-25260-5 (pbk.)
1. Advertising copy. 2. Advertising layout and typography. I. Title.
HF5825.J46 1994
659.13'2—dc20 94-34874

To Belle, Melissa, Scott, Maki, and Mom—who was born in Russia, who lived and died in Washington D.C., and who would have been thrilled to see this book appearing in yet another edition

About the Author

A. JEROME JEWLER is a tenured full professor in the College of Journalism and Mass Communications, University of South Carolina, Columbia, where he teaches undergraduate and graduate courses in advertising. He is a graduate of the University of Maryland, with a B.S. in Journalism and an M.A. in American Civilization. He worked as an advertising copywriter before beginning his teaching career in 1972.

He taught briefly at the University of Tennessee, spent a summer with McCann-Erickson, Ltd., London, on a visiting professor fellowship, spent another summer in research at the Center for Advertising History at the Museum of American History and Technology of the Smithsonian Institution, and still another summer teaching creative strategy to nineteen American students in England.

He previously served as co-director for instruction and faculty development for the USC freshman seminar and has led workshops on teaching at the University of Hawaii, the University of Prince Edward Island (Canada), the University of Tennessee at Chattanooga, the Art Institute of Houston, and The George Washington University. He and John Gardner are the co-editors of *Your College Experience, College Is Only the Beginning,* and *Step by Step to College Success.* He has an avid interest in film and theatre, and has performed in a number of community theatre productions.

Contents

Preface

If you ask what's changed about advertising since the last edition of this book appeared just a few years ago, you'll have to read more of this book than the preface! In the last three years, marketers and advertisers have embraced a whole new world of ideas, employed new communications technologies, and realized the need to build lasting relationships with the most diverse group of consumers in modern times. The economic crunch of the '90s has produced consumers who are skeptical of product claims, who doubt they'll ever have it as good as their parents, and who want value for every dollar they spend. To complicate matters more for the advertiser, consumers may be white, African-American, Asian-American, Hispanic-American, a Boomer, a Generation X-er, or a 50-plus. And if that were not enough diversity, advertisers are realizing that each market segment contains people with highly different lifestyles and values. One couple in their late fifties may enjoy a sedentary life, while another may work out regularly at the local athletic club. One African-American family may place a high value on entertainment, while another spends its income on things for the home.

This new edition reflects the diversity in people and technology that have brought sweeping changes to the advertising industry and had an impact on the creative process in advertising, which is what this book is about.

In the very first chapter, you'll learn about many things that are changing the face of advertising: new media, new narrower targeting of audiences, new generations of consumers with dramatically different reactions to commercial messages, new concerns about privacy as the direct response market grows at a superhuman rate, new relationships the smarter advertisers are building with consumers so as to keep them loyal to their brands and services, a new respect for the consumer as a thinking human being as the vast baby boom generation enters middle age—all this and more.

Chapter 2 is a general introduction to the advertising creative process, while in Chapter 3 you will find a new guide to digging for the information you'll need before you can begin the creative process.

Chapter 4 brings you one step closer to writing advertising with the all-important concept of strategy. You'll take the information you have gathered, add your own marketing insight, and write a strategy statement that forms the basis for your creative plan. Chapter 5 shows you how to make the leap from strategy to execution in print and electronic media.

The next five chapters take you through the specific methods for advertising in the traditional major media. Chapter 6 is on writing for print. Chapter 7 is on designing for print. Chapter 8 discusses how computer design has changed not only the look of advertising, but added speed and flexibility to the production process. Chapter 9 on radio and Chapter 10 on television complete this segment.

Beginning with Chapter 11, which traces the emergence of direct marketing as a strong new force in the advertising arena, you will explore the special markets of advertising. Following direct marketing, Chapter 12 explains the difference between writing retail advertising for stores and national advertising for products and services. Chapter 13 provides information on reaching a minority market, while Chapter 14 addresses the growing importance of the 50-plus market and Chapter 15 notes the special peculiarities of writing for the business-to-business market. Finally, Chapter 16 takes a more personal note to tell how to present your creative work as well as how to prepare yourself for the job search in ad creative.

Spaced between the chapters are ten creative spots, explaining how such advertisers as Coca-Cola, Bali, United Air Lines, Cover Girl, and *Mother Jones* magazine achieved their creative goals with advertising that struck a nerve with the consumer target. You will find a slew of new ideas for writing assignments in the revised appendix, including a final project assignment.

My thanks to Van Kornegay for updating the chapter on computers, to Bonnie Drewniany for her new chapter on the over-50 market, in addition to her updated retail chapter, and to Sharon Brock for her new chapter on minority consumers.

Thanks also to the following reviewers:

Peggy Kreshel, University of Georgia; Nancy Mitchell, University of Nebraska; Barbara Mueller, San Diego State University; James Tsao, University of Wisconsin-Oshkosh; Suzette Heiman, University of Missouri; Jon Shidler, Southern Illinois University at Carbondale; Kevin Keenan, University of Maryland.

No doubt advertising is a business in a constant state of flux. What doesn't change, however, is the creative process. It still begins with information, continues with insight, and demands hard work and critical thinking along the way. While obviously challenging, the road to creating successful advertising can be filled with excitement and a profound feeling of having done something in a distinctive way that possibly no other individual could duplicate. Work hard, have fun, and never forget that, while a dull idea probably won't catch anybody's eye, "clever" in advertising is never enough. It has to sell, too.

A. Jerome Jewler
Columbia, South Carolina

Creative Strategy in Advertising

Fifth Edition

Steps in the Advertising Creative Process

Information Gathering

Planning the Strategy

Exploring Creative Options

From Information and Strategy to Tactics

Revisions, Revisions, Revisions

Presentation of Finished Ads and Commercials

More Revisions

Etc., Etc.

CHAPTER 1

A 1990s Framework for Creating Advertising

Good advertising makes relevant and unexpected connections in order to build a relationship between a brand and a prospect. As you read the following headline ideas, jot down what is relevant, what is unexpected, and what you believe the relationship to be. We'll get back to this idea later.

If you think Paris is sophisticated, wait'll you see Pittsburgh.

(ad tells potential visitors and corporations about Pittsburgh's rebirth as a cultural, business, and transportation center.)

Darlene and Tom Robinson were run off the highway, rolled their car, and took the rest of the day off.

(ad for the Saturn automobile, using real people and real events to emphasize positive benefits of owning one.)

SIMPLE INSTRUCTIONS
FOR CHANGING YOUR
SPARE TIRE.

(for Nordic Track exercise machines.)

He hasn't missed a day of work in ten years. Without insurance, he can't afford to get sick.

(announcing a new opportunity for uninsured people.)

It brings a lot to the party. It'll even bring the party.

(the Accord EX Wagon.)

After A Day Of Competition,
You Deserve A Hotel That Has None.

It's what Shakespeare would have used on a flight to the coast.

(the IBM laptop.)

THIS SEASON WE'LL POISON A VIOLINIST, CREATE A MONSTER, AND WATCH A CATERPILLAR TURN INTO A CHICKEN.

(Scientific American PBS program . . . the concert violinist injected with poison to relieve a muscle disorder, making movie monsters, and the caterpillar which screams for help when attacked.)

From here, you can easily take your business in any direction.

(Essex House, Hotel Nikko, New York.)

This winter surround yourself with warmth. And our weather isn't bad either.

(Ritz-Carlton Hotel, Naples.)

Rent Mother Nature.
Lease a sugar maple tree or sap bucket for one year.

Come to New Hampshire this winter and we'll make you feel good inside and out.

Great headline ideas, but what makes them so? What made them interesting to read? What were the writers trying to do? Why didn't the writer who penned "Lease a sugar maple tree or sap bucket for one year" simply leave it at that? Why did she add "Rent Mother Nature"? What does Shakespeare, for goodness sake, have to do with an IBM laptop computer? Paris with Pittsburgh? Why would Saturn tell you that one of their owners rolled their car? Why did Nordic Track refer to your "spare tire" instead of your gut?

Remember what we said at the start of this book? It's worth repeating: good advertising makes relevant and unexpected connections in order to build a relationship between the brand and the prospect. What do we mean by a relevant connection? That's easy to explain. Any good ad begins with a strategy, as we will soon learn, designed to cause the desired audience to feel positively toward the product or service or idea being offered. If we were IBM, selling the idea of a computer that could go practically anywhere, we'd probably try to present the product in situations where you couldn't take just any computer—on a flight to the coast, for example. But other companies make laptops that are just as portable. Sad to say, most brands are very much like most other brands. That's where the unexpected connection becomes a must. Note that the headline above doesn't say, "It's what the smart person takes on a trip to the coast," but claims instead:

It's what Shakespeare would have used on a flight to the coast.

That's unexpected. That's also relevant. They have to work together, and when they do, great advertising can happen.

What about "building a relationship between the brand and the prospect?" In some instances, the relationship may simply be the transmittal of positive information to the prospect in a clever way that entertains as it informs, the result being a positive feeling toward the brand. Today, most marketers are interested in building relationships that are more lasting, and they do this in a number of ways: by relating their brand to an interest or cause shared by the prospect (sponsoring an environmental cause if prospects tend to value such actions, or offering catalogs of merchandise that support consumer interests, such as a manufacturer of dog food for hunting dogs offering hunting clothing and gear for the hunter), and by maintaining and updating databases of attractive market segments for future messages and offers.

Advertising Stays the Same and Keeps Changing

When the first edition of this book was published in 1981, who would have guessed how advertising would change in little over a decade?

The economic crunch of the past several years has done more than create a scarcity of jobs in our profession. It has also made consumers more selective in their buying habits. No longer content to spend hard-earned dollars on an image presented in striking virtual reality, ingenious animation mixed with live action, or by some holier-than-thou superstar voicing empty promises for a sizeable check, many would-be buyers are demanding more. More information, more details, more truths. Naturally, they want those details presented in a compelling way, else they might simply ignore them. Nonetheless, if we don't do our homework, chances are we won't create a change in attitudes, which is what good advertising usually seeks to do.

An example of how advertisers are suddenly providing more information is a TV commercial for a new kind of toothbrush. Using sophisticated computer animation, the advertiser spent a lot of time explaining how the manufacturing process of this brush is unique and how the bristles are designed to conform to the way teeth are shaped. No high concept pitch here, yet a clever animated demonstration that, if not the most exciting message of all time, is certainly both memorable and believable.

More than that, it positioned this brand as unique from the competition, and in a market segment that one could hardly term "exciting."

If advertising is providing more information these days, it also is changing in other ways. Look around you. And listen too:

- Thirty-minute infomercials on television selling everything from spray-on hair to nationally advertised products;

- Integrated marketing communications campaigns that include advertising as part of a total communications strategy, not only to reach, but to keep, potential purchasers;

- Direct response messages, not only taking shape in print but also on videocassette, narrowly targeted to the best prospects;

- Concerted efforts by major advertisers to distinguish themselves, not only as marketing the finest products, but doing the most for people in general;

- Focused efforts to reach ethnic and racial minorities, whose reasons for purchasing often differ in meaningful ways from the white majority.

One study, for example, determined that, while African-Americans tend to choose quality over price, Hispanic-Americans tend to be brand loyal, and Asian-Americans seek the best value for the money.

On the other hand, the creative process which produces the best advertising hasn't changed much at all. It existed centuries before advertising was invented, and it still works. All we have done is apply the basic rules of creativity to media such as print, radio, television, direct mail, outdoor, point of purchase, and a slew of new media that range from videos on shopping carts to entire TV channels dedicated to selling goods. Advertisers are following the tried and true formulas for creativity and applying them to new ways of thinking.

What are some other factors which have caused changes in the ways advertisers are thinking?

1. ***The search for real value.*** Value is what much of America is seeking these days, and this quest spans nearly all income groups. The more disposable income, the higher one's purchasing aspirations may be, but the best value for the money remains a major consideration. That "best value" isn't always the one with the lowest price. It may be the one that communicates through advertising messages that the buyers are getting the most for their money.

2. ***An intent to build positive relationships with consumers.*** Other evidence suggests advertising approaches are not the same as they were even a year or two ago. Wal-Mart, for example, has unveiled in Lawrence, Kansas, its first environmentally friendly store. Compared to other Wal-Marts, the store is brighter and less cramped, built with wood beams instead of steel, and has skylights to allow natural light to help illuminate the interior. The air conditioning system uses no fluorocarbons. The store recycles its own waste and even allows customers to use its recycling center for paper, aluminum, glass, and other materials. After paying for purchases, customers are encouraged to discard the packaging at a recycling area near the checkout. Signs throughout the store carry such messages as "Reduce, reuse, recycle" and "We're committed to the air, land, and water."

FIGURE 1-1
Once the computer wars heated up in the late eighties, both IBM and Macintosh, the two leading systems, sought ways to carve new niches for their respective brands in the expanding home usage market while at the same time working together behind the scenes to forge new links in system compatability. This delightful ad for the Macintosh Performa series, positioned as "the family Macintosh," employs a strategy which suggests that children will be more apt to use a computer that's "easy to learn and use."

Will a personal computer give your kids an edge?

That all depends on the computer.

To kids who are trying to make sense out of quadratic equations or subjunctive clauses, trying to figure out a complex PC can be a scary proposition.

But a computer that's easy to learn and use – like

Unlike complex PCs, a Macintosh Performa computer makes it easy to turn out impressive-looking homework.

a Macintosh® Performa® computer – can help your children in many ways.

A more personal way to learn.

A Performa computer makes it easy for students to learn at their own pace, to explore in detail those topics that interest them most, or brush up on (and ultimately master) topics that give them trouble.

A Performa – combined with any of hundreds of Mac® educational programs – makes learning interactive, involving and enjoyable. It encourages students to polish up their homework projects (because making changes is so easy). And because Performa makes it incredibly simple to combine text with artwork, photographs and charts, ordinary reports and term papers can look extraordinary.

More schools use Apple computers.

More likely than not, your kids are already using Apple® computers to help them learn (indeed, Apple has been in classrooms for a total of more than 15 years). A Performa offers all of the Macintosh benefits that schools enjoy – plus a few special benefits: Basic word processing, spreadsheet and other software is preinstalled, along with a program called At Ease™ that makes it easy for families to share the computer.

Toll-free phone support and a year of in-home service* are also included at a very affordable price.

Performa computers make educational software easy to use And help kids study everything from Egypt to econometrics.

Some models even include a modem.

A Performa makes it easy for your kids to discover the most important edge anyone can have. The power to be your best.®

Performa
The Family Macintosh

3. ***Ventures into new media.*** Venerable retailer R.H. Macy announces plans for a 24-hour home shopping cable TV service. Some describe home shopping programs as a long advertising format, which is what fashion is all about.

4. ***A growing interest in database marketing.*** Magazine publishers are stepping up their database marketing efforts. Condé Nast, for example, offers an 11-million-name database to advertisers seeking more targeted programs.

American Express is making a major foray into database publishing with the development of *a hybrid newsletter/catalog/magazine for fashion conscious female cardholders. The Style Report* was developed by its Custom Media Group and was scheduled to debut with five sponsors and a controlled circulation of 750,000, another example of how a company with an extensive database is finding new ways for its merchants and other marketers to tap in. Plans were to mail *The Style Report* free to women in 11 major markets who were identified by researching AmEx's cardholder database as *"having a common denominator of a passionate interest in fashion, shopping, and style."* The audience, editorial content, and frequency of publication were developed using cardholder spending patterns and other quantitative and qualitative measures.

5. ***New technology offers new choices.*** Changing technology is also changing the face of advertising. A New York Times/CBS poll indicates most Americans are willing to pay for the privilege of controlling what is shown on their television, and soon they will be able to do so. Recent technology combines the capabilities of television, the telephone, and the computer with satellite uplinks to multiply the flow of information.

Already major cable companies and phone companies are scrambling to get a piece of the pie. TCI, the world's largest cable TV operator, is prepared to market a new cable decoder that can deliver up to 540 channels. Companies are building their own interactive networks so anything the customer wants to see will be as close as a phone call or the button on a TV set.

The role of existing broadcast networks may be taken over by libraries of information owned by businesses, which can relay the data anywhere in the world by satellite. This will more than likely be a pay-per-use system.

6. ***A growing awareness of, and interest in, global markets.*** As American markets become more competitive, U.S. advertisers are looking to foreign markets to help them achieve sales goals.

Advertising is reaching across the globe with campaigns promoting American goods and services, following the lead of American films, television, and music to create what some foreign nationals are calling a "cultural invasion." The French people are actually protesting the introduction across Western Europe of Ted Turner's 24-hour TNT and Cartoon Network. "It's intolerable that certain North American audiovisual companies shamelessly colonize our country," decried a former French culture minister in the fall of 1993. The French communications minister added that "culture can't be considered just another type of merchandise. It's a question of creativity and our cultural heritage."

7. ***Today, consumers are different, too.*** The '90s are:

a. Not a rerun of the fifties, when cigarette smoking was fashionable and abortion was illegal. Separate but equal treatment of blacks was not considered discriminatory. Women, minorities, older Americans, and gays had no employment rights.

b. Not a decade of affluence. Even though Baby Boomers will be bringing in more money than ever before, a dollar won't buy as much as it did for their parents at the same age, and most Boomers will never call themselves affluent.

c. A time when women will continue to work, due to household financial needs. It now takes more than one earner to maintain the average household's standard of living. The Bureau of Labor Statistics predicts that women workers ages 25–54 will represent 82 percent of women by 2005, up from 74 percent in 1990.

Female Stereotypes Change Slowly[1]

Flip the TV dial during a weekday and you'll discover a different world with its own phrases: soap scum, dingy whites, occasional irregularity. In this world, women seem to live only to cook and clean and please children and husbands. It seems to be a man's stereotype, wanting to position women as childlike and passive and dependent.

Lynn Jaffe, a marketing professor at Northwestern University, showed women two sets of mock commercials, one depicting modern roles, the other a throwback to the fifties. On average, the modern ads drew a rating nearly 42 percent higher than the traditional ads. Furthermore, when Jaffe posed the question to women who identified themselves as traditional, they showed no clear preference for either of the two images. Jaffe concluded that advertisers who use modern positioning are going to capture a lot of women who want to see that, and they won't alienate the traditional group.

So the big question is, Why perpetuate the stereotype?

She and he are under the weather. But there's only one dose of Nyquil left. You take it, she says. You have a big day tomorrow. Later that night she's still miserable. I just hope my coughing doesn't keep you awake riddled with guilt, she tells him. No chance of that; he's almost sound asleep.

Dad has a sore throat and his little girl wants a bedtime story. Sorry, he tells her. Leave it to Mom. By quietly slipping him a couple of Sucrets, Mom gets Dad back in the running, so he can become a hero to his daughter.

She's taken care of her kids, her house, her man. What's left? Why the cat, of course. She tries Sheba, the gourmet cat food. She sniffs it—heavenly! Tabby digs in with pleasure! At last she will receive her due for a job well done. Not from her kids or her husband. From Tabby. They snuggle. She is happy at last.

Uh-uh.

[1] The *Washington Post* national weekly edition, February 15–21, 1993.

The ad industry knows that men aren't good for much around the house. And though 3 of 5 women with children under 18 hold jobs outside the house, they wind up doing most of the work at home as well. According to a Yankelovich study, 83 percent of married men in 1992 reported that the woman did most of the cooking, grocery shopping, and dishes. That means she is still responsible for most of the household purchases, and the most efficient way to reach her is on daytime television, where 56 percent of all viewers in this time period are adult women 18–49, the prime consumer years.

But the real reason for lack of change is that stereotypes change slowly. Others claim the commercials continue to reflect the deep-seated fears, longings, and social condition of many women because women continue to respond to them, despite the research.

A current Rice-a-Roni ad interweaves shots of a little girl leaving school and a man with a briefcase heading out of his office. "They'll be home soon," says the announcer, as a picture of hot Rice-a-Roni appears. This ad scored high with women. Whether she has a paying job or not, the woman is still expected to put dinner on the table. A stay-at-home mother in California says those ads do mirror her daily life. But in some ads, women are shown deriving pleasure only from pleasing those around them.

Some ads do appear to be trying to go beyond stereotypes, though. In a commercial for Motrin IB, a father is able to spend time with his young daughter after Motrin helps him fend off a headache. And dad fetches his own Motrin, too. Cheer is successfully using a chunky bald man who wordlessly describes the product's cleaning power, with nary a woman in sight.

Jaffe admits that product category may have much to do with the way women respond to depictions of themselves, preferring modern women when it comes to a product like financial services. But the same rationale might not work for a product such as household cleaners. In the end, because women's roles are more diverse than ever before, a portrayal of the traditional role, while representing a smaller part of the overall mix, may still be effective.

---

d. A time when some men are doing the housework. Much of this increase is due to the fact that never-married men are a growing share of all men. Husbands and fathers are participating more in child care and shopping, but not cleaning.

e. An era in which kids are as smart as always. And the share of high school graduates who go on to college has increased steadily since the 1940s. Children from all walks of life have greater access to higher education.

f. A time without a major baby boom. As baby boom women edge out of the childbearing years, the number of births will decline. The number of births in 1991 was lower than in 1990.

Courtesy Health-tex, Inc.

Babies tormented by their clothes. On the next Oprah.

Can you see it now? A vocal crowd. A panel of experts. And lots of babies. Then, national hotlines. Self-help books. Until, finally, harmful baby clothes become the most-talked-about issue of the presidential campaign

We're kidding, of course. But considering the way babies are treated by their clothes, it's not far from the truth.

That's why here at Health-tex, we try to make dressing your baby easy.

With nice, wide neck openings.

Snaps in hard-to-maneuver places like the crotch.

And a soft, durable cotton/poly blend that doesn't shrink or fade, and requires little or no ironing.

Just call the number listed below to learn more. Of course, our operators won't be nearly as entertaining as your average talk show host. But, they'll be full of information that you can actually use.

Rodeo Rex

Health-tex

A VF COMPANY. A LEADER IN QUALITY APPAREL ©1992 Health-tex, Inc.

If you'd like to know where to find Health-tex, just give us a call at 1-800-554-7637 for the store nearest you.

FIGURE 1-2

We hope you read the copy in this ad, for it's a hoot. How did the writer make a connection between maddeningly tight baby clothing and the world of TV talk shows? Doesn't matter, because the ad is a winner. Admit it, could you pass up this ad after being grabbed by the outrageous headline? And read the opening copy: "Can you see it now? A vocal crowd. A panel of experts. And lots of babies. Then, national hotlines. Self-help books. Until, finally, harmful baby clothes become the most talked-about issue of the presidential campaign. We're kidding, of course. But considering the way babies are treated by their clothes, it's not far from the truth."

g. A time to realize the power of the older market. While Americans are getting out of their homes more than ever and spending more of their dollars on food prepared away from home, older Americans seem particularly lively. While people ages 45–64 make up only 25 percent of adults, they constitute 43 percent of frequent leisure travelers. The Bureau of Labor Statistics predicts that during the 1990s more men and women over 55 will be in the work force.

8. ***In today's market, the magic words are "use lifestyle data to target narrowly."*** Robert Rueff, director of marketing and account services for Clarity, Coverdale, Rueff, Minneapolis, writes that demographics alone won't help you reach a target audience.

Women 25–49 isn't a target audience, he writes; it's a female convention. A clearly defined target segment means just that—a segment. And a segment is a percentage of consumers. The tighter and more focused the segment, the smaller the percentage of the population it represents.

Most marketers make two mistakes, trying for the largest segment possible and defining segments by demographics alone. Consumer attitudes and behavior are not demographically driven and in some cases not even demographically related. The segment a marketer is seeking might span a wide demographic definition even though the true target is a much smaller number of people.

Not all Baby Boomers, for instance, are health and nutrition conscious.

Not all people over 55 behave alike as consumers, either. Some drive BMWs and some Chevrolets. Some are fitness conscious, some couch loungers. Some are interested in financial services, while others rely on their pensions.

Rueff urges advertisers to recognize the limitations of demographics, learn more how lifestyle data can be applied, seek services that give the whys as well as the hows of consumer behavior, and have the courage to target the narrow segment that often results from this process.[2]

9. ***The concept of preparing and presenting a total communications package that stems from a common strategy is gaining new respect in an era when it is much more difficult to find a competitive advantage in the marketplace.*** That's a major reason for what is popularly known today as "integrated marketing communications."

Tom Duncan, director of the IMC graduate program, University of Colorado, Boulder, explains that integrated marketing communications stresses the advantages of synergy, where the whole is greater than the parts, which is a vintage management concept.[3] When all brand and corporate messages are strategically coordinated, the effect is greater than when *advertising, sales promotion, marketing, PR, packaging,* etc. are planned and executed independently, with each area competing for budgets and power . . . and in some cases sending out conflicting messages.

[2] *Advertising Age,* February 4, 1991.
[3] *Advertising Age,* March 8, 1993.

That misplaced apostrophe in our name is a boo-boo from the early days, when our quality control was (obviously) a little skimpy.

Lots of people, especially English teachers, have taken us to task for it. It makes us cringe today. But in a funny way, that out-of-place apostrophe has served our customers very well.

You see, every time we think about it, it reminds us that we're only human. And that we can't ever be *too* careful about what we sell or how we deal with the good folks who favor us with their business.

Truth is, we depend on their trust. As direct merchants, we sell by catalog–classic clothing, soft luggage, home furnishings. Folks have to feel that anything they see in our catalog will deliver as promised.

Still, we know that occasionally we *will* goof. So, we add one more feature to our product line, the Lands' End guarantee:

We accept any return, for any reason, at any time. Without any conditions.

We want no mistakes about *that*.

Guaranteed. Period.® *©1993, Lands' End, Inc.*

JV

If you'd like a free catalog, call us any time, 24 hours a day, at **1-800-356-4444**
Or mail this coupon to: 1 Lands' End Lane, Dept. JV, Dodgeville, WI 53595

Name ____________________

Address ____________________ Apt. ______

City ____________ State ______ Zip ______

Phone ( ) ____________ Day/Night (*circle one*)

Courtesy Lands' End.

FIGURE 1-3(A)

Selling through direct response catalogs, Lands' End publicizes its goods through print ads such as these. Even the typeface used in the ads mirrors that used in the catalogs, but the similarities hardly end there. Consider the personal tone of the copy in these advertisements as well as in the catalogs themselves, a style responsible in part for the overwhelming success of this leading direct response company. The Lands' End charm is nowhere more self-disparaging than in "To err is human. To guarantee divine." There, the writer compares the misplaced apostrophe in the company name. ("a boo-boo from the early days") to the quality control that "was (obviously) a little skimpy" in the early days of the company, but which resulted in the company's unconditional guarantee of quality.

You'll find our Mesh Knit has more of nearly everything–except flies, slubs and crocking.

If you make a cotton Mesh Knit shirt – and you're as finicky as Lands' End – there are a *zillion* things to watch for.

Cotton comes from the field, after all. You can card it, and comb it, and still have *stuff* left in it. When that's knit into the cloth, the result is flies and slubs – tiny bumps and imperfections, like hiccups in the fabric. They're unsightly and weaken the Mesh.

So, we do our darndest to weed out flies and slubs. Matter of fact, we have *seventy* fly- and slub-inspectors.

A fine Mesh we're getting you into.

Our Mesh Knit is made of 100% American grown cotton. It's spun into an 18 singles yarn: a yarn so fine that it takes *4.3 miles* of it to make one Lands' End Mesh.

Now obviously, what makes a Mesh so comfy is that it *is* a Mesh. It's "ventilated" with thousands of tiny air holes that let it breathe. (Don't ask us how *many* thousands, please – we gave up counting 'em!)

But to make our Mesh Knit even comfier, we add thoughtful little details. For example, side vents. So, you can wear the shirt outside your pants, without its catching around the hips.

We also tape the neck band to keep the edges from chafing and rubbing you the wrong way.

And speaking of rubbing, we hate when a shirt's color rubs off – on other clothing, for instance. That's called *crocking*. We try and avoid it by using reactive dyes. These get chemically "married" to the yarn – the two become nearly inseparable till death do them part.

The price is the clincher.

Our Mesh is only $19. (A little more for Tall, Men's XXL, or with a pocket or stripes.) And that's not much for such quality.

Of course, the Lands' End catalog has lots more – from classic dress and casual clothing, to our original soft luggage, children's things and home furnishings. It's all fairly and honestly priced.

And it all comes with our unconditional guarantee. In two words–"Guaranteed. Period."

Send for our catalog. Better yet, phone us – 24 hours a day, any day or night.

You'll find no flies in our service. No slubs, either.

©1993, Lands' End, Inc.

YM

If you'd like a free copy of our catalog, call **1-800-356-4444**
Or mail this coupon to:
1 Lands' End Lane, Dept. YM
Dodgeville, WI 53595

Name__________
Address__________
City__________
State_____ Zip_____
Phone ( ) Day/Night (circle one)

FIGURE 1-3(B)

Our seamless neck. It's enough to convince you that not all turtlenecks are cut from the same cloth.

We could tell you tons about a Lands' End turtleneck. But today, let's focus on the neck. Because what we put into *that* is enough to make you feel warm all over.

For one thing, our neck is rib-knit to size in a *single piece.* So, there's no need for a seam. Now, if you've ever worn a turtle that has a seam here, you know how it can rub and chafe you. Doesn't happen with ours.

Another thing: our neck, like our body, is made of 100% long-staple cotton, or a cotton/poly blend, if you prefer. But we add a touch of Lycra® spandex to it. This lets the neck s-t-r-e-t-c-h. You can roll it into a turtleneck, and wash it time and again – and it won't sag or poop out like some.

A neck is not a neck is not a neck.

A neck has a hard life. Just think of the trauma it goes through every time you pull it over your head. So, we add another bit of Lycra® spandex where the neck connects to the shoulders. When you squiggle through, it *gives* a little.

(Some turtlenecks use a piece of cotton tape here. It doesn't stretch the same way; it's likely to pucker and tear.)

We could tell you lots more about the neck – and obviously, about the rest of our turtle. It's neck and shoulders over anybody else's. We'll just mention one other thing: the price.

"What? Only $15?"

It's only $15 for men's or women's regular: same as it's been for four years now. (Tall and larger sizes are a little more.) That's astounding when you think of everything we put into these beauties.

But it's not astounding when you know Lands' End. You see, we've built our whole business on giving our customers quality products, at a fair price. And that's as true of our sweaters and buttondown shirts, our soft luggage and home furnishings, as it is of our turtles.

In fact, we're so eager to do right by you, we make an unconditional guarantee. In two words: Guaranteed. Period.®

See for yourself. Simply call us here in Dodgeville, Wisconsin, any time, day or night, and ask our friendly operator for a catalog.

Then go shopping in it whenever the spirit moves you.

©1993, Lands' End, Inc.

FK

To get our free catalog, call
1-800-356-4444
Or mail this coupon to:
1 Lands' End Lane, Dept. FK
Dodgeville, WI 53595

Name________________
Address________________
____________ Apt. ______
City________________
State________ Zip________
Phone ( ) ________ Day/Night *(circle one)*

FIGURE 1-3(C)

Once the marketing mix is strategically on target, the communications strategy can be determined, driven by a big idea. It may originate with sales promotion, public relations, advertising, or even packaging. Remember L'eggs and its breakthrough egg container?

But there's more, as Duncan goes on to explain. Many companies that have enjoyed rapid growth—Ben and Jerry's, The Body Shop, Nike— have had a *strong corporate culture that has intuitively integrated and focused all corporate as well as marketing activities,* resulting in high brand awareness and *strong customer relationships . . . or loyalty.*

UC's IMC graduate program has identified these four levels of integration as they apply to marketing communications:

a. **Unified image.** This one look, one voice approach made Coke one of the leading brands in the world. Marlboro is another example. The primary focus is on having a strong brand image.

b. **Consistent voice.** Concern with how one talks to all audiences, including the trade, the consumer, employees, suppliers, and stockholders. Even though it must say different things to each audience, the messages are consistent in overall tone and look.

c. **Good listener.** This level maximizes feedback from current and potential customers by using databases and encouraging consumers and other "stakeholders" (employees, stockholders, suppliers, competitors) to talk to the organization through 800 phone numbers, consumer surveys and panels, seminars, and trade shows.

d. **World-class citizen.** Such organizations are socially and environmentally conscious and have strong company cultures that guide them in their relationships not only with stakeholders but also with a wider community. They are good neighbors and world-class citizens, like Ben & Jerry's and The Body Shop. The Body Shop does not use animal testing. It requires employees to do a certain amount of community service on company time and buys as many ingredients as possible from developing countries. Ben & Jerry's provides child care. It returns a percentage of its profits to its state and community. These policies have resulted in extensive positive media coverage. Although neither company spends much on advertising, their brand awareness and acceptance are higher than most brands in their categories.

While levels one and two are primarily concerned with sending messages in order to influence purchase, one might define levels three and four as "the process of strategically developing and controlling or influencing all messages which customers and other stakeholders use in forming an image of, and maintaining a relationship with, an organization."

10. ***The consumer, especially the group called "Generation X," consisting of 46 million consumers ages 18–29, are more skeptical than ever of most advertising claims.*** Maybe they've seen too much advertising for too long. Whatever the reason, Karen Ritchie, senior vice president for media at McCann-Erickson Worldwide, Detroit, warns advertisers that younger adults, non-Baby Boomers, are not replacing aging Boomers in the audiences of major media.[4] They have very little in common with Boomers, in fact. They turn off their TV and turn away from magazines because there is little to interest them there. It's like the sixties. As one 28-year-old put it, "They skipped me completely. They went straight from 'thirtysomething' to '90210.'"

While the Boomers, whose anthem was "sex, drugs, rock and roll," have been called one of the most repressive and reactionary generations in history, their kids are Generation X, the no-brand generation, the kids with the purple hair. By 2000, Generation X will have grown to 62 million strong, and by 2010 will overtake the Boomers as the primary market for virtually every product category—beauty, fashion and fragrance, packaged goods, travel, and home furnishings. It is a fragmented generation in just about every way.

To start with, it is racially and ethnically diverse. Eventually, it will have four minorities: African-Americans, Hispanic-Americans, Asian-Americans, and whites. Minority marketing will have little relevance because all marketing will be minority marketing. Boomers represented the last WASP generation in America. Generation X'ers will have to share economic and political power with other nations. Fortunately, they seem more conciliatory about such things.

Still, they are angry. They are unhappy that Boomers have all the good jobs, frustrated that the American dream is out of their reach, and outraged that we seem to be squandering the resources of our economy and our planet before they can inherit them. They are tired of living at home with Boomer parents, frustrated about AIDS and its effect on sexual intimacy, and bored by Boomer-driven high-tech consumer hype.

How do we reach people who cry out, "I am not a target market!"

By facing facts. Generation X watches less TV. And cable isn't doing much better, unless it's MTV or the Comedy Channel. And it is not reading the same magazines as Boomers. Some media are reaching out to it, like the Fox network and *Spin* and *Details*. This is where you will find the leading edge advertisers and marketers.

11. ***Other actions of advertisers fly in the face of good judgment and taste.*** A major automotive brand is charged with rigging a demonstration in a television commercial, causing most Americans to doubt there is "truth in advertising." Many people believe advertising is promoting material values (wear expensive clothes and you will be happier) over spiritual ones (do something good for the earth and you will be a better person). Advertisers who have jumped on

[4] *Advertising Age*, November 9, 1992.

the goodness bandwagon, touting recycled packaging and environmentally safe chemicals, may already be out of date. Women—the "megaconsumers" of our society—take offense at how their gender is portrayed in ads and commercials that often cast them as window dressing on the street of life. Minorities question the pseudo-integration of advertisements, where people of color often seem to be added in passive roles as a numerical afterthought, rather than as part of an overriding strategy.

What Kind of Advertising Are You Going to Create?

Cereals that cure flab. Cigarettes that keep you slim. An airline fleet as new as its last overhaul. Such are the kinds of deceptive claims decried by the Center for Science in the Public Interest, a private consumer advocacy group.

Small wonder, since there is so much advertising, that there is so much criticism of advertising. Advertising is indeed ubiquitous. It's everywhere. Some say we can never escape it. Worse, much advertising plays the role of "miracle worker," promising miracles through the use of products. The images of advertising—physically perfect humans in idyllic settings— often seem to replace reality in the lives of many. Some advertising capitalizes on our fears—fears of aging, fears of not being socially acceptable, fears of looking less than dazzling—with products offered as ways to avoid our most common anxieties. Certain advertisers have been scolded for marketing questionable products to those who can least afford them. Some have toyed with the truth, daring to cross the line separating exaggeration from outright lies. Others have promoted bad taste on a major scale. Still others have disguised their advertising as "something else" in order to sell something.

In E. L. Doctorow's novel *The Book of Daniel,* set in the 1950s, the author offers a condemnation of the medium of television:

Everyone is digging the commercials. That's today's school, man. In less than a minute a TV commercial can carry you through a lifetime. It shows you the baby, the home, the car, the graduation. . . . It makes you laugh and makes your eyes water with nostalgia . . . telling you how cool you are and how cool you can be. Commercials are learning units.

And learning units they are, literally. Marketers have installed video advertising units above public telephones in schools, and offered twelve minutes of news and free TV sets, satellite dishes, and wiring to classrooms in exchange for two minutes of commercials. Around the world, from Europe and the Middle East to the Pacific Rim, American advertising has made its mark on societies as different from ours as night and day. In some cases, consumers from other nations have had difficulty separating the fantasy world of American commercials and sitcoms from the realities of American daily life.

While advertisers claim they offer the consumer a number of choices for the satisfaction of needs, critics say they offer only one: purchasing a commodity. As early as 1930, one trade magazine claimed advertising "helps to keep the masses dissatisfied with their mode of life, discontented with the ugly things around them. Satisfied customers are not as profitable as discontented ones."

And how do we change reality? We retouch images to manipulate and perfect what is imperfect. We appeal to feelings and discourage thinking. We create advertising that, on the surface, is only selling a product. A closer look may reveal other messages, intentional or not, that suggest that we must have certain products in order to measure up to some fabricated "status quo." Dreams abound in ads and commercials. The high tech appeal of sports cars is so powerful that some people apparently fantasize about being sports cars. At least, the agency for Porsche thought so as it asked, "If you were a car, what kind of a car would you be?" The TV commercial based on this idea uses a subjective camera to depict a Porsche-eye view of the road as it scurries around one curve after another.

In modern ads for dandruff shampoos, deodorants, mouthwashes, and laundry detergents, our nightmares are exploited. From a historical perspective, advertising seems even worse. Brochures published in England in the seventeenth century to lure settlers to the New World were full of hopeful overstatements, half truths, and downright lies.

So what is fair and what is downright dishonest? Should profit or prudence prevail when surveys indicate that Hispanics, women, and African-Americans are prime targets for cigarettes and spirits in an age when the general population is cutting back? Should a commercial for a well-known pain reliever explain that the reason more hospitals choose their brand is that they supply it so cheaply that they are in effect paid to use it? Should an automobile manufacturer show one of its sports models outracing a jet plane in an age when highway speeding kills daily?

Or consider this casting imperative for the homemaker role in a major advertiser's television commercials: She should be blond—or if brunette, not too brunette. Pretty but not too pretty. Midwestern in speech, middle-class looking, gentile. If they're using blacks, they want waspy blacks. Husbands? Same thing. But the husband is getting to play the jerk more and more in American commercials.

Perhaps a spoof on *Saturday Night Live* sums up the cliché-ridden world of advertising best. A middle-class woman, dressed in a polyester pantsuit, crashes through the café-curtained dutch door of a kitchen and addresses the camera: "I'm a nuclear physicist and Commissioner of Consumer Affairs," she begins. As she starts to put her groceries away, she explains, "In my spare time, I do needlepoint, read, sculpt, take riding lessons, and brush up on my knowledge of current events. Thursday's my day at the daycare center, and then there's my work with the deaf; but I still have time left over to do all my own baking and practice my backhand, even though I'm on call twenty-four hours a day as a legal aid lawyer in family court." As she hurries to put more groceries away, the announcer asks, "How does Ellen Sherman, Cleveland housewife, do it all? She's smart. She takes Speed. Yes, Speed—the tiny blue diet pill you don't have to be overweight to need."

One hopes this isn't the way you're thinking about writing advertising.

How Will You Prepare Yourself for the Task?

Lisa Duke, creative supervisor and writer for the Rich's Barbeque campaign, claims it takes endless curiosity, a strong ego, and resiliency to work in advertising. She explains that without her natural curiosity, she might never have visited the East Bend barbeque restaurant, where the idea for "Ruby" (see pp. 30–38) first sprang forth. As for a strong ego, she reminds us that copywriters and art directors face daily rejection of ideas they have personally nurtured to fruition. "You can come up with lots of good ideas, as we did with this campaign," she recalls, "and still the work is very subjective." As for resiliency, she warns would-be ad creatives that there will be good days and bad days, even good and bad years, for everyone in the business. Being able to exult in your successes will make the not-so-smooth times bearable.

Advertising has no room for mediocrity. What it does have room for are bright, energetic, self-assured people who find excitement in the art of creative persuasion and who can use truth to their advantage in helping their clients sell products. The advertising profession also demands communications skills far superior to those of the average person and the ability to use those skills brilliantly.

Moreover, such individuals must also possess a good sense of humor and a flair for the dramatic. It helps to know something about art, music, film, and theater, as well as to have some understanding of what motivates people to respond to a suggestion. College courses in literature, psychology, and the humanities can be a big help.

Dick Joel, former head of the Department of Advertising at the University of Tennessee, says, "If your goal is creative advertising, remember that you can constantly learn from the life around you. Wherever you go, whatever you do, you should keep your eyes and ears open and a pad nearby to record what you see and hear."

So read all you can, not only about advertising, but about people and places. Absorb the great literary techniques of the best novelists and writers of nonfiction. Catch all the good films and TV programs and notice how the story line progresses and how character development is achieved, as well as how camera and sound work to enhance the mood as well as the meaning.

Cultivate a taste for a variety of music: from Madonna to Beethoven, Gershwin to Hamlisch, Streisand to the Grateful Dead. Become more eclectic in your tastes; sample a little bit of everything. You may learn, in the process, why different people enjoy different things, and why some ideas will work only with certain groups of people.

A Day in the Life of Writer and Designer

So here you are, sitting at your desk at 8:30 Monday morning, and a glance at your calendar reminds you that you're to attend an account group meeting at 9 A.M. to discuss a new campaign for Satin Margarine. The account supervi-sor has sent you a memo to prepare you for the meeting. Reading it, you have learned that this fairly popular brand, positioned in the market as "the smoother spreading stick margarine," is now being reformulated with 15 percent butter to provide what the client calls, "real butter flavor with no cholesterol." Butter, you know, is extremely high in cholesterol, but on the other hand, nothing beats it for flavor.

The Satin account group includes the account supervisor, the client's main contact with the agency, who is responsible for knowing the marketing environment in which the brand is sold. Also in the group is the art director, with whom you have worked on a number of other projects; a media analyst to recommend where and when advertising is to be placed; and a researcher or planner to conduct and interpret primary research (consumer focus groups, telephone surveys, in-store questionnaires, and so on), as well as to present existing information on the brand category. In fact, the planner has provided you with copies of three recent articles: "Current Preferences Among Margarine Users Indicate Decline in Cholesterol Scare," "Margarine Market Goes Soft as Buyers Perceive All Brands to Be Alike," and a report of a test done by a competing brand in Kansas City, which indicated that flavor is still a major factor in purchasing behavior among 54 percent of the target market.

The meeting runs until 10:30. Afterwards, although you have a few other assignments you're working on, you and the art director get involved in a bull session about Satin Margarine. Some initial decisions have been made in the meeting; among them is to position the new brand as "the best of both worlds—real buttery taste yet lower in saturated fats." You certainly aren't going to use those weary words in the advertising, but at least you have some focus and direction for your thinking.

By now it's 11:30, and a colleague from the traffic department runs a couple of type galleys by your desk and waits as you check them for typographical errors. People in the traffic department keep things moving on schedule within the agency, and they must pay particular attention to media deadlines so that enough time is allocated for the many layers of approval within and beyond the agency for all work on any particular account.

After a quick lunch, you begin some personal brainstorming on Satin Margarine. At this stage, you work best alone, and you and your art director agree to this approach. Later that afternoon, the two of you will get together to discuss approaches that each of you has been thinking about. Many of the best creative ideas result from such an exchange—when two people, one who has "a way with words" and the other who has "a way with design and visual communication," trade ideas in a cooperative, noncompetitive spirit.

FIGURE 1-4

Because so much insurance advertising is formulaic, this series for Mass Mutual glows with originality. It's fresh, packs an emotional wallop like few insurance ads do, and best of all, it's upbeat: While much insurance advertising talks about the negatives, this series stresses the joys of life and promises to be just as reliable and faithful to its policyholders as they are to their own friends and family. Lovely sentiment, isn't it? And probably just right for attracting believers, too.

A promise never to say, "Chris, I mean Bobby, I mean Tim."

A promise matching sailor suits will never come near your closet.

A promise to be there for you. And you. And you.

Nothing binds us one to the other like a promise kept. Nothing divides us like a promise broken. At MassMutual we believe in keeping our promises. That way all the families and businesses that rely on us can keep theirs.

MassMutual®

We help you keep your promises.®

©1992 Massachusetts Mutual Life Insurance Co., Springfield MA 01111.

By now it's mid-afternoon and your art director knocks on your door. It's time to share your ideas: she has her sketch pad filled with doodles, headlines, rough layouts, and loose drawings; you have pages of copy paper scribbled top to bottom with phrases, sketches, design ideas, and theme lines. She has hit on an interesting headline that might be the theme for the entire campaign, and you've thought of a unique way to show consumers' "flavor response" in print and on television. You review all the ideas: those with potential go in one stack, those that might have potential go in a second, and ideas that just don't work go in a third. Both of you will review your ideas many times before arriving at a decision. Then you'll proceed to rough copy and layout to see how your idea works in all the media covered by the campaign. Chances are that you won't ask your creative director to review your work until you have several good approaches to show, and each approach will include several ideas for each medium.

If you were working in a British ad agency, an account planner would have provided you with a "creative brief," or strategy statement, to help you focus in on the task. For now, just remember that it's difficult to proceed with even rough ads and commercials if no one has agreed on the strategy or plan of action. Is the Satin campaign to emphasize flavor and smoothness, flavor only, or something else? Is there a danger that "health-conscious" people will be turned off by the butter story and switch to another brand? Or are there perhaps "health-conscious" people who secretly long for real butter flavor and are willing to buy the new product, provided the butter content is low? A strategic decision is called for before you embark on any creative work.

The day is winding down, but you decide to stay after hours to work while your ideas are still fresh in hand. You check your calendar and realize you're going to be out of the office all day tomorrow to travel to another client's offices to present a preliminary strategy report on next year's campaign. Another of your accounts requires new work, and you'll be briefed by that client toward the end of the week.

Some days never seem long enough in the advertising business, while others never seem to end. If you find yourself in a lull between jobs, you can still find something productive to do at the agency. You could contact the library or research department and obtain the files on the accounts to which you've been assigned. You could look at previous advertising, or at ads for competing products. You might read any research that has been done on the brand or the market category in the last several years; perhaps your agency library can lend you a clip file of articles about the brand and market category. If the account supervisor has some time, you could make an appointment to discuss the history of the brand. The more you know, the more you'll have to draw from when time arrives to be "creative."

Suggested Activities

1. Reflect on the many changes in advertising over just the last several years. Check your library or reading room for recent issues of *Advertising Age, Ad-*

week, and other consumer and trade publications that discuss advertising and marketing. What other trends can you spot that excite you? Disturb you? Make you question whether advertisers are going too far to reach target audiences? Make you commend advertisers for their ingenuity in targeting so precisely? Write a paper in which you summarize your feelings and findings. Write it as if you were attempting to persuade others to understand your opinions. Present this in class and let it be the basis for a discussion of what good advertising should be.

2. Take inventory of the number of advertising messages you see or hear in a single day. How many did you count, how many do you remember vividly, and what were some of the more unusual places in which you found advertising?

3. Find examples of advertisements that you believe (a) promise "miracles" through products, (b) offer stereotypes of people to sell products, (c) play on fears to convince us to buy, (d) state questionable "truths," and (e) are in bad taste. What could the advertisers have done to eliminate such qualities without diminishing the impact of the selling message?

4. A good creative person is one who has a natural curiosity and diverse interests in reading, the arts, and popular culture. In the following exercise, you are asked to inventory your "creative resources" and seek new worlds to conquer. First, make a list of your favorite films, entertainers, music, fiction and nonfiction books, magazines, live plays and musicals, live concert performances, television programs, and things you enjoy in your spare time. Share these with classmates and your teacher. Now make a concerted effort to add something different to that list. If you watch TV sitcoms, spend an hour or more watching a nature program, a ballet performance, or a historical documentary. If you like country music, try a symphony. What did you learn about yourself as a result of this exercise?

5. After reading what this chapter has to say about the qualities of a good creative person, what do you regard as your strengths in this area? Your weaknesses? How can you capitalize on the former and work against the latter?

6. The basis for good creative work is a storehouse of knowledge. Although some might argue that ordinary products simply are not that interesting, seasoned advertising people will shout at you, "Boring is no excuse!" Writer James Gorman obviously agrees. In a magazine article on the pencil, Gorman spends the better part of three magazine pages exploring the mystery of this basic writing tool. An excerpt from his work follows. After reading it, you might:

a. Try your hand at writing an ad for the pencil. Use the Pencil Makers Association as the advertiser and use the advertisement to remind your audience that pencils are versatile writing tools.

b. Do research on your own for an equally basic commodity, such as table salt, a plumber's friend (plunger), a hammer, nails, sugar, flour, bread,

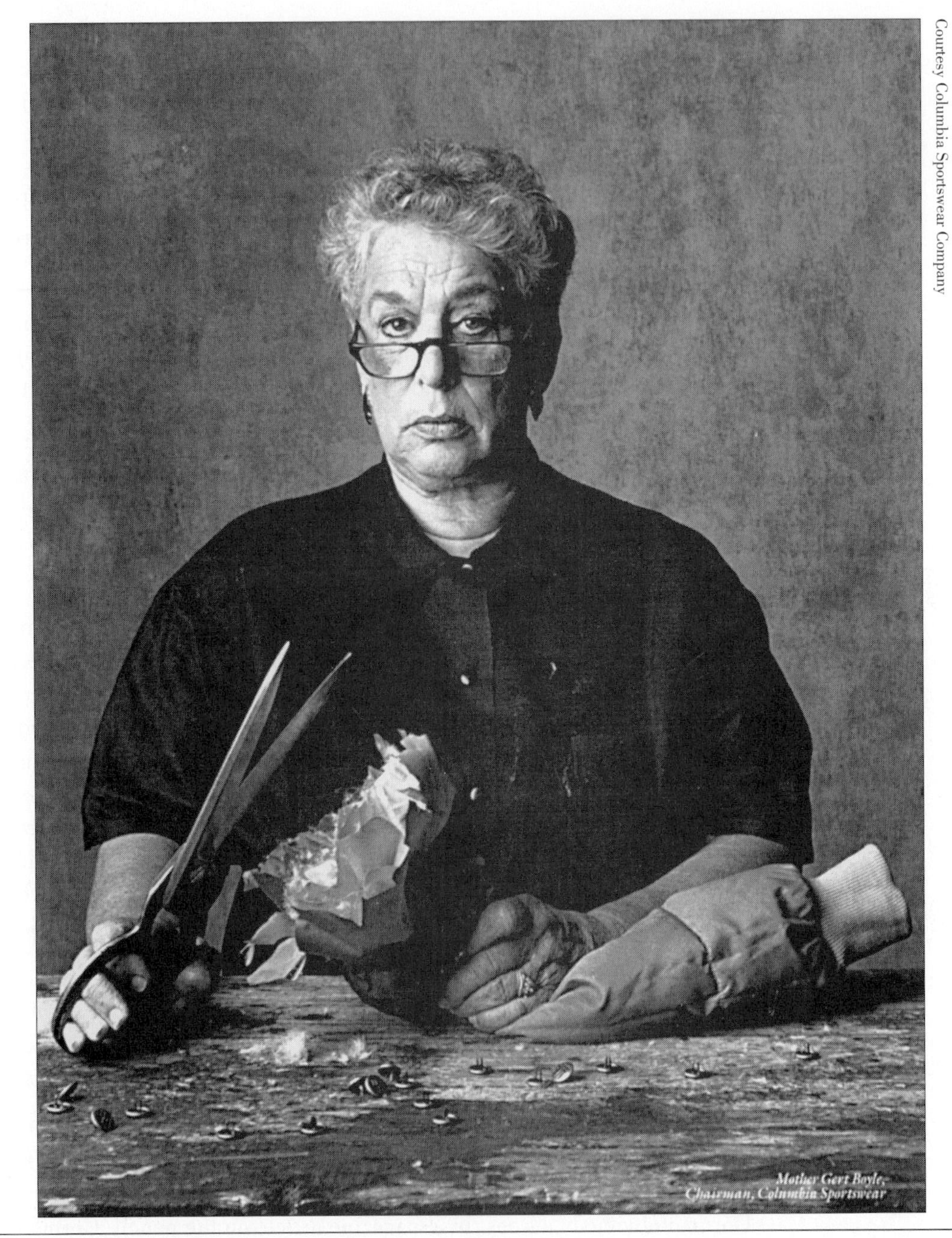

Courtesy Columbia Sportswear Company

FIGURE 1-5

As chair of Columbia Sportswear Company, Mother Gert Boyle is also instrumental in positioning the company's outerwear as the most carefully stitched and sewn in the industry. Note the familial tone in the copy as Columbia president Tim Boyle uses his own voice to extoll the superiority of his product, acknowledging the persistent demands of Mother. We suspect Mrs. Boyle allowed the copywriter to make her seem more abrasive than she really is—all for the good of the advertising. Note the care the photographer has taken to match the visual

"SHE SNAPS NECKS AND HACKS OFF ARMS."

–By Tim Boyle, President, Columbia Sportswear

My Mother, Columbia Sportswear's chairman, will stop at nothing to get what she wants–superior outerwear.

In fact, the mountains around Portland, Oregon, frequently echo her sharply barked commands. "When I say a snap closed neck and storm front, that's what I expect to see!" Or, as she hacks away at an inappropriately attached sleeve, "All seams are to be double sewn!"

What, you may ask, is the end result of having such a, uh, vociferous chairman? The Columbia Interchange System,™ for one. It lets you brave multiple weather conditions with one jacket by matching a zip-in, zip-out liner to a weatherproof shell. They may be worn separately, or together.

Take our Ponderosa Parka™ pictured here. The outer shell is 100% Technicloth II™–a soft blend of cotton and nylon woven into a durable rib fabric, oiled to keep water out. To hold warmth in, the bomber-style Zap Fleece™ liner is quilted with Thermoloft™ insulation.

All in all, it's easy to see why not just any parka can survive Mother's rather pointed demands.

Columbia Sportswear Company

6600 N. Baltimore, Portland, Oregon 97203. For the dealer nearest you in the U.S. and Canada, call 1-800-MA-BOYLE.

FIGURE 1-5 Continued.

image with the verbal one. While some might argue that the headline doesn't tell the reader a whole lot about the product, others would contend that it says a whole lot more than most sportswear ads—and commands instant attention, too.

lumber, etc. Write a paper about it, then use the paper as a basis for writing an advertising message.

Gorman writes:

Remember pencils? Remember the smell of cedar shavings, the pleasure of writing on clean paper with that first, sharp point, the sense of guilt and personal inadequacy that comes from seeing the gnawed and stubby evidence of your own anxiety neurosis next to some obsessive's long, sharp points and untoothed hexagonal pencil bodies? I had forgotten about pencils until recently, when I overdosed on computers and decided I needed a rest cure. Pencils. Do people still use them? Are there living pencil devotees? Or have the laser printer and the felt tip pen conquered all?

I called the Pencil Makers Association in Moorestown, New Jersey, to ask those very questions. . . . Pencils are doing fine. There's no runaway surge in pencils, mind you, no graphite valley where pencil nerds drive Porsches and hop from company to company with their new designs, but growth has been steady. About two billion pencils are made each year by U.S. companies. In fact, pencils are one of the few manufactured goods that the U.S. still knows how to make. We may not know how to make televisions or cars anymore, but we make great pencils. . . .

Pencils got their start in 1564, when a particularly good graphite deposit was discovered in England. Gradually, people figured out what to put around the graphite and what to mix it with and how to cook it to make it a stronger, better writing substance. Ernest Hemingway and Walt Whitman used pencils to write. So did Vladimir Nabokov and Herbert Hoover. Henry Thoreau ran a family pencil-making business. And my favorite item of information: "You could eat one every day without harming yourself."

Gorman explains that in 1971 many newspapers ran stories about a child who got lead poisoning from chewing pencils. Pencil makers called on a pediatrician for an official statement, and he told the world, "Here's how safe the pencil is. Any human being, regardless of age, can eat at least one pencil a day without suffering any injurious effects to health." Actually, Gorman explains, there is no lead in a pencil, only graphite. He then explains how modern pencils are made.

What modern pencil companies do is glue two wooden pencil halves together with the lead inside. . . . A top-quality pencil is bonded, or "wood clinched," which is to say that not only is the wood glued together but the wood is also glued to the lead. This avoids the problem of lead falling out of a sharpened pencil."[5]

[5] "Pencil Facts, from James Gorman," adapted from *Wigwag*, February 1990. Used by permission.

Gorman's essay concludes by revealing that certain pencil users prefer certain types of pencils, and are quite picky about their preferences. He mentions the major pencil companies: Faber-Castell, Empire-Berol, and Dixon Ticonderoga—makers of Venus Esterbrook and Eberhard Faber pencils. His lengthy and engaging story certainly breathes new life for most of us into this rather mundane writing instrument. Can you do the same in advertising copy?

How to Heat Up Frozen Barbeque

Lisa Duke,
Creative Supervisor

Brian Marshall,
Account Supervisor

Long, Haymes and
Carr Advertising,
Winston-Salem, N.C.

LISA: Where I live, people think you only reach hog heaven by way of Lexington, North Carolina, barbeque capital of the world. So you can imagine our trepidation when Rich Foods, based in Buffalo, New York, enlisted the help of our agency to introduce a frozen barbecue to be sold in supermarkets.

BRIAN: The scene had been polluted by the cut-rate, refrigerated barbeque already in grocery stores. People tried them, and they just didn't match up to anything available in restaurants. But this Rich's Barbeque was the real McCoy, hand pulled pieces of meat in a thick sauce. Rich's even made chicken barbeque for the health conscious.

LISA: Once you do a little research, you realize there are as many ways to make barbeque as there are to spell it. In my native South Carolina, the real thing is bite-sized pieces of pork in a mustard-based sauce. In North Carolina, you chop it up fine and add a few dabs of vinegar-tabasco sauce. Out West, it's not pork at all, it's beef. Say "barbecue" in Owensboro, Kentucky, and you'll get mutton. Beyond the fact that this was a flash-frozen product made by a bunch of Yankees, this was going to be a tough sell.

On the plus side, barbeque's a great feel-good food for the masses, like pizza and burgers, that little kids won't turn their noses up at. And like pizza, no one in their right mind tries to make it from scratch. If you want good barbeque, you bundle up the kids, climb in the car, and make the required trek. We had a significant advantage. With Rich's, you could have hot barbeque in your hands with the flick of a microwave.

BRIAN: Research told us that people actually liked Rich's better than their local barbeque. Our job was to get them to try it. From these early focus groups and taste tests, we developed the creative strategy, "Rich's is Authentic Southern Barbeque." We learned that people go to barbeque restaurants because they're fun and unpretentious. We had to capture that fun in the advertising. If we could convince people that Rich's Barbeque was authentic, unlike the other grocery store imitations, we could sell all the client could make. But "authentic" is one of those tricky words like "quality" . . . the more you say it, the less people believe it.

LISA: We went to see the product being made, which I truly dreaded. Fortunately, the plant only processed whole pork shoulders that were delivered by truck. They

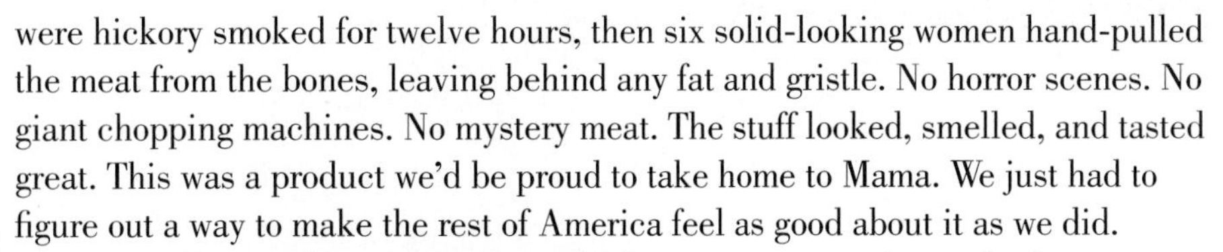

were hickory smoked for twelve hours, then six solid-looking women hand-pulled the meat from the bones, leaving behind any fat and gristle. No horror scenes. No giant chopping machines. No mystery meat. The stuff looked, smelled, and tasted great. This was a product we'd be proud to take home to Mama. We just had to figure out a way to make the rest of America feel as good about it as we did.

For inspiration, the art director and I drove out to a truck stop/barbeque restaurant I knew about near East Bend, North Carolina. The place was packed, and as we soon learned, it wasn't because of the food. It was the waitresses. Barbeque waitresses are a unique species. They have high hair and low shoes. Everyone calls them by their first names. And they speak with a familiar, homespun authority that lets you know up front that they are to be trusted.

The creative equation was simple. Authority = Authenticity. If you want an authority on barbeque, you don't want Julia Child. You want one of those waitresses from East Bend. We brainstormed executions, trying to find the right one. We did the barbeque waitress taste test. We did the barbeque waitress words of wisdom: "You can always tell a good barbeque place by the number of pick-up trucks in the parking lot." Barbecue waitress true confessions. Maybe our waitress should sing. We bought tapes by country music stars and bluegrass bands, searching for our sound. We found it on an old blues tape by Muddy Waters. Scratchy. Mournful. Funky. Real . . . authentic, even! But why would a barbeque waitress be mournful? She'd lose some tips if people ate at home more, sure. But what did she have to lose compared to, say, pigs? If Rich's Barbeque took off, they're the ones who'd really be blue. So we did the Rich's Barbeque Blues, a tune we called "Long Gone," sung by a real pig who decides it's time to leave home when the farmer who owns him starts bringing home Rich's. We could have a whole revolt, with pigs carrying signs saying, "Eat fish!" Pigs disguised with berets and paste-on mustaches, boarding buses for New York, where no one eats Southern barbeque.

It was risky. With the notable exception of Charlie the Tuna, it's generally not a good idea to show a cute critter in the same commercial as his processed cousin. On the other hand, we decided if we made our pigs cartoon-like as Charlie, in their abilities and thoughts, they would be accepted as characters in the consumer's mind—and not tomorrow's doomed dinner.

BRIAN: Our testing in six locations throughout the Southwest showed people didn't mind looking at pigs in barbecue commercials. In fact, they liked the "Long Gone" commercial better than the two others we tested. But the spot didn't communicate the brand's name clearly enough for a new product. We knew our introductory commercials had to hit hard and sell quickly, or the product would languish on the shelves, and we'd be out of a budget.

LISA: With the launch of the product only four months away, we had to come up with something fabulous and fast. Then we remembered our original idea with the waitresses. The true confessions bit. What if we focused on one waitress, who's so passionate about Rich's, she has to hide the fact from the world . . . and especially from her employer?

COMM'L. NO.: RWB 8040

"MUFFIN"

RUBY: It's hard work waitressin' at the Pork-O-Rama . . . Thank ya' Muffin.

So . . . when I get home,

I don't do diddly- squat.

Keep new Rich's Southern BBQ Sandwiches on hand at all times.

Got your hickory smoked pork, and for a nice change, even chicken!

Don't have to buy buns.
Don't have to buy sauce.
Just sit home and chew.

I do love the leisure life . . . Thank ya' Muffin.

So pick you up Rich's Southern BBQ Sandwiches from your grocer's freezer . . .

Just please don't tell 'em Ruby sent ya!

Courtesy Rich's Southern Barbeque

COMM'L NO.: RWB 8014

"FORBIDDEN LOVE"

RUBY: I'd look you in the eye and say this, but bein' a waitress at the Pork-O-Rama,

my true identity must remain . . . unidentified.

Puts me in a real predicament . . .

To have fallen for Rich's Southern BBQ. Found it in my grocer's freezer . . .

And it's been forbidden love ever since. All that pure lean pork . . .

Hickory smoked 11 hours in a tangy Southern sauce.

Like to make my knees buckle!

So pick you up a box of Rich's Southern BBQ . . .

Just please don't tell 'em Ruby sent ya!

COMM'L. NO.: RWB 8020

"BOTH SIDES"

RUBY: Ever see a BBQ waitress talk out of both sides of her mouth? Watch this . . .

(ONE SIDE) I am a loyal employee of the Pork-O-Rama . . .

(OTHER SIDE) But my real true love . . . Is new Rich's Southern BBQ in your grocer's freezer!

All that pure lean pork. Hickory-smoked 11 hours in a tangy Southern sauce.

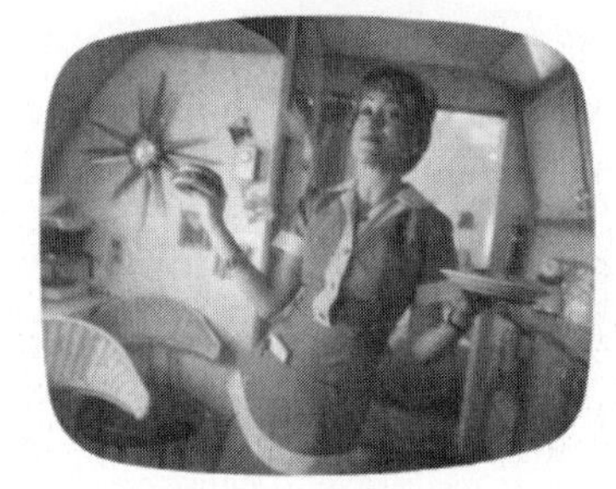

Rich's lingers on your lips,

Puts a wriggle in your hips!

And both sides of my mouth agree on that.

So ya'll pick up some Rich's Southern BBQ.

Just please don't tell 'em Ruby sent ya!

COMM'L. NO.: RWB 8030

"DISGUISE"

RUBY: I'm a well-known BBQ waitress . . . And master of disguise!

See, I can't just go to my grocer's freezer . . . For Rich's Southern BBQ.

I've got a career at the Pork-O-Rama to consider!

But then I get the cravin' . . .

(GASP)

. . . for Rich's pure lean pork . . . Hickory smoked 11 hours . . . In that tangy Southern sauce . . .

Before long, I'm in my blonde bouffant and dark sunglasses . . . Revvin' the truck and headin' to town.

So if you see me pickin' up some Rich's Southern BBQ . . .

Remember, I'm really a lot cuter than that. And please, don't tell 'em Ruby sent ya!

Courtesy Rich's Southern Barbeque

BRIAN: The creative and account teams worked over the weekend to pull together two different television executions. One had the waitress, whom we dubbed Ruby, singing voice-over as she sat in the broom closet at the "Pork-O-Rama" where she works, sneaking her Rich's fix. The other was an on-camera testimonial/confession, with Ruby trying to balance her zeal for the product with her desire to hide her identity. The spot ended with her appeal. "So y'all pick up a box of Rich's Southern Barbeque. But PLEASE . . . don't tell 'em Ruby sent you!"

LISA: Our creative director, Bob Graham, felt we could push the campaign to make more of the character. With his encouragement, we added three more spots to the campaign: "Both Sides," in which Ruby literally talks out of both sides of her mouth; "Master of Disguise," with Ruby dressed in her bouffant wig and dark sunglasses for a midnight grocery run to satisfy her Rich's craving; and "Muffin," featuring Ruby's pampered poodle. Our client in Buffalo fell in love with the "Please don't tell 'em Ruby sent you!" campaign and wanted production to start immediately.

We got two lucky breaks that made the spots magic. First was the availability of a talented young director named Matthew Harris, who loved the spots and went all out to add the "magic" touches that make a spot special, right down to rebuilding a 1950s style Airstream trailer from parts for Ruby's home. The second stroke of luck came when our agency producer, John Briley, remembered an actress named Connie Schulmann, who had appeared in the play *Steel Magnolias* off-Broadway. He brought her in for the casting session, and when we saw her, we were stunned. She wasn't what we had in mind at all. Tiny, flat-chested, young . . . with short, spiky, bleach-white hair. But when she spoke, you heard a pure, sweet Southern accent Meryl Streep couldn't top. After we cast her, we discovered she came to New York after dropping out of beauty school in Tennessee. Perfect.

The finished spots won a silver award at the International Film and Television Festival, and *Advertising Age* designated "Muffin" as the best commercial in the food category for 1988.

BRIAN: With the advertising running and in-store product sampling, the product was jumping from the shelves. The pork barbecue accounted for 80 percent of sales, with chicken at 20 percent. In fact, sales were so strong that stores were selling out of initial orders during the weekend. Even more encouraging than the initial purchases were the high repeat sales. Follow-up research in the test markets showed the advertising was driving trial [purchases] and that the product was living up to Ruby's claims.

LISA: Rebecca Cohen, art director on this project, is always quick to point out that the success of the spots was the result of a harmonic convergence of good luck with bad breaks. A collection of clients, creatives, and account people who resisted becoming a committee to become a team. And the Tennessee beauty school teacher who flunked Connie.

This is the first in a series of creative case studies scattered throughout this text to demonstrate real-life applications of the creative process in advertising. A listing of all such "Creative Spots" appears in the table of contents of this book for easy reference. Here are some things to keep in mind as you review the Rich's Barbeque case:

1. The role of research in the creative process. Ideas do not thrive in vacuums. Lisa and Brian began their work by finding out as much about barbecue and the people most likely to buy barbecue—their target audience. But research can involve more than reading. Visits to the plant and to a local barbeque restaurant provided important insights for the creative team of writer and art director.

2. Coming up with a strategy was difficult, but it was only the beginning. Once they decided on a direction, the monumental task of expressing their idea in a memorable way had just begun.

3. The creative team tested several approaches in six Southeastern markets. They noted that while one of the commercials seemed popular, brand registration was not as strong as they deemed necessary for a new product introduction.

4. Pressured by time, their months of long work paid off when they returned to the idea of the barbeque waitress.

5. Lisa rightfully pays tribute to the director who added touches to make the spots "special," and to the agency producer who found the perfect "Ruby" for the campaign. The storyboard is not the commercial. Only the commercial is the commercial, and plenty can go wrong between concept and production. In this case, everything went right.

6. Lisa's comments about "harmonic convergence" are important. The best creative work happens when everyone on the team pitches in. Possessive personalities don't make important contributions to great creative work; friendly collaboration does.

FOLLOW-UP

1. Reread the "Ruby" campaign. What do you learn from this case about how creative people work? What do you believe are the most important steps to follow in coming up with an idea to sell a product or service?

2. Even though you may not have experience in writing advertising, you might want to try the following two assignments as practice. Later in the course, come back to your work and refine it using what you have learned:

a. The client is thrilled with the "Ruby" campaign, but would like to move more chicken barbeque. Try your hand at writing a radio or television spot that might do this.

b. To capitalize on the television blitz, the client asks for a newspaper ad with a 25-cents-off coupon. Ruby is to be featured, of course. What will the headline read? What will the copy say?

CHAPTER 2

Capturing Your Creative Potential

Many great advertising campaigns succeed because they were able to make contact on an emotional level with the targeted consumer through an unexpected yet relevant approach to selling a product, service, or idea.

Product, Service, Idea
Health-Tex Children's Clothing
(see Fig.1-2)

Target Audience
Mothers frustrated by toddler clothes that don't fit properly.

Unexpected Yet Relevant Connection
"Agonizing" true stories on TV talk shows

In such cases, the advertising can actually *become* the product. A fragrance by any other name is just another smell, but the sensuous advertisements for Obsession, Eternity, Poison, or Lauren create unique images and allude to intangible benefits that a quick whiff from a sample at the cosmetics counter might never do.

What are some of the relevant, unexpected connections that have strengthened our feelings as consumers about certain products?

A hand pours Bombay Sapphire Gin into a goblet and, instead of splashes, the droplets appear to be cut gemstones. The tagline reads, "Pour something priceless." (See Figure 2.1.)

A box of Tang Juice Beverage makes its claim as a Vitamin C enriched drink kids will love, using a headline, "Clever new ways to disguise nutrition." Beside the product are a fast food container of string beans, a candy bar wrapper around a slice of Swiss cheese, and a candy box labeled "Beanets" with lima beans spilling out.

Courtesy Carillon Importers, Ltd.

FIGURE 2-1

When there's not much to say about a product, a general rule of thumb is not to say it, but to use visual imagery instead to give the message impact and meaning. The combination of exquisite photography, a simple and clever verbal statement, and the splashes of gin magically transformed into cut sapphires is quite irresistible.

Federal Express runs a magazine ad promoting the idea that it hires good people, regardless of race or color. The rather startling headline is stacked as follows:

We don't hire Blacks.
We don't hire women.
We don't hire Hispanics.
We don't hire Asians.
We don't hire Jews.
We don't hire Disabled.
We don't hire Whites.

The copy begins: "We hire people."

The first two pages of a three-page magazine ad read like a scene from a spy thriller. Only when you get to the third and final page do you read the clincher: "And as the billowing smoke began to tear at my nostrils and burn my eyes, I realized that it was something much, much worse than an overheated engine. It was my chicken pot pie burning in the kitchen, the charred, inedible victim of my engrossment in Mitsubishi's Home Theater with Dolby Surround Sound." (See Figure 2.2)

A series of ads for the Oster Kitchen Center, one of those all-in-one kitchen helpers, has readers doing double takes on purpose. Shown mixing cake batter, the ad reads: Makes Great Salads. With its food processor slicing carrots, the ad reads: Makes Great Shakes. The final ad in the three-page series shows all attachments, with the headline: Makes Great Sense. (See Figure 2.3.)

Neutrogena, the transparent facial bar, doesn't tell you to wash your face. Too predictable. "Once a day, purify your skin," reads the headline beside a graphic display of the bar popping out of its wrapper. (See Figure 2.4.)

Even a cigarette company finds a way to capture attention in a most unusual way. Claiming "there's a difference between people who smoke Merit and people who smoke other cigarettes," the ad carries a long list of statements that have fun with words. For example, people who smoke Merit "know that consommé isn't what a French couple does on their wedding night, know that Plato is not some distant planet . . . or some silly dog, know that a megabyte isn't treated by an orthodontist, and that you won't find Chateaubriand on a wine list."

Finally, an ad for Interplak, a "home plaque removal instrument," headlines its ad, "How can a person who puts high technology on his head put low technology in his mouth?" The headline nestles between a hi-tech stereo headphone and a plain toothbrush.

Before you read on, go back over these examples and identify the unexpected element in each ad. Does each of these elements pass the test for relevance? Does the addition of each element add a touch of entertainment to the ad message, and how critical is this entertainment value in attracting the attention of

The insane laughter faded away behind me. To one side of the clearing sat a deserted house, as decomposed and forgotten as the people who'd once lived there.

The door opened, and I was in the front room, a room so dark I felt I could reach out and run my fingers through its inky stillness.

From outside the window came the sounds of the night. Owls. Crickets. And from across the room...drip, drip, drip.

Courtesy Mitsubishi Electric Sales America, Inc.

FIGURE 2-2 (A)

My eyes, adjusting to the light, made out what appeared to be a coat hanging from a hat rack, but as the haze dissolved from my sight I saw that from the neck of the coat stared the lifeless face of Kuperman, his eyes frozen in horror. A shrieking laugh, as inescapable as a nightmare, rang out around me.

My heart, already shaking at the cage of my chest, exploded as a hand fell upon my shoulder.

FIGURE 2-2 (A) Continued.

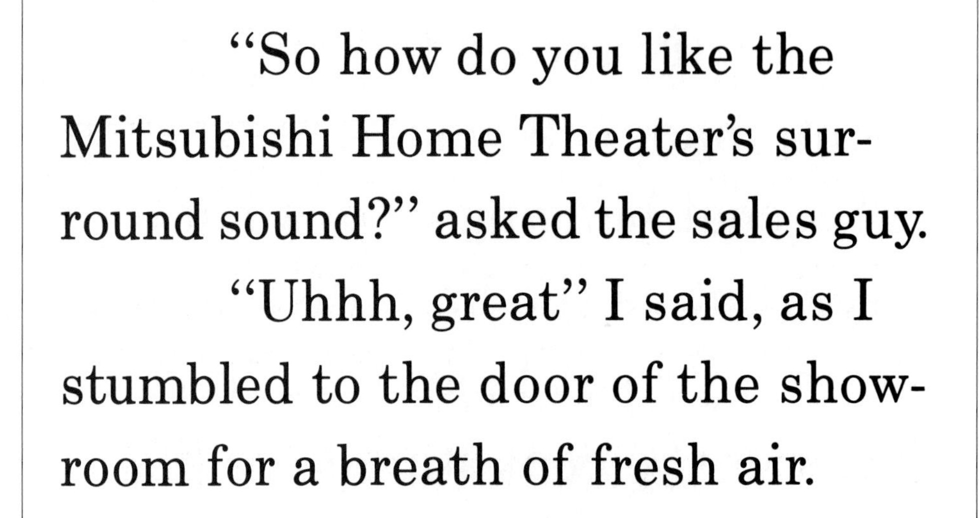

FIGURE 2-2 (A) Continued.

The sound of a single bullet buzzed straight past my ear.

I didn't have to look at the rear-view mirror to know that Dubrov was back on our tail. Our only avenue of escape was through the street market up ahead.

The brightly colored patchwork of stalls rushed up to meet us as Johnson put his foot to the floor. A crate of watermelons exploded wetly against the car, the pink juice streaming across the windscreen.

I stole a quick glance in the mirror. Dubrov's gleaming black limo was getting closer by the second.

It was then that I sensed the first hints of acrid smoke. The stink of a grinding, dying engine.

Our car was going to go, and with it, all our chances.

And as the billowing smoke began to tear at my nostrils and burn my eyes, I realized that it was something much, much worse than an overheated engine. It was my

chicken pot pie burning in the kitchen, the charred, inedible victim of my engrossment in Mitsubishi's Home Theater with Dolby Surround™ Sound.

Mitsubishi's Home Theater brings you an experience so lifelike, you'll feel as though you're right in the middle of the action. And because we make a whole range of components, you can create the system that suits you best. The example above features the VS-5004R 50-inch big screen TV and the E-5300 Dolby Surround™ audio system components. For your nearest authorized dealer, call (800) 527-8888 ext. 245

MITSUBISHI

TECHNICALLY, ANYTHING IS POSSIBLE®

Courtesy Mitsubishi Electric Sales America, Inc.

FIGURE 2-2 (B)

Swimming at night had never bothered me before. But as I watched the sun retreat behind the horizon, an overwhelming sense of loneliness swept over me.

I peered into the heavy black water and knew that this was now an alien world, no longer a turquoise playground, but something dark, mysterious, uncaring.

The peaceful murmur of waves and seagulls, sounds I usually found so comforting, had taken on a sinister and mocking air.

Suddenly, there was a splash somewhere off to my right. I turned, but could see nothing. My breath quickened as I heard another ripple, this time behind me.

I was fighting to keep the rush of adrenaline from pushing me into a blind panic when, my God! I felt something brush against the soles of my feet.

As my terror found voice in a bellowing scream I realized it was

only my cat Columbus, and that watching a movie such as this on a Mitsubishi Home Theater with Dolby Surround™ Sound was not, repeat not, good for my nerves.

Mitsubishi's Home Theater brings you an experience so lifelike, you'll feel as though you're right there in the middle of the action. And because we make a whole range of components, you can create the system that suits you best. The example above features the CS-3521R 35-inch direct-view TV, the E-5300 Dolby Surround™ audio system and the HS-U52 Hi-Fi VCR. For your nearest authorized dealer, call (800) 527-8888 ext. 245.

MITSUBISHI
TECHNICALLY, ANYTHING IS POSSIBLE®

Courtesy Mitsubishi Electric Sales America, Inc.

FIGURE 2-2 (C)

the target audience? (Remember that "entertainment" may consist of things other than humor, such as shock value.) Do you think it is better to add an element to the ad that will restrict its interest to the intended audience (such as the Merit ad, which is obviously targeted to more educated smokers), or should advertisers avoid such practices in order to reach the widest audience possible?

The answer to the last question should be obvious. A cardinal rule of advertising is that it is far more efficient to target advertising messages to very specific, well-defined groups of people—the most promising prospects for the advertised goods or services. Anything that captures the attention of this select group by establishing a relationship between them and what the advertiser is offering for sale is going to be beneficial in the long run.

Guidelines for Effective Creative Work

The following are offered merely as guidelines and should not be considered hard and fast rules, as the first "rule" points out. Nonetheless, keeping these points in mind may help you rule out certain approaches to creative problem solving.

1. Frankly, there are no hard-and-fast rules for creating great advertising. Quite often the exception is the best choice. Be forewarned that, before you begin making exceptions, you should learn how to play the game.

2. Most products and services are not unique, despite what clients may tell you. That is why your advertising must be.

3. Unfortunately, your advertising message is the least important thing in the life of your consumer. That's why how you communicate is just as important as what you communicate.

4. Remember that you are not trying to convince your client—the manufacturer—of the value of the product. They are already convinced and may be the worst judge of your campaign strategies for this very reason. Remember that you are trying instead to establish a relationship with a very special group of other people, those who are most likely to buy.

5. People often hesitate to tell you the real reasons they like or dislike a product, so in most cases you'll have to figure this out based on what they choose to tell you—or ask more questions. A mother in England told a market researcher that milk was best for her kids and soda pop the worst. When he asked what she bought for them, her reply was, "Soda pop. They hate milk."

6. People tend to be highly irrational creatures. Most goods and services, therefore, are purchased for irrational or emotional reasons. That's why all advertising should rely to some extent on emotional appeal, and why some advertising should completely rely on emotional appeal.

7. An advertisement doesn't sell the brand so much as it establishes a relationship between the brand and one consumer, which may result in a purchase. To do this, the advertisers imbue brands with personalities. Baby powder is gentle, soothing, and caring. A man's cologne is subtle or bold or irresistible—or all three! Breakfast cereals are friendly, household cleaners are as fussy about dirt as you are, and automobiles want to make you feel like ruler of the road. Such human qualities attributed to products through advertising can build a relationship between the product and an individual, which may result in a purchase. Think of this relationship as a sort of friendship between two things: a person and a brand.

8. Clichés in advertising are like boring people: they tend to be tuned out. Using the same words, the same headlines, the same illustration, the same joke—the same anything too frequently will reduce the potential of your campaign after the first few encounters by the target audience.

9. There is always a better way to sell something. Even a small child can write "advertising" in minutes, and many grown people claim to have similar abilities. The truth is that many can write bad or ordinary advertising, but few can write great advertising. Every day of your life, you will see or hear a great number of rather mundane commercial messages. Fortunately, if you're lucky, you'll remember the few great ones you also saw or heard. And that's the point. Those few standouts are the ones everyone knows and responds to. Great ads require fewer media dollars because each time they run, they work harder. In advertising, that's efficiency. If you were paying for the advertising, what kind of ad would you demand?

Courtesy John Oster Mfg. Co.

FIGURE 2-3
Oster delivers a triple whammy with its clever use of three consecutive right hand pages to promote its Kitchen Center appliance. What makes the series all the more brilliant, though, is the deliberate discordance within the first two head and visual combinations, followed by the winning message of the third and final headline. Someone pulled out all the creative stops for this effective piece of work.

What Constitutes Creativity in Advertising?

"Different, unique, unusual, out of the ordinary," are some of the spontaneous definitions advertising students provide when asked to define "creativity." "Creativity has no boundaries," one student adds. "If you don't practice on a regular basis, you can lose your touch." Another claims that "creativity is a method that offers a unique perspective about a certain thing."

But the comment I like the most is this one: "Creativity is all from me."

Defining creativity is not as easy as it seems, as Patricia Hutchings of Alverno College discovered when she discussed the topic in the context of teaching college students. She quotes author Arthur Koestler's definition of creativity: "The bringing together, for the first time, of previously unrelated matrices of thought."

Ann Dreher, an acting teacher at the University of South Carolina, says, "People love certainty and creativity is just the opposite. You just have faith that the creativity is there and summon the guts to use it. In the simplest sense," she adds, "creativity is nothing but problem solving."

Harry Miller, another professor at USC, hates the word "creativity." He prefers to call it innovative problem solving. "All you do all your life is solve problems and if you say you're not creative, what you mean is you're a bad problem solver."

Bill Mould, director of the USC honors program, says, "Being creative means a willingness to put your soul on the line and requires an enormous amount of self-trust."

One behavioral expert defines creativity as "novel but appropriate behavior." Professor William Seidel of San Francisco State University, who teaches a course

FIGURE 2-4
Had this headline read, "Use Neutrogena once a day to purify your skin," we would have answered, "Ho hum." Instead, the writer invites the reader to complete the thought by making a connection with the prominent brand name on the package. Such involvement is the stuff that powerful advertising is made of. Note, too, the dynamic thrust inherent in the visual, with the product seemingly jet-propelled from its package and, not incidentally, nicely framing the text for the reader.

Courtesy Neutrogena Company. Photographer: Rudi Legname.

called "Developing, Patenting, and Marketing New Ideas," begins his course by asking students to raise their hands if they believe they are creative. According to Seidel, "Usually, a daring few put their hands up. Then I tell how, during the 1973 oil embargo, a major oil company decided it needed more creative executives. So it hired a team of psychologists to determine exactly what makes a person creative. After a great deal of study, the psychologists reported this:

"People who think they are creative are. People who think they aren't aren't.

"Then I ask the class to raise their hands if they think they are creative, and if every hand doesn't go up, I tell the story again."

Strategies for Creativity

Hutchings lists three strategies for approaching creativity. Each has a critical application to the creative process in advertising.

1. ***Risk-Taking.*** Also known as "the right to fail." The problem many of us have with this strategy is that throughout school we have been urged not to take risks, but to come up with the right answers, so that we "succeed." Therefore, risk-taking is in sharp contrast to conservatism, which prefers traditional solutions, puts old principles to work in tried-and-true ways, and distrusts any shifts in emphasis. Yet the right to fail is essential to creativity, just as the prevention of failure is the essence of conservatism. The creative act must be uninhibited and marked by supreme confidence; there can be no fear of failure. Nothing inhibits so fiercely, or shrinks a vision so drastically, or pulls a dream to earth so swiftly, as fear of failure. If you take risks, you may get an A or an F on a creative assignment. If you play it safe, however, chances are you will always get just a safe, average grade.

The effective advertising copywriter or art director is never afraid to take a chance with an idea. As Oscar Wilde once said, "An idea that is not dangerous is hardly worth calling an idea at all."

2. ***Divergent Thinking.*** The use of more open-ended, divergent, ambiguous modes of thinking often contributes to creativity. Many of us know the story of Albert Einstein failing math. That he would rather ask questions than fill in the blanks is often offered as the explanation for this phenomenon. He was a divergent, rather than a convergent, thinker.

When Hutchings asked a group of her students who were completing internships to describe their work sites, she got predictable, dull papers: "There are two secretaries in the front office and a row of private offices down the corridor." But when she asked each student to find a metaphor to describe the work site, the results were dramatically different. One compared her site to the four stomachs of a cow, with information passing from one stage of digestion to the next; another compared her site to a popcorn popper in which events continued to explode in almost random fashion.

Metaphor—using one unrelated idea to describe another—forces us to see things in new ways and to make observations that raise questions, rather than answer them. How would you describe corn flakes if you were told to use the metaphor of a personal computer? How would you describe a popular shampoo or toothpaste in terms of the Caribbean Sea? How many other product-metaphor combinations can you come up with, and how far can you take them? Looking for a new way to open a can, you might ask: "How does nature deal with openings?" After considering such cases as the opening of a flower, a mouth, or the earth in an earthquake, you might eventually come to the peapod, which opens easily because of a weak seam. It was from the peapod, so the story goes, that the idea of the pop-top can was born.

FIGURE 2-5
These two ads for Smith Corona Personal Word Processors attest to the compelling nature of cleverly turned words and phrases. Not only are the headlines lightheartedly clever, but the same lilting tone takes hold in the copy and moves the reader swiftly and smoothly to the ultimate conclusion: why aren't you using one of these machines? Note how the uniformly crisp design and consistent type styles add to the campaign look of these ads, proof that every detail is important in putting together an advertising message.

Courtesy Smith Corona Corporation

3. ***A Sense of Humor.*** A fair amount of research links humor and creativity. Creative people, for example, tend to have better senses of humor than noncreative people. Humor appears to create an atmosphere conducive to the kind of risk-taking necessary for creativity, for humor requires the same kind of shift in perspective—or new slant, or sudden, unexpected change of direction—that is crucial to creative problem-solving.[1]

Unfortunately, there is no way in the world to order a person to "Be creative!" In fact, this sort of ultimatum is a surefire way to inhibit creative thinking. So if

[1] Patricia Hutchings, "Break Out, Be There! Thoughts on Teaching Creativity," *College Teaching* (Spring 1987): 43–48. Copyright 1987. Published by Heldref Publications. Used with permission of the Helen Dwight Reid Educational Foundation.

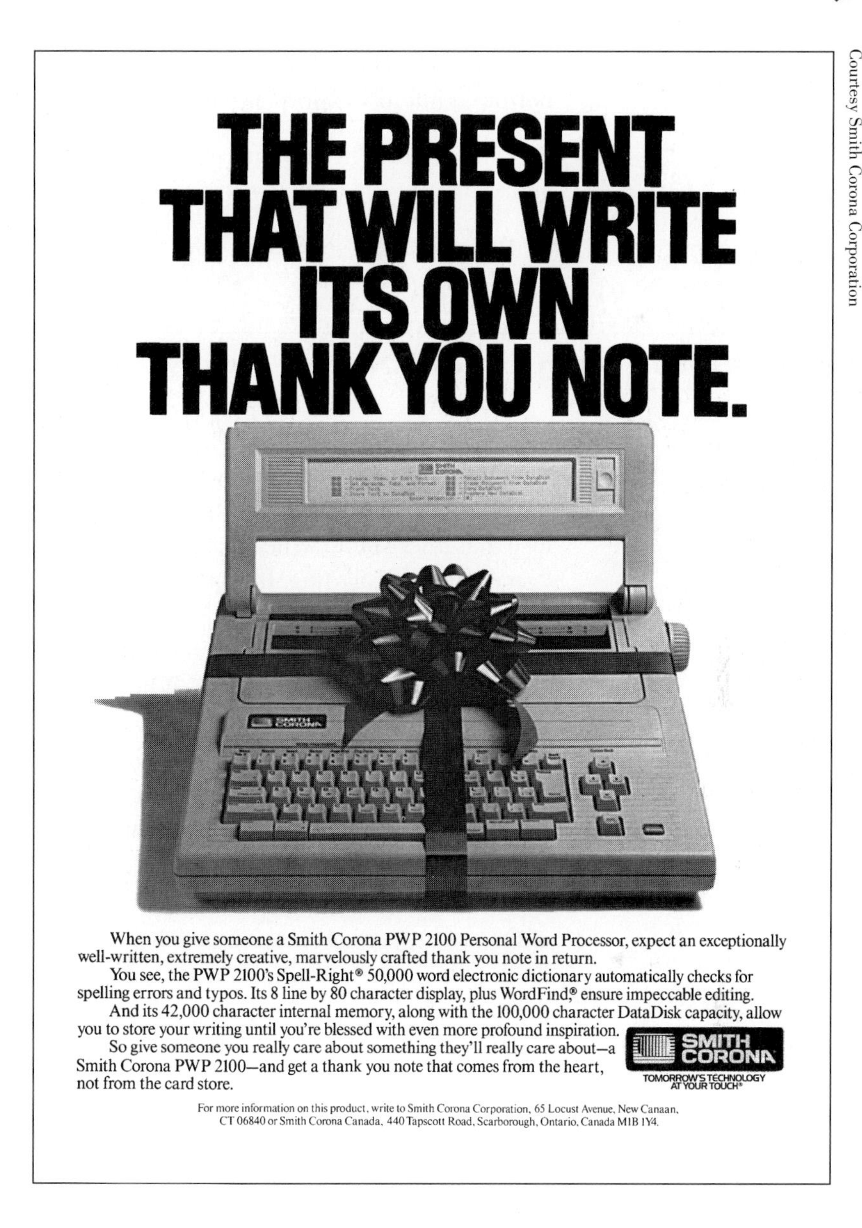

Courtesy Smith Corona Corporation

your advertising professor refuses to settle for adequate work and tells you, "This won't do. Try something new. Take a risk. Be creative," take heed. Receiving permission to take a risk is wonderful motivation for doing so. You might surprise yourself.

Lisa Duke, speaking to advertising students, offers more advice on creative thinking. "Don't flinch at the new and unfamiliar," she advises, "but make it familiar to the client and to the prospect. Appeal to the emotions. Draw from the world of *un*common sense. Make the old new, the uninteresting interesting, and do it—sometimes—in just 30 seconds. Bat ideas back and forth with a creative teammate; it will help both of you to refine your thinking." She adds that at Long, Haymes & Carr, the agency where she works, three criteria for good creative thinking are:

1. Is it right? The right idea is true to the product as opposed to one which uses borrowed interest to draw attention to it.

2. Is it powerful? A powerful idea changes you, informs you, even transforms you.

3. Do you want to see it again and again?

Other Ways to Recognize and Develop Creative Potential

Although some argue that creativity is something we are born with, others claim it can be nurtured by those who feel they lack creative insight. Later in this text, you will be asked to explore your creativity through a writing exercise that frees you to write what you feel without stopping to judge whether it is "good" or "bad" writing. If it is true, as Patricia Hutchings states, that creativity involves some risk, it is also important to know that taking risks is not without its limits. A prudent risk, one that generally isn't going to get you in serious trouble, is probably the best kind to take. While risk-taking is a sign of creativity, there are other signs as well.

Creative people tend not to think in terms of right and wrong or black and white. For them, the answers to problems lie somewhere in between. They tend to be showoffs. Many say they would enjoy spending an entire day alone, just thinking. They tend to be open with others about their true feelings, think of themselves as nonconformists, ask questions frequently, demand a good deal of themselves, enjoy observing the behavior of others, and enjoy the challenge of finding a solution to a problem. Most of them have a good sense of humor, and many tend to forget details, such as names of people and streets.

Does any of this sound like you? If not, remember that even without these traits, you may be a very creative person nonetheless.

What Makes Ads Work?

1. Does the ad gain my attention without confusing me? Would it stand out in a magazine or newspaper full of ads (or amidst the clutter of all the other television or radio commercials, or all the other mail in the mailbox?

2. Does the ad show empathy with the target audience? Is the target clearly defined? Is there a sense of involvement, i.e., "That's me they're talking about"?

3. Does the ad clearly communicate the key benefits? Is there a reason to consider purchase, whether rational or emotional, overt or implied? If implied, is it clear enough?

4. Does the ad use a memorable device to make you remember it?

5. Does the ad make you feel positive about the product, the ad, the manufacturer, and yourself?

6. Is there anything about the ad, however small, that might be improved? How could it be improved?

7. Does the idea lend itself to other aspects of integrated marketing communication? How?

People who make ads ought to know how to critique ads. If you can look objectively at another's work, you also should be able to apply those rules to your own efforts.

There is value in having your work evaluated by someone else. First, the other person comes to your idea with a clear and unbiased mind. There's no vested interest in saying this works or this doesn't work. Second, if your evaluator knows advertising, chances are he or she can judge your work as both consumer and professional.

The key to the critique is objectivity. This means critique the work, not the person. First look for positive elements, then question those that may not seem clear or strong. Finally, talk about things that don't seem to work well for you. This is best done by questioning, as opposed to "telling" what you think is wrong ("Do you think most people would understand the idea?" instead of "Most people wouldn't understand it.") It's also important to use "I statements" as opposed to "you statements" ("I feel this isn't working" is much closer to the truth than, "You didn't make this work.")

Ogilvy & Mather tells its account people to ask the following questions when evaluating creative work:

1. Is it on strategy? What did you get from the advertising? Was that *net impression* a good or bad one? Why? Remember to be a human being. React to this advertising as a consumer, not as an advertising person. Does this ad address the right group of people? Is the tone consistent with the strategy?

2. Is it a good execution? Is the promise visualized effectively? How? Is the brand name up front enough? Is the core selling idea clear? Does the execution lend itself to a total campaign? If so, what might be some other executions? Does something make you stop, look, listen quickly? What is it?

More Guidelines for Good Advertising

Make certain your ideas develop from a sound strategy. Make a meaningful promise to your target audience, but avoid overpromising. There is a difference between exaggeration for comic effect and promising more than the product can deliver. While the first can become a memorable device, the second is doomed to failure once the prospect tries the product the first—and only—time.

Stress benefits over selling points. A selling point is an attribute of a product or service. A benefit is the satisfaction gained by using the product or service. "Women don't buy lipstick, they buy hope," is how Revlon founder Charles Revson puts it. Tires promise safety and a smooth ride, not unique tread design. Macintosh promises user-friendliness in a computer, not sophisticated circuitry.

Never risk offending your audience. A joke in questionable taste may destroy years of brand image building. Instead of telling people what they should do, write in a way that makes them feel they have made the decision themselves. Finally, make the idea seem simple, even if it was tough to create. If it seems simple and it works, chances are it wasn't easy to invent.

Suggested Activities

1. Find a product or service as a topic for the following exercise. Some suggestions:

   a. Locate a product at your local grocery or general merchandiser that isn't advertised extensively. Look especially for cleaning products, foods, hardware, appliances, and health and beauty aids. Read the label to find out what the product offers. Examine competing products on the shelf to find out how they differ.

   b. Use library resources to find out more about the product category (shampoos, microwave dinners, toaster ovens, etc.).

   c. Consult market research data such as that found in MRI (Market Research, Inc.) to learn more about the product category, including demographics and lifestyle characteristics of the heavy user, share of market, competing products, etc.

   d. Interview local people who use the product or competing products to gain additional insight.

2. Now make a presentation to the class in which you:

   a. Describe the product/brand. Share what you know of its history (current uses, current target market, key selling points, current advertising approach).

   b. Discuss the competition for this product. Include not only similar products but other types of products/services that might compete for the same consumer dollar.

   c. Speculate as to whether this product, through a shift in the advertising approach, might be targeted to other audiences. If you see new opportunities, explain them. If you see no new opportunities, defend the current position of the product.

   d. Ask others in the class to help you clarify your goals in advertising this product.

Changing People's Minds Without Changing the Client's Image

Andy Ellis,
Creative Director

Hawley Martin Partners,
Richmond, Va.

Most seasoned creative people I know cringe at the mention of the term "bank advertising." Somewhere in their careers they were assigned to a bank account and spent months at a drawing table or keyboard trying to come up with yet another way of saying, "Yeah, our interest rates on long-term certificates of deposit aren't the worst in town."

It's a highly competitive category littered with mediocre, me-too advertising. After all, in the public's mind, there really is little that differentiates one bank from another.

But the Riggs National Bank is an exception. It's the oldest financial institution in Washington, D.C., and can claim first families as customers as far back as the Lincolns. In a town that has more embassies than lawyers (well, maybe not), Riggs is considered the leader in international banking. They helped finance the construction of the Capitol dome, a boatload of *National Geographic* expeditions, and even America's purchase of a piece of real estate known as Alaska.

When Hawley Martin acquired this account, everyone in the creative department begged to be assigned to it (some even brought baked goods). We were all aware of the strong, solid advertising Riggs had been running over the last ten years and were anxious to see if we could do the previous agencies one better. Copywriter Peter Sheldon and art director Art Webb were given the task.

Now as you might imagine, when you're the banker to presidents, diplomats, and potentates, your perceived image is going to fall somewhere between highfalutin and hoity-toity. And Riggs wasn't exactly out to dispel this image. Neither was their advertising. Every ad was tagged with the theme line, "Bankers to the most important money in the world." But as regulations, and the banking industry as a whole, began to change, Riggs realized a need to appeal to a broader base of potential customers.

The highly affluent (top 15 percent of the market) already saw Riggs as "their bank." The challenge now was to convince the next market tier of the same. So Riggs began opening branches in the suburbs surrounding the District of Columbia. It had an impact, but there was still a slight problem.

Research told us that many people who were indeed potential customers didn't see themselves that way. If they had a family income of $75,000 a year, they thought they needed to earn $100,000 to bank at Riggs. And those folks who were pulling in $100,000 believed they needed an income of $150,000. In other words, there was a large, affluent contingent out there believing it was

Courtesy Riggs National Bank

SURROUNDING A PICTURE OF THE OVAL OFFICE OF THE WHITE HOUSE, the copy for this ad reads: "When Abraham Lincoln needed a checking account, he came to Riggs. As did Theodore Roosevelt, Harry Truman and so many others who've made the White House their home. Leading some to believe you have to be written up in history to bank at Riggs. When, in truth, you just need to be someone who writes checks. RIGGS. Bankers to the most important money in the world. Yours."

not affluent enough to bank at Riggs. That unless this group was interested in trust services, estate planning, or some other sophisticated bank offering, Riggs wasn't interested in it.

Our job was to take these people's brains and turn them around 180 degrees. To convince them that their most basic banking needs (checking, savings, etc.) are just as important to Riggs as Socks' trust fund.

At the same time, it was important to maintain Riggs' heritage. The "aura," as we refer to it, had been well established. And while people viewed this aura as rich and well-to-do, they also felt it connoted stability, safety, and traditional values. Given that the country was beginning to head into a recession,

Courtesy Riggs National Bank

AROUND A MONTAGE OF NATIONAL GEOGRAPHIC PHOTOS FROM AROUND THE WORLD, this ad states, "For over a century, Riggs has helped send National Geographic to some of the most extraordinary locations above, below, and upon the face of the earth. You should see some of the places we've helped send families. RIGGS. Bankers to the most important money in the world. Yours."

it would have been foolish for us to have walked away from those attributes.

So what it all boiled down to was that we were going to have to walk a fine line between changing perceptions and reinforcing the known. Not an easy task. I remember Peter and Art complaining at this point that whenever they shook their heads, they heard the sound of washers bouncing around inside empty coffee cans.

Three weeks (and several chocolate doughnuts) later, "the boys" showed up in my office with a number of campaign ideas, including the campaign that was eventually accepted by the client and subsequently produced.

What they proposed was to take the history of Riggs and turn it around in a

Courtesy Riggs National Bank

FRAMING A COLLECTION OF FOREIGN COINS, this Riggs ad tells readers, "Around Washington, there's one place to go to turn pesos into pounds into rubles back into pesos. That knows the value of the franc, be it French, Rwandan, or Cameroonian. Yet if you live around, say, Rockville or Arlington or Fairfax and have a problem as simple as an unbalanced balance, we can explain it to you. In just plain English. RIGGS. Bankers to the most important money in the world. Yours."

way that asks potential customers for their business. For example, the first television commercial centered around the "bank of presidents" theme. That Lincoln, Truman, and others had come to Riggs for checking accounts. "Leading some to believe you have to be written up in history to bank at Riggs. When in truth, you just need to be someone who writes checks."

The other commercials leverage their expertise in international banking with quality service, their history of security with savings accounts, and their support of *National Geographic* with their ability to help on personal loans. The magazine and radio ads take a similar approach. Please note that in the ads shown

Courtesy Riggs National Bank

THE CAPITOL DOME WOULDN'T BE THE CAPITOL DOME," reads this Riggs ad, "without frescoes by Brumidi, the Freedom statue from Rome, hand-sculpted Corinthian columns and assistance from Riggs. But even if all you need is cement, shingles, and two-by-fours from the corner hardware store, we can help with that, too. RIGGS. Bankers to the most important money in the world. Yours."

here we did add one important word to the Riggs tag line. It now reads, "Bankers to the most important money in the world. Yours."

I guess there's a more important reason I wanted to share this particular case study, other than the fact that I like the creative product. The Riggs image campaign is a good example of the world's second oldest profession (prostitution is said to have been first, advertising second, and interior decorating third). This is advertising in its purest form; communication designed to change perception. And what I particularly appreciate about this campaign is that it doesn't ignore what the public already perceives about the client.

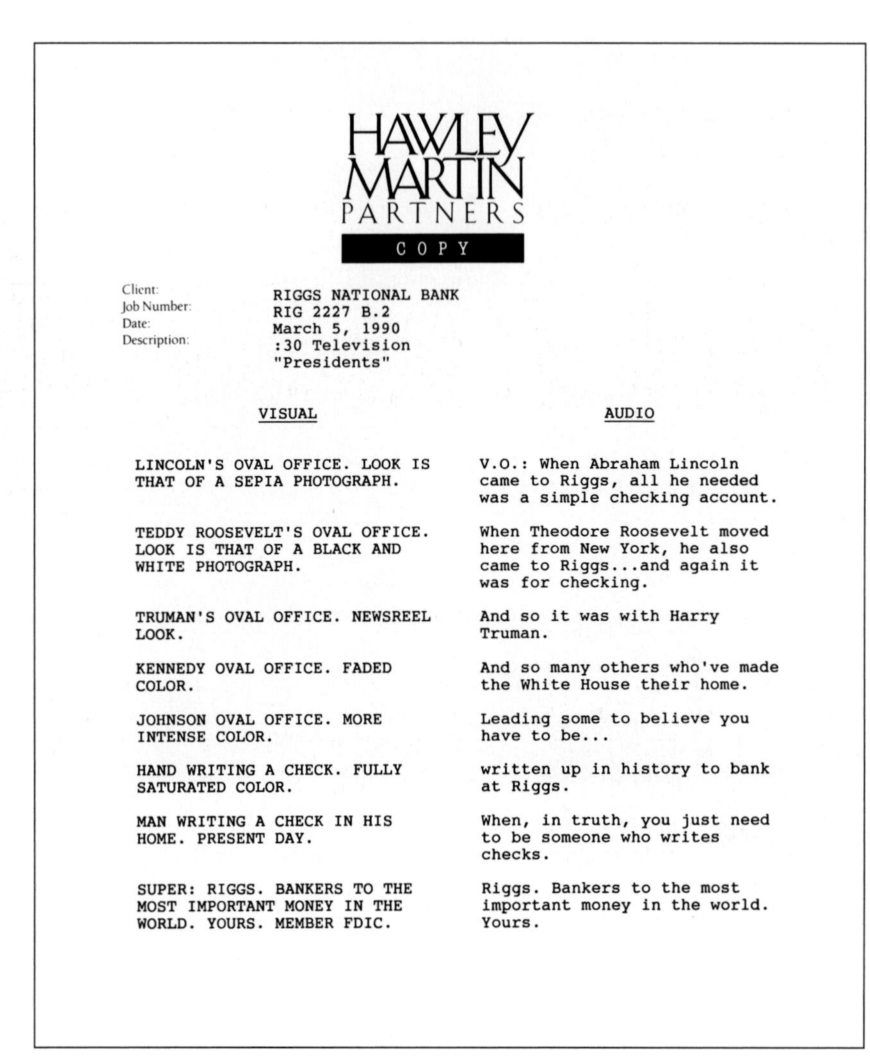
HAWLEY MARTIN PARTNERS

COPY

Client: RIGGS NATIONAL BANK
Job Number: RIG 2227 B.2
Date: March 5, 1990
Description: :30 Television "Presidents"

VISUAL	AUDIO
LINCOLN'S OVAL OFFICE. LOOK IS THAT OF A SEPIA PHOTOGRAPH.	V.O.: When Abraham Lincoln came to Riggs, all he needed was a simple checking account.
TEDDY ROOSEVELT'S OVAL OFFICE. LOOK IS THAT OF A BLACK AND WHITE PHOTOGRAPH.	When Theodore Roosevelt moved here from New York, he also came to Riggs...and again it was for checking.
TRUMAN'S OVAL OFFICE. NEWSREEL LOOK.	And so it was with Harry Truman.
KENNEDY OVAL OFFICE. FADED COLOR.	And so many others who've made the White House their home.
JOHNSON OVAL OFFICE. MORE INTENSE COLOR.	Leading some to believe you have to be...
HAND WRITING A CHECK. FULLY SATURATED COLOR.	written up in history to bank at Riggs.
MAN WRITING A CHECK IN HIS HOME. PRESENT DAY.	When, in truth, you just need to be someone who writes checks.
SUPER: RIGGS. BANKERS TO THE MOST IMPORTANT MONEY IN THE WORLD. YOURS. MEMBER FDIC.	Riggs. Bankers to the most important money in the world. Yours.

It would have been very easy to have created ads for Riggs about checking accounts, savings accounts, and so on without ever mentioning presidents, *National Geographic*, or international banking. But the campaign is stronger because it mentions all these things. The reader sees the ad and says, "Oh yeah, that's Riggs, I know them," and then we turn that perception on its ear so the reader concludes, "Well, I never knew they were interested in my business before." And while research data is still coming in, preliminary reports tell us this is exactly what is happening.

I wish there were some little turn of phrase I could come up with to encapsu-

Riggs National Bank
"Presidents" :30 TV

1 V.O.: *When Abraham Lincoln came to Riggs, all he needed was a simple checking account. When Theodore Roosevelt moved here from New York, he also came to Riggs . . . and again it was for checking.*

2 *And so it was with Harry Truman. And so many others who've made the White House their home.*

3 *Leading some to believe you have to be written up in history to bank at Riggs.*

Courtesy Riggs National Bank

4 *When, in truth, you just need to be someone who writes checks.*

5 *Riggs. Bankers to the most important money in the world. Yours.*

late what we learned from this experience. I mean, there should be a moral to this story, right? Something like, never try to change your client from apples into oranges overnight. Or always strive to say the expected in an unexpected way. Or better yet, you can't run with the big dogs if you're asleep under the front porch.

Words to live by, huh?

AUTHOR'S NOTE *In addition to thanking his talented copywriter and art director, Ellis credits the following individuals for the excellent work that went into this Riggs campaign:*

Client:	RIGGS NATIONAL BANK
Job Number:	RIG 2227B.1
Date:	March 5, 1990
Description:	:30 Television "Safekeeping"

VISUAL	AUDIO
STOCK FOOTAGE OF DOUGLAS MACARTHUR REVIEWING TROOPS.	While General MacArthur fought to keep his country free, he kept his belongings safe. By shipping them to Riggs.
PAN ACROSS MASONS CEREMONIOUSLY PASSING A GAVEL.	When George Washington's gavel needed a secure home, the Masons of Potomac Lodge Number Five proudly brought it to our door.
PAN ACROSS CUB SCOUTS RECITING THE PLEDGE.	So when Andy Martin needed a place to keep his son's college fund, the choice was simple.
PULL INTO TO ONE VERY SINCERE CUB SCOUT.	Because you can't trust the education of America's first switch-hitting, brain surgeon, astronaut to just anyone.
SUPER: RIGGS. BANKERS TO THE MOST IMPORTANT MONEY IN THE WORLD. YOURS. MEMBER FDIC.	Riggs. Bankers to the most important money in the world. Yours.

At Hawley Martin: Jo Watson, account supervisor; Cathy Bendall, strategy development and research; Elaine Cappiello, account executive; Linda Locks, print production; Amy Daniels, TV production; Christie Dowda, traffic.

At Riggs National Bank: David Palombi, Vice President for Corporate Communications; Suzanne Duncan, Advertising Manager.

Everybody Else: Marc Chait, TV director, Red Dog Films, Los Angeles; Carol Chaffin, TV & radio music. In Your Ear, Richmond; Steve Bonini, photography, Portland, Oregon.

Riggs National Bank
"Safekeeping" :30 TV

1 V.O.: *While General MacArthur fought to keep his country free, he kept his belongings safe . . . by shipping them to Riggs.*

2 *When George Washington's gavel needed a secure home . . .*

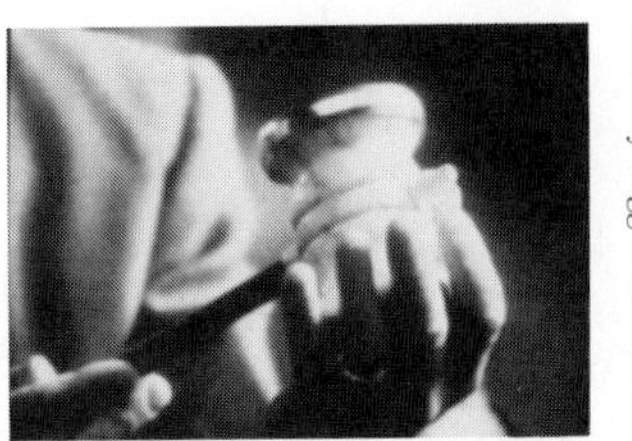

3 *. . . the Masons of Potomac Lodge Number Five proudly brought it to our door.*

Courtesy Riggs National Bank

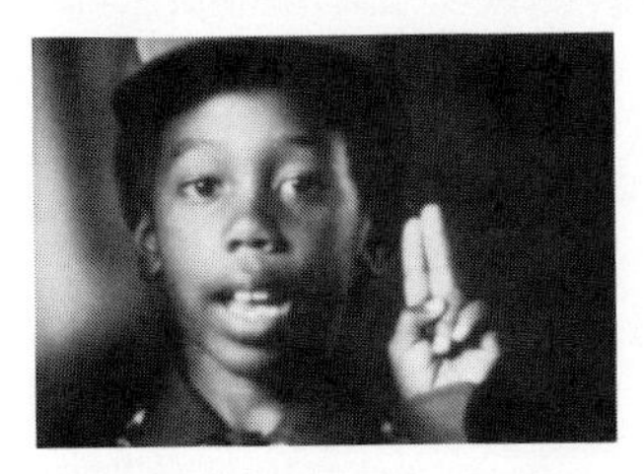

4 *So, when Andy Martin needed a place to keep his son's college fund, the choice was simple. Because you can't trust the education of America's first switch-hitting, brain surgeon, astronaut to just anyone.*

5 *Riggs. Bankers to the most important money in the world. Yours.*

FOLLOW-UP

How closely does the creative strategy solve the communications problem? Because banks are pretty much alike, bank advertising can be a challenge to the creative team. For the next week or two, clip ads from your local paper for financial institutions. When you have enough samples, comment on how each attempts to distinguish itself from its competition in the market. How many are successful at doing so? What's the difference in the advertising of those that succeed and those that do not?

Client: Riggs
Job Number: RIG 2227B
Date: March 5, 1991
Description: :30 Television
"National Geographic"

VISUAL	AUDIO
FILM OF POLAR BEAR WALKING ACROSS ICE.	
FILM OF PENGUIN WALKING ACROSS ICE.	
FILM OF MOUNTAIN CLIMBERS.	
FILM OF CATERPILLAR CRAWLING UP STICK.	
QUICK CUTS BETWEEN FILM OF TIGER IN TREE AND RHINOS.	
SNAPSHOT OF TIGER.	SFX: CLICK OF A 35MM CAMERA.
FILM OF MINARETS.	
FILM OF BABOONS.	
FILM OF BUTTERFLY.	
FILM OF LANDSCAPE.	V.O. For more than a century, Riggs has helped send National Geographic...
SNAPSHOT OF PAGODA.	SFX: CLICK OF A 35MM CAMERA.
FILM OF FISH SWIMMING.	to some of the most extraordinary places
FILM OF EEL SWIMMING.	above, below and upon
FILM OF FLAMINGOS FLYING.	the face of the earth.
FILM OF CHIMPANZEE.	
SNAPSHOT OF CHIMPANZEE.	SFX: CLICK OF A 35MM CAMERA.
SNAPSHOT OF RED SQUARE.	SFX: CLICK OF A 35MM CAMERA.
SNAPSHOT OF VOLCANO ERUPTING.	SFX: CLICK OF A 35MM CAMERA.
SNAPSHOT OF EASTER ISLAND.	SFX: CLICK OF A 35MM CAMERA.
FILM OF RHINO.	
SNAPSHOT OF RHINO.	SFX: CLICK OF A 35MM CAMERA.
FILM OF WHALES.	
SNAPSHOT OF WHALES.	SFX: CLICK OF A 35MM CAMERA.
FILM OF WHALES CONTINUES.	

FILM OF AGRICULTURE SCENE.	
SNAPSHOT OF AGRICULTURE SCENE.	SFX: CLICK OF A 35MM CAMERA.
SNAPSHOT OF FAMILY AT ARCHES NATIONAL PARK.	SFX: KA-CLICK OF INSTAMATIC CAMERA. V.O.: You should see some of the places we've helped send families.
SNAPSHOT OF FAMILY BY WINNEBAGO WITH RIBBON ON IT.	SFX: KA-CLICK OF INSTAMATIC CAMERA.
SLIDE OF FAMILY BY SECOND HOME.	SFX: KA-CLICK OF INSTAMATIC CAMERA.
SUPER: RIGGS. BANKERS TO THE MOST IMPORTANT MONEY IN THE WORLD. YOURS. MEMBER FDIC.	V.O.: Riggs. Bankers to the most important money in the world. Yours.

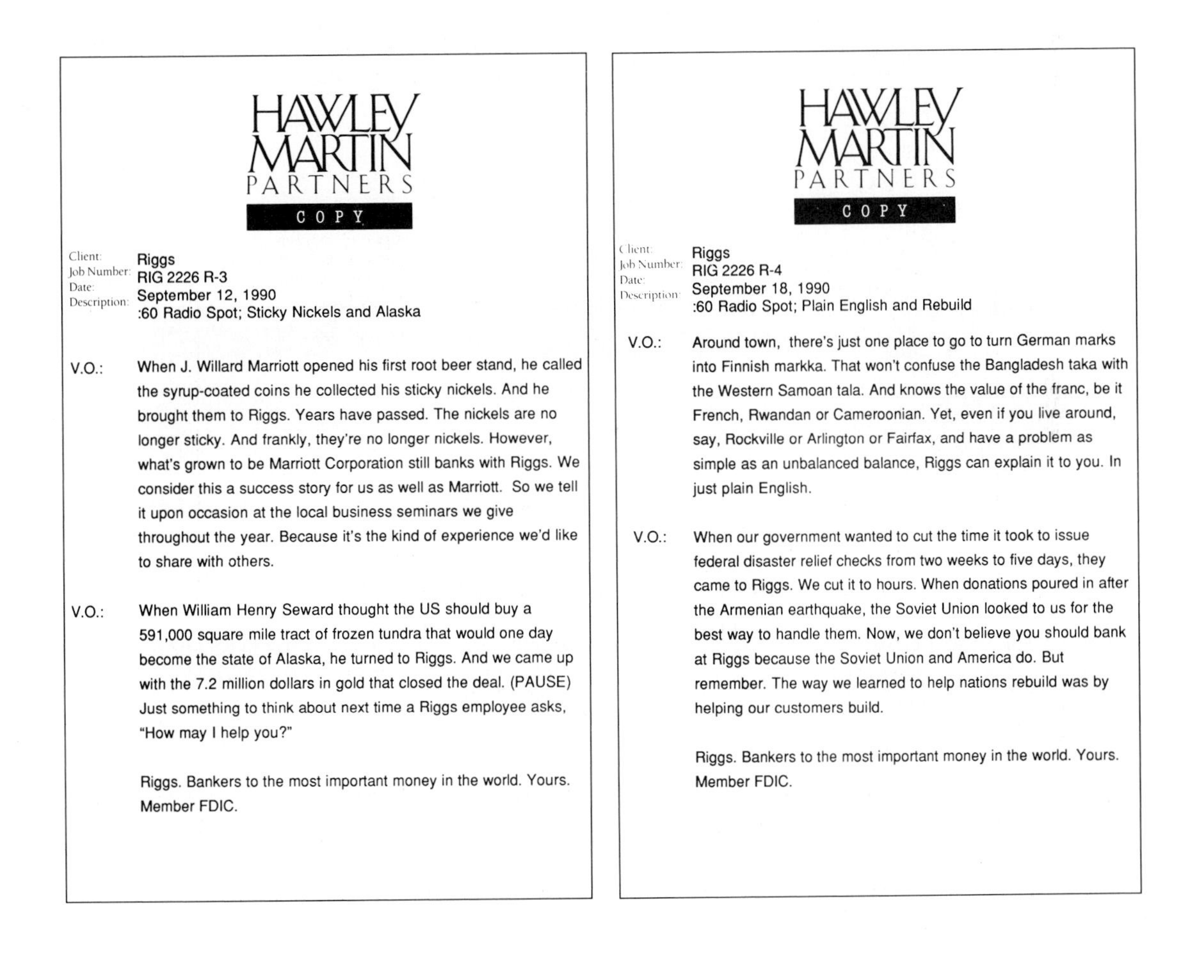

HAWLEY MARTIN PARTNERS

COPY

Client: Riggs
Job Number: RIG 2226 R-3
Date: September 12, 1990
Description: :60 Radio Spot; Sticky Nickels and Alaska

V.O.: When J. Willard Marriott opened his first root beer stand, he called the syrup-coated coins he collected his sticky nickels. And he brought them to Riggs. Years have passed. The nickels are no longer sticky. And frankly, they're no longer nickels. However, what's grown to be Marriott Corporation still banks with Riggs. We consider this a success story for us as well as Marriott. So we tell it upon occasion at the local business seminars we give throughout the year. Because it's the kind of experience we'd like to share with others.

V.O.: When William Henry Seward thought the US should buy a 591,000 square mile tract of frozen tundra that would one day become the state of Alaska, he turned to Riggs. And we came up with the 7.2 million dollars in gold that closed the deal. (PAUSE) Just something to think about next time a Riggs employee asks, "How may I help you?"

Riggs. Bankers to the most important money in the world. Yours. Member FDIC.

HAWLEY MARTIN PARTNERS

COPY

Client: Riggs
Job Number: RIG 2226 R-4
Date: September 18, 1990
Description: :60 Radio Spot; Plain English and Rebuild

V.O.: Around town, there's just one place to go to turn German marks into Finnish markka. That won't confuse the Bangladesh taka with the Western Samoan tala. And knows the value of the franc, be it French, Rwandan or Cameroonian. Yet, even if you live around, say, Rockville or Arlington or Fairfax, and have a problem as simple as an unbalanced balance, Riggs can explain it to you. In just plain English.

V.O.: When our government wanted to cut the time it took to issue federal disaster relief checks from two weeks to five days, they came to Riggs. We cut it to hours. When donations poured in after the Armenian earthquake, the Soviet Union looked to us for the best way to handle them. Now, we don't believe you should bank at Riggs because the Soviet Union and America do. But remember. The way we learned to help nations rebuild was by helping our customers build.

Riggs. Bankers to the most important money in the world. Yours. Member FDIC.

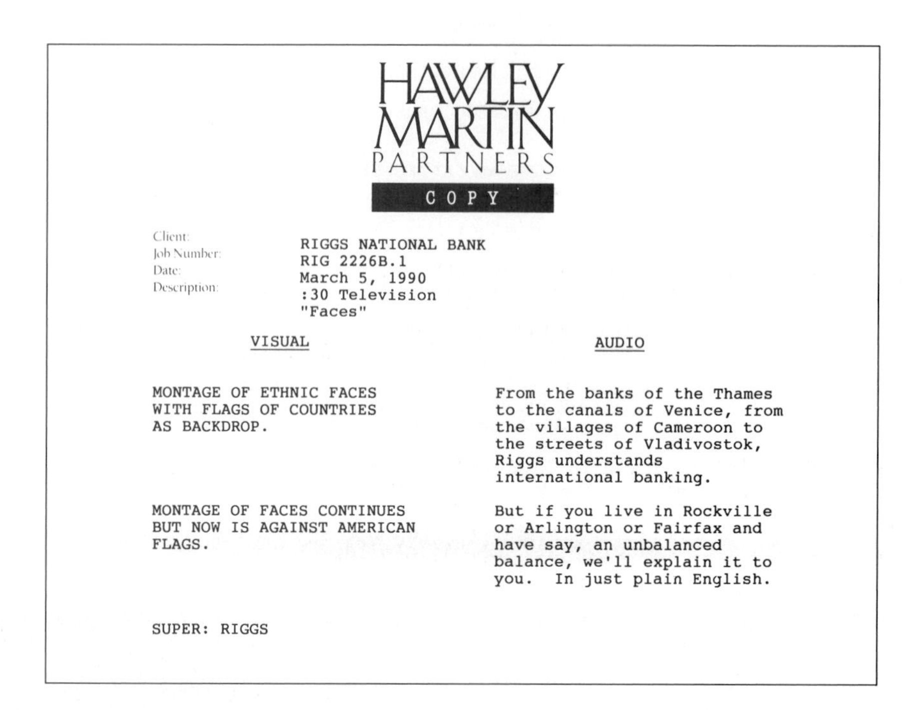

HAWLEY MARTIN PARTNERS

COPY

Client: RIGGS NATIONAL BANK
Job Number: RIG 2226B.1
Date: March 5, 1990
Description: :30 Television
"Faces"

VISUAL	AUDIO
MONTAGE OF ETHNIC FACES WITH FLAGS OF COUNTRIES AS BACKDROP.	From the banks of the Thames to the canals of Venice, from the villages of Cameroon to the streets of Vladivostok, Riggs understands international banking.
MONTAGE OF FACES CONTINUES BUT NOW IS AGAINST AMERICAN FLAGS.	But if you live in Rockville or Arlington or Fairfax and have say, an unbalanced balance, we'll explain it to you. In just plain English.
SUPER: RIGGS	

Riggs National Bank
"Faces" :30 TV

1. V.O.: *From the banks of the Thames to the canals of Venice . . .*

2 *From the villages of . . .*

3 *. . . Cameroon to the streets . . .*

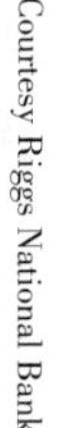

Courtesy Riggs National Bank

4 *of Vladivostok, Riggs understands international banking.*

5 *But if you live in Rockville or Arlington or Fairfax and have, say, an unbalanced balance, we'll explain it to you.*

6 *In just plain English.*

CHAPTER 3

Fact-Finding: The Basis for Effective Creative Work

In the world of TV sitcoms and sexy novels about the advertising business, creative ideas spew forth at the drop of a hat. It isn't that way in real life. In fact, chances are that the simpler the creative idea appears to be, the more blood, sweat, tears, and frustrations were involved. Because advertising is created with a business goal in mind, you must begin the process by finding out as much as you can about the product or service, the target audience, the competition, the things that make people want or need goods and services, and the prevailing trends of the moment. Consider this list of questions as a start:

WHO is the most likely prospect for the product?

WHY is this person the most likely prospect? Should specific wants or needs be appealed to? Emotional? Rational?

WHAT product features can satisfy the consumer's needs?

HOW should this be communicated? What style, approach, or tone should be used in the campaign, and what will the copy say?

Although traditional library searches may not work when you're searching for fairly current marketing data, we list the typical steps involved in an information search at a college library. Be aware that some of your best sources will probably turn out to be demographic and lifestyle studies of consumer audiences, and articles from current consumer periodicals and marketing/advertising trade journals. Of course, you should be familiar with the product or service itself. If you're researching a product, purchase it and use it. If a service, try it out. If you're lucky enough to be near the corporate headquarters of a company, you might call its marketing or advertising department and ask if you could meet with some of its members to work on a class project. In any event, use your college library to:

1. Consult a general encyclopedia, such as Britannica. Check the index volume first to find out how your topic may be listed. Start with specifics and check broader entries if these efforts prove fruitless. For example, if your product is Snapple natural beverages, begin with something such as "soft drinks" or "foods, natural." Try "beverages" and look for "soft drinks" or "natural" under the more general listing.

2. Ask the reference librarian if there is a "subject encyclopedia" dealing with marketing, manufacturing, consumer goods, advertising, etc. Search it for listings.

3. Check the Readers' Guide to Periodical Literature for article listings. Check a recent volume first, then check several years back.

4. Check the Business Periodicals Index, which is a "subject index," to look for additional listings. Ask the librarian if there are other "subject indexes" in this field you should check. Pay particular attention to citations from periodicals such as *Advertising Age, American Demographics, Journal of Advertising, Marketing Communications, TV/Radio Age, Sales and Marketing Management,* the *Wall Street Journal,* the *New York Times, AdWeek, Journal of Advertising Research, Journal of Marketing,* and *Broadcasting.*

5. Check the Library of Congress Subject Headings to find how many ways your topic might be listed in the library catalog. Then use a computer terminal to check the subject headings you have found in the LOC Subject Headings.

6. If you're interested in opinions and points of view and your topic is the sort that might spur editorial comment (tobacco and alcohol products, health issues, etc.), also check the Editorials on File volumes in the reference section.

7. Ask the reference librarian if you should check other sources. You will get better information if you are prepared to tell the librarian what your topic is, what you are trying to find out, and how much information you need.

8. Check MRI (Market Research Inc.) data, a compendium of updated information on the characteristics of product and media audiences, or demographic and lifestyle data from other market research as available. If your library does not subscribe to these, consider calling one of the larger advertising agencies or market research firms in your area to ask if you could search through their copies.

You will find a number of other resources on products and consumer demographics in your library. Here is a representative listing of books you might find helpful. Be certain to look for others as well.

Almanac of Consumer Markets. Ithaca, N.Y.: American Demographics Press, Inc. (annual).

Barry, Thomas E. *Marketing and the Black Consumer: An Annotated Bibliography.* Chicago: American Marketing Association, 1976.

Bikson, Tora K. *Product Decision Making Among Older Adults.* Santa Monica: Rand, 1978.

Channels of Communication for Reaching Older Americans. Washington, D.C.: National Council on the Aging, 1985.

Demographics of Minority Markets. Ithaca, N.Y.: American Demographics Press, Inc., 1993.

Demographics, U.S.A., New York: Market Statistics (annual).

Encyclopedia of Consumer Brands. Detroit: St. James Press, 1994.

Francese, Peter K. *Capturing Customers: How to Target the Hottest Consumer Markets of the '90s.* Ithaca, N.Y.: American Demographics Press, Inc., 1990.

Hitschler, Pamela B. *Spending by Older Consumers: 1980 and 1990 Compared.* Washington, D.C.: U.S. Department of Labor, Bureau of Labor Statistics, 1993.

Loden, D. John. *Megabrands: How to Build Them, How to Beat Them.* Homewood, Ill.: Business One Irwin, 1992.

Lazer, William. *Handbook of Demographics for Marketing and Advertising: Sources and Trends on the U.S. Consumer,* Lexington, Mass.: Lexington Books, 1987.

Lifestyle Market Analyst, The. (annual)

Makower, Joel. *The Green Consumer Supermarket Guide.* New York: Penguin, 1991.

Marconi, Joe. *Beyond Branding: How Savvy Marketers Build Brand Equity to Create Products and Open New Markets.* Chicago: Probus, 1994.

Martin, David N. *Romancing the Brand: The Power of Advertising and How to Use It.* New York: Amacom, 1989.

McGrath, Molly Wade. *Top Sellers, U.S.A.: Success Stories Behind America's Best Selling Products from Alka Seltzer to Zippo.* New York: William Morrow, 1983.

McNeal, James U. *Children as Consumers: Insights and Implications.* Lexington, Mass.: Lexington Books, 1987.

Michman, Ronald D. *Lifestyle Market Segmentation.* New York: Praeger, 1987.

Minority Marketing. Chicago: Crain Books, 1980.

Moschis, George P. *Marketing to Older Consumers: A Handbook of Information for Strategy Development.* Westport, Conn.: Quorum Books, 1992.

Murphy, John M. *Brand Strategy.* Englewood Cliffs, N.J.: Prentice-Hall, 1990.

Randazzo, Sal. *Mythmaking on Madison Avenue: How Advertisers Apply the Power of Myth and Symbolism to Create Leadership Brands.* Chicago: Probus, 1993.

Rossman, Marlene L. *Multicultural Marketing: Selling to a Diverse America.* New York: American Management Association, 1994.

Strasser, Susan. *Satisfaction Guaranteed: The Making of the American Mass Market.* New York: Pantheon Books, 1989.

Successful Marketing to U.S. Hispanics and Asians: Players, Agencies, and Media: An American Management Association research report on target marketing. New York: AMA Membership Publications Division, American Management Association, 1987.

Weinstein, Art. *Market Segmentation: Using Demographics, Psychographics, and Other Segmentation Techniques to Uncover and Exploit New Markets.* Chicago: Probus, 1987.

World's Greatest Brands: An International Review. New York: Wiley, 1992.

Beyond your library search, talk to people, whether individually or in focus group sessions. Talk to users, nonusers in your target audience, people who sell the product, and, where possible, those who manufacture it. Ask users what they like best about the product, what they would change if they could, and what brand they buy (and why) when they can't find your brand. Ask nonusers what their preferred brand is and why they chose it. Ask about different ways to use the product. Once you have gathered enough information, you're ready to move on to step two in the creative process, planning the strategy.

Assignment 1: Gathering Information

Choose one of the categories below, which were taken from MRI data. Look under the appropriate product first, then use campus libraries to assemble as much information as you can find about the product category: who uses it, current industry trends, top brands in the market, product differences, how the product is used and for what, other use options for product, where category is headed in the near future, etc. (Bold headings refer to volumes in MRI where product data can be found.)

ADULT PERSONAL CARE
Toothpaste
Mouthwash
Electric shavers
Shampoo
Personal care soaps
Hand and body cream
Deodorants/anti-perspirants

BAKED GOODS, SNACKS, DESSERTS
Frozen yogurt
Frozen desserts
Crackers
Cookies

MEAT AND PREPARED MEALS
Frozen pizza
Mexican foods
Prepared dinners

REMEDIES
Indigestion aids
Athlete's foot remedies

SOUP, FRUIT, VEGETABLES
Canned or jarred soup
Flavored/seasoned rice

HOUSEHOLD SUPPLIES
Air freshener sprays
Cleaners
Glass cleaners
Fabric softeners
Charcoal

PET CARE AND BABY PRODUCTS
Baby shampoo
Packaged moist dog/cat food
Packaged dry dog/cat food
Canned dog/cat food

BEVERAGES
Instant iced fruit tea
Energy drinks
Bottled water and seltzer

HEALTH CARE AND DRUG PRODUCTS
Contact lenses
In-home pregnancy tests
Sunburn remedies
Suntan and sunscreen products

Assignment 2: Is Clear Communication Possible?

How much of what we see, read, or hear reaches us the way the creator of the message intended it to? How much of the meaning do we add to the message? What affects how we interpret messages in the media as well as messages from one another?

Here is an exercise that will deal with the intricacies of clear communication. As you know, most ads communicate both visually and verbally. So do cartoons. For this exercise, find a cartoon (the *New Yorker* magazine is your best source). Look at it for a few moments, then put it away and respond to the following points. Rather than answer "by the numbers," write this as a narrative.

WITHOUT LOOKING, describe as much as you can remember about the drawing and the caption: details of the drawing, wording of the message, the "joke," whatever else comes to mind. What came to mind as you first looked at the cartoon? What information did you need to know in order to understand the message? What experiences might have helped you to understand the message more clearly and completely?

NOW LOOK AT THE DRAWING AGAIN. How well did you remember details? What did you forget? What does looking at the cartoon once more do to enhance the meaning for you?

Does this visual work without the caption? Does the caption work without the visual? How does the message change when you omit one or the other?

Now write a few words about what this cartoon or the exercise itself has made you think about in connection with your own life experiences. Don't worry if the connection seems far-fetched.

CHAPTER 4

Strategy: Finding a Way to Communicate

The other day I was reading that, after more than several years of flat sales, olive oil is making a comeback. This comeback is attributed to increased advertising that highlights the product's versatility, as well as a virtual freeze on prices.

Bertolli, the leading brand, increased ad and promotion budgets more than threefold, compared to expenditures in recent years. Together with promotional offers, including a recipe booklet, new ads focus more on the product than previous Bertolli efforts. "Before, we said, 'Eat well, live long, be happy,'" said a company spokesman. "Today we're using recipes and photos of prepared meals to show people this is what you can do with olive oil."

The product is going from a commodity, or "olive oil category," image to a series of brands, each touting its particular image. Print and broadcast ads for the Pompeian brand highlight how Pompeian olive oil adds "taste" to food. Industry leaders say advertising has been quite successful in getting consumers to use olive oil in more varied ways.

Olive oil recently passed corn oil to become the No. 2 pourable oil after vegetable oil, proof that the industry has been successful in getting olive oil used beyond the special occasion. While corn and vegetable oils are polyunsaturated, olive oil is monounsaturated, but just as cholesterol-free.

Yet despite volume growth there has been only a slight increase in household penetration, from 21.1 percent in 1991 to 21.3 percent in 1992. This suggests that the category's growth has been fueled by increased usage, rather than by acquisition of newer users. The industry would like to expand its penetration of households as a way to give the market a boost.

In strategic terms, olive oil falls in the low importance/thinking category (see the FCB grid in this chapter, page 86), yet the decision to purchase is surely influenced by emotions as well (the Italian heritage of the brand, etc.) A strategic plan should probably appeal to both reason and emotion. Perhaps one could stress versatility by offering new recipes. Or underscore the subtle flavor enhancement that olive oil adds to foods. That approach could lead to a strategy that suggests, "you're doing more to please the family by choosing olive oil over other oils. It's versatile, healthy, and it even enhances the flavor of your foods." Since price is less of a factor than in the past, why not remind prospects that olive oil is cholesterol-free, competitively priced, and suitable for virtually all cooking oil needs? Since its image has suggested it be used only for certain foods or on special occasions, perhaps there's a need to add an "everyday" image.

So strategic thinking for the #1 brand, Bertolli, might sound like this:

Position the brand as the logical choice because of its popularity, health-related benefits, and flavor enhancement. Combined with a reasonable price, these attributes put olive oil at the top of the list. To differentiate the brand, make the prospect feel proud to have chosen Bertolli, the best of the best (best seller in olive oils, best flavor enhancer of all oils, and a smart choice health-wise, too.

In other words:

Bertolli olive oil puts healthy, flavorful cooking within your reach. To explore this theme in advertising, play on the cook's reward for providing meals that are both healthy and flavorful, while paying no more and using what is perceived as a superior cooking oil. "I cared enough to cook with olive oil, and I chose the best selling brand, too."

Strategy is a way to sell the product as opposed to putting the words together.

It's saying what you're going to say, even before you've found the precise way to say it.

It begins with facts. But mere facts are not strategic. Saying that olive oil enhances flavor isn't strategic. Saying that because it enhances flavor, the family cook can feel better about fulfilling his or her role is strategic. The difference is what *you* add to the facts. The difference is insight.

A young copywriter wrote me once in answer to a letter I had written to *Advertising Age* regarding advertising education. He chided educators—all of us—for bothering to teach budding writers and art directors about strategy. "I get the strategy from the account people and then I go to work expressing my creativity," he explained. "I don't care what the strategy is as long as I can work with it." Yet others would say that a good copywriter or art director can help shape a strategy by learning to think like a marketing person. As a result, ads can be not only highly original, but highly on target.

O'Toole's Three-Point Approach to Strategy

John O'Toole of the American Association of Advertising Agencies says there are three things to consider when determining a strategy.

1. ***Who or what is the competition?*** To find a unique position or personality for your brand in its product category, you need to know what other brands are saying. Remember, too, that competition may go beyond the brand category. For

a home exercise machine, the competition may be health clubs as well as other brands of machines. It might also be diet supplements, a person's predisposition to run or swim, or any number of other related things. For Sunkist, greater usage of its frozen and concentrated juices resulted only when the brand realized it had to compete against snack foods as well as other brands of similar products.

2. ***Whom are we talking to?*** Are we targeting users of another brand, consumers who have never used any brand in our category, or perhaps consumers who use a related product but might be switched to ours? The answers are not simple. Kleenex Facial Tissues were developed in the last century as a replacement for cloth towels used to remove a woman's makeup. Then someone had the urge to sneeze with one in hand, and the rest is history. Much of our audience information is demographic: age, sex, marital status, income, occupation, owner or renter, user or nonuser of product category, and so on. But demographics alone cannot help the creative team of copywriter and art director see the real person they're trying to reach. Much more valuable is a profile of how that person lives, and such things as values, leisure time activities, attitudes towards work and family, stresses of everyday life. All advertising is partly emotional; some advertising is purely emotional. Never exclude emotions as a potential trigger. Remember "You deserve a break today"? Those five words revolutionized perceptions of fast food joints.

3. ***What do we want them to know, to feel, and to understand?*** Read some of the great advertising and discover for yourself what the advertiser wants you to know, to feel, and to understand about their company and their products or services. IBM wants you to know of its innovations in computer technology, to understand they've harnessed that technology into "user friendly" computers for the family, and to feel that, since prices are getting more competitive, it's probably not smart to buy a PC clone when you can get the real thing. Benneton wants you to know of their commitment to a world without prejudice, disease, and war. They want you to understand that, although they sell fashion, they have a deeper side, and they want you to feel that wearing their clothing helps publicize and support their causes.

McCann-Erickson's Role-Playing Approach

A prominent American advertising agency, McCann-Erickson, suggests we get inside the head of the consumer by acting as if we were that person, writing our responses to the first six questions below in his or her voice, and completing the last question in our own.

1. Whom are we talking to?

2. Where are we now in the mind of this person?
3. Where is our competition in the mind of this person?
4. Where would we like to be in the mind of this person?
5. What is the consumer promise?
6. What is the supporting evidence?
7. What is the tone of voice for the advertising?

Writing in the first person to explore a strategy for IBM personal computers, you might answer number 1 this way:

"I'm Jed Powers, 35, married with two children, 8 and 10. I use an IBM computer at work. My wife has never used a computer. My children are using computers at school. I'd like to be able to justify buying a reasonably priced computer for the home, so I could work there, so my children could improve their learning skills, and maybe if it's in the house, my wife could find ways to use it for family finances, schedules, and other things."

For the answer to question 2, Jed might talk about how he admires IBM capability in the office, but isn't sure if it might not be too high tech for home. And there's the matter of cost, not a small issue.

For question 3, he might discuss his perception that other brands are cheaper, or that maybe the kids could do without, or maybe he could find a way to borrow his office machine if he wants to work at home. Or maybe a new washer and dryer are more important at this stage than a computer for the family.

For question 4, he would speak as if he'd just read some of your as yet nonexistent advertising which has convinced him that it may be time to think about a purchase. Somehow your message has motivated him. How?

For question 5, state the consumer promise as simply as you can. It might be, "Imagine me with not just any computer, but an IBM computer at home that the whole family can use for self-improvement."

For question 6, he might support the promise with such evidence as, "I'm now convinced that all the good things I've been hearing for years about IBM—that they practically invented the computer, that they stand behind their reputation, that they have been constantly improving the capacity and versatility of their machines—take on a new meaning in the light of more competitive pricing and a greater degree of simplicity of use. They really seem to want to help me give my family the best in a home computer."

Finally, for question 7, the tone of voice might be described as, "friendly, conversational, works to make IBM seem less impersonal through use of personal situations with genuine people. Maintains balance between authenticity of IBM know-how and desire to use that knowledge to help families use its products for an enriched life."

FIGURE 4-1 (A)

Berlitz shows with stunning exactitude how often their famous travelers guides are updated by recreating editors' notes in red handwriting. The idea carries through to the tag line with the insertion of the word "very." The playful headlines are perfect for the brash mood of the series. Finally, the format includes a cover photo of a specific guide book which, like the headline, is matched to the text running in the ad. For the "leave your heart" headline, the guide book shown is San Francisco, for example, while the "wine country" book is for France.

If you're going to leave your heart somewhere, make sure you have the most current address.

'93 Revisions

SHOPS AND SHOPPING 205

them. Innovative women's clothing by European designers is carried at **Vivo**, at 2124 Union Street. Within a nearby courtyard at 2166 Union and up a ramp, you'll find **UKO Japanese Clothing** for men and women. Across the street is **Enzo Valenti**, a place for seriously discounted Maude Frison shoes for women and bargain Italian shoes for men.

Turn down Fillmore Street and you'll find many more interesting shops, among them **Artifacts**, for contemporary art and crafts, and the **Silk Route**, with a marvelous selection of tribal rugs, clothing, carved masks, and jewelry from all over the world. If you are intrigued by hardware shops, **Fredericksen's**, 3029 Fillmore, has been pleasing do-it-yourselfers since 1896. At number 3131 is **T.Z. Shiota**, a shop that has been dealing in Japanese porcelains and prints for 94 years (the last 20 in Cow Hollow). Back on Union Street, **Vandewater & Company** offers delivery of their distinctive gifts. Nearby, at number 2254, is **Coco's Italian Dreams**, which carries women's one-size-fits-all, romantic, washable, handmade Italian clothing. The creations are all lacy, whipped-cream fantasies, designed by a German and manufactured in Italy.

Masquerade, 2237 Union Street, the only vintage-clothing shop on the street, has a great stock of Hawaiian shirts from the 1930s to 1950s. If you have something more elegant in mind, there's **Ofelio**, 2213 Union, where the merchandise is refined menswear, most of it from Italy. **Three Bags Full**, at number 2181, is a wonderful sweater shop, and nearby **Tampico** is part of a complex of courtyard stores. The specialty at Tampico is handmade, natural-fiber clothing, and antique and vintage jewelry. In the same complex is **Helen of Troy**, stocking sexy European lingerie. On the next block, carrying dramatically styled women's clothing, is **Farnoosh**; its next-door neighbor, **Shaw**, focuses on pricey, high-fashion shoes. **Annalisa Antiques**, 1861 Union Street, offers a handsome selection of German country-pine and Biedermeier furnishings.

Haight-Ashbury

This part of San Francisco between Golden Gate Park and the Civic Center caught the public's eye during the psychedelic 1960s, and although the mood is substantially more subdued now, this remains one of the most intriguing shopping areas, still much favored by the counterculture. It boasts a remarkable concentration of used-clothing stores

The Lighthouse, nearby, is a fine place to browse through books on a variety of metaphysical subjects.

the Trojanowska Gallery, which mostly shows works by San Francisco artists, and

Mark Harrington, a small but choice shop specializing in crystal and glassware was established in 1932.

/gift baskets.

& Main Street Music Box Co., at the corner of Fillmore and Union, has a sensational collection of music boxes, from the whimsical to the serious.

/features

PSC, a few doors down the street, specializes in baseball cards and other sports memorabilia.

; across the street at number 2001, carries stylish women's clothing;

tr to next page

, and even dismantled European farmhouses.

The Berlitz Travellers Guides 1993 San Francisco

In trying to deliver up-to-date information, most travel guides leave a lot to be desired. We at Berlitz Travellers Guides make sure that our writers are the best informed and most knowledgeable in the area about which they are writing. **To order: (800) 257-5755.**

Distributed by the Macmillan Publishing Group.

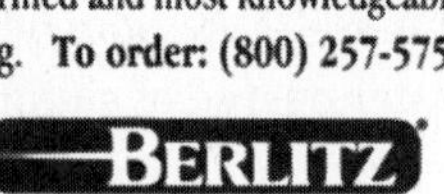

The Berlitz Travellers Guides

The very last word in travel...year after year.

Courtesy Berlitz Publishing Company, Inc. and Friedman Benjamin, Inc.

FIGURE 4-1 (B)

In London, it isn't only the Guard that changes.

'93 REVISIONS

142 LONDON

the first hotel in the world to be lit by electricity and the first hotel in London to have elevators. Another brilliant advance in civilized life, but nothing to do with Mr. D'Oyly Carte, was the invention of the martini in the **American Bar**. Next to this popular gathering spot is the **Savoy Grill**, a favorite place for after-theater suppers.

The Strand, WC2R 0EU. Tel: 836-4343; Telex: 24234; Fax: 240-6040; in U.S. and Canada, (800) 223-6800; in New York State, (212) 838-3110; in Sydney, (02) 233-8422; in the rest of Australia, (008) 22-20-33. £270.

Bloomsbury

Hotel Crichton. This 19th-century house across from the British Museum in Bloomsbury is a well-run hotel, and is understandably popular. The large breakfast (included in the price) is a good start to a day of sightseeing.

36 Bedford Place, WC1B 5JR. Tel: 637-3955; Telex: 22353; Fax: 323-0018. £50.

Grays Hotel. An elegant Victorian town house opened as a hotel in 1987, in an area on the edge of Bloomsbury where there are very few hotels, Grays has great style, with a luxurious, intimate atmosphere enhanced by sumptuous furnishings and flower-filled rooms. There are just eight double bedrooms, but if you want to be pampered in this corner of London at moderate rates, this hotel is for you.

109 Guilford Street, WC1 N1DP. Tel: 833-2474; Telex: 25335; Fax: 439-0820. £66.

The Kenilworth Hotel. This recently refurbished hotel on the edge of Bloomsbury close to the British Museum caters to business meetings and small conferences. Even so, it's well equipped for tourists, and is a good value.

97 Great Russell Street, WC1B 3LB. Tel: 637-3477; Telex: 25842; Fax: 631-3133; in U.S., (800) 447-7011, or (800) 44-UTELL; in Ontario/Quebec, (800) 268-7041; in Toronto, (800) 387-1338; in Vancouver, (800) 663-9582; in Australia, (008) 22-11-76. £165.

Covent Garden/Soho

Fielding Hotel. If you are visiting London to wallow in opera or the ballet, this is the hotel for you, as it is situated in a quiet, gas-lit alley one minute from the Royal Opera House. Even if the delights of the opera are not for you, the Fielding is still a delightful place to stay: Being in

Handwritten notes in the margins:

Scandic Crown Hotel. Opened in the early 1990s, this hotel is close to the major railway stations of Euston, King's Cross, and St. Pancras, convenient if you are travelling to the north. It is large and beautifully decorated in the Scandinavian manner, and the rooms are well appointed. The winter garden conservatory, The Terrace, offers light food all day, while the restaurant serves a wider choice during normal dining hours. 17-18 Upper Woburn Place, WC1H 0HT. Tel: 383-4105; Fax: 383-4106. £110–£125.

Britain to provide private bathrooms. ... is the hotel's association with the 99.9 percent perfect dry martini. Enjoy one.

63-SAVOY

£180–£240

£46–£48

Radisson

Canada, (800) 333-3333

£145–£186

Keeping up with changes in the world's most visited cities means going beyond simply describing the attractions. It requires the first-hand updates that only the on-site writers of Berlitz Travellers Guides can give. **To order: (800) 257-5755.**

Distributed by the Macmillan Publishing Group.

LONDON

The Berlitz Travellers Guide

1993

BERLITZ®

The Berlitz Travellers Guides

The very last word in travel...year after year.

FIGURE 4-1 (C)

When traveling through wine country, it's helpful to have a guidebook that hasn't aged.

TOURS 353

the end of July. The Touraine music festival is staged in late June at the **Grange de Meslay**, a 13th-century ensemble of farm buildings, 10 km (6 miles) north via A 10.

Dining and Staying in Tours

Dining is most expensively done in Tours at **Jean Bardet** (Tel: 47-41-41-11), a bright and airy restaurant that consistently wins rave reviews for exemplary up-to-the-minute cuisine. Sequestered in a tiny park on the north bank of the river, Bardet also offers 15 rooms and suites in its early-19th-century villa—as well as a heated pool. Cooking courses in English are offered here off-season. Within walking distance, at 101, avenue de la Tranchée, the venerable **Barrier** (Tel: 47-54-20-39) continues to serve impeccable classical dishes in its hush-hush formal dining room. In this same neighborhood of gastronomical delights is the **Jardin du Castel** (part of the Hôtel de Groisòn), at 10, rue Groison. Try the "menu surprise" created by master chef Guy Tricon in his most attractive dining room (Tel: 47-41-94-40). If you've spent too many francs on such glorious meals, stay at the nearby hotel **Italia** at 19, rue Devilde. What it lacks in aesthetics it makes up for with the friendliness of its kind hosts and rock-bottom prices.

Near the Tour de Guise at 19, rue Lavoisier, less extravagant local fare is offered at the rustic **Les Tuffeaux**, including *blanc de turbot au vin de Layon et melon* (turbot with sweet white wine and melon). Master chef Jean Sabat turns out irresistible pastries (Tel: 47-47-19-89).

Centrally located on the wide boulevard Heurteloup, the old-fashioned **Univers** is perhaps Tours's best choice of accommodations in a city with many good hotels. Travellers in search of serenity (and who don't mind then having to drive into town to sightsee) would prefer the **Domaine de Beauvois**, a lovely 15th-century manor house, and its fine restaurant, 13 km (8 miles) west of Tours in Luynes. Beauvois, with its knowledgeable staff (particularly the good-natured British concierge, Brian Byron), draws lots of American and English guests. Done up in comparatively bright colors, this is one manor house where you can wear jeans and not worry about offending history. Tennis, fishing, swimming, and ballooning are offered on the immense wooded estate, along

Travel guides are *not* like fine wine. A good one can't be left to age. That's why the Berlitz Travellers Guides are made fresh every year with extensive revisions and the most current information. **To order: (800) 257-5755.**

Distributed by the Macmillan Publishing Group.

BERLITZ

The Berlitz Travellers Guides

The very last word in travel...year after year.

Aim for One or More of the Basic Human Needs

Another way to check your strategy is to see whether it touches one or more basic human needs: to be popular, attractive, wanted; to have material things; to enjoy life through comfort and convenience; to create a happy family situation; to have love and sex; to have power; to avoid fear; to emulate those you admire; to have new experiences; or to protect and maintain health.

Choose a Strategy Type Based on Your Goals

Charles F. Frazer, professor of advertising at the University of Colorado, Boulder, cites seven different types of strategic approaches and suggests that one of them should be appropriate for any advertising situation.[1]

1. ***The Generic Strategy.*** Best used when you are the dominant brand in the category. Makes little or no claim of superiority. Does not acknowledge the competition. Generic strategy is best suited to cases of monopoly or extreme dominance of a product category, or to cases in which a new category is created by the introduction of the new product. Usually such exclusivity is short lived as other brands introduce their own versions of a once unique product. While the product is truly an exclusive, a generic strategy is well suited to it and can remain effective as long as the brand strongly dominates the category.

2. ***The Preemptive Claim.*** Although not a unique claim, the preemptive claim has not yet been exploited in competing advertising and therefore appears to be unique. One pain reliever fights pain fast. One glass cleaner cleans a whole lot more than glass. Other brands do as well, but their advertising strategies have never addressed such points. Obviously, this type of strategy is best used by products that have little to distinguish them in their category. A classic example is the Federal Express campaign, which, through highly imaginative advertising, made you think of the company as the only one assuring next-day delivery, although competitors also offered this service.

3. ***The Unique Selling Proposition (USP).*** This type of strategy, once popular, is used less frequently today because most products are not unique. A USP is based on a lasting competitive advantage, or a unique physical characteristic or benefit. Rather than a unique selling proposition, perhaps we should ask that a strategy produce a "unique consumer response."

4. ***The Brand Image Strategy.*** This strategy claims superiority that is based on factors that are extrinsic to the product or service. The differentiation between our product and competing products is psychologically based, rather than

[1] Charles F. Frazer, "Creative Strategy: A Management Perspective," *Journal of Advertising* Vol. 12, No. 4 (1983): 36–41. Used by permission.

physically based, and the strategy's emphasis is on emotions rather than facts. A brand image is an attitude people have about a product or service, one that is carefully nurtured by advertising: Ford is the motor company that takes special care to build cars right; Chevrolet is dedicated to giving America what it wants; and Coke is the All-American choice, whereas Pepsi is for a new generation of Americans.

5. ***Product Positioning.*** This approach gives the product a place in the mind of the consumer that is relative to the place of competing products in the mind. It stresses how this brand is different from and superior to the competition and is particularly well suited to new entries in a product category or to brands with relatively small market shares that wish to challenge market leaders. The most famous positioning campaign was done by Avis Rent-A-Car when it was a small force in the market compared to category leader Hertz. Avis's "We're only number two. We try harder" approach turned it into a major contender in the field and was based on the knowledge that Americans love to root for the underdog.

6. ***The Resonance Approach.*** This approach requires that the communicator deeply understand the kinds of information and experiences that are stored in the minds of the audience and the processes whereby certain stimuli evoke this stored information. The resultant advertising does not focus on product claims or brand images, but rather is designed to present situations or emotions that evoke positive associations from the memories of the respondents. Much of the advertising for Hallmark greeting cards relies on such familiar situations and people. This strategy is most suited to situations in which little product difference exists.

7. ***Affective Strategy.*** The intent of this strategy is to make contact on a purely emotional level. Such a reaction can break through indifference to change the consumer's perception of the product. An example of this approach is the Chanel No. 5 perfume commercial, "Share the Fantasy," in which a series of images are cut together, which, cognitively speaking, make little sense but clearly suggest the emotions of love and romance.

Linking Strategy with Importance, Thinking, and Feeling

Advertising strategists at Foote Cone & Belding offer still another set of guidelines for establishing strategy. Their model is based on two facts: (1) some purchasing decisions are based on rational thinking or logic, while others are based on feelings or emotions; and (2) some purchasing decisions are extremely important to us, while others may be of relatively little importance. Furthermore, between logic and emotion, high and low importance, are varying levels of the purchasing decision mix.

This model can be visualized as a grid formed by two perpendicular axes: a vertical line that represents a continuum for the importance of purchasing

FIGURE 4-2
While the name Sutter Home Winery calls attention to the uncommercial positioning of the brand, the ads further embellish that personality by focusing not on the wines, but on the wonderful foods that, like fine wines, deserve to be served on the best tables in the land. Just as the burger and chile ads suggest that wine is the perfect complement to either, the wild mushroom ad compares the uncommon fungi to the uncommon varieties of Sutter Home wines. Curiosity gets the best of you, you read about the featured foods, and maybe you're hooked on the wine, too.

Courtesy Sutter Home Winery, Inc.

FIGURE 4-2 (B)

New Mexico Red
Medium to very hot. Despite the pain, it triggers endorphins that cause a euphoria people yearn for.
Cayenne
The darker and skinnier the chile, the hotter it'll be. Obviously, these little bullets can make you go ballistic.
Güero
The best cure for a chile's bite is to drink milk. With the hottest of the güeros, two gallons ought to do it.
Bullets From Hell.
Poblano
The nicest thing you can do to poblanos is throw them in a fire. Let char, then peel; the thick flesh is ideal for chile rellenos.
Habañero
The wickedest chile of them all. Hot enough to cause temporary faint deafness so, according to one man, "you can't hear your own screams."
Some fear wine will be overpowered by the sharp bite of a chile. On the contrary, the hint of fresh berries and the crisp, clean finish of a chilled glass of Sutter Home White Zinfandel is a delightful counterpoint to these fiery devils. It makes the prospect of biting the bullet infinitely more pleasurable.
Dried Anaheims
Earthy flavor is brought out by roasting. One expert suggests using a blowtorch. Say, that's a gourmet touch...
Serrano
Hottest of common chiles, good in salsas. Packs a searing sting, followed by a numbing burn, sweats, and tearing eyes. Bon appétit!!!
SUTTER HOME
WHITE ZINFANDEL
SUTTER HOME. IF YOU'RE GOING TO DO IT, DO IT RIGHT

FIGURE 4-2 (C)

Lobster
Great in stews. For heartier portions, try that mushroom found in Michigan. It's 40 acres across and weighs 22,000 lbs. (You may have leftovers.)
Oyster
Good news! They're virtually calorie-free. Bad news! They're best with port and cream, or in puff pastries.
Chanterelle
Collected in the Northwest. Good collectors earn $200 a day on them. Good cooks spend that much a day on them.
Better Living Through Fungus.
Wood Ear
Protein-wise, they're closer to meat than to vegetables. Forget Meat & Potatoes; stick to Ears & Potatoes.
Morel
Among the finest fungi, they often appear after forest fires. So 18th century German women, naturally, set fires. Anything for a good veal sauce.
Once you taste a wild mushroom, you can't go back to common varieties. The same is true of Sutter Home Chardonnay. The ripe apple and citrus aromas, crisp fruity flavors, and the dry, lingering finish enhance any moment. It's one of the treasures that can make life more enjoyable... that, and a good fungus.
Shiitake
Dried, their smoky pepperiness is potent. 4 or 5 slices can permeate an entire soufflé. Never underestimate the power of the fungi.
Enoki
Japanese delicacy, best raw. The Japanese also breed mushrooms tasting like steak, with patty-size crowns. Fungus burger, anyone?
SUTTER HOME
CHARDONNAY
SUTTER HOME. IF YOU'RE GOING TO DO IT, DO IT RIGHT

FIGURE 4-3
The Foote Cone & Belding strategy planning model

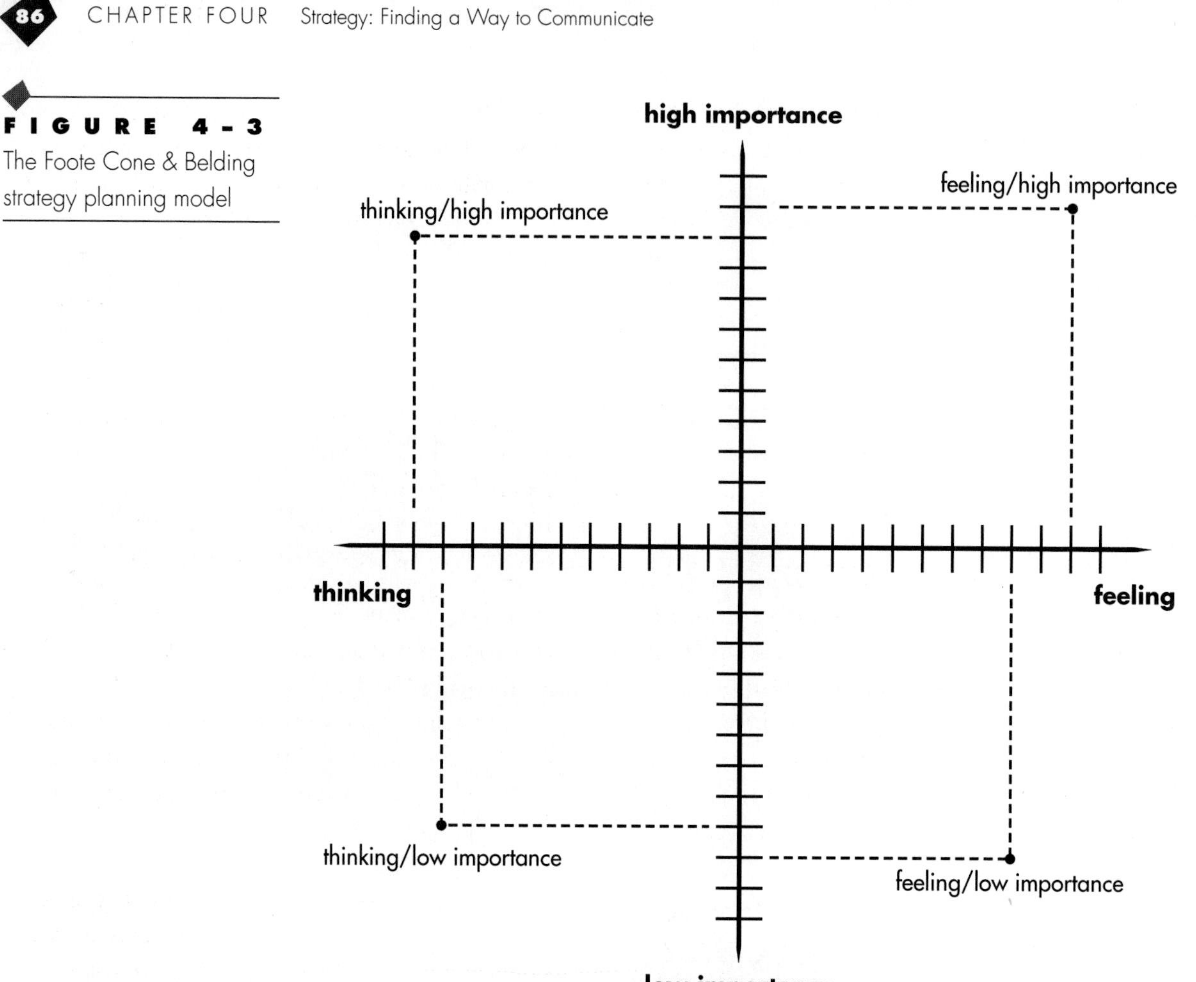

decisions, and a horizontal line that represents a continuum for the importance of thinking versus feeling as a factor in the purchasing decision (Figure 4–3). Depending on where a product or service is on the grid, a certain type of advertising approach may be appropriate. The following examples, one from each quadrant of the grid, should provide some insight into this model.[3]

1. ***Thinking/High Importance.*** This approach, also called the informative model, regards the consumer as thinker, an individual who needs a great deal of information because of the importance of the product and the logical issues related to it. Examples in this category would be cars, home furnishings, and new products. Long copy, specific information, and possibly a demonstration would be appropriate for such advertisements. This approach incorporates the economic model of the consumer: learn-feel-do.

2. ***Feeling/High Importance.*** This approach, also called the affective model, regards the consumer as feeler, an individual who relies less on specific information and more on an attitude or holistic feeling, because the importance of the

[3] From *How Advertising Works: An FCB Strategy Planning Model.* A Foote Cone & Belding Talk Piece. Published internally for members of the agency and its clients. 1978. Used by permission.

product is related to the person's self-esteem. Examples in this category would be jewelry, cosmetics, fashion apparel, motorcycles. Image-oriented ads which communicate on a nonliteral basis with dramatic executional impact would be appropriate. This approach uses the psychological model of the consumer: feel-learn-do.

3. ***Thinking/Low Importance.*** This approach, also called the habit formation model, sees the consumer as doer, an individual who makes product decisions in this category with minimal thought. Since this individual buys certain products as a result of habit, simply inducing a trial purchase, as with a coupon, can often generate subsequent purchases more readily than pounding home undifferentiating copy points. Examples in this category would be food and household items. Messages that serve as a reminder of the product might be sufficient. This approach employs the responsive model of the consumer: do-learn-feel.

4. ***Feeling/Low Importance.*** This approach, also called the self-satisfaction model, views the consumer as reactor and is reserved for products that satisfy personal tastes. Many products here will fit group situations, since most people like to enjoy themselves as part of a group, and logical interest is hard to hold and short-lived. Examples in this category would be cigarettes, beer, liquor, candy. Messages are designed primarily to gain attention. This approach employs the social model of the consumer: do-feel-learn.

You should note that the category depends on the advertised product or service, not on the consumer. Consumers buy a variety of goods and services but may fall into one of the four models at any given time, depending on a specific purchasing decision. Using yourself as an example, think of what it would take to make you want to purchase a certain brand of candy bar as opposed to a certain brand of stereo equipment.

Richard Lyon in *Guts* says a strategy is "a carefully designed plan to murder the competition." He adds: "Any premise that lacks a killer instinct is not a strategy. Any premise that doesn't reflect or include a consumer's crying need is not a strategy. Any premise embalmed in stiff, predictable language is not a strategy. Any premise that addresses the whole world, women 3–93 is not a strategy. Any premise interchangeable with that of another product is not a strategy."

"The true test of an advertising strategy," he concludes, "is to let another human being read it. If that person can't say yes, that's me, or yes, I need that, or yes, that's my problem—throw it away."

Norman Berry of ad agency Ogilvy & Mather says "Give me the freedom of an extremely tightly defined strategy." What does he mean by that?

Reviewing Things to Consider for an Effective Strategy

1. Make unexpected yet relevant connections that work to build a relationship between the brand and the prospect.

2. Choose a type of strategy appropriate to the task, which may be a type no one else in the product category is using.

3. Think about how the type of purchasing decision (high or low importance, thinking or feeling) may affect the choice of strategy.

4. Check to see that the strategy addresses one or more of the basic human needs.

Writing Your Strategy Statement

The strategy statement, or platform or brief as it is called by some groups, sets forth the creative approach on paper for the account team and the client. If you are asked to write a strategy statement, platform, or brief prior to creating individual ads and commercials, you might try the following outline, which is designed to help you explain the problem, the goals, and the probable solutions.

Here is the general outline for your strategy statement, with an example in italic type of how one student, James Webber, wrote his strategy for Sony Micro Headphones.

Creative Platform and Strategy for (Name of Product, Service, or Organization)
Sony Micro Headphones

1. Who are we trying to reach?
Suggestions: Brief lifestyle/attitudinal descriptions. Some demos, but not as important as lifestyle descriptions for many products. Users, heavy users, nonusers, users of competitive brands? Relationship to other product/service usage?

Our target market consists primarily of owners and users of portable tape and compact disc players who want quality and compactness in a headphone. MRI shows that a large number of portable stereo users are males 18–34, with heavy users falling into the 18–25 bracket. Women 18–25 also comprise a substantial share of this market. This group has invested a good deal of money in portable stereo equipment and puts quality and convenience before price.

2. What is the big idea we must convey to them?
Suggestions: Product will represent, accomplish, replace, change, satisfy a need, protect family, etc.

Sony Micro Headphones are the most comfortable and compact available, yet also offer superior sound reproduction.

3. Where are we now in the minds of our prospects? Or, what is the key consumer problem?
Suggestions: They don't know us, they know us but don't use us. They prefer another brand because . . . . They don't understand what our product can do for them. They don't use us for enough things, etc.

Our product isn't well known. This is a fairly new Sony item and has not had the time to benefit from long-term user trial. Similar products exist, but the response to these has been less than favorable, primarily because of the poor sound quality and uncomfortable fit, the latter attributed to the design of the earpiece.

4. Where is our competition in the minds of our prospects?
Suggestions: They prefer Brand G because . . . Other brands have created more positive images through advertising . . . perceived as stronger or gentler or tastier or. . . .

Our competition obviously is not well liked. Other headphones are either too bulky and uncomfortable or offer poor sound quality . . . or both. Until our product, the consumer has not believed small headphones can offer the same quality sound as the better yet bulkier phones.

5. Where would we like to be in the minds of our prospects?
Suggestions: Product is positioned as. . . . Product is the best choice because. . . . Now they know product will . . . etc. (the ideal answer, stated so positively that it probably won't make for believable advertising.)

"These are the finest micro headphones I've ever heard. Can hardly believe I'm getting topnotch sound from such a small and comfortable earpiece. I don't have to give up comfort or sound quality anymore."

6. How can we get there, and through what key selling idea?
Suggestions: Reposition as . . . stress such features as . . . clarify image of brand as . . . emphasize . . . steer away from such words, ideas, as . . .

We will show what you don't have to go through just to get quality sound from portable headphones. We will challenge target audience to give our headphones a try before giving up on micros.

7. What will the tone of the advertising be?
Suggestion: Warm, family values, startling, high tech, sobering fact, induce mild guilt, etc.

Create ads that inform, yet entertain through mild sarcasm directed at the competition.

Suggested Activities

1. Using the strategy outline above, write a strategy for a product, service, or organization.

2. Collect several advertisements for a single product, service, or organization. How much of the original strategy can you infer from what the ads say and how

they say it? Is the target audience apparent? What is the consumer problem and how do the ads address its solution? How would you categorize the type of strategy? What are the relevant yet unexpected connections in the ads? Which of the basic human needs are addressed? If the strategy is evident, does that make it a better ad? Why or why not?

3. Psyching out the auto market: How might creative people use this information to come up with a strategy for the Ford Escort? The Acura Integra? The Chevy Lumina? The Saturn sports coupe?

a. ***Purists***
Not brand loyal, skeptical, like cars and driving, like sporty but not sports cars. High percent of laborers, Asian-Americans. Age, 33.8. Average income, $31,660. 4 percent of new car buyers.

b. ***Gearheads***
Enjoy driving and working on cars. Believe a car says a lot about its owner. Men, craft workers, blue collar. Love domestic and Japanese sports cars. Age, 38.7. Average income, $34,130. 17 percent of new car buyers.

c. ***Negatives***
Car is necessary evil. Colors, options immaterial. Want no upkeep costs. High education. Average income $75,000+. Small to midsize imports. Age, 40.4. 16 percent of new car buyers.

d. ***Epicures***
Equipped, comfortable cars that seem elegant. 2nd highest percent of women of all types. Luxury sports convertibles. Age, 41.8. Average income, $31,900, but many earn $100,000+. 26 percent of new car buyers.

e. ***Functionalists***
Sensible, fuel efficient transportation. Conservative, law abiding. Have children. Small and mid-sized domestics. Age, 43.5. Average income, $29,020. 12 percent of new car buyers.

f. ***Road Haters***
Safety minded. Large domestic cars. Don't enjoy driving. Know little about cars. Highest percent women of all groups. Highest median age. Lowest median income. Age, 44.4. Average income, $27,970. 26 percent of new car buyers.

Always Coca-Cola

Early in 1993, Coca-Cola stunned the advertising world with an unusual new campaign from an unusual source. The campaign? Always Coca-Cola, spearheaded by an unprecedented twenty-six different television commercials which were as diverse as the audience for the world's number one brand itself. The source? A combination of long-standing Coke advertising agency McCann-Erickson and Hollywood talent shop Creative Artists Associates.

Some called Coca-Cola's new strategy daring but risky. Just two of the twenty-six commercials were made by McCann-Erickson Worldwide, New York, which was also credited with the "Always Coca-Cola" theme.

Thematically, the campaign reinterprets the famous "real thing" concept for the frenetic '90s with spots representing a dramatic departure from previous Coca-Cola advertising. For the first time, the brand chose to drop its traditional "one sight, one sound, one sell" approach in favor of advertising tailored to specific audiences, media, and even seasons. The company said the strategy followed the global trend toward fragmented media, adding that in this age of media clutter it is imperative to make ads that are personally relevant and that are so visually stimulating as to make the audience want to watch them.

Coca-Cola can claim that since its introduction in 1886, the only promise ever made by the brand was that "an ice cold Coke is delicious and refreshing." The company now adds that this theme needs reinterpretation for each succeeding generation, so that the essential promise remains fresh and contemporary.

The commercials for the new campaign have such diverse names as: Ice Pick, Spaceship, Dancing Clothes, Timeline, Glassblower, Digging Dog, Neon, Big and Small, Car Tire, Bottles and Bikes, Polar Bears, Deprogrammer, and Real Things Last. Each is designed to reach a segment of the broad soft drink market, using new media and various dayparts to reach more diverse and segmented groups of people. Although each commercial is unique, each is written to highlight the three brand icons: the red disk graphic, the contour bottle, and the "Always" theme line.

Many have applauded Coca-Cola's willingness to throw out the rules. Others call the strategy "subliminal," explaining that the campaign will reinforce Coke as the world's drink by the nature of its unusual execution, by the line "Always Coca-Cola," and by the media employed.

FIGURE 4-4
Evidence of the diverse themes in the Always Coca-Cola campaign are these frames from five TV commercials, along with the red disk graphic icon which appears in all of them. Following the "Logo," the frames are from "Glassblower," "Neon," "Polar Bears," "Deprogrammer," and "Ice Pick."

GLASSBLOWER
An attractive woman has wandered into a workshop where a handsome artisan is fashioning a Coca-Cola bottle. She watches intensely as he demonstrates the glassblower's art.

NEON

You are looking at the only scene in this commercial. We watch a neon sign flashing the "Always Coca-Cola" message as the theme music plays in the background.

POLAR BEARS

This highly popular spot provided Coca-Cola with opportunities for a spin-off commercial, as well as a merchandising opportunity to offer stuffed polar bear toys.

DEPROGRAMMER
Try as it may, this sinister duo finds it impossible to convince its subject that he should change his favorite brand of soft drink.

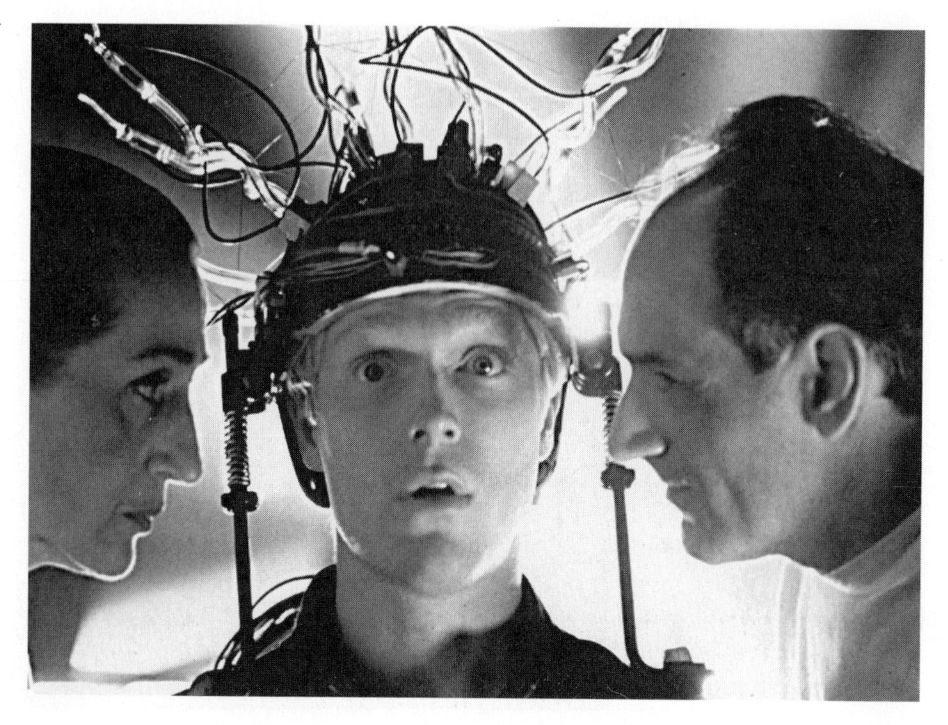

ICE PICK
To an upbeat version of the theme music, men hack away at blocks of ice to reveal ice cold Coca-Colas in the familiar bottles.

5

Strategy to Execution

You know who you want to talk to. You know what you want to say. You have an idea about the tone the advertising will take. And you're certain that the key selling idea is on target.

What now?

Now you want to translate your strategy into words and visuals that will stop prospects, make them believe what you say, and start thinking about your brand over others.

In his introduction to *The Compleat Guide to Advertising,* Barry Day offers some pertinent reminders about the nature and challenge of the task.[1]

Great advertising, claims Day, starts with the way people think and feel, and then it finds a way to interpret whatever it happens to be selling to fit that context. That way, an ad can fit into someone's life and create a real relationship.

All advertising must in some way reassure. It has to provide a point of reference. Advertising is not of itself innovation; in its use of language—and particularly in its attitude—it must express even the new in terms of the familiar.

An ad should be a small reward. The reward can sometimes be the surprise of new and welcome information. It can equally well be the quiet confirmation of a long-held view from an old advertising friend, which is a frequent strategy of brand-leader advertising. The great ad can—in its small way—crystallize the temper of the times. It can give shape to what people are thinking, often unwittingly, so that the ad becomes a small but important thing to hang on to.

Only when all of these characteristics are present does advertising technique become important. Then and only then does it matter that the product is the focus of the ad, the picture sharp and clear, the words touching and true, and the balance of the elements aesthetically pleasing. And then it matters one hell of

[1] Barry Day, "Introduction," in Torin Douglas, *The Complete Guide to Advertising* (London: Guild Publishing, 1985), pp. 6–9.

a lot. Finally, Day suggests, the advertising is right there in the product. All we have to do is coax it out.

Perhaps one way to "coax it out" is to think of what makes a good news story and to compare that to what constitutes good advertising. As Kathy McAdams and John Sweeney argue, writing advertising copy and writing news copy require similar skills. They explain that well-written news competes for the reader's attention just as ad copy must and claim that both kinds of writing require techniques that catch and reward readers with concise, informative, pleasurable reading. They further suggest that both advertising and news copy share five common features:

1. They must be written with specific audiences in mind.

2. They must distill large amounts of information into limited space or time. News leads and headlines are written to attract the reader. The headline and visual are designed to do the same in advertisements.

3. They must bristle with vitality. Great writing is involving and rewarding for the reader. It entertains as it informs.

4. They must possess substance. Strong writing presents facts and feelings. Shortness or longness in advertising copy seems to have little effect on readership. What counts is the power of the content, whether hard facts, emotional promises, or some of both.

5. They must be presented with reader ease in mind. If not, the words may never be read. That's why both newswriting and copywriting emphasize short words, short paragraphs, and simple sentences. Good writers know that simplicity invites readers to stay with a story and that white space invites the eye to keep on reading.[2]

Others claim good advertising copy must possess some or all of the following qualities:

1. It has fun with words, playing with word meanings and using them in unusual ways.

2. It reads like a conversation between the sender of the message and the recipient, rather than like a formal essay. In so doing, it builds a relationship. If the ad were a friend, it would be a special friend.

3. It communicates so as to empathize with the recipient, to elicit a response such as, "Hey, that's me they're talking about."

[2] Kathy Mc Adams and John Sweeney, "Copywriting and Newswriting Need Similar Skills," *Journalism Educator,* Vol. 41, No. 4 (Winter 1987): 38–40. Used with permission.

4. If the ad were a person, you would describe it as charming, fun, conversational, friendly, empathetic, understanding, provocative, sincere, and purposeful.

5. It shows the writer cares about the subject. Genuine caring is far more powerful than playing games with language.

6. It gets to the point and moves forward in a simple, easily followed, chain of events.

The VIPS Formula

David Bernstein, noted British advertising executive, claims that effective advertising can be summed up in four words: *visibility, identity, promise and simplicity.*[3]

Visibility. A good advertisement works hard to stop the casual reader who might be a target for your message. What will you do to make your advertisement stand out from the clutter of thousands of other messages sent to the prospect? Leo Burnett, founder of one of the major U.S. advertising agencies, writes:

Best attention comes from the entirely natural interests of the reader, built around the results of the product advertised. Being different from others is not an asset if the others are right. An ad may get attention and fail completely in getting anything else. An able show window designer once said, "The thing to avoid is drawing a crowd. The hard thing is to catch the eye of every possible customer and keep the others walking past." It is better to attract the serious attention of possible buyers than, through an exaggerated and clever headline, to attract other possible readers who won't be interested in the message anyway.[4]

Identity. In addition to gaining attention through a visible device, the advertisement must register the brand name, the identity of the advertiser. Opportunities for identity include featuring the product package in a major visual, using the name in the headline, mentioning the name several times in the copy, and featuring the name and package prominently in the logo or signature. In radio and television commercials, it's important to name the brand with some frequency and to emphasize it in the closing seconds.

Promise. Inherent in any advertisement is a promise to the recipient: the promise that potatoes are low in calories and good for you; the promise that

[3] David Bernstein, *Creative Advertising* (London: The Creative Business Limited, 1974), pp. 155–202. Used by permission.

[4] Leo Burnett, from a memorandum to his creative staff, November 13, 1947. Reprinted in *Communications of an Advertising Man—Selections from the Speeches, Articles, Memoranda, and Miscellaneous Writings of Leo Burnett*, Copyright 1961 by Leo Burnett Company, Inc., Chicago. For private distribution only. Used with permission.

Lands' End clothing is subject to dozens of quality checks so you'll have few, if any, complaints; the promise that Ultra Clear eye drops will brighten, whiten, and refresh tired-looking eyes; and the promise that a toothpaste will give you "sexy teeth."

Simplicity. Finally, the point must be made clearly. As in a good story with a beginning, middle, and end, the advertisement must stay on target, progressing logically from start to finish.

Now you're ready to do some advertising. In the next chapter, we begin with print, the medium from which all others sprang forth.

Finding a Vision for the Bali Brand of Intimate Apparel

Robert F. Graham
Vice Chairman,
Chief Creative Officer,

Long Haymes Carr Lintas,
Winston-Salem, N.C.

Bali is a department store-dedicated brand of lingerie composed of bra, panty, and shapewear lines. Like the Playtex customer, Bali users tend to skew older, while Warner's, Maidenform, Vanity Fair, and Victoria's Secret users tend to skew younger.

While Bali brand awareness is strong among users, it is weak among nonusers due to a sustained absence of consumer advertising. When asked to characterize Bali, nonusers' comments speak positively of the brand as fashionable, stylish, pretty, even sexy. These attitudes suggest an opportunity for Bali to develop the 25–34-year-old segment of department store shoppers.

The agency and Bali recognized a significant opportunity to fuel brand growth by positioning the brand with relevance to younger women in a manner that also consolidated loyalty among current users. Our key challenge was how to define the new Bali positioning. Research made it clear to us that many women use varied expressions of femininity to help define their sense of self, personally and for others. We also found that the cycle from high to low involvement with intimate apparel is both rational and emotional. On the rational level, women seek quality, fit, comfort, and value. These benefits are essential for any brand to be competitive. Emotionally, her choice of intimate apparel may reflect a woman's desire to get in touch with the sensual, intimate side of her femininity.

We found that Bali's greatest opportunity was among women ages 25 to 34 who were not loyal to a particular brand, yet demonstrated an affinity for the emotional benefits of intimate apparel.

These were the questions we asked ourselves as we began the Bali creative challenge:

1. ***Intimate apparel is a complex, multidimensional product category.*** Few categories of products have more levels and layers of meaning to the consumer. Aging boomers will make this the Decade of Gravity. AIDS will make this the Decade of Personal Fantasy. *How can we factor all this into one simple, powerful selling equation for Bali?*

2. ***Intimate apparel is a product category that is rapidly changing and will continue to change.*** New colors, fabrics, styles. Growth of mass merchandiser sales. Specialization. Orchestrated selling environments like Victoria's Secret. Declining service advantage to department store sales. Growth of promotion dependence and (hopefully) the decline of that dependence. These trends can be confusing to the marketer as well as to the consumer. *How can we put this dynamic to work positively for Bali?*

3. ***Intimate apparel is an "inside out" product category.*** It's a means, not an end. It's a beginning not an ending. It changes your body. It changes your perceptions about yourself. It changes other people's perceptions. It changes how clothes look on you. It changes your potential. *How can Bali capture this power of personal change?*

4. ***Intimate apparel is a product category in which consumers need and want change dramatically as they move up the age curve.*** The very nature of the body changes. You are not the same yesterday as today, this year as last year. How women feel about aging is in transition. Tomorrow's older woman will be "younger" than ever before. *Can we do a better job than the competition in talking to women at the right time in the right way?*

5. ***Intimate apparel is a product category which develops unparalleled product loyalty.*** A woman can buy the same bra for seven years and be furious when her style is dropped. A woman can be loyal to various styles and to various brands. *How can we break the competition's loyalty cycle and strengthen it for Bali consumers?*

6. ***Intimate apparel is a product category in which the majority of purchase decisions are wrong.*** Up to 75 percent of women are wearing the wrong bra size. Because of bad advice. Because of habit. Because they changed and the bra didn't. Or they didn't change and the bra did. Size options like small/average/fuller figure make a difference. *How can we make Bali feel more right as a brand?*

7. ***Intimate apparel is a category driven by both physical and psychological comfort.*** The bra has to fit the woman in both style and size. *How can we clarify the real nature of the Bali fit?*

8. ***Every woman is many women.*** Over the course of a week. Or a day. The difference between night and day. Between a desk and a dance floor. *How can Bali speak to more than one of these intimate apparel personalities?*

9. ***The Bali name is evocative.*** Different than competitive names. More mysterious. More associational than Olga or Warner's or Playtex. It is easier to attach meaning to a name with edge. *Can the Bali name work harder for us?*

10. ***Most bra advertising underachieves.*** There is no story value. Magazine articles on bras are more entertaining than most bra advertising. This is a high touch product. *Can feeling play a bigger role in Bali advertising?*

11. ***Most advertisers are bound by limiting selling conventions.*** Maidenform changed the rules by breaking them, first with their male celebrity viewpoints campaign, then with their thinking women's bra campaign. Energizing and politicizing their brand with woman's issues. Playtex has a new creative platform much broader than before: "Fashion lingerie for real life." Attitude and ideology are becoming more important in intimate apparel advertising. Can we capture the spirit of the times in Bali terms? *Are there other rules that should be broken in Bali advertising?*

©1993 Bali Company

To be a sensual person means...

To let your passion show?

Or is it so much more.

To not be made up,

but to be your own certain creation,

the perfect expression

of the woman within.

Find yourself in BALI.

Lots of Luxury™ Collection

Courtesy Long Haymes Carr LINTAS.

In this case study, the writer expresses the Bali brand personality with these words: *I am the spirit of sensuality. My beauty comes from within. It is refined yet effortless, soft and subtle yet unmistakable. Some say there is an intriguing mystery about me, that you can know me, but never know all of me. I can take you to a place where life moves to the rhythms of nature . . . a place you will love to return to again and again.* How well does this magazine advertisement express that personality? How much of the idea of "essential femininity" comes through in the visual and the copy? How has the creative team employed the "Bali mystique" so that the typical consumer in this target market can relate to it? What qualities does the model chosen for the ad possess that contribute to the image desired by the advertising agency and client?

12. ***The consumer thinks she knows exactly who Bali is.*** Bali has relatively high awareness levels for not having actively advertised in recent years. A change in position and greater presence will attract notice. *Can we make the element of surprise work in Bali's favor?*

13. ***The unmistakable trend is toward more expressive intimate apparel.*** More expressive colors, shapes, textures, styles—all based on broader cultural trends toward self-expression that have tremendous momentum. *What is the proper Bali expression and how should it be reflected in the advertising?*

14. ***It is better to grow than to change.*** We want to make Bali mean more to more people. To feel younger. To feel like more of a value. Yet to remain high quality. High tone. To entice without offending. *Can we find a common denominator that will let us retain the present Bali franchise and invite a new one?*

A review of the situation resulted in our decision to create a new image for the brand.

◆ ***The new Bali image:*** After weighing all the evidence, our key concept became "Essential Femininity." That basic, natural, primal softness and sensuousness that resides in every woman and is interpreted through wardrobe, cosmetics, and personal style. Intimate apparel, between skin and clothes, is near the core of essential femininity and instrumental in bringing it out in a woman. Essential femininity may be hidden or lost. Bali intimate apparel helps a woman maximize hers.

◆ The name Bali evokes mystery. After all, Bali is a mysterious, timeless, fascinating tropical island in the Indonesian archipelago that has been idealized and made larger than life through popular culture. It is a symbolic representation of essential femininity.

◆ ***Creative Strategy:*** Bali gives me the freedom to enjoy and express the essence of my femininity.

◆ ***Supporting evidence or consumer proof:*** Only Bali intimate apparel is beautifully fashionable yet always naturally comfortable. The Bali brand personality is anchored in the imagery evoked by the design and beauty of the apparel as well as the romance and allure of the Bali name.

◆ ***Brand Personality:*** I am the spirit of sensuality. My beauty comes from within. It is refined yet effortless, soft and subtle yet unmistakable. Some say there is an intriguing mystery about me, that you can know me, but never know all of me. I can take you to a place where life moves to the rhythms of nature . . . a place you will love to return to again and again.

◆ ***The "Find Yourself in Bali" Campaign:*** Poetic body copy is intended to draw the reader into contemplation of her own essential femininity as recognized and shared by Bali. Future executions will support the growing segments of the Bali line of bras, panties, and shapewear.

◆ ***Consumer reaction:*** Women exposed to the print executions found them easy to understand and relate to. They seemed to understand that Bali truly understands women and can therefore make products that fit their needs. They found the campaign affirming. The "Find Yourself in Bali" line has degrees of meaning, from a call to action to wear Bali intimate apparel to the experiential benefits of discovery, expression, and beauty. Imagery was described as intense, refreshing, exotic, aspirational, and glamorous. The ads were viewed as mysterious, alluring, sophisticated yet natural.

CHAPTER 6

Working in Print

Print came first, and many creatives still feel print is the ultimate challenge and the most fun. Print is what creative directors want to see most when you make the rounds with your book. Print lacks the sounds of radio, the sounds and movement of television, the size of outdoor, the narrow targeting of direct response. As a member of a creative team—art director and copywriter—your task is to fill a blank sheet of paper with a message that is intrusive visually and verbally.

A Visual Look at Print

We will be talking more specifically about the design process in the next chapter. For now, what's important to remember is that how an ad looks and what an ad says are both part of the creative process, can contribute equally to the effectiveness of the message, and should be agreed upon by both writer and artist.

That means if you're the art director, you'll be having thoughts about what the headline says as well as how it looks and what the accompanying visual will be. If you're the copywriter, you'll be thinking about how the entire ad will look at the same time you're writing rough concepts for headlines. You'll find it almost impossible not to think of the visuals to accompany each headline idea, just as the art director may find it difficult to design an ad without a headline/visual concept in mind. So to begin the creative process in print, though we'll be talking first about headlines, we also want you to visualize how the headlines you write will relate to the rest of the ad.

Here's how to do that. Using a soft lead pencil or a fine, roller-ball black pen, draw a number of small horizontal rectangles (about 2″ wide by 3″ deep) to represent the general shape of a magazine page. Don't bother with making the lines straight, just freehand the rectangles. Within each rectangle, begin placing your ideas for headlines and visuals. Scribble the words of the headline in the space and, if you can't draw, use simple stick figures and such. Indicate body copy with a series of rough lines and place a rough logo at the bottom, probably in the right hand corner. This is your "thumbnail rough," the first stage of a print lay-out. As you place other headlines in other rectangles, you'll probably begin thinking of still more ideas for words and pictures. Good! Don't stop until you have exhausted your topic, even if some of the ideas seem bizarre or ridiculous. Remember that it's easier to pull back from extremes than it is to push forward from mediocrity.

Headline and Visual: Important Choices

Advertisers know that most people who read periodicals never spend much time with most of the pages devoted to advertising. The great majority will glance in passing at an ad while seeking the next feature in the magazine. A smaller number may look at the visual and read the headline. An even smaller number may note the brand name, while a percentage of those may read some of the text, or body copy. The smallest number will be so interested they will read most or all of the copy.

Since we know that those who read the most represent our best prospects, we need to do all we can in the headline and visual to get their attention and keep it. Here are a number of headlines that do just that.

THE BEST REASON YET TO CHOOSE COUNTY 17 INSTEAD OF THE INTERSTATE. SAAB INTRODUCES THE 9000 CSE.

In the visual, a Saab is tooling along a bumpy road. What are the headline and visual saying to the reader? What do you imagine is the key selling idea?

To suggest that you've created "the renaissance of the American car" takes incredible nerve.
Or, in our case, an incredible car.

Revise Your E.T.A.

This advertisement for the Lexus sport sedan shows only the car. What is it saying about the car?

The Jenn-Air Range Makes a Great Lemon Souffle, Grilled Mahi-Mahi, Beef Wellington, and First Impression.

We changed the way you listen to music. Now change the way you change it.

This is an advertisement for the Sony compact disc changer.

As they say, it's all in the genes. Introducing the ThinkPad™ from IBM. The slickest, sleekest little number that ever crunched one. A mere seven-and-a-half pounds of brains and beauty that begs you to take it anywhere. And once you own one, that's exactly what you'll do.

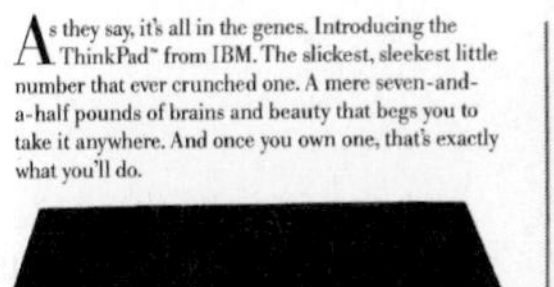

All this in only 11.7"

Introducing

ThinkPad

The top-of-the-line ThinkPad 700C sports a screaming 486 SLC™ 25 MHz processor. But it's built for comfort too. There's a surprisingly roomy interior, with a full-size, ergonomically designed keyboard. And a screen that literally bends over backwards.

Strategically placed on the keyboard is a little red spot called the TrackPoint II.™ It does what a mouse would do with a few million more years of evolution. Nothing dangles; it's part of the soul of the machine. You can operate it with one fingertip. And it lets you think on any terrain, even one without any flat surfaces.

The ThinkPad's screen is a thing of almost aching beauty. Its 640 × 480 VGA resolution is sharper than that of many desktop computers. It displays 256 colors. And it's the biggest screen on any notebook. So it's very easy on the eyes.

The ThinkPad comes standard with things some other notebooks don't even offer as options. Like 4MB of memory upgradable to 16MB. 120MB of hard disk space. Pre-installed DOS 5.0 and PRODIGY.® You can soup it up with a turbo-charged 486SLC2 50/25 MHz processor—just one of the upgrade products IBM offers. And the hard disk is removable, so it's easy to upgrade and share your ThinkPad, not to mention the great security and virtually unlimited storage.

ThinkPad blows the doors off its competition in an even more surprising arena. Price. Any ThinkPad in the line will give you more for your money—and for your psyche—than any other notebook.

If you have questions along the way, ThinkPad Models 700C and 700 are supported by HelpWare,™ an invaluable service package that includes a three-year international warranty.†

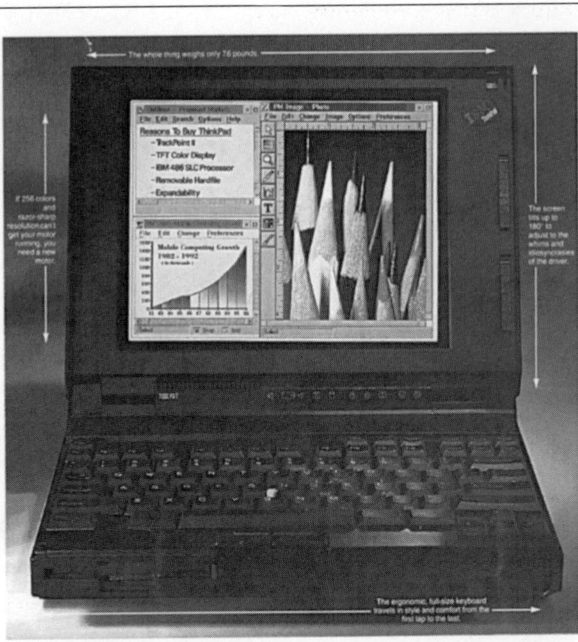

Y G H B
The world's smallest mouse.

ThinkPad	Model 700C	Model 700
Processor	486 SLC/25 MHz	486 SLC/25 MHz
Display	10.4" Active Matrix 256-Color Screen	9.5" Monochrome Display 64 Grayscale Screen
Battery Life*	2-4 Hours	3.8-7.5 Hours
Weight	7.6 Lbs. with Battery	6.5 Lbs. with Battery
Warranty	3 Years (International)	3 Years (International)
Price**	$4,350	$2,750

For more information or an IBM authorized dealer near you, call our Personal Systems HelpCenter™ 24 hours a day, 7 days a week at 1 800 772-2227.††

Then just park one in your lap and see what happens.

IBM®

*Depending on usage and configuration. **MSRP. Dealer prices may vary. †Warranty information available from the Personal Systems HelpCenter or an IBM authorized dealer. 700T warranty is available in USA and Canada only. ††In Canada, call 1 800 465-7999. IBM is a registered trademark and ThinkPad, HelpWare, HelpCenter, SLC and TrackPoint II are trademarks of International Business Machines Corporation. PRODIGY is a registered trademark of Prodigy Services Company. © 1992 IBM Corp.

Courtesy International Business Machines Corp.

FIGURE 6-1

"As they say, it's all in the genes," begins the copy for this wonderful introductory ad for the IBM ThinkPad, termed "the slickest, sleekest little number that ever crunched one." This is the new IBM, off and roaring to meet the competitive challenges of the personal computer market with a new style of advertising that adds a personal touch to a company once considered distant and reserved.

It still has four tires
and the steering wheel is on the left.
other than that, everything else has
changed for the '90s.

THE SAFETY FEATURES YOU WANT WITHOUT THE BODY STYLE OF A REFRIGERATOR.

This is an ad for the Nissan Altima sedan. What is it saying about the car? Is it positioning itself against other brands? Which brand or brands?

Live in the lap, lap, lap, lap, lap, lap, lap of luxury.

This is an ad for the 7-seat Nissan Quest van. It shows the interior seating.

Courtesy Kohler Company.

FIGURE 6-2

Copy for "Body Shop" sells the idea of an invigorating, whirlpool plunge with these alluring words of copy: "Listen, we all need it. That place to re-tune our bodies before or after the day's living. Which is exactly the idea behind every Kohler Whirlpool. But honed to a 'T.' Standing for 'technically thoughtful.' And meaning that Kohler Whirlpools don't just soothe,

These headlines and their accompanying visuals make sense in the context of what a headline and visual ought to accomplish. Effective headline/visuals quickly communicate powerful messages related to the products or services advertised. The connection is relevant yet unique. The relationship between reader and brand is meaningful. Where have you heard that before? On the first page of this book.

Nissan Quest could have headlined its ad, "We seat seven." Nissan Altima could have said, "We give you good looks and safety, too." IBM could have written, "Our new laptop combines the brains of a mainframe with the speed of a sports car." And Saab could have simply stated, "Our new model will make country roads feel like the smoothest superhighway."

But they didn't, thank goodness, for fewer people would have heard them, seen them, read them.

Headline Approaches

Some headlines defy categorizing. Sutter Home Winery's series linking its wines to good eating carry headlines such as "Better Living Through Fungus (wine with mushrooms)", "Bullets from Hell (wine with chiles)", and "Be a Burger Meister (wine with burgers)." Clinique says only "Good Riddance" in its headline for its turnaround cream. Avon, promoting its easy return policy, shows a menacing cosmetics clerk in a store next to a headline that reads, "What do you mean you want to return it?" Rather than think in terms of types of headlines, perhaps we should view the following categories in terms of the many things headlines can do and the many forms they can take to accomplish their goals. The list is by no means complete.

Benefit

People are interested in products and services that offer them something in return. Stating a consumer benefit in a headline is one way to interest prospects. It helps if that benefit is stated in an interesting way and is complemented by a good visual.

"Ethyl's new gasoline additive will keep old cars from heading for an early grave." The visual is a photograph of the famous Cadillac Ranch, where several old Caddys are buried in the dirt, noses first.

"One size fits all" shows a computer floppy disk with a coat hanger poking through the hole in the middle. The ad talks about a system that can let you add graphics to your word processing system.

FIGURE 6-2 Continued.
relieve, relax and gently ripple away the world, they do it in a way that's . . . well, you'd think we knew you for years. So, how do I find this perfect whirlpool, you ask? Just call our toll-free number and we'll snap back a book full of facts. But do it. Your personal Body Shop is waiting." Sorta makes you want to pick up the phone and dial that 800 number, doesn't it?

News

News attracts readers—hence the popularity of newspapers and other publications that tell us things we haven't heard about before. If an ad has the element of news incorporated into its headline, it can stop readers, too.

"Now I can have my favorite supper . . . for lunch." While stating a benefit, this headline also tells us something we may not have thought about doing before.

"Tartar isn't sexy. Introducing CloseUp Tartar Control Paste." This is a more obvious news headline that also adds an interesting comment up front. The visual is a huge close-up of a man and a woman about to kiss, cropped so that we see only noses and mouths and one closed eye. Talk about involving the audience.

Selective

A selective headline does something to attract a specific audience, a group with something in common. It says, essentially, if you have this problem, read this ad. If you are this kind of person, read this ad. If you're looking for this or that, this is where you'll find it. Obviously, any message that seeks its audience so deliberately will have a certain amount of appeal.

"If you have diarrhea, hurry and read this. If you have constipation, take your time and think this over." This rather startling message advertises an over-the-counter medicine, Equalactin, which claims to remedy both of these problems. The first part of the headline is under a picture of a running rabbit, while the second part is under a picture of a stationary tortoise. The copy in the ad is in two parts as well: very short under the first part, and longer under the second part. One has to give the creators of this ad credit for working hard not to offend readers, while delivering the message in an inventive and strategic manner.

"The refrigerator that's programmed to serve the needs of your family." This simply says that Whirlpool has a top-of-the line refrigerator that can tell you more than you probably ever wanted to know about the food inside. For some families, especially those with growing children, this might be a highly appealing feature.

Curiosity

A curiosity headline provides just enough information—and just enough intrigue—to whet the appetite for more. It should be relevant to the product message, for it can risk turning away the reader if it seems the least bit too confusing.

"Ever wonder why most people make love in the dark?" is surely a candidate for this category. "The most important discovery in flexible packaging was made nearly 200 years ago," reads a headline for an ad that shows a painting of two early settlers with a Native American maiden. Two of the people in the painting are holding modern-day products. Reading the copy, you discover that the settlers are Lewis and Clark, and the discovery they made has to do with working as a partnership.

"We found a new way to eat barbecued chicken in California" is a curiosity headline with the visual providing a clue to the mystery. It shows a tempting slice of barbecued chicken pizza.

"Why you should spend $250 for a pair of shoes you never heard of" is a compelling curiosity headline for J. M. Weston shoes. Ever heard of them? Want to read more? I did. The visual is a large detail of the top of the shoe.

Reverse Benefit

The idea of stating how consumers are worse off without the product or service advertised can be an effective one, simply because the tragedies of life are often more memorable than the triumphs. If this approach seems perverse, remember that ads depicting problem situations may make more powerful connections with people than ads showing the solutions to the problems. The choice to use reverse benefit headlines depends, of course, on the strategic goals of the advertising.

"Yes, we have no banana," runs a line for California Cooler wine coolers. Four are shown: orange, citrus, tropical, and peach.

"Most immigrants came to America through New York. Today's tourist doesn't have to make the same mistake," reads this rather caustic headline for Chicago tourism. The visual is of the Chicago skyline during sunset over Lake Michigan.

"This woman didn't pay enough attention to her eyes."

"Tartar isn't sexy."

"Most multivitamins don't know you from Adam."

"Unfortunately, there are some running problems even the Brooks Sojourn can't solve." This ad for a running shoe features a huge visual of a snarling dog.

"If only typewriters let you proofread your work before they printed it on a page."

Puns

Plays-on-words attract attention, provided that the pun is universally understood, as in the following examples: "Underware for your kitchen" (undercounter appliances), "Holiday on ice" (Bailey's Irish Cream being poured over ice cubes in a stylish goblet), "Fight cavities with a stick" (for a sugar-free gum), "Some vegetables have all the fun" (a glorious batch of french fries in an ad promoting potatoes), and "Grounds for owning a Subaru" (mud, snow, rough gravel, and other tough road surfaces). Puns can be delightful solutions for sprucing up tired ideas or tired products. Even the corniest ones that elicit a groan from the reader can make contact. But be careful.

Remember that these categories are only guidelines. Many of the best headlines fall into none of them, such as "The other white meat," an ad promoting pork. Another, for an office copier, shows a classic Volkswagen beetle, and the headline reads, "It came back as a copier."

If you get stuck trying to write a headline, write body copy first, and then go through your copy. You may find a clue to a headline somewhere between the opening and the concluding lines.

FIGURE 6-3 (A)
It's true that some ads do quite well with a minimum of copy. About all this copy tells you is how to get more information on the recliners shown. But the headline and visual nearly say it all: timeless elegance and timely comfort in the same piece of furniture.

Courtesy The Lane Company, Inc.

Deciding What to Illustrate

You don't have to include a visual in every print ad. Some advertisements are quite successful without them. Readership studies indicate, however, that ads with visuals outpull those without them. A typical magazine reader may skim the issue before reading specific articles, stopping momentarily to glance at the pictures and headlines. The same reader also glances at the ads in a similar way. A good visual can enhance the drawing power of a good headline, and vice versa. Here are some suggestions for strong visuals:

FIGURE 6-3 (B)

The Product

Why not feature the product? Ads that introduce new products usually feature the product to familiarize consumers with the package. Changes in packaging and labeling may be additional reasons to show the product by itself. Often, showing additional props with the package can suggest other messages.

Part of the Product

If a certain detail of the product warrants emphasis, single it out. Show the upper half of the Reach toothbrush to feature the curve in the handle and the unusual bristles. Highlight the texture of a cut orange to suggest luscious flavor. Display the detail in a piece of furniture to suggest fine quality. Bringing the reader closer to what the illustration depicts is a good involvement strategy.

The Product Ready for Use

Take the food out of the package and put it on the serving dish in pleasant surroundings. Show a brush dipping into an opened can of paint, a toothbrush with toothpaste flowing onto its bristles from a tube, or a hot steak just off the grill. If you remove the product from the package, remember to show the package elsewhere in the ad for the sake of brand identity.

The Product Compared with the Competition

One way to make this comparison is to show the two products side by side in an appropriate setting. Another way is to consider the competition to be "non-use," like the Johnson & Johnson ad "Sundown vs. sun damage," which compares one side of a face protected by the product to the other side that was not.

The Product Being Tested

An ad for a nail polish shows a billiard ball, after hours of play, still wearing a perfect coat of polish. An ad for a brand of carpet shows a child spilling his food on the thick, textured pile.

The Product in Use

A woman smiles with satisfaction as she drives her new sports car. A man looks refreshed as he uses his new soap. Children laugh with excitement as they try their new game.

The Happy Results of Using the Product

A woman who has just lost weight shows off her new body. A student with a new computer looks pleased as he gets his term paper back with a grade of "A."

The Unhappy Results of Not Using the Product

A commuter misses his train because his watch was slow. A lawyer has a bad haircut because he went to the wrong place. An executive is "drowning in paper" because her office isn't equipped with an adequate communications system. Paired with a reverse benefit headline, the result can be quite lively.

Writing Advertising Copy

What are the elements of good copy?

1. Have fun with the words. Be playful and your prospect will enjoy what you write.

2. Converse with the prospect. Keep it personal, one on one.

3. Show empathy with the problems of the prospect.

4. Stick to the point; be of single mind.

5. Keep the message logical. Be certain to use transitional statements that move the copy smoothly from one point to another.

6. Write in short, easy takes that are seamlessly fastened to one another.

7. Be provocative. What does this mean? It means sexy, but sex has little to do with it.

8. Tell the truth. People know when you make promises you can't support. Be believable and sincere.

9. Tell a good story in an unconventional way, beginning with the visual and headline you choose.

10. Never, never risk offending the people you need to reach.

11. Break long copy with subheads.

12. Think of your message as a story with a beginning, middle, and end.

13. Be engaging, conversational, friendly, charming. Think about how *you* would like to hear this story.

14. Be specific where you can. Where you can't, play on feelings.

15. Make it read easy and sound easy.

16. Don't be afraid of long copy or long headlines.

17. Make each ad a complete sale. Only the advertiser reads all the ads in a campaign.

18. If the headline asks a question, try to answer it quickly in the copy.

19. Reward the reader for finishing the copy with a quip or clever comment, or a pat on the back.

20. Use emotion to overcome the negatives.

21. Be clear about what you want the reader to do after reading the ad.

22. Always check the strategy to make certain every ad and commercial is attending to it. If not, change them or rethink the strategy. Be certain the whole campaign is single-minded.

Here is an advertisement for the Saab 9000 CSE automobile that does a wonderful job of telling prospects why they'll admire the car, from the headline to the last word. (See Figure 6–4.)

The headline says:

Roads talk to all cars. Saabs just listen better.

Now read the text. Read every word of every sentence. We will interrupt only to comment on the way each part of the copy works to drive the key selling point home.

Courtesy Saab Cars USA, Inc.

ROADS TALK TO ALL CARS. SAABS JUST LISTEN BETTER.

Roads speak a language of infinite subtlety. And few cars understand the dialects of curves, hills and asphalt better than the Saab 9000 CSE.

From the performance of its low-profile tires to the spring tension in its driver's seat, the 9000 CSE has been carefully tuned to connect, rather than separate, the driver and the road.

The chassis, for example, is 25% more rigid than ever before. An improvement that gives you a tactile sense of the car's progress through a tight turn.

And while you're in touch with the road, the Saab Traction Control System* monitors it for slippery conditions. The instant the drive wheels begin to spin, computers make split-second power adjustments to each wheel. So you get traction comparable to that of many four-wheel-drive cars.

Of course, you'd expect a car preoccupied with holding the road to come with anti-lock brakes and nimble rack and pinion steering. The 9000 CSE does not disappoint.

But since it is a Saab, the 9000 CSE doesn't just listen to roads, it also speaks to the needs of drivers. Which is why it has one of the roomiest interiors of any imported sedan. And more safety features than any preceding 9000-Series Saab; cars routinely ranked among the safest in their class.**

To experience the sports sedan that offers not just higher horsepower, but a heightened awareness of the road, ask your Saab dealer for a 9000 CSE test drive. Or, for more information, call 1-800-582-SAAB.

*WITH AVAILABLE 2.3-LITER TURBOCHARGED ENGINE. **BASED UPON STUDIES OF INSURANCE INJURY CLAIMS CONDUCTED BY THE HIGHWAY LOSS DATA INSTITUTE. ©1993 SAAB CARS USA, INC.

FIGURE 6-4(A)

Here's what the Saab ad looks like. Can you analyze the copy in the second Saab ad as the author has done in this chapter with the first ad?

YOU HAVE A HEART, A MIND AND A CONSCIENCE. SO SHOULD YOUR CAR.

Take a five-speed stick, alloy wheels and the usual performance options and you can build yourself a sports sedan. But it won't be a Saab 9000 CSE. Not without the three ingredients that make a Saab a Saab.

The heart of every Saab is its rally heritage, a thirty-year tradition of competition-bred performance reflected today in the 9000 CSE. With a 200-horsepower engine* and a 25% stiffer chassis, the 9000 CSE is the most spirited and agile Saab ever built.

Its mind is the 9000 CSE's enlightened use of information. Performance data is scrutinized by an advanced electronic engine-management system, computerized anti-lock brakes and Saab's traction control system.* The 9000 CSE doesn't just follow the roadways. It thinks its way along them.

Its conscience lies in Saab's comprehensive approach to safety and the environment. New steel reinforcements in the passenger compartment offer improved side-impact protection. Interior air filters prevent pollen and dust particles from entering the car. And Saab's new CFC-free air-conditioning helps protect the atmosphere outside the car.

Heart, mind and conscience: Mix these elements in proper proportion and you get a well-rounded human being. Or one of the most perfectly balanced sports sedans you can buy.

See for yourself through a Saab 9000 CSE test drive. Or, for more information, call 1-800-582-SAAB.

*WITH AVAILABLE 2.3-LITER TURBOCHARGED ENGINE. © 1992 SAAB CARS USA, INC.

FIGURE 6-4(B)

Roads speak a language of infinite subtlety. And few cars understand the dialects of curves, hills and asphalt better than the Saab 9000 CSE.

Note how, in the bridge from the headline/visual to the text, the writer sticks to the main point, adding more elaboration to hold the reader's interest.

From the performance of its low-profile tires to the spring tension in its driver's seat, the 9000 CSE has been carefully tuned to connect, rather than separate, the driver and the road.

This second paragraph adds still more information on the same point, that the car is engineered to help the driver guide the car effortlessly on practically any type of road.

In the paragraphs which follow, the copy moves from the "bridge" to the "elaboration of benefits" function:

The chassis, for example, is 25% more rigid than ever before. An improvement that gives you a tactile sense of the car's progress through a tight turn.

And while you're in touch with the road, the Saab Traction Control System* monitors it for slippery conditions. The instant the drive wheels begin to spin, computers make split-second power adjustments to each wheel. So you get traction comparable to that of many four wheel-drive cars.

Of course, you'd expect a car preoccupied with holding the road to come with anti-lock brakes and nimble rack and pinion steering. The 9000 CSE does not disappoint.

But since it is a Saab, the 9000 CSE doesn't just listen to roads, it also speaks to the needs of drivers. Which is why it has one of the roomiest interiors of any imported sedan. And more safety features than any preceding 9000-Series Saab; cars routinely ranked among the safest in their class.**

Finally, we come to the "urge to action," the part of the advertisement which tells, directly (as in this case) or indirectly, what the reader should do next.

To experience the sports sedan that offers not just higher horsepower, but a heightened awareness of the road, ask your Saab dealer for 9000 CSE test drive. Or, for more information, call 1–800–582–SAAB.
SAAB
*With available 2.3 liter turbocharged engine.
**Based upon studies of insurance injury claims conducted by the Highway Loss Data Institute. © 1993 Saab Cars USA, Inc.

Go back over the copy again and see how the writer has invited readership by breaking the text into short paragraphs. Note how each paragraph is the logical answer to the previous one. The first two paragraphs open up the headline concept. The third paragraph gives an example of the general idea expressed in the second paragraph (connecting the driver to the road) by explaining how the chassis is improved to give the driver the feel of the road.

The fourth paragraph uses a transitional clause (. . . and while you're in touch with the road) to introduce the Saab's computer monitoring system. The last sentence of this paragraph links the idea of the system to the benefit: traction similar to four-wheel-drive cars.

The fifth paragraph summarizes other attractive features in a way that indicates that Saab would never leave such things out . . . or it wouldn't be a Saab.

The sixth paragraph uses another transitional device (. . . but since it is a Saab, the 9000 CSE doesn't just listen to roads, it also speaks to the needs of drivers) to talk about the benefits of interior space and safety.

All in all, a powerful story which tells people who value safety and engineering that this car can deliver on both counts.

All this sounds easy, but how do you begin? If you're having trouble writing headline ideas, start writing the body copy first. Often a great headline will spring from the middle of a piece of copy. If you experience writer's block writing copy, pretend instead that you're writing to a friend, extolling the virtues of a product or service or company. Sometimes forgetting that you're writing an ad will make the words flow more easily.

In any event, don't write it once and consider the job done. Effective writing is a process that begins with rough ideas committed to paper, proceeds through a series of drafts, and culminates in a final draft that is ready to be seen by others. Spend ample time on your "private" writing, and your "published" piece will be much more convincing.

Guidelines for Writing

First, check your copy to make sure you've stated your argument as clearly as you can. Remember your reader probably isn't as close to the product as you are, so think what it would be like to be your prospect, trying to understand what you wrote.

Write so that each point you make draws the reader into the point which follows. Although you can't say everything about the product in one ad, be certain nothing critical is omitted. Above all, check to see if your words agree with your strategy. Great copy that's off strategy will be hard put to accomplish your goals, even if it attracts readers.

Finally, keep these general writing guidelines in mind.

1. ***Stick to the present tense whenever possible.*** It keeps your message active. For example: "Our copiers aren't fancy. And maybe they're not especially pretty. But they'll never let you down. In fact, we guarantee it in writing."

2. ***When possible, use singular nouns and verbs.*** You are talking to one consumer at a time about one item at a time. For example: "We do things a little differently in California. Like prepare gourmet meals atop a delightfully crisp, chewy pizza crust. One bite from any of them tends to make converts out of even the most die-hard traditional-style pizza addicts."

3. ***Active verbs mean action.*** Avoid passive construction in your sentences. In the example above, you wouldn't say, "converts are made after one bite from any of them," or "Things are done a little differently by us in California." Hear the difference? The active construction is lively; the passive is deadly.

4. ***Stick to familiar words and phrases.*** Some of the best writing in the world touches readers because it speaks their language. Five dollar words often don't work nearly as well as ten cent ones. Write directly to your audience, never up or down to them. It's amazing how much you can say—and say well—with everyday, conversational phrases.

5. ***Vary the lengths of sentences and paragraphs.*** Several short sentences followed by a longer one give your words a pleasing rhythm. A mixture of short and long paragraphs looks more inviting (remember the importance of being visually appealing?).

   Note how some ad copy even makes use of a single word or phrase as a paragraph. Such a technique can add emphasis where it's needed. As with any technique, this one can be overdone; if you consciously attempt to write in short and long takes, the results may sound artificial and insincere. Initially, just write. As you revise, look for ways to vary lengths.

6. ***Punctuate properly, even in headlines.*** Commas and periods serve important purposes in written communication: They signal readers to pause and

Courtesy Houghton Mifflin Company.

Why should she have to struggle with the same difficult and confusing dictionary you did?

Now, she doesn't. The *American Heritage College Dictionary* is designed in an airy, wide-margin format that makes finding words much easier. And unlike your old dictionary, we list the most common definitions first, to save her even more time.

The *New York Times* says it's "surely the most pleasurable dictionary ever published in this country, and one of the most useful."

Pick up a copy today. You'll help the succeeding generation succeed a little faster.

THE
AMERICAN
HERITAGE
COLLEGE
dic·tion·ar·y
THIRD EDITION

The new American Heritage College Dictionary. There is a difference.

Why should you have to wade through the same difficult and confusing dictionary your folks use?

Now you don't. The new *American Heritage College Dictionary* is designed in an airy, wide-margin format that makes finding words much easier. And unlike their dictionary, we list the most common definitions first, to save you even more time.

The *New York Times* says it's "surely the most pleasurable dictionary ever published in this country, and one of the most useful."

Start a new family tradition. Pick up an *American Heritage* today.

The new American Heritage College Dictionary. There is a difference.

FIGURE 6-5

An interesting use of one message to reach two targets are these ads for the *American Heritage College Dictionary.* While the ad with the young woman runs in publications her parents would be reading, the ad showing the parents appears where young women would see it. In both cases, the messages make sense and make a connection to the right audience.

collect their thoughts. Avoid leaders....... and extensive use of dashes — — . They not only look sloppy, but suggest a certain laziness on your part. Semicolon? Perhaps, but a period will do nicely in most cases.

7. ***Refrain from bragging.*** Just as talking down to your readers can be insulting, bragging about your client's "100 years of service" may be a quick turnoff if done in the wrong manner. Your prospects are mainly interested in what's in it for them. Tell them, and generate excitement by showing how excited you are when you talk about your merchandise.

8. ***Avoid superlatives, vague words, and clichés.*** Superlatives are those absolute words that describe your product as the best, the biggest, the most, ad nauseum. Superlatives send a warning to the prospect that you're exaggerating. Be certain that you aren't before you use one. Vague words like *quality* and *craftsmanship* and *service* communicate very little. Use more precise words to tell what constitutes the quality or craftsmanship. Clichés, through overuse, make reading copy a wearisome task. Drop the following phrases from your advertising vocabulary: *a breakthrough, you'll be glad you did, a (product) for all seasons or all reasons, unbeatable values, sale of the century, unbeatable deal,* or any other word or expression that has been used to death. It will never be recognized as yours.

9. ***Support improbable, unbelievable facts with evidence.*** A testimonial can accomplish this, as can a series of laboratory tests. Most of us are skeptical of exaggerated claims; providing hard evidence may be just what is needed to change our perceptions.

10. ***Involve the reader.*** Write your copy as if you were writing a letter to a friend. Use *you* whenever possible. You may have been told to avoid this "second person" in essay writing, but use it now. *You* is the name of your prospect. Don't leave his or her name out! As much as possible, put yourself in your readers' shoes and show that you understand their problems. Show them you know how your product or service can help them solve their problems, and show that you care about helping them. If the information about your product is complex, explain it in terms they can understand. When the first microwave ovens appeared, the more effective ads did not explain how they worked; they just told the prospect that these ovens could cook a roast for guests in only thirty minutes. Did the first ads for compact disc players explain how they worked? What do you think will be stressed in advertising for the new digital audiotape players?

11. ***Don't set out to make an advertisement.*** If you do, chances are you'll write something that looks and sounds very much like all those other ads out there. Instead, remember that you are writing something that will draw the attention of the prospect and give him or her a good reason to consider purchase.

12. ***Revise, revise, revise.*** It is reported that author Truman Capote once said, "I know when my book is done. The publisher grabs it out of my hands." If famous writers can always find ways to make their work better, surely you can improve your words and pictures through meticulous editing. In a visual context,

FIGURE 6-6
An ad with a simple message is told in the clever way that Volvo advertising is famous for. Yet with all its creative flair, the way to get a Volvo overseas and save money is amazingly clear: just dial that 1–800 number.

IT'S AMAZING HOW FAR SOME PEOPLE WILL GO TO GET THEIR HANDS ON A VOLVO.

Courtesy Volvo Cars of North America, Inc.

850 OVERSEAS DELIVERY • 1-800-631-1667

Purchase an 850 here in the States, and pick it up at any of ten European locations, and you'll save thousands on the price of a car* that, as Car and Driver put it, "grabs the pavement and consumes it."†

Better yet, your authorized Volvo dealer makes all the arrangements.

For a booklet containing complete details on the 850 Overseas Delivery Program, as well as the name of the authorized Volvo dealer nearest you, just call 1-800-631-1667.

Then, ask yourself how far you'd go to save on a very new, very different kind of Volvo.

Drive safely. **VOLVO**

*1994 Manufacturer's Suggested Retail Price compared to 1994 Overseas Delivery price. Prices subject to change without notice. †November, 1992 issue of Car and Driver. ©1993. Volvo Cars of North America, Inc. Drive Safely is a trademark of Volvo Cars of North America, Inc.

editing means moving in on the focal point and cropping away extraneous detail. Close-ups tend to be more effective in most cases because they focus attention on what you want readers to see.

13. ***Tell the reader enough.*** No one can tell you how long copy should be. Certain types of products demand long copy; others do not. A stereo enthusiast will read every word of long copy about a new set of components, but a detergent user usually wants a brief summary of benefits, period. The same is true of headlines. Some of the best-read headlines are also some of the longest ever written.

14. ***Make the strange familiar and the familiar strange.*** Most margarines have basically the same message to communicate: We taste like butter. That's

FIGURE 6-7 (A)

Jeep advertising works hard to define the brand as the ultimate 4-wheel driving machine, capable of taking you "virtually anywhere you want to go." It is evident in both of these Jeep ads that a main thrust is to distinguish the full line of Jeep vehicles as separate and distinct from anything else in the industry. The standard driver's side air bag is the unique quality of the Grand Cherokee, while the ad selling the Jeep line focuses on the ability of the vehicle to roll across land of practically every description.

Courtesy Jeep, a Division of the Chrysler Corporation. Jeep is a registered trademark of Chrysler Corporation.

familiar, and also dull. But when Chiffon margarine said, "Our taste even fooled Mother Nature" (who, in some delightful television commercials, raised her arms in defiance and exclaimed, "It's not nice to fool Mother Nature!"), or when Parkay introduced its talking margarine tub that keeps saying "butter" when the user says "margarine," the results were memorable.

15. ***When you have a revolutionary idea to promote, on the other hand, it may be more effective to play it straight.*** Polaroid did that when it hired Sir Laurence Olivier to demonstrate its then revolutionary SX-70 camera for the television audience.

FIGURE 6-7 (B)

There are still a few places on the planet that you won't find a Jeep. But barring the vast expanse of oceans and endless miles of seas, a Jeep vehicle will take you virtually anywhere you want to go.

At the heart of this incredible range is four-wheel drive. Jeep defined it. Jeep refined it. To set these vehicles apart from everything else on the face of the earth. And you apart from the rest of the world. Jeep makes 4WD available to you on the legendary Jeep Wrangler. The classic Jeep Cherokee. And the award-winning Jeep Grand Cherokee.

Of course, the only way to truly appreciate the capability of a Jeep is to experience it firsthand. Please call 1-800-JEEP-EAGLE for test drive information. Then let your sense of adventure take you to the ends of the earth.

There's Only One Jeep®... Jeep Eagle
A Division of the Chrysler Corporation.

16. **Use understatement.** While overstatements can cause doubts, understatement is often a charming way to sell effectively. Good salespeople know this, and as a copywriter, you should know it, too. When Volkswagen first introduced its car in this country, it was perceived as an ugly, cramped, underpowered vehicle in an era when horsepower, tail fins, and chrome sold automobiles. The Volkswagen ads could have used trick photography and fancy settings, but what would that have accomplished once the prospect walked into the showroom? Bill Bernbach of Doyle Dane Bernbach, Inc., Volkswagen's ad agency, asked this question, too. The actual ads dramatized the truth instead. They showed the car in stark

simplicity and called it a bug. They admitted it was small and odd looking, and they turned those negatives into positives by convincing the American consumer that the car was also economical and dependable.

The same agency solved a similar problem with Heinz ketchup. Because this leading brand is thick, it's difficult to pour, so the agency suggested turning thickness into a virtue. The result was a campaign, "the great ketchup race," in which Heinz always lost to a competing brand whenever the two were poured side by side. The ads quickly point out, however, that speed was not especially important in the ketchup business, but thickness was. This unique positioning has been so successful that Heinz advertising still uses it today. Although the commercials tell different stories, they hinge on the fact that the ketchup comes out of the bottle slowly. Which brand do you think of when you think of "slow ketchup?" What does "slow" indicate in terms of ketchup quality?

17. ***Be honest and sincere.*** Neither honesty nor sincerity can fail you in advertising. Listerine once bragged its mouthwash had the taste people hate—twice a day. Other advertisers have also discovered that being less than perfect is often a virtue because it shows them to be honest.

18. ***Stir in a heaping measure of imagination.*** When Sony introduced its first lightweight portable color television, it could have simply announced, "Sony introduces lightweight color." Instead the headline read, "The color portable that won't give you a hernia." "American Express travelers' checks make traveling safe" was the idea; "How to behave in a holdup" became the headline under a picture showing a businessman with hands held high.

Someone complained recently that writers don't seem to be able to write any-more, that they may put the words down and say the right things, but not in new and different ways. No one seems to care much, the complaint goes on, about exploring new styles or using words in provocative new ways. Advertising des-perately needs more innovators. Clean, vivid, hard-hitting active words can still move people. When you add it all up, advertising works hard because someone worked hard to write it.

Print Copy Checklist

1. ***Concept:*** The major premise of the ad is ______________________________

____

_______ a. The ad concept works to communicate the major selling premise effectively.

_______ b. The concept emphasizes the product or service being advertised.

_______ c. One doesn't have to read the entire ad in order to understand the major premise.

2. ***Visual***

_______ a. Works to gain attention by depicting something unusual, new, provocative, attractive.

_______ b. Relates to headline and copy.

_______ c. Shows the product.

_______ d. Does not show the product; however, the brand name is emphasized strongly elsewhere in the ad.

_______ e. If people are shown in the visual, they are appropriate for the message, the product, and the target market.

3. ***Headline***

_______ a. Offers a benefit (reason for using).

_______ b. Announces something new.

_______ c. Selects the audience for the ad.

_______ d. Arouses curiosity without totally confusing readers.

_______ e. Works with the visual to draw readers into the copy. Strong headline-visual relationship.

_______ f. Mentions the brand name.

_______ g. Identifies the type of product, service, or company.

4. ***Body Copy***

_______ a. Divided into readable paragraphs of varying lengths (unless very short copy).

_______ b. Avoids complicated words, unless full explanation is given.

_______ c. Written in loose, comfortable, yet intelligent style.

_______ d. Uses the word *you* as an involvement device.

_______ e. Begins as a logical outgrowth of the idea expressed in the headline and visual.

_______ f. Ends with an urge to action, a summary of the main idea, or an open-ended statement designed to provoke the reader to action.

_______ g. Avoids bragging but does exhibit honest enthusiasm about what is being offered.

_______ h. Tells readers what they need to know without becoming boring.

_______ i. Gives readers reason to take action.

_______ j. Makes frequent use of the brand name.

5. ***Other Elements***

_______ a. Logo is prominently displayed.

_______ b. Package is clearly shown (package goods).

______ c. Tone and style of ad are appropriate to what is being sold and the target market addressed.

There you have it: a list of the essential ingredients for good print advertising. No magic formula exists. But if you are missing too many of these elements, it's time to go back over the copy and take care of the weaknesses. Obviously, it is not always possible (or advisable) to get the brand name into the headline or visual. A headline cannot always offer a benefit, announce news, select its audience, and arouse your curiosity in one shot. Yet if it does none of these things, it may not be a very good headline. Ads are not written according to hard and fast rules, just as great literature is not written to conform to a set of standards. Yet any form of writing develops its own criteria, and advertising copy is no exception. If you ignore the rules totally, you may yet succeed in writing moving copy, but you may also be gambling with your client's budget.

As a copywriter, you live in a world of what might be, not what is. Don't misunderstand: You must never distort the truth. But you must find a way to make the simple facts of life about soap and shampoo, cereal and soup, soft drinks and spring waters, interesting. You must involve and persuade. Just as Alka Seltzer became not a headache relief but a cure for "the blahs" in one famous campaign, so your copy ideas must work to ease the blahs of life.

Honest enthusiasm can be far more effective than the most superficially clever try-it-today copy.

Print Format

Figure 6–9 on page 128 shows how your copy should be typed when you prepare a print ad for presentation. This copy should always be accompanied by a full-size layout of the ad. Note that the copy draft begins with a three-line slug in the upper left corner. The first line identifies the advertiser. The second line states the size of the ad and the medium. The third line is the ad's working title (in quotation marks), which will be used to facilitate production of the advertisement. Virtually every advertisement or commercial needs a simple working title so that the agency and client can distinguish each ad in a series from the others. Once the ad reaches the public, of course, the title does not appear.

The copy should be double-spaced, with roomy margins on all sides for comments and suggestions. If the ad is to contain a visual, type "visual" in capital letters, followed by a colon, and briefly describe the idea of the visual. Do not go into extreme detail; state simply and concisely what the reader will see.

On a new line, type the word "headline" in capital letters, followed by a colon; then type the headline in capital and lower case letters, with proper punctuation at the end. Use exclamation points sparingly, if at all. A statement is no stronger with one of these at the end if it wasn't strong in the first place. Capitalize only proper nouns and the first letter of the first word. If the headline has more than one sentence, capitalize the first letter of each sentence.

FIGURE 6-8
No question as to what BVD wants you to know about their "not-so-brief briefs." They last. And what a delightful way to drive that point home. While competing brands may talk comfort, fit, or fashion, this brand knows how to stand apart from the rest.

Courtesy B.V.D. Licensing Corporation.

Notice that the copy in Figure 6–9 is paragraphed, and the opening line of each paragraph is indented. Note how the use of paragraphs of varied lengths makes the page more inviting to the reader by opening it up with white spaces at the paragraph indents and at the ends of paragraphs.

A Guide to Outdoor, Transit, and Point-of-Purchase Advertising

Outdoor

If brevity is the soul of effective copy, the outdoor board is the final proving ground for audience involvement. How much time can a person spend with your outdoor message? Mere seconds, when they are cruising down the interstate,

Courtesy SAAB Cars USA, Inc.

SAAB

Full page, magazine

"Saabs listen better"

VISUAL: Saab from side/rear view on narrow, winding country road.

HEADLINE: Roads talk to all cars. Saabs just listen better.

COPY:

Roads speak a language of infinite subtlety. And few cars understand the dialects of curves, hills and asphalt better than the Saab 9000 CSE.

From the performance of its low-profile tires to the spring tension in its driver's seat, the 9000 CSE has been carefully tuned to connect, rather than separate, the driver and the road.

The chassis, for example, is 25% more rigid than ever before. An improvement that gives you a tactile sense of the car's progress through a tight turn.

And while you're in touch with the road, the Saab Traction Control System* monitors it for slippery conditions. The instant the drive wheels begin to spin, computers make split-second power adjustments to each wheel. So you get traction comparable to that of many four wheel-drive cars.

Of course, you'd expect a car preoccupied with holding the road to come with anti-lock brakes and nimble rack and pinion steering. The 9000 CSE does not disappoint.

But since it is a Saab, the 9000 CSE doesn't just listen to roads, it also speaks to the needs of drivers. Which is why it has one of the roomiest interiors of any imported sedan. And more safety features than any preceding 9000-Series Saab; cars routinely ranked among the safest in their class.**

To experience the sports sedan that offers not just higher horsepower, but a heightened awareness of the road, ask your Saab dealer for a 9000 CSE test drive. Or, for more information, call 1–800–582–SAAB.

LOGO: SAAB

BASELINE: (none)

MANDATORIES: *With available 2.3 liter turbocharged engine.

**Based upon studies of insurance injury claims conducted by the Highway Loss Data Institute.

© 1993 Saab Cars USA, Inc.

FIGURE 6-9

An example of a typewritten copy draft. Note the use of a working title, double-spacing, and adequate margins on all sides.

only seconds more on a city thoroughfare—all the more reason an outdoor message must be bold in design and intrusive in concept. All the rules for creating effective advertising apply, only more so. Here's how to work for optimum reaction to your outdoor messages:

1. Keep them graphically simple. One large headline. One major visual. Some boards are all type with no visual.

2. Make the type bold and big. Your message is to be read from hundreds of feet away. Don't waste it.

3. Think of the visual as a close-up on television. Remember the magic of the close-up? It focuses attention on what we want the consumer to see. Sometimes your outdoor concept may call for a more panoramic view but consider getting close as a way to bring the message closer to the moving audience.

4. Get the product or company name/image in there prominently. As in all advertising, if you miss out here, you've missed it all.

5. If nothing else seems to work, merely using your campaign theme as the headline can link outdoor advertising with your ads in other media.

In preparing your outdoor layout, follow the same procedures as for other print layouts. Standard outdoor posters (paper pasted to existing structures) are scaled to a proportion of 1 to 2¼. Outdoor bulletins, painted on boards, are usually proportioned 1 to 3½. This translates to a 4 × 9 inch layout for the poster and a 4 × 14 inch layout for the painted bulletin.

Transit

Transit advertising appears on the inside and outside of public transportation as well as in bus, rail, subway, and air terminals. Like outdoor advertising, it works best when the message is short. It differs from outdoor advertising in that the audience can choose to spend more time with the message. For this reason, many transit ads include "take one" cards or other literature attached to the ad.

Point of Purchase (POP)

Advertising at the point of sale—in the retail store where the buyer is about to choose between one brand and another—is justifiably recognized as the last chance the advertiser has to affect the outcome of the purchase. Window posters, permanent signs inside and outside the store, special merchandise racks and cases, wall posters, and "shelf talkers," those ubiquitous messages popping from the actual shelf where the advertised product is stocked, are common forms of POP. The medium has become more sophisticated with the addition of coupon dispensers at point of sale, signs on shopping carts, in-store videos, and coupons printed at the checkout counter to try to switch you from the brand you just purchased to a competing brand.

Suggested Activities

• 1. Go through several recent magazines and cut out advertisements that contain headlines and visuals that fall into the categories listed below. If the same headline accomplishes several things, note them all (some of the best often do). As you complete your search, also note why some ads attract you and why others do not. Write about these positive and negative qualities in a brief essay to accompany your ad collection.

a. Headlines to look for: benefit, selective, news, reverse benefit, pun or play on words, curiosity.

b. Visuals to look for: product, part of the product, product ready for use, product compared to competition, product being tested, happy results of using product, unhappy results of not using product.

2. If you find headlines and/or visuals that do not fall into these specific categories, but are effective nonetheless, clip them and write about why they work so well.

• 3. Using the creative platform that you wrote earlier as a guide, write two pieces of print copy. Be sure to describe any visuals you plan to use and include a thumbnail sketch of the ad along with your copy. Try writing headlines for the ads as well as body copy.

• 4. Present this ad to the class, pretending that you are a member of an agency creative team addressing the client. How will you explain your strategy and concept? How will the rough layout help you make the presentation more vivid? Will you read the copy word for word or paraphrase it? Why?

5. Find a national advertisement that you feel exemplifies effective copy style. Write a brief analysis of its merits and recommend any changes that you feel would improve the copy and the concept. Mention the headline and visual as well as the body copy.

6. Find several advertisements (print or broadcast) that make optimum use of the VIPS formula (visibility, identity, promise, and simplicity) to drive their messages home to their prospects. If you cannot find such examples, tell how the ads you have chosen in their place might have improved their drawing power by adhering more closely to the VIPS formula.

7. Find a teammate and work out a series of advertisements for a local business establishment in your town. These ads should be suitable for your local newspaper. First gather ideas individually, then meet to bounce them off each other. Finally, use the arts of compromise and cooperation to determine which ideas work best. When you have agreed on a specific approach, develop a series of three or four ads based on this approach.

Beauty from an Ugly Blue Jar: The Genesis of Clean Makeup

Cosmetic copy is the sappiest writing in the industry, but you can't be a sap to write it.[1]

[Author's note: This advertising history, from the archives of the Center for Advertising History of the Smithsonian Institution, fascinates me because it is a clear example of how to launch a successful brand and, through strategically crafted advertising, keep it successful through decades of change. As one of the principals in the story has said, it's not that the makeup itself was so special. Makeup is makeup. It was the concept behind the brand that made it special initially, and it's the consistency in that concept that has given Cover Girl makeup and its line extensions such a long and successful life. If prudent risk-taking is the essence of success in advertising, this is one brand that proves that point beautifully.]

In the 1940s, virtually every medicine cabinet in America contained three staples: witch hazel, Vaseline, and Noxzema Skin Cream in its klutzy blue glass jar. Although people knew and believed in the greaseless white cream with the heavy scent of camphor, they simply weren't using much of it.

And no wonder. Unless you were suffering from eczema, a nasty skin rash from which the product derives its name (*no eczema*) or had stayed out in the sun too long and needed a cooling balm to soothe your burning skin, you had little need for this household staple.

George Bunting, a Baltimore pharmacist, created the product we now know as Noxzema Skin Cream in 1914. In 1917, he established the Noxzema Company and began to sell his pungent recipe, and by 1938, the product was in national distribution. When letters from satisfied users indicated many men were shaving with the cooling balm, the advertising agency for Noxzema, SSC&B, New York, convinced the company to begin marketing a shaving cream.

In time, the Noxzema Company was renamed Noxell, and SSC&B continued to seek innovative ways to increase product usage. One of the Noxzema assignments fell into the hands of Mary Andrews Ayres.

Mary Ayres, as remembered by George Poris, a creative director at SSC&B who worked on Noxell business, was tall, thin, blonde, and attractive. Arriving in New York from the Midwest, she attended night school and earned a business degree. Beginning as a secretary, by 1958 she had become one of the few female

[1] From one of the oral interviews in the Cover Girl collection, Center for Advertising History, National Museum of American History, Smithsonian Institution.

vice presidents of an advertising company. Poris describes Ayres as a hard-working, self-made person who was not always ingratiating but was always prepared. "She had a good analytical mind, a great marketing mind, and a strong copy instinct," he recalls. She was, in essence, a "good strategist."

Ayres had earned an early reputation for marketing ingenuity when, seeking a way to increase the use of Noxzema, she repositioned the brand through advertising as a beauty preparation and increased sales dramatically. Poris recalls that Ayres realized this opportunity to expand usage when a letter from a user who soaked her feet in Noxzema and warm water made her aware that the brand was water soluble. Recalling that women also were beginning to use Noxzema to treat chapped skin, she created the "nurse's home beauty treatment" in the late thirties. It was a 1–2–3 regimen: First, wash with Noxzema to remove makeup (instead of creaming with cold cream, which had to be tissued off). This gave the skin a pleasant, tingly sensation. Second, apply the cream as a moisturizer to keep facial skin smooth and velvety. And finally, use the brand as a night cream to soften skin. Ayres had little trouble convincing the company that a woman who followed this ritual religiously would be using the brand a minimum of three times a day.

By 1957, Noxzema Skin Cream was being advertised as "the complete complexion cleanup." To position the brand as unique, advertising stressed the original Noxzema line, "It's medicated," and deliberately retained the original blue glass package and the familiar camphor and menthol aroma as validation of the product's serious "medicinal" origins.

Noxzema was selling well, but the company realized it was not going to grow without new products. By 1958, it was apparent that something new was needed, and Ayres had another idea: Why not introduce a line of cosmetics that capitalized on the "medicated" image of Noxzema Skin Cream? Her original concept consisted of three premises: promote the brand as "medicated makeup" and make it smell vaguely like Noxzema Skin Cream, sell it at a popular price in mass-merchandise stores instead of in department stores, and offer only three shades.

In restricting the brand to three shades, Ayres realized that no mass merchandiser would allot shelf space for twenty-four shades of makeup. Remember, this was before the days of extensive mass merchandising of cosmetics, and manufacturers' racks and blister packs were nonexistent. To find an answer, she commissioned a study, which revealed that 80 to 85 percent of competitor Revlon's makeup business was in only three of its twenty-four shades. Thus, the new line was introduced with three shades, creatively named Light, Medium, and Dark, and in two forms, a compact with puff and a liquid. Dubbed Cover Girl, the new makeup became the first to be sold in grocery chain stores, where, incidentally, the bulk of mass makeup is now purchased.

At this time, the agency believed the key to the success of Cover Girl was Noxzema's history of treating blemishes. Accordingly, the brand was targeted toward teenaged women and positioned as a flesh-colored cover-up makeup. Before long, the agency realized the brand had the potential to reach a broader audience, and for a while there were two separate campaigns running for Cover Girl: one directed to teens, the other directed to adult women. An analysis of sales soon convinced the company to drop the "blemish" campaign in favor of a full-fledged effort targeted to young women.

Interestingly, the name "Cover Girl" was chosen to suggest "cover-up" rather than "cover girl beauty."

In its early years, Cover Girl was advertised as "glamour that's good for your skin." But the basic premise from the start was that beauty should take precedence over the "cover-up" idea. Advertising was now declaring, "So natural, you won't believe it's makeup," and making reference to the now-famous line, "A Cover Girl complexion."

Cover Girl was an instant success. Poris says the company made its first-year sales goals in the first month and went national immediately. He adds that, since none of its competitors believed the idea of a mass-merchandised makeup would work, no one took steps to compete with the brand until it had captured a major share of the market.

The original idea for the television campaign was to use actual magazine covers and models. The covers would come to life in the TV commercials. After being refused by most magazines, who feared other cosmetic companies might pull their advertising from the publications, the agency finally convinced *Cosmopolitan* magazine to agree, which in turn convinced several other magazines to join the campaign. In time, with the brand selling on its own reputation, Cover Girl successfully introduced line extensions of eye makeup and lipstick.

John Bergin, creative director at SSC&B from 1974 to 1981, also credits Mary Ayres with the development of the Cover Girl brand personality and its "clean makeup" concept line, adding that in creating Cover Girl she took a $20 million company and turned it into a giant with hundreds of millions of dollars in sales annually. Although the phrase "clean makeup" was in itself not exciting, the idea within it was compelling. It was a challenge to the concept of the "painted lady" of rich society promoted by Maybelline. Cover Girl showed women who looked like the daughters of society, the Ivy League. White on white ads became part of the creative strategy to stress the clean look.

Another player in the success of Cover Girl was Malcolm McDougall, vice chairman of Jordan McGrath Case & Taylor, New York, who joined SSC&B in 1980, replacing John Bergin as creative director and moving on to the agency's presidency. McDougall calls the advertising for Cover Girl a classic example of how to manage an account, for these reasons: The client and agency had a great working relationship, the brand idea essentially came from the agency side, and the positioning—clean makeup from Noxzema—was clear, concise, and smart. That positioning, McDougall says, is the fundamental reason for the success of the brand. Cover Girl knew what it was from the start, and the notion to take cosmetics into mass merchandising was probably "the strongest idea in the history of cosmetics." As Mary Ayres had said from the start, "We're going to look pretty and talk tough."

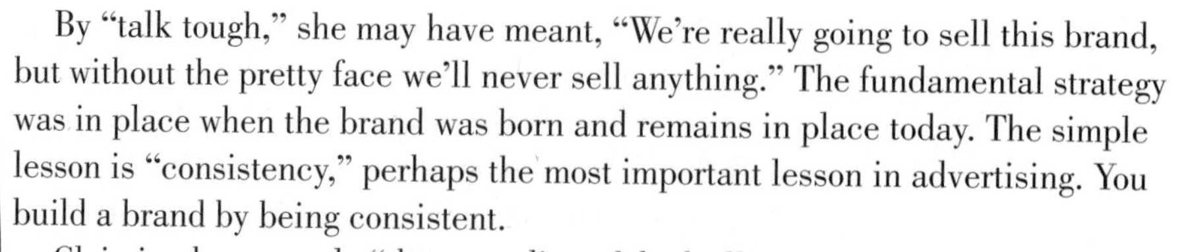

By "talk tough," she may have meant, "We're really going to sell this brand, but without the pretty face we'll never sell anything." The fundamental strategy was in place when the brand was born and remains in place today. The simple lesson is "consistency," perhaps the most important lesson in advertising. You build a brand by being consistent.

Claiming he was only "the custodian of the brilliant thinking passed down to me," McDougall wrote a personality statement for Cover Girl to define what the brand should be. The statement specified that this was the first cosmetic a young girl might use, establishing it as a traditional brand in many American families. This indicated that, in Cover Girl advertising, sex was out. Part of the formula for the advertising was to be as different from other cosmetic advertising as one could be.

How do you keep an idea fresh and yet consistent?

Cover Girl doesn't win creative awards, yet year after year it has been a consistent seller. It is the only brand that has kept the advertising idea pure for thirty years. Of course, there have been changes, but not in the basic premise.

Lynn Giordano, executive vice president and executive creative director, Lintas New York, successors to SSC&B, joined the Noxell team in 1981. "I was given a chance to work on Noxzema Skin Cream," she recalls, "which is where they started everyone. If you could make that jar of skin cream come alive to another group of pimply faced teens, maybe you were good enough to work on Cover Girl."

Working under the tutelage of Fran Harrison, Giordano helped breathe new life into the old blue jar with the phrase "Beautiful skin begins with Noxzema." Recalling that she grew up with Cover Girl in the 1960s as a college student, she disputes the myth that college women of her era cared little about their looks. No matter how radical her politics, Giordano claims, the sixties college woman wanted to look good. She might claim she used no makeup, but for most of them it was a "no-makeup look," exactly the sort that Cover Girl was promoting. It added to the brand's success, a sort of accidental case of being in the right place at the right time with the right look.

And what of today's woman? Giordano believes most women say "I know I can't look like Christie Brinkley, and I don't want to." The truth, she claims, is that everyone wants to look better. "We found that out through research. During the seventies, the brand chose models that weren't 'models.' They were friendly types who talked and had personality. That was the look of the seventies. In the eighties, that look went out."

If you look at Cover Girl on its simplest basis, it's every girl's dream of being discovered. It is not a startling turnaround or great new product idea. It's keeping her young, looking good, relevant, and desirable.

And by the nineties, the Cover Girl had a new face, in keeping with the changing times. All of a sudden, one sees her wearing jeans. She no longer wears that perfect white blouse. Showing just the face isn't enough anymore.

Cover Girl still has the Noxzema smell. There is still that relationship. And Cover Girls still dream of being discovered, but now they dress like Madonna. In commercials they must do more than "spin like props" to relate to women today. So you might see a Cover Girl model sticking out her tongue at the photographer, indicating she's a real working model and needs to lighten up her day, just as you do. It's just that she looks like a million bucks, but there's much more to her than looks. She eats a hot dog during the commercial, not only to appear more human, but to show that Cover Girl lipstick lasts. Remember, we're talking advertising here.

FOLLOW-UP

Okay, you might remark, so what's so beautiful about coming up with an ideal like clean makeup? Pretty simple, really. But take yourself, if you can, back to a time when most makeup was sold in department stores. Picture yourself working for the advertising agency handling the Noxzema Skin Cream account. What evidence during that time might convince you to do what Mary Ayres did as she recommended a bold new step for a small pharmaceutical company in Baltimore? To get a feeling for how you might react, pretend you are asked to write a recommendation to the account executive on Noxzema for a new brand of makeup with ties to the familiar cream in the blue jar. Write the memo as persuasively as you can, following Mary Ayres's line of reasoning or one of your one.

CHAPTER 7

How Design Contributes to the Advertising Message

Today's copywriter and art director work as a team to produce the most effective communications possible. They begin by exchanging ideas on content and approach, then proceed to work out the problems. The design idea may come from the writer; the headline from the art director. Nobody worries about defending territories; the only important thing is finding the best answer to the client's problem.

Of course, such teamwork implies that each partner has some understanding of and appreciation for the other's talent. While we may not all be great artists, we certainly should be able to understand the principles involved in arriving at a graphic solution. If we're uneasy about our writing, we can still appreciate words that sizzle and question words that puzzle.

If you think you're all thumbs when it comes to visualizing, think again. You're probably saying, "But I can't draw. But I can't draw. But I can't draw." So what if you can't draw? That has no bearing on your ability to evaluate and make suggestions. How often have you commented on a film you saw? That's a design judgment. Do you choose the clothes you wear each day? Another design judgment. And just as surely, you can talk about the way a product is displayed in an ad, or how type could dominate the page to solve a problem. You can talk about the relationship of color to the mood of the copy, and you can decide whether a long shot or medium shot or close-up of the product is the best choice. You may not think so, but yes, you can.

In fact, the design process is very much like the process of writing copy. You have to put your imagination to work in order to produce vibrant headlines and powerful text. You're even thinking visually, whether you know it or not, when you attempt to find the right words to explain the product benefits. So when you start to think about how you want the campaign to look, just make believe that someone else will be doing the finished artwork and dig in with your own fresh ideas . . . in rough form.

The process of design is very much like the process of writing. Each consists of finding a solution to a problem and each begins with ideas. The toughest part of the process is at the beginning, when thinking skills play a major role in seeking the answers. Unfortunately, many people stick with the first thoughts that enter their heads. A good copywriter or art director, on the other hand, will spend lots of time playing with words and phrases or shapes and lines, trying one approach after another. The thinking processes are the same; it's just that the medium is different.

What Is Good Design?

Good design depends on the arrangement of each element with regard to every other element in the design. If one element were to be removed, the entire design would fall apart. Remember that a layout is designed to make the message easier to comprehend. It must function as communication, not merely as art. If it does both, so much the better, but art for art's sake has no room in advertising. It isn't the layout that should be the hero; it's the message the layout and copy transmit.

This suggests that you would use different design approaches to sell hairspray and garbage bags; yet the primary function of each layout would be the same. To be certain the reader can absorb the information, you may decide to keep the type organized in blocks and columns, and to keep the ad free of unnecessary visuals that only add clutter. A layout designer is like a good editor. To clarify a point, the editor often takes something out. Your layout may have many elements in it, but it should "read" as one unit.

What Is a Layout?

A *layout* is a pleasing arrangement of elements into a meaningful message. In an ad, this includes headline, body copy, illustration, other design devices, and white space. When these elements are placed in such a way as to make the ad pleasing to the reader, and the message is easily understood, you have a good layout. Placing elements on the page in a serendipitous manner will rarely result in good design. Layouts take a good deal of planning to be effective, and you should exercise great care in executing them. A good idea poorly presented will rarely get the client, or the consumer, excited.

In another sense, layout means two things: (1) the laying out of the component parts of a print advertisement; (2) a blueprint for the mechanical, or paste-up, and thus a guide for the printer. Above all, it is the plan of an ad.

When we speak of planning a direct mail piece, the term used is *dummy.* When we speak of planning a television commercial, the term is *storyboard.* All three terms—*layout, dummy,* and *storyboard*—refer to plans that are to be carried out in very specific ways.

A layout is a way of visualizing an ad, visualizing where the copy goes and where the headline is placed, along with the illustration or photograph, logo or store name, and the size or importance of each of these components with respect to one another. This might also be viewed as determining how much weight to give each element in the advertisement. The basic components of any print layout are headline, copy, visual, and logo. How you arrange them will have a great deal to do with the success or failure of your ad to communicate.

What element in the ad should be emphasized? Copy? Illustration? Product name? Again, there is no single right answer. It all depends on the message. To give a simple example, if a store is having a sale, the price would be most important. If an automaker is unveiling his new models, the visual will probably be the most prominent element in the announcement ad. The copy, in the latter case, would play a more supporting role.

Consider this, also: Is the ad you are designing part of a series or campaign? If so, your layout must be able to accommodate many different visuals and headlines and must have enough flexibility so that it can be enlarged or reduced in size. Above all every ad in the series should have a "family" look for instant recognizability and a feeling of continuity. Such a series of ads can build equity in the mind of the potential customer. He or she will recognize the advertiser by the very look of the ad, regardless of the difference in message or illustration.

You should also remember that many layouts have a certain symbolic function or make an emotional contact with the consumer. This function has everything and nothing to do with the product or service advertised. Everything, because it is linked to the product or service. Nothing, because it is a design communication rather than a verbal communication. Imagine an ad for a sporty wristwatch aimed at the younger set. Now imagine an ad for an insurance company. They would send out highly different messages, apart from the message about the watch or the insurance. The watch ad would be lively, with lots of inherent action. Not so the ad for insurance. This message must look more serious, for insurance is a serious topic for most people, and even the design of the ad must speak to this. Thus, if you look at layout designs in the abstract sense, they communicate different messages, their symbolic interpretations vary, and the resultant emotional impact on the reader is different, even before you begin to consider what the words say.

White Space

A layout can be thought of as "packaging an idea." Therefore, the package must be as inviting as possible. One of the most relevant elements for the building of an effective design "package" is the use of white space. By *white space* we mean blank, or "negative" space. There are many guidelines in advertising design, but not many rules. There is, however, a rule concerning the use of white space: *always throw white space to the outside of your layout.* Allow white space to invade the center of your layout, and you are inviting a scattered, uncohesive design. Use lots of white space, a great expanse of white space, and what is the result? Often, it's a feeling of exclusivity.

White space is particularly important in newspaper ads because of the way it will contrast with the gray editorial content surrounding your ad. The judicious use of white space can set the ad apart from its surroundings. It can protect the ad from the encroachment of other material. In magazine advertising, white space draws our attention to the ad in which it is used, whether in full color or black and white.

Gestalt

The term *gestalt,* applied to design, means the whole, or complete figure. If you feel your early tries at design are scattered, try throwing white space to the outside of the design and notice how the components begin to form a group. You don't want to crowd them together too much, so leave some breathing space between the elements, but don't leave too much, or they may lose their relationships with each other. Once you begin to group the illustration(s), copy, headline, and logo, and see them as a whole (or gestalt) against the white space, you're on your way to designing a layout that works. As you thumb through magazines in the next few days, look for this kind of advertising design. You should find many. This approach to layout, incidentally, owes a great deal to the figure/ground or positive/negative space theory of the fine arts.

One other thing to be aware of when you group these elements: see the white, or negative, space as a shape in itself. In a good design, it is the sense of dynamics between the positive and negative areas that can evoke interest and excitement. (See Figures 7–1 and 7–2.)

Other Design Elements

Here are other design elements you should think of as tools with which to build your layout.

Balance

After white space and gestalt, this is the first element to consider. Will your layout have a formal or an informal balance? Will a symmetrical layout best serve the message of your ad, or would an informal (asymmetrical) balance serve it better? A layout using formal balance has the same weight on either side of the page. With formal balance, there is a strong sense of a central axis, or vertical line, with elements distributed evenly on either side of the axis. An informal, or

FIGURE 7-1
Gestalt. Seeing the whole, not the parts.

FIGURE 7-2
A stunning example of graphic design selling watch design, this Tiffany & Company advertisement makes use of a bold silhouette to show off three of its classic offerings. The understated headline, upper right, tops off the message fittingly: What endures is what matters.

Courtesy Tiffany & Co.

asymmetrically arranged, layout has the components arranged irregularly on either side of this imaginary line. An asymmetrical layout has a more dynamic feeling and is favored in contemporary advertising design.

To help you find your way through this thicket of formal vs. informal balance, remember the following:

- An irregular shape has more weight than a regular shape.
- Dark has more weight than light.
- Larger elements appear heavier than smaller ones.
- A shape with texture has more weight than a smooth shape.
- Color has more weight than noncolor.

After working with layout and design, you will begin to develop an instinctive feeling about the use of balance, and you'll begin to feel the rightness or wrongness of the balance in the design.

Point, Line, Shape

A *point* can be the convergence of lines or it can be the enlarged letter at the beginning of a copy block. You can think of it as the optical center of the ad, which is about five-eighths of the way up from the bottom and slightly right of center. If you have many points together, they form a shape. If the points are in a row, they form a line.

A *line* is the path of a moving point. It can be an actual line, as in the line of type that is the headline. It can also be a short copy block. A line shows direction and movement. While it does not exist in nature, we view it as a demarcation between adjoining values. Laying down lines in a deliberate pattern is the simplest way of developing a visual image. The imaginary line we mentioned in discussing balance is the axis of the design, running through the layout, to which component parts of your ad will connect, hinge, or overlap.

A *shape* can be defined in terms of tone, value, or texture. Shape is *defined space,* whether regular or irregular. Groups of words can form shapes. It is important to realize that we impose three basic shapes on everything we see: the square, the circle, and the triangle. Of course, there are endless variations and permutations of these. Placing these shapes together, apart, on top of one another, or juxtaposed to one another gives us certain innate feelings about the resultant pattern. For example, a triangle communicates something innately dynamic. When we tilt the triangle, the feelings of uncertainty and excitement increase. The square is strong, solid, and calm. What about the circle? Is it a hole? A disc? Or the most compelling of all geometric shapes, a target?

Proportion

Proportion is the relationship of one element to the other. As soon as you put a stroke of pencil to a piece of paper, you have established a proportion, that of the pencil mark to the edge of the paper. Dividing a layout exactly in half may be

FIGURE 7-3
Repetition of shapes.

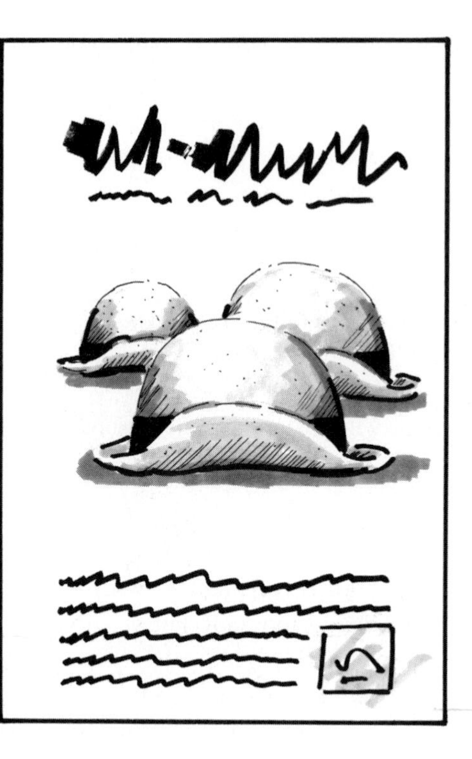

desirable for a design which must "say" dignity and solidity. But dividing an ad so that proportions are three to two, for example, will produce a more exciting appearance. You will acquire a natural sense of proportion and know what looks interesting, what works, and what doesn't through the application of actual layout elements. Once you begin pushing them around in this way and that, the right proportions will be evident.

Repetition of Shapes

Rhythm, harmony, and movement can be achieved through repeating shapes within a design. When a shape is repeated, the eye continues to follow the series of shapes. Such repetitions produce a certain rhythm in the ad, and the rhythm in turn produces a feeling of harmony (see Figure 7–3). Another way to produce a cohesive design is to line up the elements in an ad. You can do this simply by overlapping elements, or by lining up edges of, say, the right hand edge of a copy block with the left edge of a photograph. The eye will automatically make the connection. All of this will make the ad easier to read and therefore more accessible to the reader.

Sequence Direction and Gaze Motion

These ideas are related, though somewhat different in application. *Sequence direction* means the way in which the eye is led through the layout. Sequence direction may use all of the design elements listed above. One of the most common sequence directions is the reverse "s." This takes advantage of our natural propensity to read from left to right. In a reverse "s," the eye would scan the headline, turn down through the visual, swing left through the copy, and end up

FIGURE 7-4
Gaze motion.

down in the lower right hand corner where the logo rests. Next time you leaf through a magazine, see how many reverse "s" layouts you can spot.

Gaze motion has a simple rule: Never have the model or product facing away from the copy. Always have the model either gazing toward the copy, gesturing toward the copy, or facing straight ahead, but never away from the copy (see Figure 7–4). The theory behind this rule is that the reader's eye will naturally follow the gaze or thrust of the model or product, and be led into the copy.

To sum up, all of these guidelines, or design elements, can be employed to manipulate the eye movement of the respondent through the layout.

Thumbnails: The Search for the Right Design

Every designer gets started on ideas with little sketches called *thumbnails.* After you've had reasonable design experience, you may begin designing on a computer, but professional designers prefer to use the computer as a production, rather than as a design, tool. These small layouts, perhaps 1 × 2 inches, allow you to experiment comfortably and quickly with many design options. Many students resist doing thumbnails because they are forced to think of several ideas at once. But thumbnails are important; think of them as the warm-up exercises an athlete might do before he or she begins competition. Thumbnails loosen up the mind, helping it get rid of the junk that is always there when we start a project. Thumbnails don't require the talents of a Michelangelo. In fact, one thing to avoid in thumbnails is spending too much time on them. If you're trying to make them look like miniature works of art, you're working too hard to think of too few ideas.

Thumbnails are small, quick, "jot 'em down" sketches of your ideas. They are not refined pieces of art and often the headlines are roughly drawn with no attempt at detail. The copy is indicated by rough lines in one area, while the visual may be a shape, such as a circle or oval. Let your mind flow. Keep asking yourself, "What if?" and then jot down that image.

As you begin, try something really far out. Try ideas you think may not work, can't be done, or would give the client cardiac arrest. You'll usually have to tone down your concept, but that's easy. What's impossible is taking a dull idea and trying to breathe life into it. At this point, reject nothing. Don't stop to evaluate, just go on to the next little sketch and the next after that. You'll find yourself looking at earlier thumbnails as the basis for later ones. That's fine.

Which comes first, design or words? The answer is that the idea comes first, whether it's in words, pictures, or some of each. To prepare for your assignment, find out as much as you can about the product or service you're advertising. Saturate your mind with good ads in magazines to get some inspiration from the way others have used type for headlines and body copy, white space, illustration, and logos. As your idea begins to take shape, think about the kind of typeface that would go best with the idea. Type has its own voice and personality and can set the tone for the words. Are you trying to shout or be soft? Eloquent or informal? Will the letters be set tightly together—which seems to be the style of most ads currently—or will you open up the letter spacing to give a feeling of openness and classicism? Begin looking at typefaces in other ads and rough in your choice in the thumbnail you're working on.

What about the illustration? Will it be the product dominating the entire ad? The product in an unusual situation? What will it take to consummate the marriage between copy and design to answer the client's needs? You can work such ideas out in your thumbnails.

Often the idea will come from the headline. Other times, something buried in the copy will start you off. By the time you've designed the ad, you may have a new headline in mind. Don't worry; that's the way great work gets done.

For inspiration, get your hands on copies of these magazines at your college library: *Communication Arts, Print, How,* and *Step-by-Step.* No one works in a vacuum, and the more you look at, the more easily good ideas will come.

Now That You Have the Concept: The Rough Layout

Once you choose your best thumbnail idea, it's time to refine it to a rough layout. A *rough layout* is the actual size of the final ad. It is a more detailed layout than the thumbnail and reveals whether you have an idea worth pursuing to the end.

You'll have to make some adjustments from your thumbnail to the rough, since most thumbnails have an excitement of their own. Once you begin enlarging and refining those small images, you'll find some of this excitement vanishing. This doesn't mean the idea isn't exciting; it's just a necessary step in the evolution of the design, so don't worry. (See Figure 7–5.)

In the rough you'll work with pencil to make certain each element works with every other element. You'll further define your headline type, body type, and spacing. You'll tighten up the illustration. You will also check that all elements of the design work together, and that no single part stands alone. The visual may get the reader's attention, but other elements must support the visual and reinforce the message you want to communicate. A beautifully shot photograph will go down the drain if the message is ignored, just as a headline set in an overpowering typeface may obscure what the words say. It's like seeing someone across the room who looks attractive, and discovering there's nothing beyond his or her looks that interests you.

The one element that dominates your design will depend on your approach to solving the problem. You certainly don't want to confuse the reader with too many domineering elements that distract her from the real message. That would be like hearing a symphony orchestra playing out of harmony. Instead of hearing the orchestra, you'd be distracted by violins competing with oboes competing with trumpets competing with kettledrums. Can you imagine the noise?

The Finished Layout for Presentation

The *finished layout* is the rough taken to a more finished stage. This is the version you will be presenting to the client; therefore, it must be clean and crisp so that it gives a clear impression of what the final ad will be like. In order to accomplish this, take care in drawing, or tracing, the illustration and letter in the headline in the style of the typeface you have chosen. In other words, everything should be done so that the client will understand how the finished ad will look. Along with this layout, you will also be presenting the typewritten copy, double-

FIGURE 7-5
Thumbnail to full-size rough.

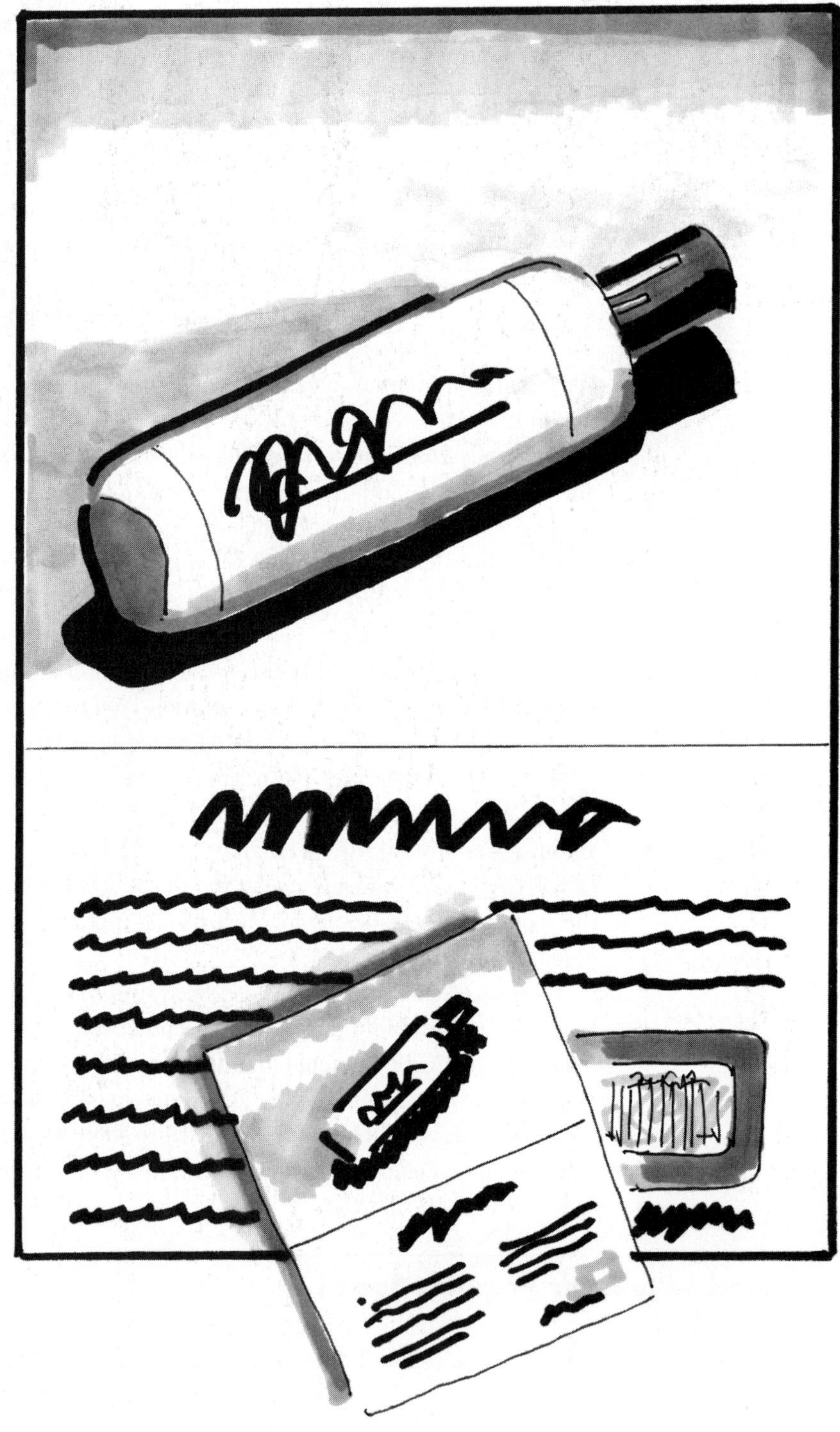

spaced on a separate sheet of paper or typeset directly in position on your layout.

If your ad will be in color, it should be rendered in color. For one thing, color gives an added dimension and weight to your layout. One medium to use for this is colored markers. Remember, you are not attempting to do a finished illustration, but rather a clear indication of how the finished ad will look. Thus, when you use colored felt markers, it isn't always necessary to fill in every bit of the paper with color, but rather to allow the white of the paper to shine through in ways that make it work for you. Letting white show through can add a highly desirable quality of transparency and lightness to your layout.

For presentation purposes, you can mount your layout on black or gray matte board or on foamcore. In lieu of hand lettering, you'll probably want to set type on a personal computer and either paste it into position, or position it on the computer screen so that you can print it out in its proper place.

A fourth layout stage, the *comprehensive,* may be necessary if the client demands a more precise interpretation of the proposed ad. For the comprehensive, or comp, actual photography may be shot and type may be set for the copy as well as for the headline. Comps are also frequently used in new business presentations, the idea being that the extra effort and expense may be justified by the situation.

Layout Patterns

The basic layout patterns are shown in Figures 7–6 through 7–16. Although many ads are a combination of several styles, this list should get you started.

Mondrian

This pattern is named after the Dutch artist, Piet Mondrian, whose paintings consisted of squares of unequal sizes of varied, pure colors. Ads emulating this style have the advantage of being logical, well organized, and easy to follow. Each section of the design is designated for art, text, or headline. The key is to make the different sizes fit into an organized pattern which tells a story.

Grid

Some designers will not start a job without laying out a grid. They begin by dividing the page into a series of equal rectangles, then assign art or type to each rectangle. Grid layouts can be exciting when the designer plays with variations on the grid theme. The result can be an organized and appealing ad.

Picture Window

A highly popular arrangement, the picture window has the visual dominating other elements. The visual often takes up two-thirds or more of the space and is accompanied by a small, single-line headline over limited copy space which is often divided into two or three columns of equal width. Since the picture is the dominant element, it had better be a compelling one. Variations of this style include placing the visual at the bottom, or employing a full-page visual with the

FIGURE 7-6
Mondrian.

type overprinted or reversed. Picture window layouts are used for a vast array of products and services. You will see this familiar arrangement in ads for everything from cars to cosmetics to computers.

Copy Heavy

In a copy heavy layout, the emphasis is just the opposite of the picture window. Big headline, long copy, and small or no illustrations are its trademarks. The body copy may be set large. Subheads and/or secondary headlines are often used to break up the "gray matter."

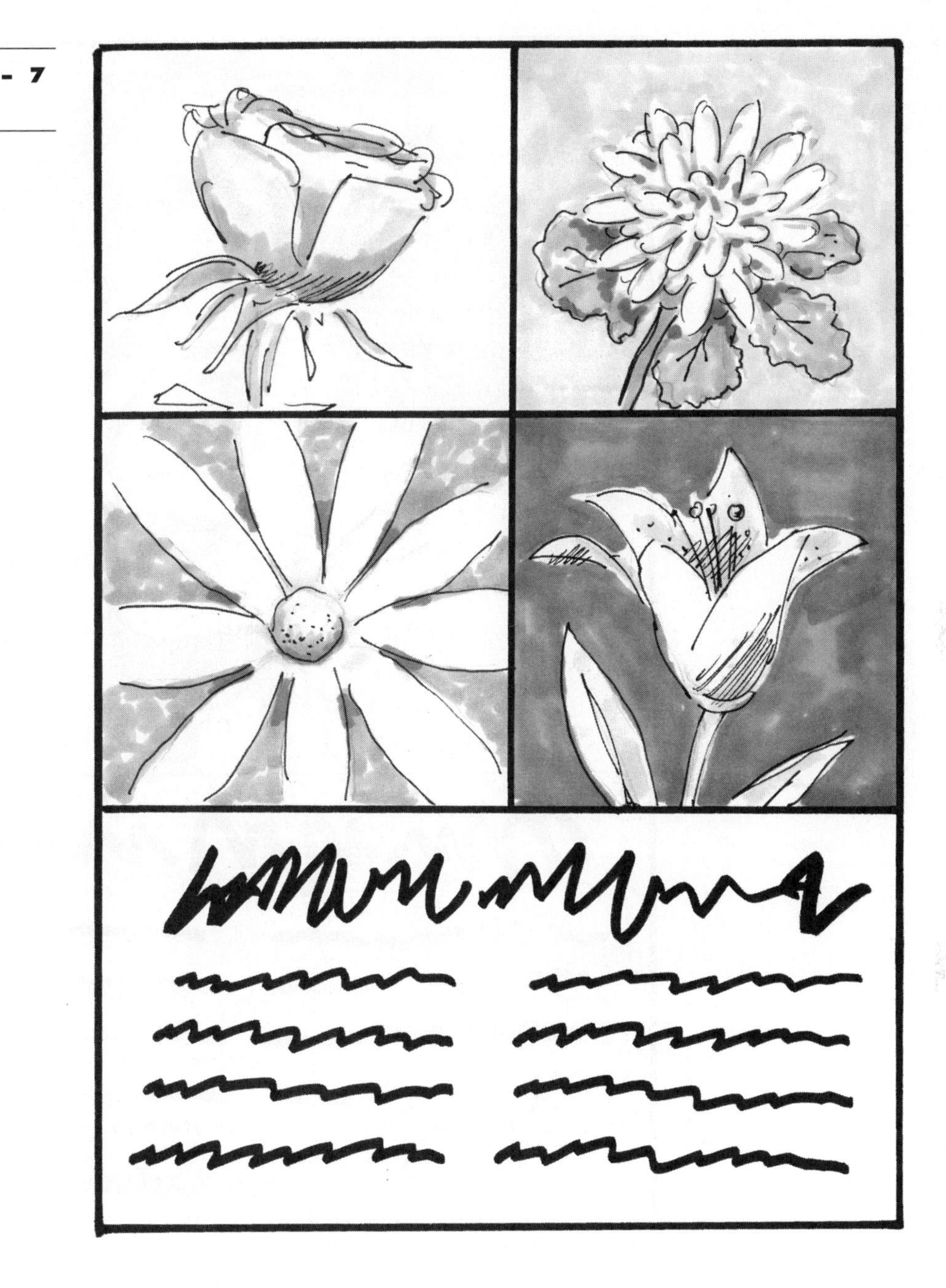

FIGURE 7-7
Grid.

Frame

A frame layout is an offbeat arrangement in which the visual frames the copy, or forms a cul-de-sac in which the copy is nestled. An arrangement where the copy frames the art may also be termed a frame.

Circus

If Mondrian and grid layouts have a strict design pattern, the circus layout is designed to lend a feeling of excitement and "organized disarray" to the page. The circus layout is a combination of art and type mixed in orderly confusion and may include silhouette and angled photographs as well as a variety of type

FIGURE 7-8
Picture window.

displays. In the right hands, the result can be sparkling; otherwise, the page will look like a horrible mistake. Having a gestalt in a circus design is most important.

Silhouette

Here the image is generally as large as in the picture window layout, except that it stands alone without a background and the type usually follows the lines of this irregular shape. White space is used for dramatic emphasis, but the effect is that of a silhouette with the white space on the outside. Take care that the elements are not too far apart, or the design may fall apart.

FIGURE 7-9
Copy heavy.

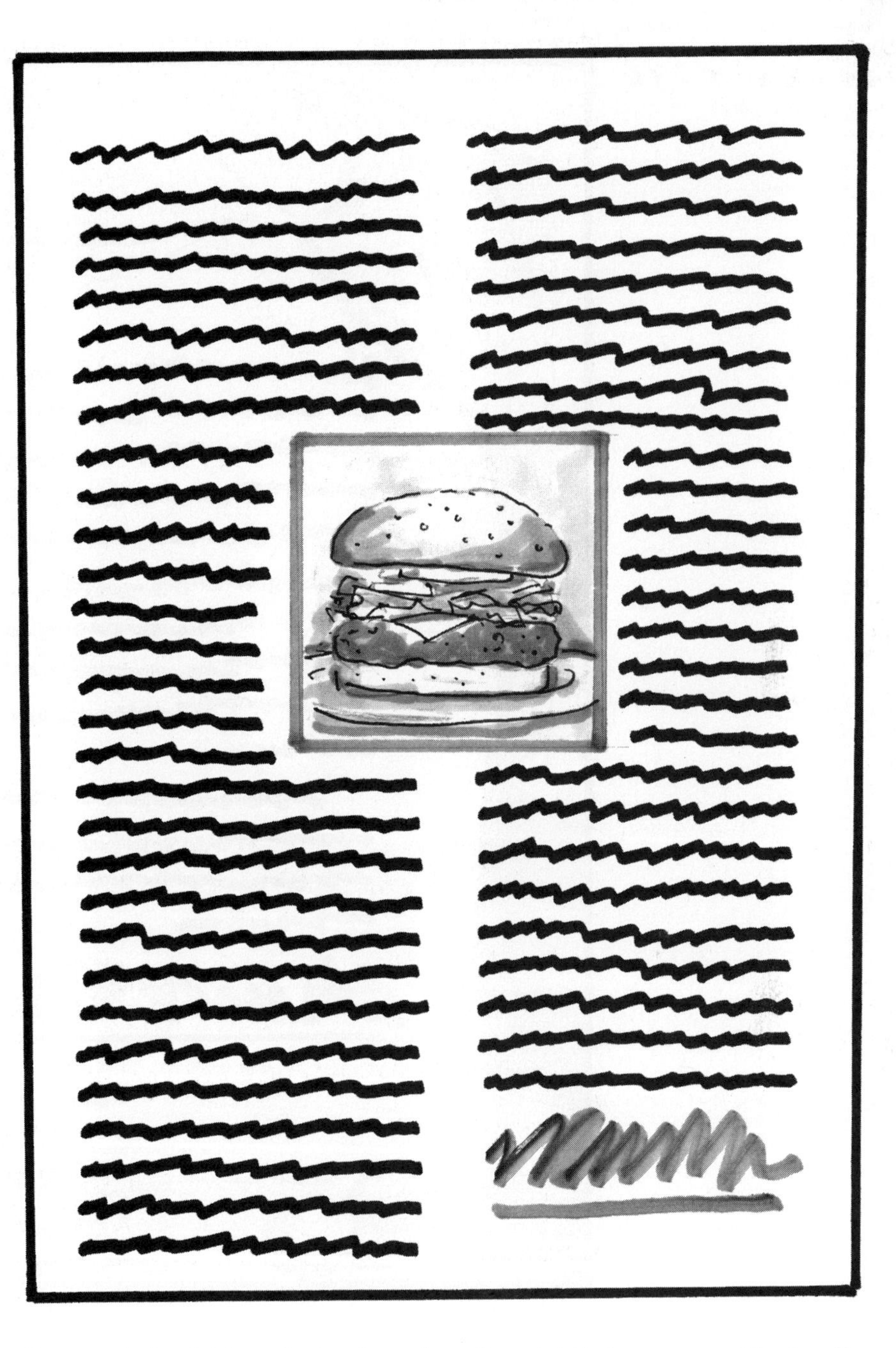

Type Specimen

Characteristic of this style is a large headline with little or no art. The headline dominates and is the major visual attention-getter; therefore, the style of type chosen is extremely important. You may notice this type of layout in newspaper airline ads, as well as in ads for banks, computers, and insurance.

Color Field

This style is always treated as a bleed ad, and is often a double-page spread, with one large photograph dominating. It is always in color, relying on large areas of color to make its impact. It may also contain substantial copy. Automobile advertising makes extensive use of this style.

FIGURE 7-10
Frame.

Band

The band layout lines up all elements, except for one, with the latter lying outside the "band." The benefit of this arrangement is its simplicity. When lining up the elements, be sure to leave some breathing room between them. While the components should have a strong relationship to one another, you don't want to crowd them. You will see ads for liquors and wines using this approach.

Axial

The axial layout is very similar to the band layout, except that it has more than one element emerging from the "vertical stack." Think of the axial layout as a tree trunk with various branches spinning off it. Again, do not crowd the ele-

FIGURE 7-11
Circus.

ments. Leave breathing room and be aware of how the white space operates in relationship to the component parts. You may see this type of arrangement used for a great variety of products. Often the "branches" are short lines of copy explaining various points in the visuals.

All of these layout variations are time tested and have served designers and layout artists well through the years. Think of them as starting points. Perhaps you will come up with an entirely new design!

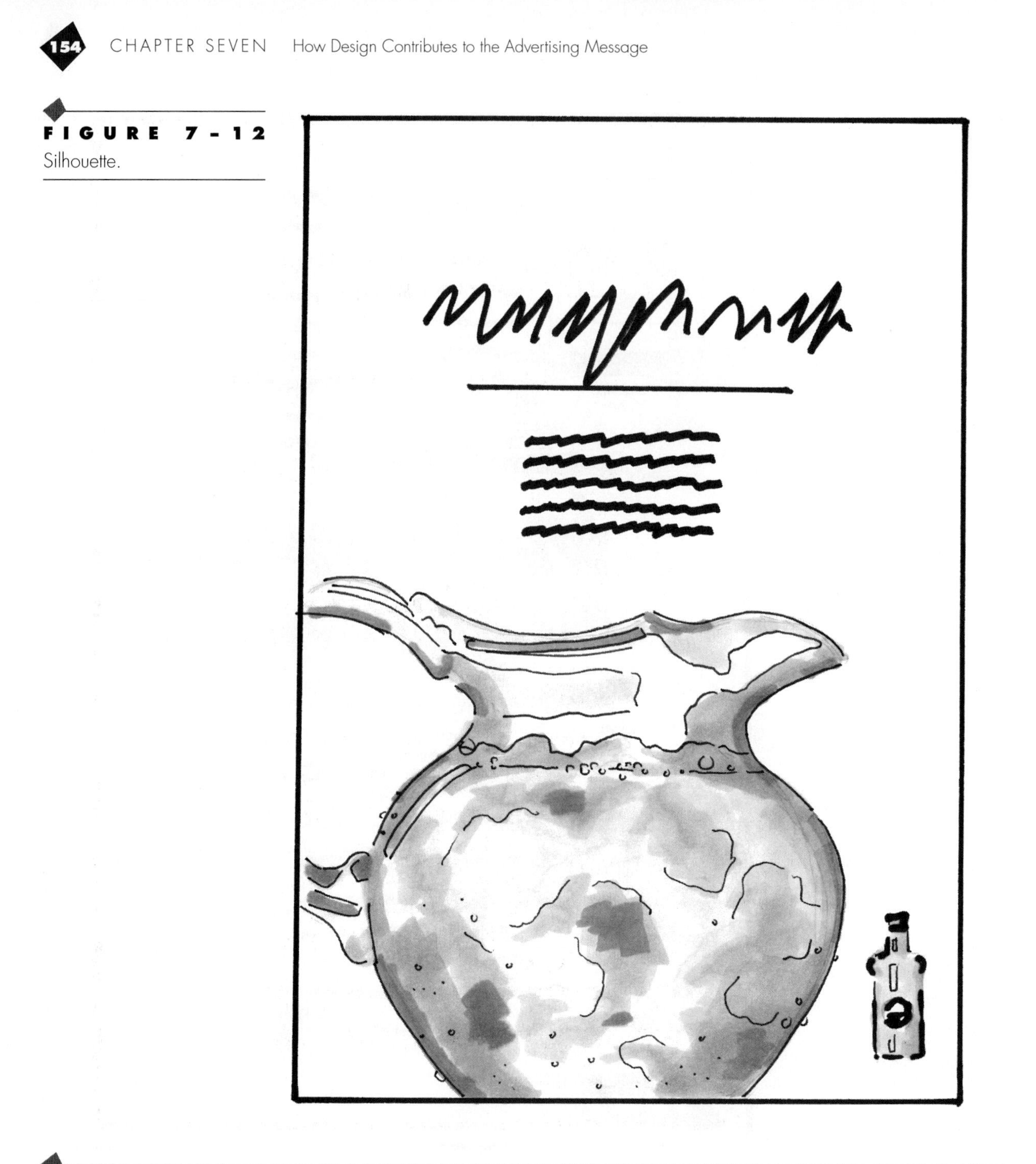

FIGURE 7-12
Silhouette.

Swiping

One of the most useful adjuncts to your list of supplies is your own swipe file. This is simply a collection of photographs and illustrations that can be useful to you. You can put a scrap (as a photo or drawing is called) under your layout paper and, using a pencil, sketch it in, changing hairstyles, clothing, sur-

FIGURE 7-13
Type specimen.

roundings, etc., as you see fit. While these scraps are "swipes," plagiarism is not the goal here. The idea is to use these drawings to save time doing a layout. If you are uncertain as to the effectiveness of a certain scrap, trace it first on a separate sheet of paper, making the changes you want. Once satisfied the drawing is appropriate, put that tracing under your layout paper and retrace it into

FIGURE 7-14
Color field.

position. If you cannot access a computer for setting display type for your layout, swiping can provide an alternative. Find several alphabets in varying sizes and trace the letters you need, first on a spare sheet of paper. Then move the tracing around under your layout until you have it positioned properly, and retrace.

In using a piece of scrap, sometimes the figure or product is facing the wrong way. To correct, simply trace the figure on tracing paper, flip your tracing, and retrace it onto your layout. A light table will help you see the image more clearly and one of the enlarging-reducing art projectors will allow you to adjust the size of a scrap until it works in your design.

FIGURE 7-15
Band.

Doing the Layout

After doing scores of thumbnails and choosing the one that best solves the advertising problem, it's time to begin the full-size layout. To do any layout, you will need the proper tools, which include: bond or vellum layout paper, at least 14 × 17 inches; a T-square to keep your lines straight and true; an assortment of soft and hard black drawing pencils (4B, 2H, 2B), all freshly sharpened; a ruler

FIGURE 7-16
Axial.

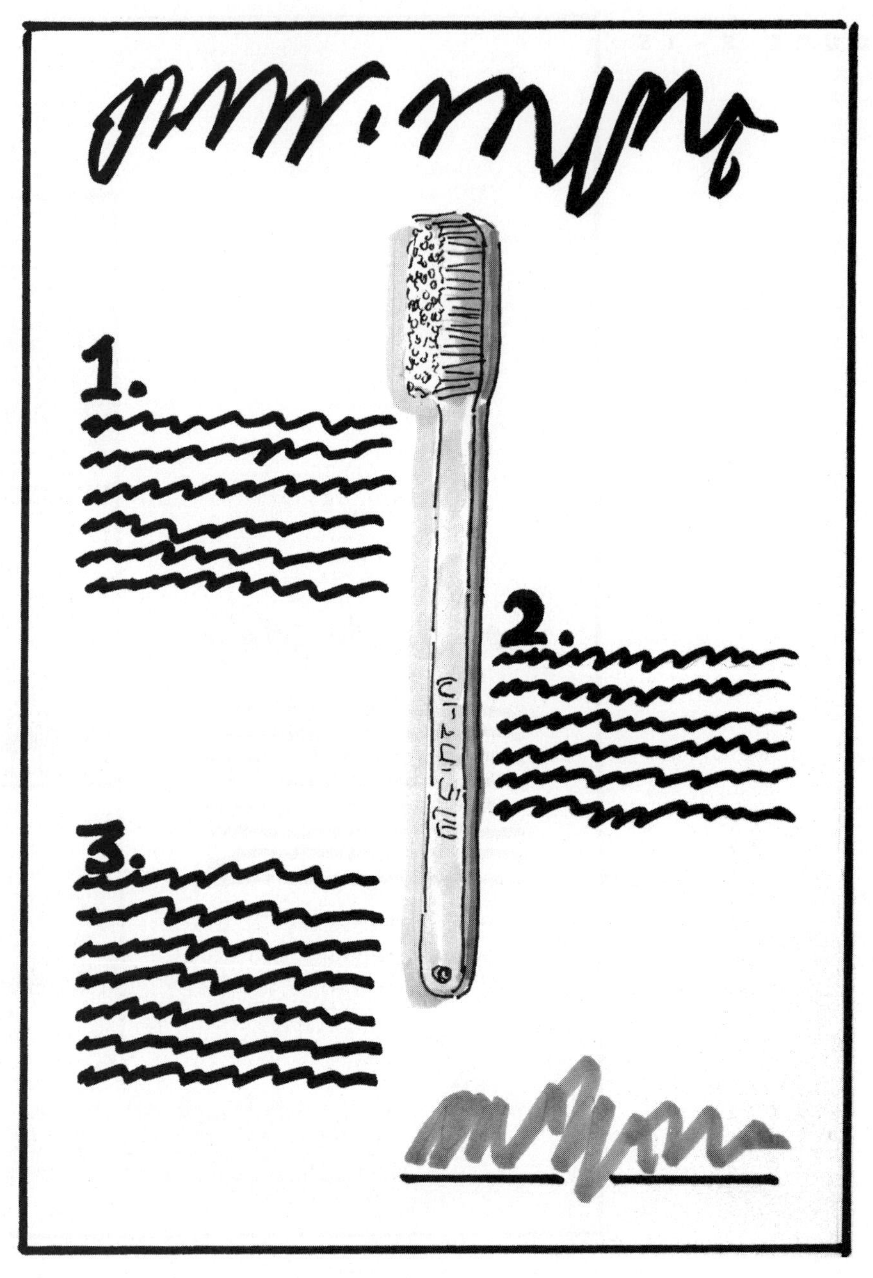

for measuring; tracing paper for tracing art and type; and masking tape to hold your paper in position. First, draw the trim size of the ad on your layout paper. Always begin in pencil.

Be aware that many standard magazine pages consist of the following dimensions:

Trim size: 8 × 11″
Nonbleed and type area: 7 × 10 ″
Bleed: 8 1/4 × 11 1/4″

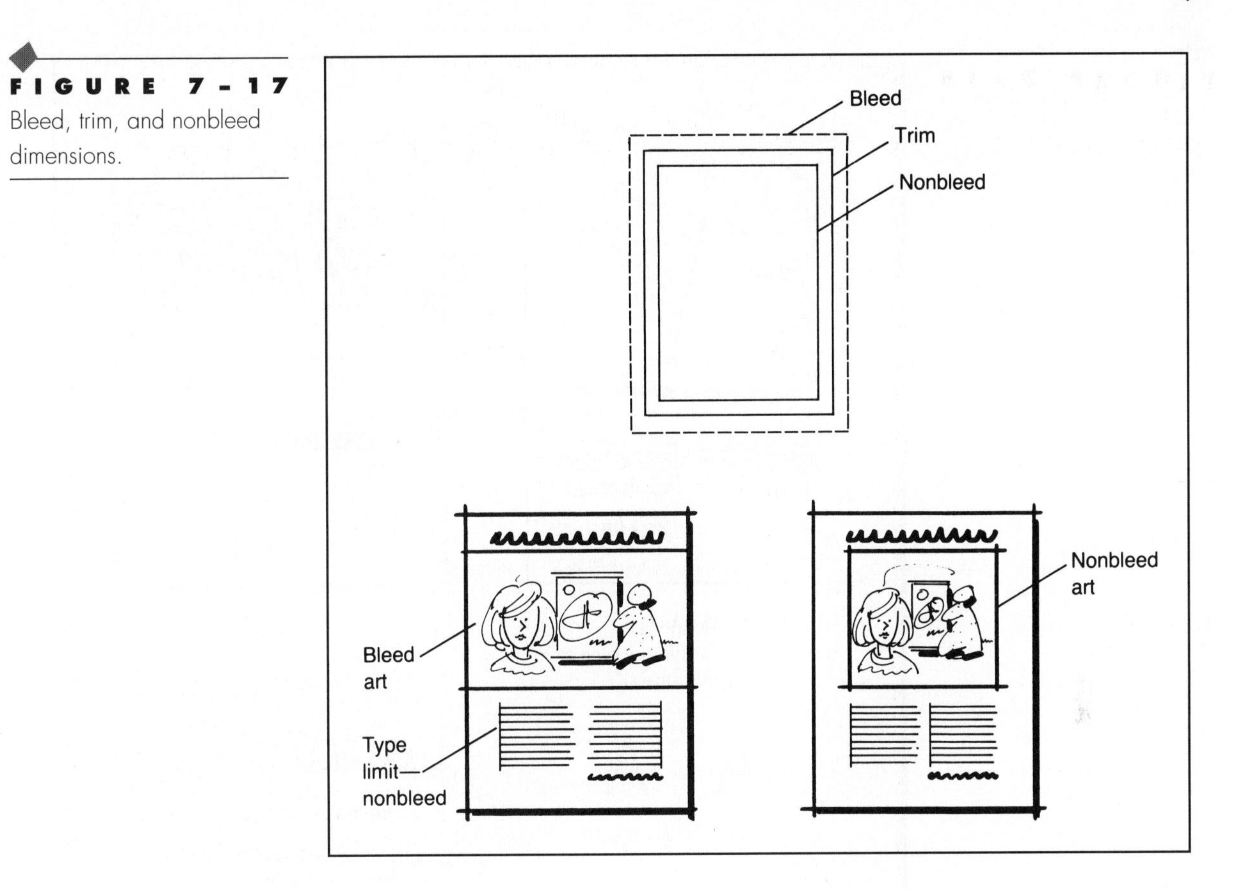

FIGURE 7-17
Bleed, trim, and nonbleed dimensions.

The trim size represents the finished size of the page after the magazine has been trimmed at the printing plant. It is the size of the page when it reaches the subscriber or newsstand. Your layout should be drawn to this size if you are designing a full-page ad. Be aware, however, that magazine sizes may vary slightly, and always check the mechanical specifications for each magazine. (See Figure 7–17.)

A bleed ad is one that runs all the way to the trim on one side or more. A nonbleed ad is contained within the nonbleed page limits, so that it has a standard white margin surrounding it on all sides. Whether your ad is designed to bleed or not, you should keep all type matter within the nonbleed limits. Setting type too close to the trim runs the risk of having a letter or two trimmed off, which could make your copy illegible. You might want to lightly indicate the nonbleed limit as a second frame *within* the frame you draw to establish the trim. This will remind you to keep all type within the inner frame, or nonbleed area.

It's not essential that you be able to draw in order to produce an attractive advertising layout. If you own or have access to a personal computer, you'll want to use it to save time and to make your layouts look as professional as possible. On the most basic level, you can set headlines, baselines, even text in the appropriate size and typeface and paste them into your final layout. If you're using a design program such as PageMaker or QuarkXPress, you'll also be able to

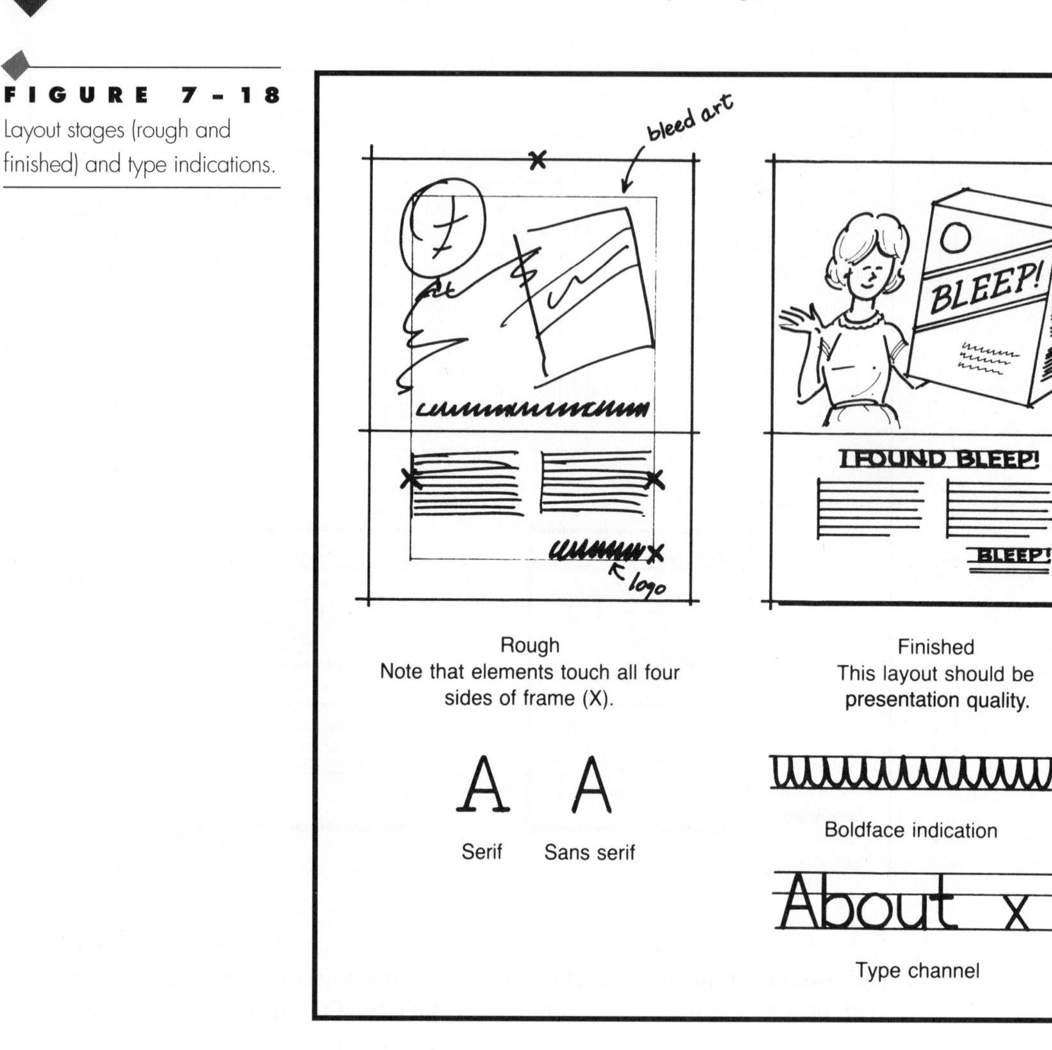

FIGURE 7-18
Layout stages (rough and finished) and type indications.

merge art and text elements into one document and print out a fairly finished advertisement.

You can also swipe art for tracing directly to paper or scanning into a computer document. If your school has an art projector, use it to project swipe art to virtually any size and trace it into your layout. Or paste the actual swipes into position and have them copied same or different size, in black and white or color. Unless you have set it in type, lightly line in the copy, keeping in mind how much copy is written for this layout. Once all elements are properly in place, it's time to go over them with black ink. After this has dried, carefully erase the pencil indications that still show (any markings that are not indigenous to the design itself).

Even after you have changed and erased and refined your ideas, the layout still may not work. The reasons are myriad. But, difficult as it may be, you sometimes will simply have to start all over again. It's not easy, but in the long run you will save time. Never present a layout that you do not believe in wholeheartedly.

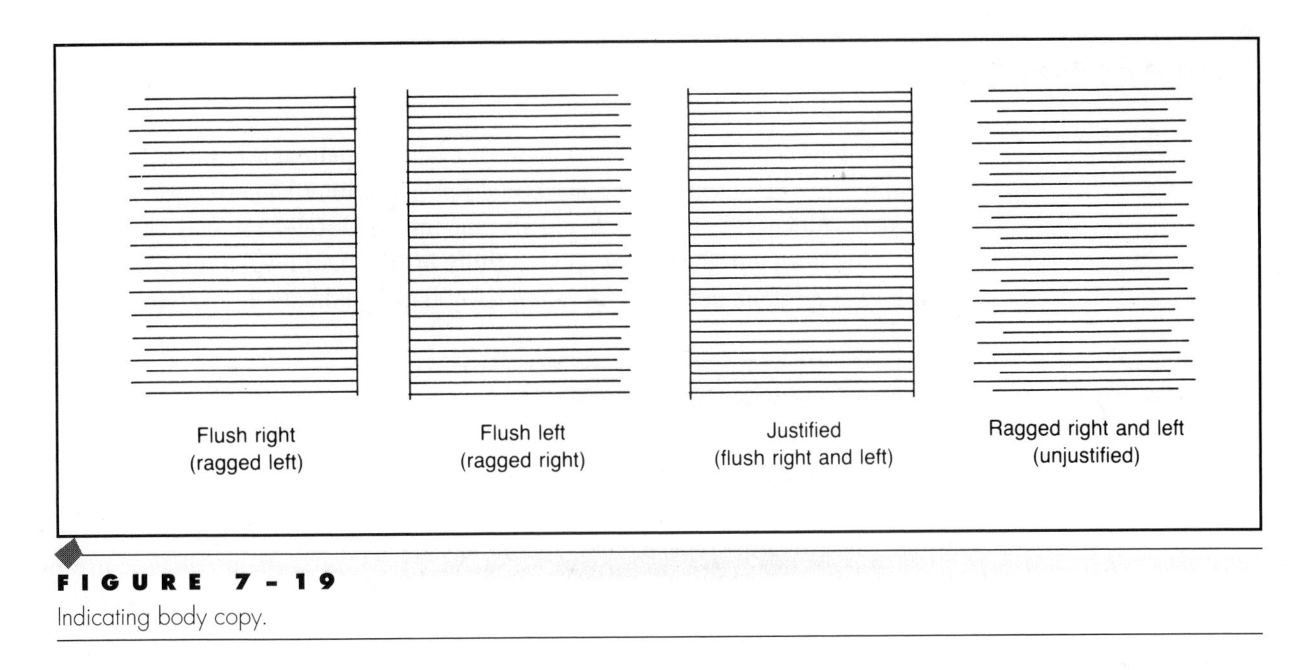

FIGURE 7-19
Indicating body copy.

Choosing Type

Type is one of the major elements in any advertising design. We use it for headlines, for body copy, and to indicate the name of our company at the bottom of the ad. Type can emphasize, direct, establish a mood, add "color" to a page, and inform and motivate. Type is the "voice" of your message.

For a novice, the hundreds and hundreds of available typefaces can be overwhelming, but a few words will help cut through the confusion. Most typefaces can be categorized as serif or sans (without) serif. The serifs are those tiny appendages or "feet" that give some individuality to letters. The sans-serif faces lack these little lines and generally look more contemporary. A good rule of thumb is to have no more than two typefaces in any ad, perhaps one for all display lines and a second for the body copy.

Strive for contrast, not for clash. A heavy serif for the display, a light sans-serif for the body copy will look fine. You can often use just one typeface throughout; a larger size for display, a smaller size for body copy. You might also choose heavy and light versions of the same typeface for contrast.

If you're freehanding type, draw a channel to the proper height. You should also add a third line between the top and bottom lines to indicate the lowercase (or *x* height) of the type. Trace the letters into the channel from your type book. If they are thick, simply outline them at this stage and save the blacking in for your finished layout.

Indicating Body Copy

If you are not setting type for body copy, run your T square down the page and draw a series of closely spaced horizontal lines. The lines should represent the intended width of the copy block and also the intended style. You may choose flush right, flush left, flush right and left (fully justified), or ragged right and left. See Figure 7–19 on page 161 for examples of how to indicate these styles.

How to Be Certain the Words Invite Readership

1. ***Don't set type wider than 39 characters.*** Any wider and you will discourage readership. Instead, break the space into two or more columns of equal width. The larger the type, of course, the wider it can be set.

2. ***Avoid setting copy in less than 10-point type.*** Smaller type becomes hard to read.

3. ***Break up long copy blocks with subheads.*** Careful paragraphing will also avoid the gray mass look.

4. ***Avoid setting body copy in reverse*** (white on black). This tends to cut down readership. Headlines may be reversed for impact, provided the type is large enough and bold enough.

5. ***Take care when printing copy over tonal matter, such as photographs.*** If you must do this, be certain the contrast is there to make the type legible.

6. ***Use lowercase when possible.*** It tends to be more legible than all capital letters, especially in smaller type sizes.

7. ***Either capitalize the entire headline or capitalize only the first word of a sentence and any proper name.***

8. ***End the headline with punctuation*** (period, question mark). Save the exclamation point for the rare occasion when it is warranted.

9. ***Align all copy elements to avoid a jumbled look.*** This is easily done in an axial layout by aligning them on a common axis.

10. ***Use normal punctuation throughout.*** Avoid leaders (. . . . . .) as they look sloppy and uninviting.

11. ***Use italics sparingly.*** They are good for *occasional* emphasis, but too many italics make copy look pale and weak, instead of adding impact and importance.

Apply this test to any layout you design: If you can remove one part of your layout and it still holds together, your layout needs further refining. A good

Courtesy Union Carbide

FIGURE 7-20 (A)-(D) (a) Rough layout

To create and produce the "Porsche" print ad for Simoniz Royale, the agency first develops a rough layout based on a copy concept (a). Once approved internally, the rough is transformed into a comprehensive layout for client presentation (b). When approved by the client, the ad goes into production. This involves ordering type, shooting photographs of the car and the product, and preparing a mechanical, or keyline (c), that combines type with art.

(b) Comprehensive layout

(c) Mechanical (keyline)

(d) Finished ad

design is one in which no single part can be taken out without the entire design collapsing. Each part has a tight and meaningful relationship with every other part. All parts must work together for the greatest impact, excitement, and consumer interest.

Suggested Activities

1. Find a black and white ad that presents strong possibilities for rearrangement, perhaps for improvement when you rearrange the components. Do not choose an ad that is a simple picture window, so that the only changes might be to put the picture below and the headline above. Give your creativity a challenge!

   After looking long and hard at the original ad, start with thumbnails. See how many different ways you can rearrange the ad. Choose your best arrangement. Now, tape the original ad to your drawing board. Draw the trim size on your layout paper, making certain it corresponds to the size of the original ad. Using your chosen thumbnail as a guide, start moving your layout paper around to trace the various components from the original. Carefully letter in the headline, and line in the copy. Shade in dark values with the side of your #2 pencil. Compare the new to the original. What do you think?

2. Find a gestalt-type print ad or one with a silhouette design. With tracing paper, draw the positive shape and shade in the negative shape. This will produce a silhouette of the positive shape (i.e., the headline, copy, and illustration) while sharply emphasizing the negative space. You should end up with quite an abstract design, and it will allow you to see the negative versus the positive shape in the original design.

3. Collect several ads that you think are effective and trace or set the headline in three other typefaces from samples you have collected. Lay the new type over the old. What effect does the change in type style have on the advertisement?

4. Take one of your ads and enlarge and reduce elements to form a new design. You can do this with an art projector that lets you adjust the size of any image. Compare your design to the original.

5. Find eight ads with different typefaces and defend or argue the choices. Does the personality of the type fit the image of the ad? Does it work with the visuals? Does the type overpower all else and work against the effectiveness of the ad?

Federal Express: When It Absolutely, Positively Has to Sell the Idea of Overnight Delivery[1]

[Author's note: This case study, developed from materials at the Center for Advertising History of the Smithsonian Institution, is a bold example of how a small, progressive-thinking company and a creative and risk-taking advertising agency worked closely together to change the concept of package delivery almost—as the service itself promises—overnight.]

In 1971, Fred Smith of Memphis created the Federal Express Corporation. Using the "hub and spoke" idea, a fleet of small airplanes would fly packages from cities across the nation each evening to a hub in Memphis, Tennessee, where parcels would be sorted and reloaded onto other planes for their final destination. Smith chose this type of routing for two reasons: to expedite delivery of the parcels and to ensure their security in the process.

Since its inception, Federal Express has employed only two advertising agencies: Ally & Gargano, Inc., New York (1974–1987) and Fallon McElligott, Minneapolis, since. Originally, Ally was chosen for its small size and entrepreneurial spirit, traits Smith is said to have believed would foster original and effective advertising to introduce the Federal Express concept. In 1971, the agency had to convince customers not only to abandon such industry incumbents as Emory Air Freight, United Parcel Service, and the U.S. Postal Service, but also to trust a newcomer like Federal Express with valuable packages.

Advertising targeted the professional community and the general public through print advertisements and television commercials. Especially in the latter medium, it used humor as its primary marketing technique, to emphasize competitors' slowness and unreliability. In 1981, the agency launched a series of widely acclaimed and highly effective commercials with John Moschitta as the "fast-talking man." The slogan, "When it absolutely, positively has to get there overnight" flashed at the close of most commercials to serve as a reminder of what Federal Express could do.

In 1948, Carl Ally was a law student at the University of Michigan, working at several jobs. He also taught flying, and one of his students happened to be an advertising executive. Seeing how hard Ally was working to support his family, the advertising executive told him he would be a natural in the advertising business. After all, the man told him, advertising, like law, uses advocacy to teach people something. You prepare a brief and you argue your cause from it. After working for General Electric, Ally was recalled to active duty during the Korean

[1] Special thanks to the staff of the Center for Advertising History, National Museum of American History, Smithsonian Institution, for access to their collections on Federal Express and Cover Girl.

War, and upon returning to the United States, began a graduate degree in English literature at the University of Michigan, with an eye toward teaching and writing. Once more, however, the need to support his wife and children led him back to advertising and the Campbell-Ewald agency in Detroit.

Moving to New York, he worked for Papert Koenig Lois until he formed his own agency, Carl Ally, Inc., in 1962 with the Volvo account. After picking up business from IBM, Hertz, Pan American Airlines, and Travelers Insurance, he was introduced to Fred Smith, who was just beginning to form the company called Federal Express. Smith's vision had led him to believe that it was time to improve package delivery. As he saw it, American business in the early seventies was depending more and more on getting the right parts and pieces from one place to another quickly, and he knew he could take anything from anywhere and send it anywhere. That was the whole idea behind Federal Express.

As Ally reminds us, real marketing looks at what is happening in society, finds a niche or hole somewhere where something going on isn't adequate anymore, and proceeds to fill the hole with a service or product. Although Smith may not have been a marketer in the strict sense, he had the vision to find the niche. That was the genius behind the idea of Federal Express. The opportunity lay in contacting people who needed the service and convincing them of its value. That is exactly what Smith and his small team managed to do.

Ally recalls his first trip to Memphis. This guy is going to fly little packages around at night in a small corporate plane, he hears. Sounds crazy, he thinks, but he goes because he is intrigued. Fifteen minutes after meeting Fred Smith in a vintage World War II wooden building at the Memphis airport, he begins to believe in the idea.

Patrick Kelly and Mike Tesch, the copywriter and art director who worked on much of the award-winning advertising, recall that the strategy at the start was "We can guarantee overnight delivery and nobody else can. So if you have to have it overnight, we're it." Nobody else had this service. It was trailblazing.

In its introductory phase, the advertising announced: "America, you've got a brand-new airline." Ally was deeply involved in this phase. "Let's not tell them about the hub," he advised company principals. "It won't mean anything to them. What do they care if it goes to Memphis? 'Don't build me a watch, customers will say, just tell me what time it is.'" The agency argued this point with the company and won.

Following the introductory campaign, advertising attacked a new situation. Competitor Emory Air Freight claimed that it was the best in the business, yet Federal Express could prove that it was twice as effective in delivering on time, giving birth to the claim "Twice as good as the best in the business." To test this claim, Federal Express shipped identical sets of packages to 200 cities, one set via Emory, the other via its own system. It was no contest. Federal Express delivered more than twice as many packages on time and cost less.

Having established credibility with its target audience, the advertising entered its third and most famous phase with the new tag, "When it absolutely,

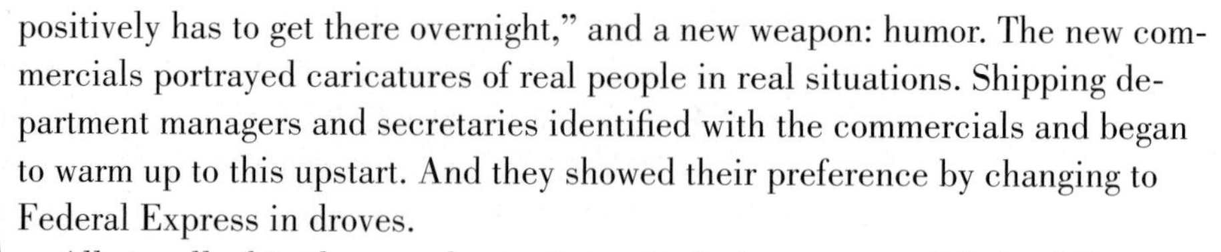

positively has to get there overnight," and a new weapon: humor. The new commercials portrayed caricatures of real people in real situations. Shipping department managers and secretaries identified with the commercials and began to warm up to this upstart. And they showed their preference by changing to Federal Express in droves.

Ally recalls this phase as the turning point in the success of Federal Express. "They had a message and it was singularly presented. It wasn't just pyrotechnics for the light it would make. It got them out of the business of being a narrowly defined service. It wasn't just the logos and such. Logos are corporate cuff links. Current advertising is drowning in form, cosmetics, and fakery these days. The real stuff is what counts. Federal Express was real."

The humor was unorthodox for the time, and, thankfully, the client trusted the judgment of the agency. The campaign caused a sensation, especially among Federal Express employees, who loved the commercials. Even the Federal Express courier loved to come into the agency, Ally remembers fondly. The glory years were glorious.

Mike Tesch, art director on the Federal Express account at Ally & Gargano, Inc., describes how the agency works. "Our agency uses a team system. The writer and art director meet with the client, along with the account executive." Good creative work, he asserts, "all comes down to two people who know what they're doing, the art director and the copywriter. But," he adds importantly, "there is major crossover. Any good writer is a visual thinker. Many good art directors are good writers. Both accept the crossover. That makes it work. We know when to keep working and when to stop working on an idea. When Patrick Kelly and I worked on Federal Express, we knew what was good for the client and what constituted good advertising."

Asked his sources for the zany ideas in the commercials, Tesch cites Mel Brooks, Buster Keaton, Charlie Chaplin, Saturday Night Live, and Woody Allen, but he also claims that a fat bus driver you remember or a guy who brought your laundry up might prove equally inspirational.

For a creative team to work, the partners must have good synergism with one another, says Tesch. "Knowing each other is very important. You don't have to waste time. You know what your partner is thinking."

His partner, copywriter Patrick Kelly, currently a director and filmmaker in his own company, Kelly Pictures, Inc., New York, says he got into advertising "by accident." A jazz drummer in his youth, he attended Kansas State University in Wichita to play in the band. Someone asked if he wanted to be on the radio, so he began taking course work in radio and TV. After graduation, he took an advertising job in Chicago because he couldn't find one in broadcasting. "I noticed that writers and art directors were having the most fun, so I started writing and they started using it." Ultimately, this led him to a job at Ally & Gargano.

"One day some guy comes down the hall and says I'm on this box account. Nobody had ever head of it. I said, 'Here's another stupid client we have to make look good.' They sent us to Memphis, and it turned out to be interesting after all. Even though it was a podunk operation then, you knew they were going to be big. Back then you sent something overnight and it took two days. Everybody accepted that. These guys figured a way to actually deliver overnight, using the hub and spoke theory."

How do you come up with a direction at this point? "We did several campaigns before we hit upon the one that worked," Kelly recalls. "They needed all fifty-two of their planes ready to go in order to stay in business. First night, they had six packages. And no advertising. We thought the best thing would be to show the planes on the runway, with the headline 'America, You Have a New Airline.'"

After the second phase, where the company proved it was twice as good as then leader Emory, came the funny stuff. Kelly had been wanting to write comedy for a long time, and, as he puts it, "packages were pretty dull." This turned out to be a rare and great opportunity for a creative team. "Most clients tell you not to rock the boat, but these guys wanted advertising that stood out and won awards." The first series of ten commercials included one called "pass it on," in which a chairman gives a package to the president, who passes it down the line, and so forth. Each in his own way says something like "If this package doesn't get to Toledo tomorrow, it's your job." This one commercial set the tone for the rest of them. The idea came from the experience of working in an office and seeing people passing the buck. At the heart of the humor is a sobering thought: The American office runs on fear, and Federal Express can provide the answer. Instead of showing positive stuff, which is boring, advertising showed the negative stuff, which is interesting. "Showing the positive is so often an overpromise and people won't buy it," Kelly reminds us. "People identify with the schlemiel; we've all been that way at one time or another. Isn't it interesting that we tend to see ourselves more in a negative than in a positive sense? The identification comes on a subconscious level. At the conscious level we see the idiot as someone else."

Another influence was commercial director Joe Sedelmaier's reel. Federal Express was his first big national campaign, but he had lots of local spots. Sedelmaier was famous for his casting of people nobody else would use. It is said that big companies would not use his bizarre casting until he became famous with his work for Federal Express.

The campaign won tons of awards for five years in a row. Federal Express quickly surpassed Emory as first in air freight. As the principal creative people say, it was unbelievable. So there was much faith in the advertising by the company. The marketing department would provide direction (such as a campaign to sell overnight letters against the post office) and the team would work on it. Commercials that tested poorly were killed. Kelly is quick to mention that tests used fully produced commercials, not storyboards or animatics. "We produced more commercials than we would need because comedy is risky and you need a margin of error," he explains. "You never know. If we needed six we would shoot nine or ten."

Like his partner, Mike Tesch, Kelly readily recognized the sources of his ideas. "I've always been a wise guy, never had a serious thing to say. I've always loved and followed comedy, and have been inspired by all major comedians, from Chaplin through Bob and Ray, Stan Freberg, and Woody Allen. Freberg started the idea of parody in advertising. Allen is a great writer. My older brother was a wise guy, a very funny guy. It's a basic Irish Catholic upbringing; it produces a lot of humor. We once did a parody of an old Sanka Coffee spot from the 'why so tense' era. Two guys are in the mailroom. One looks a lot like Robert Young, the actor who did the old Sanka commercials. 'It's these darned packages that are making me tense,' says the younger fellow. You can see where it went after that.

"We ended up doing several different styles of commercials. One group showed the negatives. Another consisted of parodies of other commercials. The ten-second ID's were all variations on the idea of something blowing up, as in, 'If I don't have that package on my desk tomorrow morning, my whole business will collapse,' and we cut to a building exploding.

"One spot we never produced because of money took place in ancient Babylon. A skinny little slave is carrying a thick clay tablet across the desert as the announcer says, 'Incredible as it may seem, it took four days for a letter to go across town in ancient Babylon. Today it still takes four days for a letter to go from one side of town to another.' The slave walks up a flight of steps to deliver the tablet to the king. He trips, and the tablet breaks. We were suggesting that 3,000 years later, the post office hadn't improved much, but the spot was going to cost too much money."

Why did Federal Express ultimately change advertising agencies? Kelly believes much of the decision had to do with the fact that the men who began the company were not there ten years later. "It wasn't funny anymore," he adds.

What of the post-Ally & Gargano work? "I think the new stuff is visually interesting, that's all," offers Kelly. "It's totally dehumanized, a bunch of robots walking around. But it's probably the perfect campaign for them now, because they have turned into this robotic type of corporation. On the other hand, I think it is a mistake because it has dehumanized the company to its audience."

It is interesting to turn to an interview with Carole Presley, senior vice president for marketing, Federal Express Corporation, who comes off in the agency version as the one who made the decision to change agencies in 1988. She recalls the last presentation Ally & Gargano made. "They presented numerous approaches. One was with Robin Williams that had no bearing on the strategy we were trying to execute. We just didn't like any of the stuff."

Times had changed and competition was fierce, says Presley. "We were looking for any form of differentiation. 'Absolutely positively' didn't do it anymore," she remarks.

In answer to the heavy criticism of advertising critics for one commercial that dehumanizes business, she answers, "Business *is* hell."

Tesch obviously sees things differently. The best of the Federal Express campaigns came out of a single-minded idea, he recalls. "Later, when the company tried to say everything, it became a mishmash." Tesch adds that, while the company wanted to talk technology, the agency felt it was more effective to sell the humanity of the company. In attempting to convince the target that Federal Express was a high-technology company, the creative team found that the humor so admired by the company and its market wasn't working. "Earlier, we could poke fun at the competition," Tesch explains. "Now our assignment was to use humor to show that Federal Express people were technologically superior. You just couldn't make fun of Federal Express people; the driver couldn't be fat; he had to look good."

At the Smithsonian Institution, where I reviewed the comments of these professionals on audiotape, I also had the rare chance to examine the creative presentation of March 19, 1987, which ended Ally & Gargano's long-standing relationship with Federal Express. It was based on a strategy on which the client and agency were apparently in agreement, that businesses should use Federal Express for all communication, not just for priority mail—a logical choice for expanding business when on-time communication is more critical than ever before. I gather that this is the presentation Carol Presley rejected in its entirety, leading to the end of the association with Ally & Gargano and the hiring of Fallon McElligott.

After reading the highlights of the presentation, I flipped through the television storyboards that were shown on that day, the ones the client rejected for not being related to the strategy. I thought they were pretty wonderful.

Then, in a sort of retrospective mood, I watched the entire Federal Express television reel. The early stuff, "Show the planes," which ran roughly from 1975 through 1977, is funny and invasive. You see planes, planes, planes. Commercials make the point that other air freight companies use the other airlines, but Federal Express is the only one with its own airline. There are many advantages to that.

Beginning in 1978, the famous tag, "When it absolutely, positively has to get there overnight," heralds the golden era of advertising for Federal Express: the fast-talking man, the people who make the wrong decisions. The paper blob. The guy who uses the wrong company and is embarrassed out of his job. The business that blows up because the package doesn't reach its destination on time. The ideas change subtly over the years, but the overall effect is brilliance and a concerted effort to stand out and sell.

In contrast, the last Ally & Gargano campaign for Federal Express, done in 1987, pales by comparison and appears to be a weak compromise with the new principals at the company. In the midst of a comical situation, a hand points a finger and a voice says, "Stop. If you use Federal Express, we know where your package is every minute. Come with me." The disembodied finger then shows several astounded folks the Federal Express truck with the computer. Or they see the late-night Federal Express counter and again feign surprise. By being forced to target technology, this campaign comes off as a parody of the great stuff that was done earlier. It made me sad to watch it.

Then, in 1988, the new agency work debuts with a new line. "Federal Express. Because it isn't just a package; it's your business." While it all has a terribly expensive look, it also strikes me as highly irritating. Let's face it, high-tech can make you nervous, especially these quick cuts and future-world approaches that dehumanize the company as an omniscient voice points out that you can't afford to make a wrong decision in today's business world. It grates on the nerves. If this is the way business sees itself, pity business. It isn't fun. The spot with the secretaries annoys me especially. They act like robots, and everything is moving at top speed. The difference between the fast-talking man and this is that we could laugh at the former, but there is nothing funny about the latter. It's the way the world really is.

At the end of his interview, Carl Ally waxes philosophical. "The successes and failures of human society all come from communication or lack of it. The great thinkers were great writers. Clear writing is essentially clear thinking. The essence of advertising is being able to distill a great thought into a simple sentence. It is a serious business, a public portrayal and discussion of the time you live in. It says what the aspirations of the people are. People don't struggle for what they need today; they struggle for what they want. This is true on a global basis today. You have 20 percent of the world consuming 80 percent of the goods. If we fail to support human society, we may disappear, too. The people in power are afraid to do something about it publicly, even though they may be upset privately."

No reflection on Federal Express, but it's something those of us who choose to make our living in advertising should remember.

CHAPTER 8

Designing for Print: Computer Production

VAN KORNEGAY
University of South Carolina

A friend in graphic design used to joke that he was a cave dweller when it came to computers, and planned to stay one. He wasn't alone among his artist friends. Creative types used to snub computers with all the gusto of schoolboys singing off key in choir. In a few years, all that has changed. A new generation of personal computer technology has transformed the field of visual communications, offering design and production advantages to just about anyone who uses art, photographs, and type. While the computer can't make you a good designer, it can enable those with design skills to execute their ideas more efficiently.

At Sawyer Riley Compton, Inc., Atlanta, every art director has given up the drawing board for the Macintosh. The business-to-business agency has disposed of those tables and the high stools that go with them, along with X-acto knives, waxers, and other cut-and-paste paraphernalia. Instead of going through normal layout and production stages, art directors go directly from hand-sketched thumbnails to computer-designed concept layouts and ultimately to full color comprehensives on screen. Once the client has approved a laser print of the comp, the image is "fine tuned" and forwarded on disk, or over a modem to the printer, with color separations already made and copy typeset electronically.

Other agencies are producing video comprehensives on the computer, adding a rough sound track, and presenting to the client in this format. Once the commercial is approved, shooting proceeds in a more traditional manner.

The computer can accommodate a wide variety of users at different levels of involvement; you don't have to be a rocket scientist to make the tool work. Some graphic artists use computers for everything and covet them the way rock stars fancy amplifiers and synthesizers, while others know little more than how to turn them on and do simple things like set type. No matter the level of involvement, complete mastery of the technology isn't a prerequisite for using a computer.

But computers are still complex tools, and it pays to know more than how to find the on/off switch. Those who understand how these machines work inevitably make the technology work better for them and their employers. They add value to their visual communications skills because they understand the system as a whole and are thus able to help manage the technology and solve problems when they arise. This chapter introduces you to some of the basics of computer terminology and how people can use computers to design and compose advertising.

Computers: Mainframe, Mini, and Personal

Three basic types of computers are capable of performing graphics functions. Mainframe and minicomputers are powerful machines used primarily in corporate, industrial, and university settings, but most advertising agency work is done on smaller, less expensive personal computers.

Personal computers are now used for creating graphics and type for overhead transparencies, slides, video, and simple animation. They are also used extensively as a prepress production tool for printed materials. With the proper software, personal computers can now create camera-ready graphics and text for something as simple as a black-and-white one-column ad in the classifieds to four-color art in the graphically demanding newspaper *USA Today*.

Components of the Computer

The Microprocessor

At the heart of every computer is a device called the microprocessor. Although the analogy may be simplistic, you could compare the role of the microprocessor to a car engine. The size of the engine governs the amount and rate of fuel consumption, which ultimately determines performance characteristics of the car. A computer's microprocessor serves a similar purpose. It regulates how much information the computer can handle at one time and how fast it can perform its operations.

In most computers the microprocessor is identified by a number. These numbers give some clue to the computer's capability and speed in much the same way the horsepower number of a car engine tells something about its performance. In general, the higher the number, the greater the performance gains. For example, earlier models of IBM and IBM compatible computers were driven by 286 and 386 microprocessors. The current models are equipped with 486, or faster, more powerful, microprocessors.

Those contemplating using a computer for graphics or page layout would do well to learn about the capabilities of the microprocessor, because they will certainly become aware of the ways it affects their computer's performance. Slower processors slow all functions of the machine, from the time it takes to rotate or redraw a graphic on the screen to the speed with which files are saved. Performance differences between different chips are especially important for users working in color, using scanners, or creating large, complicated graphics.

Memory

Random access memory (RAM) is the working active memory of the computer. It's somewhat analogous to a person's short-term memory. As each program is activated and files are created, the computer temporarily stores instructions and data in RAM and keeps the information there only as long as the computer is turned on. When the computer is turned off, information stored in RAM is lost, unless saved to a hard drive or floppy disk.

Having more RAM available, preferably sixteen to twenty-four megabytes, is a necessity for running many graphics and page layout programs. Another reason to add RAM is that it enables a user to have more than one program running on the screen simultaneously, eliminating the time-consuming task of quitting one program and opening another to work on another aspect of a job. This is an important capability for working with advertising design because you will frequently need to call upon a number of different programs to complete one assignment.

Long-Term Storage Media

Floppy disks and hard disks are the most common media used to store data permanently. Hard disks are installed either inside the central housing of the computer or as an external piece of hardware. Floppy disks are the familiar 3 1/2 inch or 5 1/4 inch plastic squares that are inserted into the computer's drive slot. A double-sided floppy disk holds about 800 kilobytes of data, the equivalent of almost 500 pages of double-spaced typewritten text. Hard disks come with a variety of storage capacities and can store many more programs and files than floppy disks. Other types of popular storage devices are CD-ROM (which stands for Compact Disc-Read Only Memory) and removable tape and optical drives. The tape cartridges or special disks that are inserted into a removable drive are small and easy to transport but can store massive amounts of information. This type of transportable data storage is a necessity for graphic artists who frequently take large graphics files to an outside service bureau for output on high quality typesetters or color printers.

The Monitor

Monitors in a variety of shapes, sizes, prices, and colors are available for almost every brand of computer. Screen size, resolution, and color capability are three of the most important features in a monitor that will be used for ad layout. Most small screens can only display sections of the actual size of a layout. This limitation forces the user to enlarge and reduce the screen view to work on one section of the layout at a time. Doing ad layouts this way can be like navigating through rush hour traffic with a periscope. It's hard to keep track of all the elements and get an overview of how the layout is progressing. A two-page display monitor, usually measuring at least 19 inches across the diagonal plane of the monitor, is adequate for most advertising layouts and can speed up production time by allowing an actual view of up to two 8 1/2 × 11 inch pages. (See Figure 8-1.)

Screen resolution and the ability to show grays and other colors are other important monitor features. High-resolution monitors provide accurate and crisp images of type and graphics without ragged edges. Color monitors also allow the designer to preview scanned photographic images and to experiment with numerous process color combinations. Whether you are working with type,

Actual size view on a small screen

Reduced view on a small screen

Actual size view on a two-page display screen

FIGURE 8-1
Monitor size is an important feature for designing an ad on computer. A small screen can restrict one's ability to view the entire advertisement, while large double-page monitors can display most layouts' actual size and in their entirety.

graphics, or photos, a high-quality monitor is crucial for providing a real life preview of what will ultimately be a finished ad.

Peripheral Devices

The computer, monitor, and its associated memory components make up the core part of the graphics hardware. But there are other devices, known as peripherals, that are important components of a well-rounded system.

Peripherals may include input devices for generating original art or importing existing images into the computer. The digitizing stylus and mouse are input devices that allow artists to use freehand drawing techniques to generate and edit images on the screen. Scanners and video cameras are input devices that can convert line art, photographs, and three-dimensional objects into images that can be displayed on the computer screen and manipulated with various graphics software programs.

Once an advertisement has been created on the computer screen, an output device is needed to convert the data into some form of "hard copy." A wide range of output peripherals, from inexpensive dot matrix printers to costly slide film recorders and typesetters, can accomplish this task. In general, laser printers and digital typesetters are the most popular devices for generating proofs and camera-ready prints for type, line art, and entire camera-ready mechanicals.

Creating and Producing Print Advertising on the Computer

Personal computers have redefined the production process for many creative materials, and their influence in print production continues to be dramatic. Before personal computers and laser printers arrived, most print ads were created in stages by a variety of people working in different places. Writers worked with art directors who specified type sizes and styles and passed their instructions to a typesetter for phototypesetting. Illustrators and photographers created visuals and the art director coordinated their placement with the type. The art was reduced or enlarged to fit the layout and usually pasted down with type on a mechanical, from which a printing plate was prepared.

With the occasional exception of the typesetter, the computer has not eliminated the need for any of these people or the skills they bring to producing an ad. But it has changed the production path an ad takes from concept to finished product and, as a result, has changed the way these people work. What follows is a description of how an ad is developed from concept to camera-ready art, with the computer playing a role in these steps. The actual advertisement was composed by an undergraduate advertising major using an illustration program, a scanner, and a page layout program.

1. ***Create a Thumbnail.*** Visual planning for any print ad begins with a thumbnail sketch, a step that should happen before you turn on the computer. The reason is simple. For most designers the computer is a production tool more than a design tool. It can offer a great deal of flexibility and opportunity for creative experimentation once an idea is in rough form, but a pencil and paper are still the ideal tools for beginning a good design.

The thumbnail is a comfortable way to experiment with a variety of options before selecting the one to serve as a loose blueprint for your layout. Your thumbnail should probably include:

a. A representation of the shape of the ad, vertical or horizontal.

b. General position of art, headline, and text. At this stage, you may use stick figures for art, squiggly lines for text.

c. A sense of proportional relationships among the elements: how big is the art in relation to copy and text?

The thumbnail is design shorthand and should be a fluid, uncritical process focusing on the development of concepts rather than details. (See Figure 8-2.)

2. ***Create a Rough Layout.*** A rough layout is a more detailed execution of the thumbnail. You should draw it to actual size and indicate more precisely where headlines and copy will be placed and how large or small they will be. The rough should also contain a more detailed sketch of any visuals in the layout. It can then serve as a more exacting guide for moving to a comprehensive rough, or rough comp, on the computer.

Designers who are fairly proficient with graphics and page layout software might find it more efficient to transfer the thumbnail directly into the computer. Novices should refine their ideas further at this stage with pencil and paper. The thumbnail is only a loosely defined concept, and making it conform to the precise parameters of the computer may stymie your creative experimentation and thwart any opportunities to further refine the concept.

3. ***Turn on the Computer and Create a Comprehensive Layout.*** Now the computer can begin to make a real difference in the amount of time you can save, as well as the chance to experiment with design options. Your comprehensive layout will be the selling tool your client will approve or disapprove, and should contain the headline and other display lines, along with a more detailed sketch of the visual. You may use lines to represent the text, or body copy, or may choose to actually set the copy and drop it into the computer layout.

Before you begin setting up a comp on the computer, decide which software tools you will be using.

a. *Selecting Software.* A wide range of software programs can be useful for putting together a layout. Most programs fit within these categories:

1) Word processing software for writing body copy.

2) Graphics software for creating illustrations.

3) Image editing software for saving and editing images from a scanner or some other video source.

4) Pagination software for combining elements created by all of the above programs into a comprehensive layout.

Most programs have special capabilities in one of these areas and limited capabilities in others. For example, PageMaker and QuarkXpress are popular pagination programs primarily used for combining copy and art from files

FIGURE 8-2 (A)

In this and the next two figures, you can follow the step-by-step creation of an advertisement on the computer. The two small thumbnails help the designer choose a format which she then draws to actual size in the full-size rough layout.

Thumbnails

created by other programs. But they also have basic drawing and word processing capabilities, which means you can use them to write body copy and generate simple illustrations.

There is no one magic software program for designing. Some art directors use a variety of programs while others stick with a single favorite. If the ad is heavy with art and light on type, you might use a graphics program to create the illustration as well as the type. If the layout has a minimal amount of art and is copy heavy, you probably will have to use more then one program:

FIGURE 8-2 (B)
Full-size rough.

graphics software for the art, word processing and pagination software to create and position the type.

Whatever program you use, you should be fluent with its basic commands before you start working. Coming up with good creative ideas and executing them is tough enough; struggling with software at the same time makes it even tougher. After reading the user's manual, you can further develop your

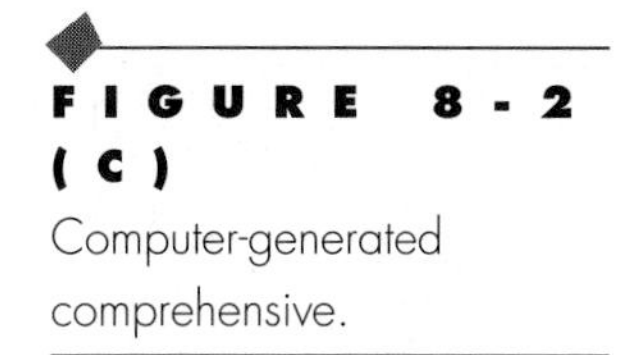

FIGURE 8-2 (C)
Computer-generated comprehensive.

proficiency with a new program by redoing an old layout with the new program, taking a class, or hiring a computer consultant to train you.

b. *Set Up Rough Dimensions in the Computer.* Before you begin manipulating type and art on the screen, you should transfer the measurement specifications of the rough into the computer. Most graphics and pagination programs allow users to set up specifications by creating a grid pattern on the screen. The

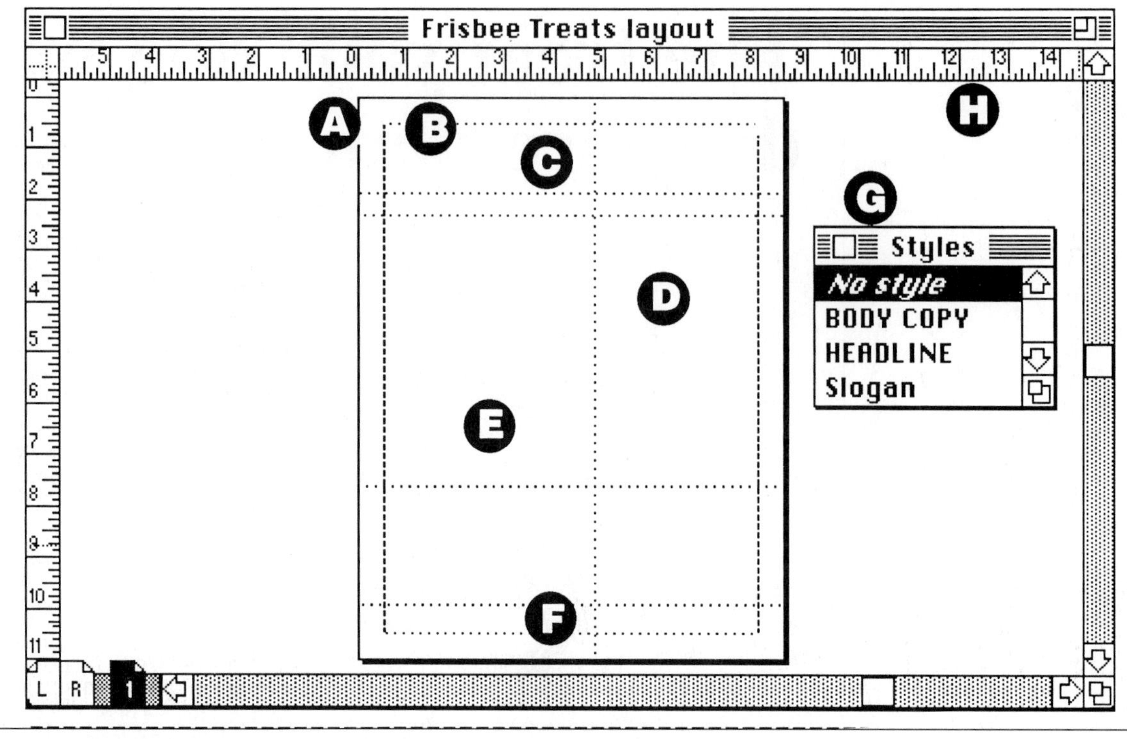

FIGURE 8-3

This actual screen for the PageMaker program shows a blank PageMaker page with grid lines drawn to aid placement of art and copy for the Frisbee Flying Dog Treats layout. Window includes:

A. 8½ x 11 inch trim for actual page size;
B. nonprinting margins for all type and nonbleed materials;
C. nonprinting grid lines for headline;
D. nonprinting grid lines for body copy;
E. nonprinting grid lines for large art;
F. nonprinting grid lines for baseline.

Palette style (G) can speed production by storing standard type specifications for body copy, headlines, and so on. By highlighting the desired style in the palette, the designer can bypass cumbersome and repetitive typesetting commands. The vertical and horizontal rulers (H) allow for exact placement of all elements.

on-screen grid will display the dimensions of the printed page; the top, bottom, and vertical margins; the number of columns, or axes, and their widths; and will allow the creation of other grid lines to mark consistent placement of graphics and text. (See Figures 8-3 and 8-4.)

You can then assign typographic style sheets to the grid, designating consistent specifications for display and body type: size of margins, number of indents, amount of leading between lines of type, and word and character spacing, as well as the font, size, and style of headline and body text. Such style sheets are especially useful whenever you plan to repeat layout formulas. For example, you might use a single style sheet to create a series

FIGURE 8-4

PageMaker page after placement of art and copy. Smaller copy sizes are displayed as grey bars due to the reduced screen view of the page.

of ads for a campaign with different visuals and text, but the same basic design.

c. *Combine Elements from Other Programs.* With the grid in place, you can now integrate art and copy into the layout precisely. Rough illustrations, logos, and photographs can be imported from graphics programs or from files containing images digitized from source materials using an optical scanner. Headlines and body copy can be set in the actual font and size in which they will appear in the finished advertisement.

4. ***Create a Finished Mechanical.*** Once a client approves the comprehensive layout you have generated with a laser printer, it's time to prepare the camera-ready mechanical. The mechanical, from which the ad is printed, should contain all of the finished elements—art, type, photography—as they will appear in the final ad.

From the mechanical, a make-ready house or the printer will produce a film negative from which a printing plate is made.

At mechanical stage, you obviously will need approved copy, finished illustrations, and final photography. If you have used a computer throughout the preparation stages, art and copy can simply be positioned on the screen, with

FIGURE 8-5
These Christmas ornament illustrations by Paul Calhoun were generated in Adobe Photoshop and Alias Sketch computer programs. All separations and illustrations were placed in a QuarkXPress file and output to negatives on a Scitex system by DG&F, Columbia, S.C., who also produced the four-color separations. Layout by Patricia Callahan, Semaphore, Inc., Columbia, S.C.

PALMETTO POWER

PROMOTING ECONOMIC DEVELOPMENT IN RURAL SOUTH CAROLINA

NOVEMBER/DECEMBER 1993

SANTA CLAUS HAS COME TO TOWN!

Everybody in the small town of Heath Springs, South Carolina, unquestionably believes in Santa Claus. Jim and Jan Shore's three year old company, Designs Americana, served by Lynches River Electric Co-op, has made sure of that. Begun in their backyard, the Shore's company employs nearly 100 people from the area in the casting and handpainting of collectible figurines—primarily ones of Santa. Gross sales have rocketed from $50,000 in 1989 to millions today. Five members of the immediate Shore family and "a lot of cousins" are involved in the company.

Christmas figures have been the bread and butter products. Ones for other holidays and still others for everyday display are also produced and sold through gift shops nationwide and national retailers such as Spiegel, Belk, Hallmark, JC Penney and Nordstrom. There is a craft line which is sold unpainted and the gift line of handpainted items. Within the gift line, there are special collector's pieces with limited production. Very popular new series include a jazz ensemble called *Hot Licks*, an Amish family and a set of African animals. Golfers and Civil War figures comprise major new collectible sets that will come off the production line in 1994. And just this year, Designs Americana was asked to produce figures of Mickey Mouse, Minnie, Goofy and Donald Duck for sale by Disney at its theme park gift shops.

Jim Shore, a mechanical engineer, has sculpted most of the originals for the current product line of more than 500 designs. Mr. Shore's talented sculpting and Ms. Shore's painting

Continued on back page.

Courtesy Palmetto Power/Semaphore, Inc.

no additional cutting and pasting of art, nor trips back and forth to typesetters for revisions.

Once final copy and art have been created and placed in the layout, you are ready to print a copy of the mechanical on a laser printer. You may want to run this by the client once more for a final check, then send the computer file to a type house that can print the file on a professional quality typesetter. Most type houses can also print files from personal computers directly to a film negative, ready for conversion to a printing plate.

FIGURE 8-6
Here is an example of how a logo was created for an organization affiliated with the Methodist Church. A statue of John Wesley, a minister who rode from town to town on horseback to start local churches, was photographed and a pencil tracing of the photograph was made. Nonessential elements and much detail were eliminated. The tracing was then scanned into the computer and imported into an illustration program, where it was redrawn so that separate computer commands could be sent to each portion of the design. Once redrawn, the image also could be enlarged or reduced, colorized, or combined with other graphics and typography.

Courtesy Van Kornegay

Original photograph of statue.

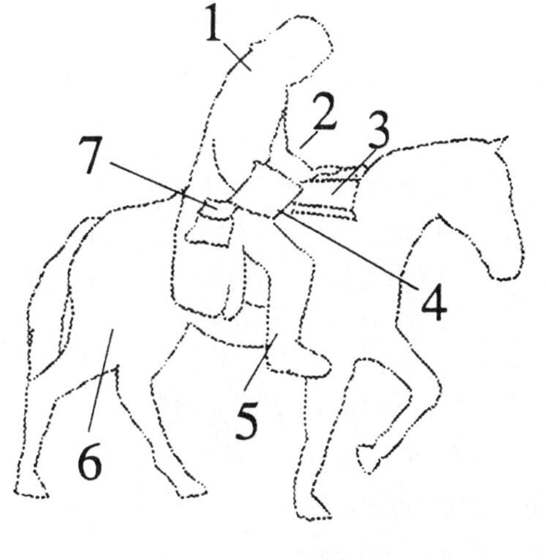

Tracing of photograph to eliminate unnecessary details.

Final design incorporating type and line art.

Courtesy Piedmont Municipal Power Agency and Semaphore, Inc.

FIGURE 8-7
Using enlarged photocopies of existing photographs and illustrations, the designer of this annual report scanned all art into a computer to create this striking collage.

Composing the Copy

Most copywriters probably already use a computer with a word processing program, and most page layout programs used for creating advertising are able to interchange or read files from these programs with minimal compatibility problems. One immediate advantage of producing advertisements on a computer is that it preempts the need for a typesetter to rekeyboard copy. The writer need only save copy on a disk, which she then gives to the designer, who can import the file into a page layout program for typesetting and design.

The writer can even compose the copy within the actual comp by using the page layout program as a word processor. Using this technique, the writer simply types the text in position, replacing the lines or "greeked" dummy text. The actual text is automatically set in the appropriate font size and style specified by the art director. A growing number of page layout programs now offer powerful word processing features that make this process easy. Typing directly into the layout can eliminate much copyediting done to make the words fit the space, for the writer can see exactly how much space is available for both headlines and text as she writes.

Creating the Visuals

A number of graphics programs can generate illustrations, logos, and other line art suitable for use in finished advertisements. When connected to a scanner or some other video input source, the computer can also display digitized versions of any drawing or photograph. Such graphics can then be integrated into a computer generated advertising layout. (See Figures 8-5, 8-6, and 8-7.)

A scanner is one of the quickest ways to transfer an image into the computer. Although it can capture any printed image and display it on the screen, black and white photographs and line art work best. Scanned line art, such as pen and ink drawings, will reproduce more faithfully than photographs. In preparing a comp, the artist might scan in a rough pen and ink sketch in order to integrate it with type and experiment with size and placement. Later, he can replace the rough sketch with a finished version.

Most scanned photographs are not suitable for reproduction in the final version of the advertisement, but are useful for showing position, size, and cropping. Scanned photographs might be placed in a layout in the comp phase for client approval. As final copy and art are placed, the scanned and integrated photograph can be marked "for placement only." In the production stage, an original print of the photo is then dropped in.

You can create original illustrations with graphics programs, as well as manipulate electronic clip art drawn by professionals. Many artists claim it can take more time to draw something on a computer than draw it freehand, but they also acknowledge that computer images have these advantages over traditional drawings:

1. Images can be reshaped, resized, and repositioned on the screen instead of using a photographic enlargement or reduction process, which usually takes longer.

2. Images can be saved on disk and used again and again without the need to redraw.

3. The artist has more freedom to experiment with shading, tonal values, and color.

4. The computer is a forgiving medium. There's no need to worry about spilled ink or slips of the knife. If you make an error, simply tell the computer to "undo" or "delete" the last command.

Beyond Print Production

The personal computer is becoming a mainstay in advertising for typesetting, layout, and graphic production, but it's also introducing new approaches for selling and distributing advertising that go beyond art and copy for the printed page.

A number of specialized advertising agencies now use computers to develop interactive multimedia ads. The ultimate in personalized marketing, these ads are graphic, text, and sound presentations on the computer screen that allow the user to interact with the message. Computer-based advertising can be distributed by disk to individual computer owners through commercial computer information networks such as Compuserve, or via information kiosks at point-of-sale displays and trade shows.

Ford and Buick are among the larger companies experimenting with computer-based advertising. Both companies have mailed computer disks with software allowing potential buyers to peruse product lines using their office or home computers. These ads allow customers to choose on-screen graphics of the models and features they want to examine, figure the monthly payments, and even print out a window sticker to take to the dealer.

Analysts predict this trend toward personalized computer-based advertising will continue to grow and become more sophisticated. Advanced computer designs will allow programs that accept the screen and keyboard responses of the user and gauge how fast he reads, which colors he prefers, and which product configurations are best suited to his needs.

Computers are also changing the way publications service their advertisers and sell ad space. Many newspapers and magazines now have systems in place which allow retail advertisers to send their own computer-generated ads directly to the publication through the phone lines. This bypasses the need to mail or hand carry camera-ready mechanicals or rely on the publication's composing facilities and personnel to create the ad from scratch.

In an effort to be more responsive to advertisers, account representatives can now carry small notebook-size computers equipped with color monitors to show clients sample ads with display type and art already in place. If the client agrees to purchase the ad, the account representative can enter relevant information, such as pricing and headlines, on the spot, and then transmit the ad over the phone to the publication's computer.

The computer can be a powerful aid for producing, selling, and delivering advertising. It can cut the time to produce a finished ad, provide greater flexibility

FIGURE 8-8
These graphics are from an interactive computer-based advertisement from The SoftAd Group. The three screens display the product, its specifications, and even provide a spreadsheet that calculates monthly payments and finance charges. Mouse and keyboard commands allow the prospective buyer to interact with the advertising by selecting menus and buttons on the screen. Computer-based ads such as this can combine graphics, animation, sound, and full-motion video with human interaction to deliver highly targeted and engaging presentations.

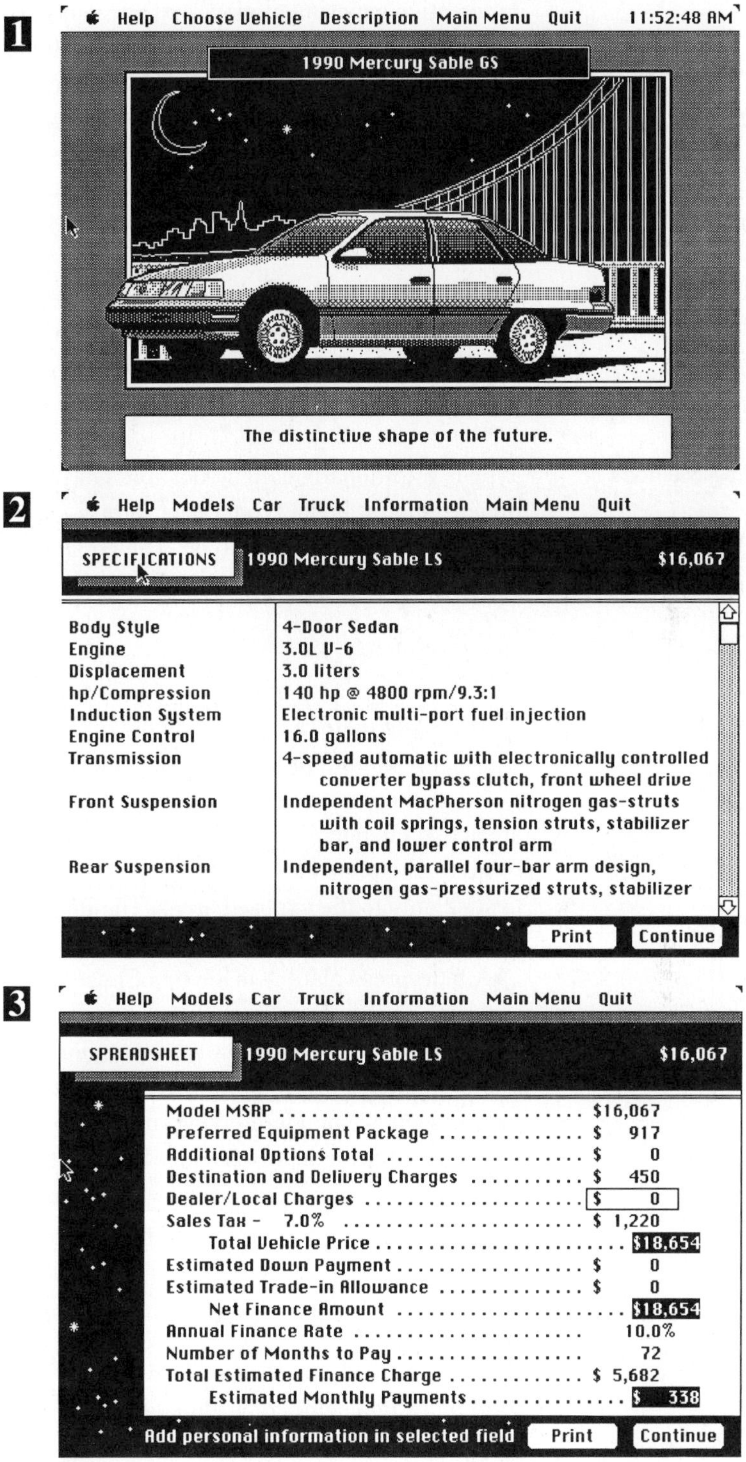

1

Help Choose Vehicle Description Main Menu Quit 11:52:48 AM

1990 Mercury Sable GS

The distinctive shape of the future.

2

Help Models Car Truck Information Main Menu Quit

SPECIFICATIONS 1990 Mercury Sable LS $16,067

Body Style	4-Door Sedan
Engine	3.0L V-6
Displacement	3.0 liters
hp/Compression	140 hp @ 4800 rpm/9.3:1
Induction System	Electronic multi-port fuel injection
Engine Control	16.0 gallons
Transmission	4-speed automatic with electronically controlled converter bypass clutch, front wheel drive
Front Suspension	Independent MacPherson nitrogen gas-struts with coil springs, tension struts, stabilizer bar, and lower control arm
Rear Suspension	Independent, parallel four-bar arm design, nitrogen gas-pressurized struts, stabilizer

Print Continue

3

Help Models Car Truck Information Main Menu Quit

SPREADSHEET 1990 Mercury Sable LS $16,067

Model MSRP	$16,067
Preferred Equipment Package	$ 917
Additional Options Total	$ 0
Destination and Delivery Charges	$ 450
Dealer/Local Charges	$ 0
Sales Tax - 7.0%	$ 1,220
Total Vehicle Price	$18,654
Estimated Down Payment	$ 0
Estimated Trade-in Allowance	$ 0
Net Finance Amount	$18,654
Annual Finance Rate	10.0%
Number of Months to Pay	72
Total Estimated Finance Charge	$ 5,682
Estimated Monthly Payments	$ 338

Add personal information in selected field Print Continue

for creative experimentation, and even serve as the medium through which an ad is delivered. With the development of artificial intelligence, high volume memory, and faster processing speeds, computers promise to provide more opportunities for greater immediacy and personalization of the advertising message.

Basic Guide to Print Production

Although graphics and word processing programs for computers have revolutionized the production of print advertisements, readers may be interested in other typesetting methods and printing processes. Here is a quick rundown of those.

Typesetting Methods

Type is traditionally called "hot" or "cold." If type is cast from hot metal and is dimensional, it is hot type. Other forms—phototypesetting, computer word processing—are termed cold type. The popular and versatile personal computer has made word processing the norm for typesetting.

Printing Processes

Offset and letterpress are the most widely used methods of printing, while screen and gravure printing are options for certain kinds of printed work.

The offset plate, a descendent of the lithographic process, is perfectly flat. During the plating process, a film negative of the material to be printed is exposed on a light-sensitive metal plate. The processed plate includes exposed areas that chemically repel water, while unexposed areas attract water. During printing, the plate is continually misted with water, which causes oil-based inks to stick only to the exposed areas. The image is first transferred—or offset—from the plate to a rubber roller, then to the paper.

A letterpress plate is made up of raised surfaces which, when coated with ink and applied with pressure to paper, produce a printed product.

A rotogravure plate contains depressions or indentations which capture the ink to produce a printed product. This process produces superior detail, and the durable plates can tolerate long runs without perceptible loss in printing quality.

Screen printing involves squeezing ink through a cloth screen on which the areas to be inked are cut out, as with a stencil. A photographic process is used to produce the screen. This process produces brilliant color work and is used for short runs of point-of-purchase materials in which halftone reproduction is generally not involved.

Halftone and Line Art

Halftone art contains shades ranging from light grays to blacks, while line art is solid black or a solid color. Photographs are halftones because they contain a spectrum of tones and therefore must be copied through a fine screen pattern to break shaded areas up into fine dot patterns for printing. Even type is termed "line art" in the production stage, unless it has been screened to reproduce in a lighter shade.

Color Printing

For each color of line art, a separate plate is required. When full color photography is to be reproduced, the color photograph must be broken down into red, yellow, blue, and black hues. This is done by shooting the original photograph through a set of color filters, each filter isolating one of the four "process" colors. The resultant four screened negatives are the basis for four printing plates, each inked on the press with the proper process color and printed in perfect registration over one another. Yellow is printed first, followed by red, blue, and black.

Type Specifications

Type is sized in points, with 72 points to the inch. Yet 72-point type is generally less than a full inch high, to allow for space between lines. Each style of type is termed a font and each font carries a name. This text, for example, is set in 11 point Bodoni Book. Advertisements are measured either in inches or in picas. The pica, a standard printer's measure, consists of 12 points. There are 6 picas to the inch.

Estimating Space for Type

Since you can now set type in actual sizes and styles on the computer, there's little need to estimate how much space to allow on a layout for type. In case you ever have to estimate, here's a simple formula:

1. Find a sample of the type font and size.
2. Measure a width on your sample which is equal to the width your text will be set and count the number of letters and spaces on the line.
3. Measure the number of lines on the sample that fill one inch in depth.
4. Now count your typewritten copy. Count characters in one line and multiply by number of lines as a shortcut.
5. Divide the answer in (4) by the answer in (2).
6. Divide the answer in (5) by the answer in (3) to determine approximately how many inches in depth your typeset copy will fill.

To check your headline, just count the number of letters and spaces in the longest line of your headline and compare that to a sample of the actual type.

CHAPTER 9

Writing for Radio

Radio offers a format for every listener as well as every advertiser: country, adult contemporary, news-talk-sports-business, oldies, religion, adult standards, Spanish language, soft adult contemporary, rock, classic rock, ethnic, classical, jazz and new age, and more.

Radio is everywhere. At home, in cars, at places of business. And radio reaches everyone from teens to the over-50 group. Radio is the niche medium of broadcasting. While television, as we shall see in chapter 10, is rapidly becoming a segmented medium, radio has held this distinction almost since the birth of TV in the late 1940s. Radio is a great stand-alone medium, or a great support for other media. Airing commercials for its Bubble Jet printer on radio allowed Canon USA to create awareness among a specific audience, the ones ready to buy a printer. Spots were aired in thirteen large markets on news/talk, sports, and classical formats. In each market, radio was supported by newspaper ads on the "best computer day," including a Tuesday "Science Times" section in one market and a Monday business section in another.

Snapple Natural Beverages claims it chose radio because of its ability to really target a specific market, along with its cost-effectiveness and the power of radio personalities to move product.

Leading advertisers find spot, or local, radio an effective way to target and localize their advertising dollars, advertisers such as Philip Morris, Anheuser-Busch, K-Mart, General Motors, PepsiCo, and Delta Air Lines.

And what do commercial radio writers love about this medium? One calls writing for radio a unique adventure that transcends the limitations and the costliness of the camera lens and the shooting schedule. Others say radio is "a lot sexier than sex" and must touch the heart to work effectively. Seasoned radio writers will remind you that radio is a visual medium, in which audiences see whatever the writer can make them see. The better the writer knows radio, the more the audience will see. To help them see more, consider providing a location for your radio spot. You could do that by simply having a voice say,

"It's lovely here in Tahiti" or "Jail sure ain't fun." Or use sounds to provide the location: waves crashing on craggy rocks, the crow of sea gulls, stalled traffic in New York City with a few well-chosen taxi driver groans thrown in for good measure. Music can make the location clear, as in the oompah-pah of a Bavarian band, the stirring finale of the *1812* Overture by Tchaikovsky, or Scottish bagpipes. Even a voice can provide a location, whether it's an exaggerated Southern drawl, a West Indies clipped English, or a New England twang.

To begin thinking about your radio commercial, think about the one big idea you need to communicate. In sixty or thirty seconds, you cannot expect listeners to remember a series of benefits. They can't go back and re-read what interests them as they can in a newspaper or magazine, so take your big idea and play it for all it's worth for the length of the commercial.

Think of the voice or voices that can best command the attention of your audience. Not specific personalities, but voice types: skeptical young woman, trustworthy old woman, genius child, conservative Vermonter, gushy Southern belle, thickheaded cave man, etc.

Think of sounds and music. Or no sounds. And no music. Sound effects should be used to further the message, not as ends in themselves. They should not be used in an attempt to duplicate reality; there is little purpose in calling for the sound of footsteps unless they have a purpose in the commercial. Sounds which do not imitate life may be more compelling; a public service announcement on child abuse uses the violent sound of doors slamming as the voice talks about how some people hide such abuse behind closed doors. A spot urging older people to remain active uses a constant background of rocking chairs squeaking on a wooden porch as the voice tells listeners to do quite the opposite. Be aware that sounds can save words and dramatize situations.

Don't be afraid to use music. Or to leave it out. If the tune has a life of its own, it may detract from what you are trying to say. Frequently, silence can be more powerful than sound, as long as it doesn't overstay its welcome. On the other hand, music can enhance a mood, but never plug it in for its own sake. And remember that obtaining commercial rights to use copyrighted music and music performances can be extremely costly.

Begin with something relevant yet unexpected to gain the listener's attention. End with something as memorable to drive home your point. Since you can't see the product on radio, be certain its name is mentioned several times in the copy, but never so intrusively that it smacks of "commercialism."

The Writer as Key Decision Maker

In radio advertising, the writer is the key decision maker more than in any other advertising medium. Production budgets tend to be comparatively low; there is no need to choose type styles or layout formats. And radio invites your imagination to run free. In fact, if you don't choose unusual techniques to break through the typical listening habits of the radio audience, they won't hear you. The happy truth is that you can easily afford to be unusual because radio audiences want to be entertained and production costs tend to be reasonable.

The Theater of the Mind

Try for a moment to think of a radio commercial you consider great. Chances are that it wasn't one of those read by a local announcer who had to rush through the copy because someone wrote too many words for the time slot. Chances are that it was a commercial that used humor, pathos, music, or intrusive sound effects as it extolled the brand name and major selling proposition. Radio has been called "the theater of the mind," and anyone who grew up in the 1930s and 1940s fully understands the meaning of this expression. In those days, without television to furnish pictures, radio writers worked hard to deliver visual impressions through the sounds emanating from the big family set, and they did it! Today you must create the same kind of cerebral pictures to be certain your radio commercial overcomes the indifferent listening habits of many radio listeners.

The radio commercial that arrives at the station on tape, ready to air, is called a "produced" or "taped" commercial. But not all radio commercials are prerecorded. Some are sent in script form to the station, where they are either read live on the air or recorded by a staff announcer. Other advertisers send no script at all; instead they furnish a fact sheet that describes the major selling points and benefits of their product or service. Before discussing the produced commercial, let's first look at all forms of radio commercials and the advantages and shortcomings of each.

The Fact Sheet

A fact sheet works best when a particular radio station has a popular on-air personality. Quite often the informal chatter of such an individual is more spellbinding to listeners than the most lavishly produced commercial. If you can send a fact sheet to someone like this, with facts numbered in descending order of importance, your announcer will not only work hard to promote what you are selling but may also go over the time limit, giving you two or more minutes of "sell" for the one minute you purchased.

Clearly, a fact sheet is only as good as the individual who uses it. Don't rely on it in markets or on stations where you cannot rely on the announcer to do your message justice without the benefit of a script.

The Live Script

Instead of furnishing a fact sheet, some local advertisers will send instead a typewritten copy of a script. These commercials are usually composed of straight announcer copy. The inclusion of sound effects, music, or additional speaking parts would require studio production.

The live script is advantageous to the local retailer who must get a message on the air in a matter of hours, which is another advantage of radio as an advertising medium.

The disadvantage of a live script is that, as the writer, you exercise virtually no control over the way your spot will be aired. It may help to underscore words for emphasis and to offer pronunciation guides for unusual names, but that's about the extent of your control.

The Combination Live-Taped Commercial

When a company has invested in an identifying sound or musical jingle, it should use it as often as possible to trigger recall of its name and to justify the initial cost. A popular format for many local and national advertisers who use musical signatures is the donut commercial. The advertiser produces a musical tape with or without singers, and in the middle portion of the tape, the music "fades under" or is reduced in volume to allow for insertion of live copy by the local station.

Since the middle of the spot contains this hole, the format is called a "live donut." Usually the advertiser will include with the tape a script which indicates the entire format of the spot and notes when the hole begins and ends. Along with the script, the advertiser furnishes live donut copy for the station announcer to read over the taped music. By substituting several different pieces of live donut copy, the advertiser maximizes the initial investment in the musical background, or bed. While the music gives the campaign a continuity it should have, the various live copy inserts work to keep the advertiser's message timely.

Local franchise owners use the donut format to insert messages tailored specifically to their markets and to provide timely information on special promotions. It is important not to overwrite such copy; once the donut ends, the music returns to full volume, drowning out everything else.

The Produced Commercial

The bulk of national radio commercials and a growing number of local commercials come to the station already produced on tape and ready to be aired. You can understand why so many advertisers prefer this approach. Like a print ad that arrives set in type, the produced radio commercial allows little room for human error once it arrives at the station. Many such commercials are designed to run five seconds short of the time purchased to give the local announcer time to add a "live local tag" (where to buy the product, sale dates, and so on). Copy for the tag should be included in script form with the produced tape.

Writing Effectively for Radio

At least three ingredients are essential for the making of an effective radio commercial: a good writer—one who understands the power of radio—to write an effective and original script; a client who grants the writer the freedom to do so; and a production company that can create a finished commercial, or "spot," using the right combination of performers, music, and sounds. In radio as in television, it isn't a commercial until it's produced.

During production, the writer should be present to review script adjustments and to work with the producer on ways to enhance the recording. Not surprisingly, some of the most memorable ingredients of a good script emerge during the production session.

Peter Hochstein of Ogilvy & Mather offers these ten rules for making better radio commercials.[1]

1. ***Identify your sound effects.*** Unless you do so, you may confuse your listener, or the sound effect may be barely noticed. The sound of rain falling in a forest is the same as bacon sizzling. Tell listeners what they're hearing, and they'll be more likely to hear it.

2. ***Use music as a sound effect.*** A brokerage house created an image of financial power with the same sounds of kettledrums Prokofiev used in *Peter and the Wolf* to conjure up hunters. Another commercial depicted a German neighborhood by playing a few bars of oompah band music.

3. ***Build your commercial around a sound:*** the sound of a crisp new cracker, for example, or thunder to represent the power of a solid bank account, or the reactions people have when food sizzles in hot margarine.

4. ***Give yourself time.*** Fight for sixty-second spots. It is often impossible to establish your sound effects in thirty seconds and still relate them to product benefits. You need time in radio to set up a scene and establish a premise.

5. ***Consider using no sound effect.*** A distinctive voice, or a powerful message straightforwardly spoken, can be more effective than noises from the tape library. People love to hear a good story. Can you spin a compelling yarn about your product and just let someone narrate it?

[1] Peter Hochstein, "Ten Rules for Making Better Radio Commercials," *Viewpoint III* (1981). Used by permission of Ogilvy & Mather, New York.

6. ***Beware of comedy.*** It's rare when you can sit down at your typewriter and match the skill of the best comedians. On the other hand, well-written and relevant humor can be a powerful advertising technique.

7. ***If you insist on being funny, begin with an outrageous premise.*** The customers at the film store are goblins who want to take their own Halloween pictures. Lake Michigan will be drained of water and refilled with whipped cream. A man puts on his wife's nightgown at 4 A.M. and goes out to purchase *Time* magazine—and the cops catch him. The premises may have been weird, but the events that grew out of them were perfectly rational under the circumstances.

8. ***Keep it simple.*** Radio is a wonderful medium for building brand awareness. It's a poor medium for registering long lists of copy points or making complex arguments. What one thing is most important about your product? That's what your commercial should spend sixty seconds talking about.

9. ***Tailor your commercial to time, place, specific audience.*** If it is running in Milwaukee, you can tailor it for Milwaukee. You can talk in the lingo of the people who will be listening and to the time of day in which your commercial will be broadcast. Talk about breakfast at the breakfast hour or offer a commuter taxi service during rush hour.

10. ***Present your commercial to your client on tape, if possible.*** Most radio scripts look boring on paper. Acting, timing, vocal quirks, and sound effects make them come alive. If you can possibly produce a commercial before presenting it to your client, it will be easier to sell. Happily, studio time and demo fees aren't nearly as costly as television production costs.

How Radio Evokes Pictures

Although you are writing for the ear alone, you must work hard to make those sounds transmit visual impressions to the brain as well. A good script works hard to help the listeners identify with the speakers and to see what they look like, how they're dressed, and where they're standing or sitting.

For example, a commercial for Aztec suntan lotion does this quickly and vividly by using a character called the Aztec Sun God. This character doesn't talk the way you might imagine a sun god would, but more as an ordinary fellow would. As he converses with a store manager, he mentions that most people don't recognize him in his corduroy suit and wing-tip shoes. Instantly we visualize two men in the store and feel the obvious agitation of the manager as the sun god begins to remove his clothes to show off his tanned body to the customers. It's not only funny and involving, but the ad also sticks closely to its main selling point: Aztec suntan lotion can make your body look like a sun god's body.

To help a listener see the product, you might describe the package as "blue and white with an easy-open top." In another commercial, the listener might even hear someone opening a can of coffee. With the "whoosh" of the vacuum seal, perhaps listeners will practically smell the aroma of freshly opened coffee as it wafts into the room.

To help your listener remember what you are selling, you must mention the name of the product frequently. Remember, there are no visuals to rely on here. An average of three mentions in a thirty-second commercial and five mentions in a sixty-second commercial may not be too frequent, as long as the repetition is not done in a forced and annoying manner. And since the last thing listeners hear is what they tend to remember longest, you want to mention the key selling idea and the brand name at the close of the commercial.

Voices, Music, Sounds

Radio offers the writer three basic tools: the human voice, music, and sound effects. Be sure to make full use of them as situations warrant. Characters on radio don't have to say they dropped the dishes—all we need to hear is a clatter of broken china followed by a groan. A bit of Hawaiian music can take us halfway around the world at minimal cost without mincing words.

Proper casting can offer clues about the type of person who would use the product being offered. In writing for radio, you have many more choices than the authoritative voice of the typical announcer. For a cake mix, there's always a grandma. To promote a new bank service, perhaps there's potential in a whining voice complaining that nothing new ever happens at the bank. The absence of pictures demands that the voices you choose help listeners "see" the characters in your commercial.

What about music? Not all radio commercials need or should have music. In fact, a moment without music on the radio may be the best way to gain audience attention. Music can be anything from a complete jingle with or without lyrics to incidental background music used to set a scene, identify some part of the country or the world, or create a mood.

A few seconds of music at the beginning of a commercial is one way to tell the audience to listen. Then the music can softly fade under the dialogue to form a backdrop to the words and action up front.

Not all music is yours for the asking. Any performance by a famous artist, as well as any song written during your lifetime, is heavily protected under copyright laws. To secure permission to use such songs, arrangements, or performances can cost a good deal of money, and such rights are usually for a limited time only. You can get by for far less money by finding music in the public domain or by using original music that you have commissioned especially for this advertising campaign. Several music companies offer public domain (PD) music for a small fee, and most radio stations have libraries of PD selections on disc or tape for the convenience of local advertisers.

As for sound effects, when everything in an advertisement is coming at you through your ears, why not use things such as crowd shouts or cheers, train whistles, barking dogs, slamming doors, and the hundreds of other familiar sounds of life that can make a situation all the more believable and vivid? As with anything else, restraint is a good rule of thumb with sound effects. Use only those you need, unless your purpose is to bombard the listener with sounds.

How Many Words?

As a rule of thumb, about two words a second is average for a well-paced commercial. You can go as high as 135 words in a sixty-second commercial and 75 words in a thirty-second commercial. If you exceed these limits, chances are your speaker will have to rush through the copy with little or no time for those pauses and special inflections that add color and clarity to the spoken word.

Rushing through copy can also have an unnerving effect on the listener. Of course, some speakers naturally tend to read more swiftly than others. In production, you may have to tailor your copy to the speaker. It's wise to premark cuts or additions on your copy of the script before you begin the production session.

Give Adequate Directions

In writing your copy, it is helpful to describe the way you want the lines read. You might call for anger, sarcasm, or humor. You might also want to describe in general terms the sort of voice you have in mind: elderly woman, crotchety old man, Viennese baker, valley girl, Teutonic warrior. Then let the actor do a reading and see if you agree on the inflection.

Using Humor in Radio

You probably already know that humor is one of the most popular devices in radio commercials today. Humor is difficult to write. Good humor has a universal appeal and is not confined to some local in-joke of the moment that will make no sense at all to the majority of listeners. Humor is elusive, and it pays to try out your funny thoughts on others before determining whether they are right for your advertising.

Some of the funniest and most effective commercials in radio history have come from the former team of Dick Orkin and Bert Berdis. Before writing a commercial, Dick and Bert would ask themselves these questions:

1. ***Does the spot relate to human experience?*** If they can get the listener to say, "Hey, that's me. I know what's going on with that character," they've got the listener hooked.

2. ***Is it really funny?*** A funny voice doesn't make a spot funny. What makes a spot funny is a real voice saying funny things or reacting to a funny premise.

3. ***Does the comedy sell the product?*** If the product is hidden by the comedy, the commercial has flopped. It's a sure sign of failure when the listener laughs but can't remember what the product was.

4. ***Does the spot treat the product with respect?*** Rather than making fun of the product, a humorous commercial should have fun with the product.

5. ***Does the spot appeal to the right group?*** Know your audience, its tastes, its aspirations, and its particular sense of humor.

6. ***Is the spot honest?*** If the product is in a parity situation with other competing products that are very good, try to find a point of difference and make a comic

situation out of it. With Rockwell minicalculators, the only difference was their large green-colored digits and rubber footpads, so Dick and Bert developed a music track with the lyrics "We've got big green numbers and little rubber feet."

7. ***Does the campaign have variety?*** A comedy spot can become familiar very quickly, so it's important to keep the impact strong by developing several spots for the campaign.

8. ***Is it simple and direct?*** A commercial that tries to do too much is confusing. A good spot must capture attention, maintain concentration, develop and resolve the concept, and also sell the product.[2]

A Guide to Radio Commercial Formats

1. ***One Voice:*** A voice which is both interesting and relevant. The words must be exceptional. If you choose to make the spot this simple, it should contain a powerful message delivered by a compelling voice. If this is the case, you'll really break through the clutter. If not, better stay away from this format.

2. ***Dialogue:*** Usually two voices in back-and-forth conversation. The danger of using this approach is that it's too easy to put dull phrases into the mouths of boring people, or, worse yet, to put decidedly pointed selling pitches into the mouths of "ordinary folks" (as in "Doris, this new detergent has a water-soluble bleaching agent which seeps through dirt to render fabrics brighter than ever!" instead of, "Doris, there must be something to this new kind of bleach in Whoosh because this stuff really gets my clothes bright and clean"). No ordinary person should be forced to make a set-up pitch for the product. To get around this, try using an announcer. The announcer can break into the conversation, give the pitch, then return us to our chatting folks. Or the announcer can speak at the very end, or in both places.

3. ***Multi-Voice:*** In this situation, a number of voices speak to the listener, rather than to one another in a variation of the "one voice" approach. When a number of voices speak for the product, the listener may infer that there must be something to all that talk after all.

4. ***Dramatization:*** Uses the structure of a play to make a point. Dialogue is written to incorporate a conflict and its resolution.

5. ***Sound Device:*** A sound—or sounds—is used repeatedly to make the point and becomes a focal point of the spot.

6. ***Vignette:*** A series of short situations linked by a repeated device, such as an announcer, a musical refrain, or a sound effect. Toward the end, the announcer usually delivers the key selling message, and is followed by a closing vignette.

[2] Hooper White, "Radio Advertising: It's a Low-Cost Powerful Sell with a New Lease on Life." Reprinted with permission from the September 1977 issue of *Advertising Age*. Copyright 1977 by Crain Communications, Inc.

7. ***Man or Woman Interviewer:*** Someone is interviewing someone, or groups of people, somewhere—on a busy street, at the top of the world, in outer space, or under a house in a Terminix spot where the interviewer is talking to two termites as they literally eat a homeowner out of house and home.

Examples of Good Radio

The casual mood you should aim for in radio copy is well illustrated in the following scripts. Read them silently, then aloud, creating the character's voices as you think they should sound. Then ask yourself what makes these commercials work and check your reasons against the "radio copy checklist" near the end of the chapter. The first spot is for Ricoh cameras and was written by Jackie End of Chiat/Day, New York, and produced by Pat Faw at Doppler Recording, Atlanta:

ANNCR: A couple of weeks ago I bought myself a Ricoh 35mm Auto Focus camera. And I take out the instruction folder and it says, "It's the camera that thinks." So I think about this, you know; and I realize it's true. When you're taking a picture with a Ricoh, it's thinking about the right exposure; it's thinking about the right focus, thinking about the film speed. It's thinking about all the things that give you a terrific picture.

But let me ask you this. What do you think a Ricoh camera thinks about when it isn't taking pictures? Does it wonder if you're gonna keep it for yourself or give it away for Christmas? Does it believe in Santa Claus? Does it think you believe in Santa Claus? Do you? When it thinks, does it think in Japanese? Does it dream? And, if so, does it dream in color or black and white? Or does that depend on the film you're using? Does it worry about being dropped? I would. Does it think you've got a screw loose thinking about all this? Think about it. . . .

The following commercial for Hormel's Less Salt Spam was written and produced by Steve Kahn of BBDO, Minneapolis, at Voiceworks, Minneapolis:

SFX: DRUM ROLL.

ANNCR: In 1985, an old American soft drink changed its formula.

SFX: FANFARE STARTS, THEN WINDS DOWN TO A STOP.

ANNCR: You were not amused.

SFX: DRUM ROLL.

ANNCR: Now, in 1986, another American favorite has changed its formula.

SFX: FANFARE AND DRUM ROLL.

ANNCR: Introducing Less Salt Spam, with 25% less salt, 25% less sodium. Taste tests prove that Less Salt Spam luncheon meat tastes great. But just in case you're not amused . . .

SFX: DRUM ROLL STOPS.

ANNCR: . . . we still have classic Spam.

SFX: PARTY HORN.

Try this one from TBWA, New York, written for Carlsberg beer by Jeff Epstein and produced by Ed Pollack at 12 East Recording, New York:

SHE: Honey?

HE: Yes, Precious.

SHE: I have a confession, Dearest.

HE: What, Buttercup?

SHE: You know the clock in the hall?

HE: The 17th-century fruitwood grandfather clock?

SHE: I knocked it over.

HE: Not to worry, Lambykins.

SHE: Oh, Porkchop, you're so understanding.

HE: It's only money.

SHE: Sweet Pea?

HE: Yes.

SHE: You know the rug in the den?

HE: The leopard skin throw in my study?

SHE: Well, when I shampooed it, the spots came out.

HE: Don't worry your pretty little head.

SHE: I'm so relieved.

HE: What's mine is yours.

SHE: Cream Puff?

HE: Yes, Marshmallow?

SHE: You know those cigars in the fridge?

HE: The hand-rolled Hondurans?

SHE: They got wet.

HE: Pray tell how, Carrot Stick?

SHE: Well, when I moved the Carlsberg beer in the . . .

HE: (interrupting) I told you not to touch my Carlsberg.

SHE: Cucumber.

HE: Just have your lawyer call my lawyer in the morning . . . Sugar . . . Plum.

ANNCR: Carlsberg beer. The imported taste that can't be touched. Carlsberg Breweries, Copenhagen, Denmark.

And finally, note how this spot for Canon typewriters from Grey Advertising, written by Jim Morrisey and produced by Bert, Barz, & Kirby, Hollywood, California, not only entertains and sells, but also reminds writers to steer clear of that lowliest of devices, the deadly cliché:

ANNCR: And now, Canon electronic typewriters present another Canon success story . . .

KIRBY: Welcome to the National Cliché Advisory Board.

BARZ: What do you do here?

KIRBY: Encourage the use of trite, hackneyed expressions in everyday speech.

BARZ: I see.

KIRBY: Our motto is, "Clichés—they're good as gold."

BARZ: So you're busy as a bee.

KIRBY: Right. But before we got our Canon AP-300 electronic typewriters, we were up the creek without a paddle.

BARZ: Yes.

KIRBY: Now we're happy as a pig in . . .

BARZ: Why's that?

KIRBY: Well, the Canon AP-300 has this phrase memory—it stores more clichés than there's tea in China.

BARZ: And it displays them right here on the optional CRT screen.

KIRBY: And there's automatic centering, bold print, underlining, and more.

They make typing a snap.

BARZ: Or a breeze.

KIRBY: Oh, let me make a note of that.

BARZ: So you'd say that Canon electronic typewriters are . . .

KIRBY: Let's hit the Canon phrase memory for an appropriate cliché.

SFX: TYPING.

BARZ: Canon—worth their weight in gold.

KIRBY: Canon—the greatest thing since sliced bread.

BARZ: Canon—gathers no moss!

KIRBY: Gathers no moss?

BARZ: Canon—a full line of electronic typewriters for every typing need. Serviced by over 600 dealers nationwide. They're in the yellow pages.

KIRBY: Uh—that should read, "Gathers no mice."

BARZ: Mice.

ANNCR: Canon—how successful companies type.

Radio Script Format

Like all copy, a radio script begins with a tag in the upper left-hand corner (Figure 9–1). In this instance, you should indicate on the second line, after timing, whether the spot is a fact sheet, live announcer copy, or is to be produced.

Notice the designation for a sound effect: *SFX*. This is capitalized and underscored, along with the entire sound-effect direction, to alert the producer to the effect and its position within the script. For this reason, too, all effects are also entered on a separate line. If the effect should come in the middle of a line of dialogue, use ellipses (. . .) to break from the first part of the line, drop to a new line for the *SFX*, then continue the dialogue on the following line with additional ellipses at the beginning to indicate resumption of the dialogue. All radio copy should be double-spaced to facilitate reading and leave room for notes and alterations during production. Names of speakers should be typed in capital letters and followed by a colon. Any directions to the speaker should be enclosed in parentheses after the speaker's name.

Music is simply another type of sound effect and should be treated as such. If a commercial is to begin with music, which is then to fade under the speakers (play softly in the background), a direction might read like this:

SFX: HARP INSTRUMENTAL (5 SEC) AND FADE UNDER

TIM: Sometimes late at night, when you wish you could talk to a special voice far away, it's nice to know long distance rates are lower after 11 p.m.

K2R SPOT LIFTER
:60 radio (for production)
"Dry Cleaner"

SFX: NOISES OF A CROWD IN A SHOP FADE UNDER.

DRY CLEANER: Okay, ladies. Get to you all in a minute. Just put your dry cleaning up here on the counter.

MARGE: Mr. Peabody, can you get this dress really clean for me?

DRY CLEANER: Sure. That's a job for a dry cleaner.

ETHEL: I need this spot out by tomorrow . . . please.

DRY CLEANER: What? Just a spot? Why bring me one little spot to clean? Haven't you ever heard of K2R Spot Lifter? K2R spot lifter is so easy. Just spray it on like this . . .

SFX: Spray.

DRY CLEANER: . . . wait a few minutes till it dries and brush it off. K2R lifts the spot clean out.

ETHEL: You mean it's that easy?

DRY CLEANER: That easy. See? No spot, no nothing. Hey ladies . . .

SFX: SOUND OF FEET SCURRYING AWAY, TRAILING INTO DISTANCE.

DRY CLEANER (becoming exasperated): . . . where are you going?

MARGE: Out to get K2R Spot Lifter. Thanks, Mr. Peabody.

DRY CLEANER: (now really upset): Oh my gosh . . .

ANNCR: K2R Spot Lifter from Texize. The home dry cleaner that works anywhere. And saves you a trip to the cleaners.

DRY CLEANER: Watch that!

ANNCR: Get K2R Spot Lifter and get rid of that spot.

FIGURE 9-1

Radio script format. Remember to double-space and to enter sound effects on separate lines.

If the music is to disappear at some point, you should indicate this through another sound-effect cue.

SFX: MUSIC OUT.

TIM: Because when you can pick up the phone . . .

SFX: CLICK OF RECEIVER.

TIM: . . . and dial your favorite person thousands of miles away. . . .

Quite often, especially if your commercial consists of a conversation between two or more people, you may want to wrap up the message by bringing in an authoritative announcer (ANNCR) at the very end. This is a good way to bring your audience back to earth, especially if you have been treating the subject with humor, and to remind your audience what you want them to remember about your message.

Radio Copy Checklist

1. ***Concept:*** The major premise of this commercial is ______________________

   ____

   ______ a. The commercial works to communicate the major premise effectively by emphasizing it throughout the copy.

   ______ b. One hears the major premise early in the commercial, again in the middle, once more at the end.

2. ***Format and Tone:*** The format used is ______________________

   ______ a. The chosen format works well to enhance the major selling premise.

   ______ b. The tone of the commercial (serious, humorous, heavy, light, and so on) is suited to the major selling premise.

   ______ c. The tone and format will not be offensive, confusing, or foreign to the target audience.

3. ***Voices and Music***

   ______ a. Voices are adequately described.

   ______ b. Voices complement the product, the selling message, and the concept of the commercial.

   ______ c. Music is described precisely.

   ______ d. No copyrighted music or performance is called for unless it is essential and cost and availability have been determined.

   ______ e. Where music is used, it does not intrude on the spoken word so as to irritate the listener or drown out the selling message.

   ______ f. Music is congruous with the message.

4. ***Timing and Pace***

   ______ a. Sufficient time is allowed for easy delivery of the message.

   ______ b. Sufficient time is allowed for all sound effects and musical bridges.

_______ c. Sufficient time is allowed for emphasis, inflection, pauses.

_______ d. Commercial times correctly.

5. ***Brand Awareness Is Achieved***

_______ a. Through repeated mention of the brand name.

_______ b. Through description of the packaging.

_______ c. Through special music or sounds that trigger the brand image or are linked with the brand name.

Radio is fun and challenging at the same time. As with all advertising copy, it isn't always easy to find the best solution. But when you hear your commercial in finished form, you'll know if it's right. A well-written lovingly produced radio spot can make a tremendous impact on its target audience.

Suggested Activities

- 1. Using the campaign theme from your print ads, write a radio commercial for the same product or service. Write it as if it were to be produced. Note as you are doing this that merely paraphrasing the text from a print ad does not always work because of the essential differences between the media. What sort of voices will work best for your message? What will be the appropriate tone? These are but a few of the new points you will be considering.
- 2. Visit a local business establishment and interview the person in charge. Devise a creative strategy for this business, indicating how radio might be used. Cover approaches, audience, mood of commercials, and expected results. Then write two or three radio commercials based on your strategy and tie them together by using a specific unifying theme or device.
- 3. For the next week, make it a point to listen to a different radio station every day. Make mental notes of the types of commercials you hear on each station. What did you learn?

Writing for an Apathetic Audience

Ed Chambliss,
Copywriter

BBDO South,
Atlanta, Georgia

It is the disease of not listening, the malady of not marking, that I am troubled withal.

—*William Shakespeare,* King Henry the Fourth, Part II

How do you talk to someone who won't listen?

I think Shakespeare hinted at the best solution in *The Tempest* when Miranda, daughter of the Duke of Milan, commented, "Your tale, sir, would cure deafness."

When it comes to writing radio commercials, you really do have to cure "deafness" in your listeners. Your "tale" has to be so fascinating that they have no choice but to listen. Sounds simple.

But look at all you have to deal with.

First, most listeners are about as interested in your commercial as you are in reading a textbook on Friday night. Even this textbook.

They've got other things on their mind. Whether the left lane of traffic is moving any faster than the one they're in now. Or which earrings go better with the black dress, the gold hoops or the diamond studs.

So what you have to do is entertain them, inform them, do whatever it takes to catch their interest. You have to reach out, grab them by the ears, and yell, "Hey! Listen to me!"

If you do catch their attention during the first seconds of the commercial, you have to keep their attention for the rest of the spot while you get your client's message across. How many radio commercials have you heard that started off great, then lost your interest as they deteriorated into someone reading a laundry list of what the product could do for you?

The secret to keeping the listener's interest is *weaving* the copy points into the spot, instead of just *dropping* them in out of the blue every now and then. Like threads in a fabric, they should be an integral part of the story you're telling. And just like a piece of fabric, if you take them away, the commercial should fall apart.

That way, when your listeners think about even a small part of your spot, they'll automatically remember the copy points as they remember the rest of your story.

Another thing you have to deal with is that many of your listeners may already have heard your commercial before. Now you have to entice them back to listen to it again. Psychologists tell us some people have to hear something as many as sixteen times before they remember it.

BBDO
SOUTH

Radio Script
(As Recorded)

Client Delta Air Lines City Various Spot No. 5710

Date 10/30/90 Job No. DLA SPO R0 3364 Type Sports Length :60

This Spot effective ______ It replaces Spot ______ Remarks: Vacation-javelin

SFX: HAWAIIAN BEACH SOUNDS- WAVES, WIND, THE OCCASIONAL TROPICAL BIRD.

PHIL: Hi there, I'm Phil Singer, baking in the Hawaiian sun for SportsQuest. Today we're on Mahakuloa Beach with Javelin Catcher Robert Rigsbee.

SFX: JAVELIN SWISHING IN THE AIR. BOB GRUNTING. JAVELIN BEING CAUGHT. BOB HITTING SAND.

BOB (lounge lizard): Hey, (SFX: FINGER SNAP) Call me Bob.

PHIL: Alright... Bob. Tell me, why javelin catching?

BOB: Well Phil, anybody can throw a javelin, but it takes a *real* man to catch a javelin. (to the side) Right ladies?

LADIES: Buzz off.

BOB: (obliviously happy) See?

PHIL: Uh-huh. So you're spending your vacation catching javelins in Hawaii.

So how do you get someone to listen to your commercial more than once?

Think about a cult movie you really like. If you're like most people, you've seen that movie possibly a dozen times. Why? Because it keeps on entertaining you. The same holds true for radio commercials. If you can make your commercials entertaining enough or interesting enough, people will keep listening to them.

One way to make a commercial interesting is to be absolutely outrageous with your premise. Like draining Lake Michigan and filling it with your client's brand of whipped cream. But an outrageous premise is only the beginning.

Another reason people keep watching the same movie over and over is because they keep seeing new things every time they watch it. The same attention to little details layered in the script can add dozens of listenings to your commercial. A weird sound effect here, a short comment by one of the voices there, and every time your listeners "perform" your commercial in the theaters of their minds, they'll "see" something new. And keep coming back for more.

SFX:	JAVELIN FLYING IN AIR. BOB GRUNTS. JAVELIN BEING CAUGHT. BOB HITTING SAND.
BOB:	Yep, caught a Delta flight from the mainland this morning.
PHIL:	Well, with service to some of the world's great vacation spots, I can see why you'd fly Delta.
BOB:	Catch some javelins, then catch some rays, that's what I say!
SFX:	JAVELIN FLYING IN AIR. BOB GRUNTS. BOB HITTING SAND. RAFT DEFLATING.
LADY:	HEY!
BOB:	Sorry about your raft. (SFX: FACE SLAP) Let me buy you a drink...
PHIL:	(sigh) Well folks, the next time you're headed on vacation, fly Delta. To hundreds of great vacations in California, Florida, the Rockies, Mexico, Europe, Asia or even Hawaii. For reservations, see your Travel Agent or call Delta.
BOB:	Check out this catch...
SFX:	JAVELIN FLYING IN. BOB GRUNTS. JAVELIN HITTING BOB.
BOB:	Ow!
PHIL:	(suddenly happy) And what happens if Bob misses?
LADIES:	Shishka-Bob!!
SFX:	LADIES CHEERING AND CLAPPING.
PHIL:	(to Bob) You know, that looks really painful...

Take, for example, these Delta Air Lines spots.

We were asked to create a radio campaign to run during the huge amount of time Delta had bought during sporting events. The cold demographic information told us that our target audience was mainly men, ages 25–54. What it didn't tell us was how attentive these 25- to 54-year-old men would be.

You think about it. How attentive do you think a bunch of those guys would be, sitting around, sucking down suds with their buddies while listening to their favorite team? You guessed it: Not very.

Add the fact that these guys could end up hearing the same Delta Air Lines spots dozens of times over the course of a single weekend. All of a sudden, instead of an easy assignment, I found a tremendous challenge sitting on my desk. How do I get through to these guys and tell hem how wonderful Delta is in solving their travel needs?

BBDO
SOUTH

Radio Script
(As Recorded)

Client Delta Air Lines City Various Spot No. 5730

Date 10/30/90 Job No. DLA SPO R0 3364 Type Sports Length :60

This Spot effective ______ It replaces Spot ______ Remarks: Business--Chess

SFX: CROWD AMBIENCE.

PHIL: Hi again. This is Phil Singer, with another installment of SportsQuest.

WILLIS (super-jock): (shouting to team) JAM HIM!!!

PHIL: Today we're in Bozeman, Montana with Willis Price, captain of the U.S. Full-Contact Chess Team.

WILLIS: (shouting to team) KNIGHT JUMPS ROOK!

SFX: SWORD CLANGS. GRUNT, AND COLLISION OF MAN JUMPING AND TACKLING ANOTHER MAN.

PHIL: Ohh, looks like a tough game, Willis.

WILLIS: Oh, It's tough, all right. Just like today's business world. What with the harsh realities of territories, helpless pawns, hostile takeovers...(to field) BOOM!

SFX: YET ANOTHER BONE-SPLINTERING HIT.

PHIL: So you see yourselves as businessmen.

WILLIS: Sure. And like any smart businessmen, we fly Delta Air Lines.

PHIL: Well, with a record of passenger satisfaction unbeaten among the largest U.S. airlines for sixteen straight years, I can see why.

WILLIS: Right. Delta makes it easy for anyone to get to their next...board meeting.

PHIL: You heard it here folks. The next time you fly on business, fly Delta. The official airline of the U.S. Full-Contact Chess Team.

SFX: TACKLE.

WILLIS: (to field) Nice work Mongo!

PHIL: Not to mention a lot of other smart business players. For reservations, see your Travel Agent, or call Delta.

SFX: LOUD TACKLE WITH SWORD CLANGS.

I started by identifying with them in the premise. What could guys like more during a break in a sporting event than more sports? So we concocted a gullible interviewer, Phil Singer, and an outrageous sports interview show, SportsQuest, and went out looking for the "stars" of some pretty weird, wacky, and completely made-up sports.

Read the spots and see how they overcome the problem I mentioned. First, they start with an ear-grabbing combination of sound effects and visual descriptions. Then, the concepts are introduced in the same humorous vein to keep the listeners listening. Finally (even though you can't tell from the printed scripts), the production team layered lots of detailed sound effects and comments into the final taping to keep listeners involved each time they heard the spots.

See how easy it is to cure deafness? Just remember the three things you have to overcome and your audience won't be apathetic. They'll be all ears.

Author's Note

Ed Chambliss earned his B.A. in journalism and mass communications from the University of South Carolina. While there, he worked on the AAF national student advertising competition, was active in the student advertising club, and wrote a lot of good—and often wildly humorous—copy for his advertising classes.

FOLLOW-UP

As Ed Chambliss points out so clearly, no one is eagerly waiting to hear your radio commercial, to see your TV spot, or to read your print ads. You have to do something to make them want to engage themselves, and that meant you need to entertain in some fashion—through humor, through drama, through some spark that touches the emotions. You also have to remember that this is advertising, not fiction writing or moviemaking, and that means you also have to persuade them to believe in your selling message. How well do you think the Delta Air Lines radio campaign achieved these goals? Could you write another spot to go with those included here?

Most local retail businesses may seem dull at first, but if you learn all you can about them—and about their customers—it will help you write effective radio to bring customers in. Make it a point to contact a local store owner and see if he or she will spend time discussing details of the business. Write at least three sixty-second radio spots and present them. Who knows? You might wind up on the air.

CHAPTER 10

Writing for Television

Computers, telephones, and cable are changing the face of television as we know it, and there will be more changes by the time you read this chapter.

In this new era of interactive communications, cable TV, telephone companies, and computer companies are in the battle for dominance in this age of interactive TV. Cable TV and phone companies are competing to build interactive electronic superhighways that will deliver movies on demand, home shopping, video phones, and hundreds of other services. Until now, two "networks" have gone into homes: phone and cable. In the future only one may be necessary. The real question is, which one will survive?

One company, for example, announced plans for a national rollout of a system that will offer news and information, interactive advertising and, potentially, coupon printers in consumers' homes. Another company not only allows viewers to perform banking chores and order pizza, groceries, flowers, magazine subscriptions, and liquor, but also offers interactive entertainment and lets viewers request more information from advertisers, all by clicking a remote control device used with their TV sets.

Telephone companies, newspapers, cable operators, and high tech marketers are ready to offer a new generation of interactive in-home services linked to TV screens. Within a few years, consumers will do much of their shopping, banking, and reading on TV, play along with TV shows, and respond instantly to commercials. Estimates call for 40 million subscribers and a $6 billion interactive TV market by 2002. Users will be charged separate fees for some services, like home banking, but sponsors like Domino's will pay for each order generated and will charge viewers the same prices as for phoned orders.

Industry observers say such services face a huge hurdle that any new medium encounters. They must first create a strong consumer market with a valuable but competitively priced service before advertisers become interested. And they must carefully balance useful services and entertainment, which attract users, with ad support, which subsidizes the service. Some say if the medium proves large enough, marketers can exploit it by focusing on the experience of interactivity.

For example, a trivia contest tied to a celebrity spot for Diet Coke could expand viewer involvement, as would a variety of other games or response mechanisms to commercials. Currently some interactive subscribers in California can guess the outcome of *Murder, She Wrote,* predict the next play in an NFL game, or compete on *Jeopardy!*

What's more commercials are picking up speed. After years of watching commercials, MTV, and video games, viewers are used to a barrage of visual stimuli. Younger viewers demand it. So commercials move blindingly fast. The fast-paced, jumpy, visually overloaded style of music videos and MTV programs has crossed into mainstream advertising. To those who grew up on MTV, it's stimulating. To people whose eyeballs are a certain age, it's exhausting. A big mistake is trying to do fast ads for eyeballs that are over 40 years old.

What's pushing this frenetic pace? *Zapping.* Viewers armed with remote controls will zap an ad that doesn't hold their interest. *Video games.* Thanks to years of playing Nintendo, kids process visual information differently from adults. They're used to being blasted with visual rather than written information. If you pack enough visual information into a commercial, kids will want to see it over and over. *Technology.* Digital film editing is beginning to replace older technologies, which allows ad makers to slice and dice their commercials faster and less expensively. The creativity, in some sense, follows technology.

The irony for advertisers is that jamming more images into a ad doesn't make for adding more selling points per commercial. If you try to pack this sort of information into the commercial, you may only baffle your viewers. You can't tell anybody anything in a second. Pictures can fly by, but you can only talk so fast.

Eventually, speedy ads may run their course. People will get bored, all ads will seem the same, and we may have a backlash—resulting in simpler images once more. Or different forms, such as Ross Perot's amazing infomercials for the 1992 presidential campaign, which had lots of advertisers thinking. Who knows? The television audience may prefer thirty minutes of sell to the traditional programming that attracts fewer viewers each season.

So television advertisers, who once considered the home screen the most mass of the mass media, are scurrying to find new ways of connecting with potential buyers. The world of 500 channels is just around the corner, with a channel for every type of interest and commercials narrowly targeted to those interests.

For the advertising creative team, this may necessitate special attention to the media recommendation for a campaign; if television is going to run exclusively on the Lifetime channel, creatives need to know about the audience on that channel as well as the market situation for the product.

As advertising creatives discover the magic of computer-generated images, new opportunities present themselves for the blending of real and surreal images on the television screen. As a result, many spectacular commercials have come into being, with perhaps just as many poor ones falling victim to misuse of the new wonder tools. It all boils down to the same venerable rule of thumb regarding creative message generation: If it furthers the strategy, use it; if it doesn't, don't. When you have only fifteen or thirty seconds to make an impression, and time is big money, strategy is still the first priority.

For many of you, writing for television may prove awkward at first, not only for the reasons above, but also because you will be shifting gears from the way you usually write. Instead of putting the words down first, it's important that you begin by thinking of the pictures, and let those pictures suggest the appropriate words. If you try writing the words first, you may end up with a radio commercial with pictures.

Here is a plan for getting into condition to write a television commercial:

1. ***Determine the key attribute you wish to promote.*** In thirty seconds, you will barely have time to communicate the major selling point, brand image, or positioning, let alone say anything else. Decide on the key attribute before you go any further.

2. ***State the major benefit of that attribute.*** In other words, determine which benefit will be most appealing to your audience.

3. ***Translate that benefit into a visual element or scene that will make that benefit memorable.*** You might think in terms of a key visual (described later in this chapter).

4. ***Using this visual element as a starting point, begin to build a scene around it that shows and says what is needed.***

5. ***When the scene is fixed in your mind, think about what will precede and follow it.***

6. ***Begin writing the commercial.*** At this point, don't concern yourself with camera angles or other technicalities. Don't even try to write a script. Just write the story of the commercial in narrative form. Describe what will happen first, and continue until you reach the last few seconds. This is your first "scenario," in which you should describe the action and the settings as well as the narration and the dialogue.

7. ***Once you are satisfied that your scenario is working, then write the commercial in proper script form.*** Don't be too hasty. You may stumble through three, four, or more revisions before deciding to commit your work to the script-writing format.

8. ***Read the script out loud and listen to the way it sounds.*** Review the timing, the clarity of the message, the visual continuity, the product identity. Are you essentially confining your story to one major point, making that point in a memorable way, and identifying your brand sufficiently? If not, take another look.

9. ***Revise and sharpen your script.***

10. ***Once you are completely satisfied, prepare a storyboard of the commercial.***

Essentials of a Good Television Commercial

Attention-Getting and Relevant Opening

The crucial opening seconds of a commercial either turn viewers off or invite them to watch the rest of the message. As writer or art director, you should work hard to make the opening seconds not only involving, but relevant to your message. If relevance is missing, you still stand to lose your audience, no matter how interesting the opening.

Single-Mindedness

Choose a major theme or benefit and stick with it. Your viewer isn't interested in trying to absorb more in thirty seconds.

High Product Visibility

Show the product on screen as prominently as you reasonably can. Use close-ups, especially the first time the product is mentioned. Show the product during the closing seconds of the commercials so that it will be remembered. Involve the product with other things in the commercial—people, settings, objects.

Closing Recap of Product, Message, Super Title

In addition to showing the product near the end, repeat the major message and consider running your theme as a title on the screen at the same time these words are voiced.

Visual Emphasis

Think about the best way to frame your shots so that you emphasize what is most important. Keeping your major concept in mind, use the necessary visual devices to keep that concept "up front" in the minds of your audience.

Good Sense of Continuity

Learn to appreciate the smooth flow of commercials you see on television. Note the cuts and dissolves, the camera moves, the angles used. Take mental notes to remember what makes a commercial seem to move naturally and logically from opening to closing.

TV Commercial Formats

Although writers and art directors do not necessarily think in terms of format, this list may help novices make decisions before trying a television idea.

Demonstration

A demonstration uses the television medium to its fullest. When the entire commercial consists of demonstrating the superiority of a product, viewers tend to watch. A classic demonstration involved one DieHard battery starting five dead, snow-covered cars. The demonstration must often be exaggerated in this way to make its point vividly. That's perfectly acceptable, just so long as the claim is not exaggerated.

Problem/Solution

A mainstay of daytime television, this format works something like this: I have a big problem and I'm upset; enter the product, the problem is solved, and am I ever grateful! Old and corny in its purest form, the idea works nonetheless, especially when a clever creative team makes use of unusual settings, characters, and anything else that will take the clichés out of this much-used form.

Product as Star

Although the product should star in every commercial, some provide greater opportunities for this to take place. A classic car wax commercial showed the can of car wax being rained upon, spattered with mud, drenched in a downpour, and frozen in ice and snow. At the end, the sun comes out and a hand wipes a new shine on the can with a cloth. No faces, no cars—just the product for thirty seconds in clever and ever changing situations that relate to the strategy.

Spokesperson

The spokesperson technique uses an individual on camera to deliver the message. Although not the most exciting method of presentation, it benefits from a strong delivery coupled with polished copy and an interesting and relevant setting. A commercial for an allergy medicine placed its spokesperson outdoors under a tree at the height of the allergy season. The camera opened on a long shot and slowly zoomed in on the speaker, who ultimately revealed a package of the product. The spokesperson may be anyone from a distinguished looking announcer to a sports or entertainment figure. The main thing is that whoever is chosen is right for the strategy and the product.

Story Line

A story line attempts to be a thirty-second feature film, no mean accomplishment. One advertiser created a nostalgic series to promote lowfat milk for adults. Commercials had viewers thinking back to their childhoods when a cold glass of milk tasted great after a day of play in the hot sun. Following this flashback sequence, an adult in the present reminded viewers that lowfat milk might be a better choice in this day and age. Although you must tell the story swiftly, a story line commercial can be as artfully conceived as a two-hour movie.

Musical

The musical hinges on a song to carry the action forward. Numerous examples exist among commercials for soft drinks, beer, and fast food. Such commercials are often difficult to present in storyboard form and are sometimes presented as concepts, rather than as frame-by-frame boards. The director, producer, and camera operator then shoot footage that remains faithful to the original concept, although they may also incorporate new elements that are discovered on location.

Vignette

A vignette commercial uses several (usually comic) situations to drive home the point. Bud Light used this format successfully in commercials showing various people asking for a "light" and receiving anything from a bulb to a torch.

Animation

Although animation might be called a technique, it represents an entirely different way of handling a concept. Animation is often combined with live action shots to enhance the message. The Star Kist tuna episodes with Charley, for example, intercut live action "appetite shots" of real people enjoying the product.

Green Giant commercials blend live action with animation in each colorful episode.

Stop Action

A cross between true animation and live action, stop action uses the animation technique to give life to inanimate real-life objects. Through stop action, California raisins can move and dance, and packages can open, shut, or take giant leaps through space.

The important thing to remember is that the format you eventually settle on must do justice to your strategy. Don't choose a vignette format just because it's fun to work with. Base your choice on what's best for the product story.

Live Action, Animation, Stop Action, Stills

Live action refers to people, places, and things recorded as they exist. The bulk of television commercials are written for live action. In animation, action is created by drawing a number of still pictures, each minutely different from another in the movement of the character or object in the drawing, and exposing them one frame at a time, on an animation stand. Animation is helpful when live action cannot communicate the message, or when competing brands are using live action and you choose animation to make your message stand out. In combination with live action, animation can produce unique and memorable effects, as when Tony the Tiger dines with a family of real people.

In stop action, the movement occurs through manipulation of a three-dimensional object. The famous California raisins go into their dance only after some painstakingly precise manipulation of the clay figures before each individual exposure of the animation camera. The Pillsbury Doughboy's playful expressions are the result of long hours by the animation artists.

Finally you might choose still photographs as the visual basis for your television commercial. Stills are often more moving than real moving pictures, and have been used with success in all types of commercials, but especially in public service messages, using real people instead of professional actors. Through pans, zooms, dissolves, and other moves and transitions, and by adding a complementary narrator and musical background, the writer and art director can create a powerful message at a minimal cost.

Visual Storytelling

Just as the look of a print ad communicates as much as the words, so the pictures in a television commercial, as well as the way those pictures are woven together, can communicate positive or negative feelings about the commercial. The pictures will always affect the message the viewer is receiving, whether intended or not, so you will need to understand how the camera communicates with the viewer.

Courtesy Texize, Division of Dow Consumer Products

ANNCR: Plastic . . .

STAINLESS STEEL

Stainless steel . . .

Fiberglass . . .

Vinyl . . . Chrome . . .

Enamel . . . Porcelain . . .

Aluminum. You need only one cleaner to clean all these surfaces.

Fantastik, the Multi-Surface Spray Cleaner.

And not only does it clean all kinds of surfaces . . .

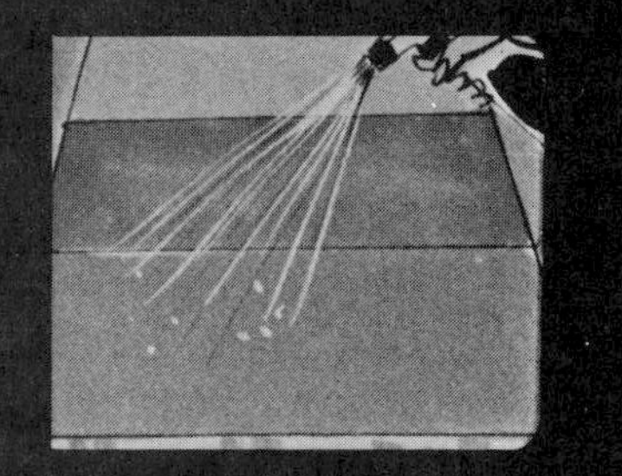

It cleans all kinds of dirt.

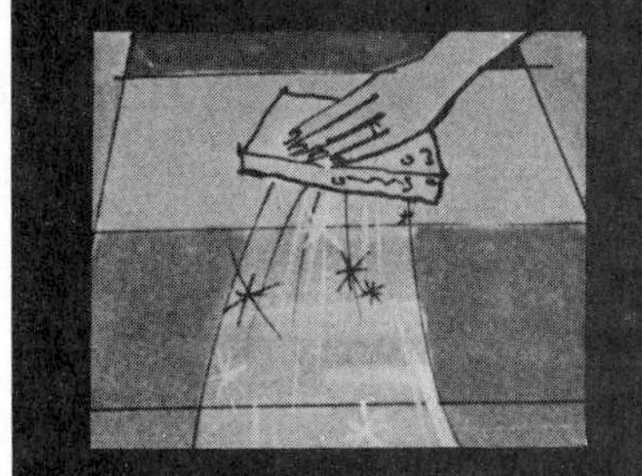

Everything from fingerprints . . . to kitchen grease.

Surface after surface, Fantastik cleans them all.

Fantastik . . . the Multi-Surface Spray Cleaner.

FIGURE 10-1

This artist's conception of a thirty-second television commercial for Fantastik Spray Cleaner was presented in the storyboard format to the client for approval. In this commercial, the product has been positioned as the "multisurface spray cleaner," using the device of a long road composed of various surfaces that the product will clean. Scenes from the resulting finished commercial appear in Figure 10-2.

"Open Road" :30

ANNCR: Plastic...

Stainless steel...

Fiberglass...

Vinyl...Chrome...

Enamel...Porcelain...

Aluminum. You need only one cleaner to clean all these surfaces.

Fantastik, the Multi-Surface Spray Cleaner.

And not only does it clean all kinds of surfaces...

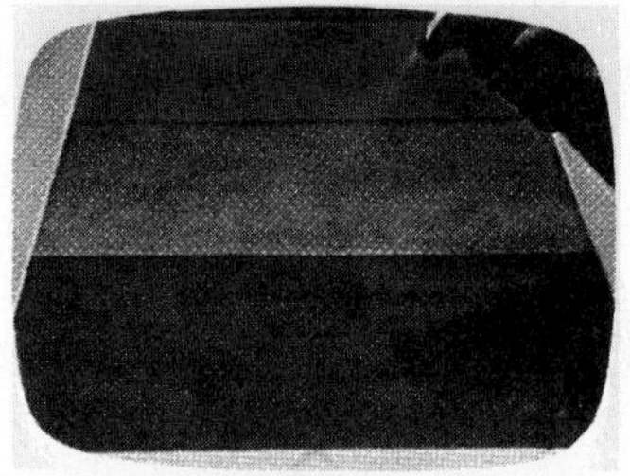
it cleans all kinds of dirt.

Everything from fingerprints...to kitchen grease.

Surface after surface, Fantastik cleans them all.

Fantastik...the Multi-Surface Spray Cleaner.

Courtesy Texize, Division of Dow Consumer Products

FIGURE 10-2

Here are scenes from the Fantastik commercial (see Figure 10-1) as actually filmed. Note the similarity between the original storyboard and the finished commercial. In some cases scripts undergo many revisions before they receive approval for production.

A shot, for example, is a continuous, uninterrupted view recorded by one camera. Each time the same action is reshot, you have a new take. A number of takes may be required before the director is satisfied that the shot works. A scene, on the other hand, may consist of either one shot or a series of shots taken from different angles or distances, yet basically related to one another by location.

To explain how you want a shot composed, you need to make decisions regarding the area included, the point of view, and the camera angle.

Camera Shots

How many shots should there be in thirty seconds? The only valid answer can be: It all depends—on the story you need to tell and on the best way to tell it. Each shot, regardless of the number in the commercial, should fulfill a specific need. Here are the basic shots to know:

ECU (Extreme Close-up)

Part of a face, a finger, a detail on a package. As close as you can get and still show what needs showing. A bigger than life glimpse at some important little detail, chosen because of its significance to your story.

CU (Close-Up)

A face fills the entire screen. We see one table setting. A product stands tall, taking over the entire screen image. The formidable close-up, an invention of necessity by the early moviemakers of this century who needed this "up close" relationship between their actors and the audience to compensate for the absence of sound, is still an extremely powerful choice in the art of the camera because it can emphasize specifics. By limiting the area of the shot, the close-up offers no distractions for the viewer; the shot commands the viewer to look at one thing and one thing only. The disadvantage of the close-up is that it masks the setting. When we are this close to something, it's hard to tell where the action is taking place. Nonetheless, the close-up remains a powerful choice for commercial messages, since it leaves no doubt about what we want the viewer to see.

MS (Medium Shot)

In the medium shot, the viewer is able to identify the location of the shot. When people are part of a medium shot, they are typically framed from waist up. A commonly used MS, is also called a 2-shot (two people). Much action is shot MS because it represents a sensible compromise in framing the action. When a close-up isn't revealing enough and a long shot is too vague, go for the medium shot.

LS (Long Shot)

Also known as an establishing shot, this framing takes in a broad area so as to reveal where the action is taking place. An LS may tell us the action is taking place in a kitchen, a classroom, or may consist of an aerial shot of an entire football field. This shot frequently appears at the opening of a commercial to let us know where we are—if that's critical to our understanding of the message that will follow. In other instances, writers deliberately fail to reveal a location, if that makes the story more interesting.

Point of View

While you may not always need to specify point of view, doing so will often help others understand what you are striving to communicate visually. If you choose the objective point of view, or objective camera, you are asking for an impersonal recording of the action. In this instance, the camera records the action from the viewpoint of an observer who is uninvolved in the action taking place. This is basically how we relate to films or theatre. The people on camera never look into the lens, as this would destroy the objective relationship between the camera and the viewers. Of course, if your actors are told to look into the camera and talk directly to the viewer, the mere shock of such action may be an effective way to get attention.

The subjective point of view, or subjective camera, records the action in a different manner. Subjective camera involves the viewer as part of the scene. Usually this is done by having the camera represent the point of view of a person in the scene. In subjective camera work, an actor can stare directly into the lens. If the situation has been established properly, the viewer will understand that, while the actor is staring at her, he's really staring at someone else in the scene who is now being "played" by the camera. Compare the rage that is directed at someone else visible on screen with the rage directed at that person through the camera, and you begin to understand the power of subjective point of view.

Camera Angle

Eye-level camera angles present a view as seen by an observer of natural height. High angle shots, which look down on action, may be chosen for technical reasons (it's the best way to see the football field), aesthetic reasons (it's a way to see something in a new and interesting perspective, as in the legendary overhead shots of dance formations in the musicals of the 1930s), or psychological reasons (to create the impression that something is of little importance because we are looking down on it). Low angle shots are used mainly for psychological impact. A foreground figure shot at low angle will seem to tower over the camera. These unusual angles should not be chosen lightly, but instead should serve an important purpose in accomplishing the strategy of the commercial.

Camera Moves

Moving the camera allows a shift from one framing to another, from MS to CU for example.

Zoom In, Zoom Out

A zoom is a movement toward or away from the subject. Actually, the camera remains in one position as its zoom lens revolves to bring the image closer or to move it farther away, as in "zoom in to CU package" or "zoom out to MS man and woman embracing."

Dolly In, Dolly Out

Similar to the zoom, the dolly involves actually moving the camera toward or away from the subject. The dolly is a slower, more deliberate move that can be extended over a larger area for a longer time. It tends to give the impression that the camera is moving, whereas the zoom gives the opposite impression—that the subject is moving toward or away from the camera. In scripting your commercial, you may choose to use these terms interchangeably. In production, your camera operator will decide which is the better choice.

Pan Right, Pan Left

In this move, the camera swivels to one side or the other while remaining in place. In a pan, the camera appears to watch the action as it passes by. Move your neck from right to left while standing still. You're panning.

Truck Right, Truck Left

Here, the camera rolls sideways to follow, or keep alongside, the action. Keep staring straight ahead as you move your body sideways, right or left, to duplicate the action of a trucking shot. As you will see, this provides quite a different perspective of the action than the pan.

Tilt Up, Tilt Down

The camera swivels up or down to create a vertical version of the pan. Move your gaze up to the ceiling, then down to the floor to see what a vertical pan looks like.

Boom, or Crane, Shot

As the name implies, this move is orchestrated by a motorized crane or "boom" which carries camera, camera operator, and often the director as they "drive" the platform over a major scene for sometimes spectacular effects. One of the most famous boom shots in film history is Scarlett's visit to the Atlanta depot in *Gone with the Wind*. As she wanders aimlessly through rows of wounded soldiers, the camera swoops up to reveal thousands of casualties and ultimately finds a tattered Confederate flag waving in the breeze. It's quite dramatic.

Video Transitions

All the shots and moves described above take place within the camera. In contrast, the following devices occur beyond the camera, and have to do with how the various shots and moves are edited into a final version of the commercial. Like camera moves, transitions carry you from one piece of action to another, but without the time required to move the camera. Transitions are essentially instantaneous, an advantage when you are dealing with thirty-second blocks of time.

Cut

This is by far the most widely used transition. The term originated with film editing when one scene was actually cut from the footage and joined to another scene which had been cut from elsewhere in the footage. For our purposes, a cut means an instantaneous visual change, from CU to MS for example, or from ECU to LS. One second we are looking at one shot, the next we are looking at another. It's important that the two shots that are cut together make sense visually and carry the action along in a logical manner.

Dissolve

A dissolve is a softer transition that looks as if a new image is slowly fading in as the former image is fading out. It can be used to suggest the passage of time, as in a story in which we see a woman shampooing her hair in one scene, then dressed and ready to go out in the next. For some reason, the dissolve helps us understand that some time has elapsed. Dissolves also work well when used throughout an entire commercial to create a soft, romantic mood. A dissolve is also the appropriate choice in compilation cutting (see below) when a series of shots unrelated in time and space (but related for purposes of telling the story) form the basis for the visual portion of the commercial.

Special Effects

Generally, special effects should be used only for special purposes. Never introduce them merely for the sake of variety, unless they add to the selling premise. Not only can they obscure the message, but they can run up production costs needlessly.

Split Screen

The screen is divided, usually in half, so that two images appear simultaneously. Useful when presenting two sides of an issue or comparing the product with a competing brand. Dull when overdone, as with any special effect.

Skip Frame

By intercutting a second image between every frame of the first, it appears that the new image is pulsating through the earlier one. Cut to the beat of music, this can be a dramatic way to show change.

Key Insert, Matte, Chromakey

These terms describe the insertion of one image into another. Advances in computer generation have made it simple to achieve even the most bizarre combinations (a tiny man walking on a giant restaurant menu as he points out the entrees, for example). Product shots are often inserted over the action at the end of a commercial, along with a super title containing the campaign theme.

Match Dissolve, Match Cut

This device can serve as a smooth bridge for what might otherwise be an awkward transition. The creative team simply chooses two objects with similar configurations—an egg and a bald-headed man, for example—and dissolve or cut from one to the other. This technique becomes gimmicky if overused, but in special situations can be quite disarming.

Super Title

Lettering superimposed over a scene is called a super title. It is most used at the end of a commercial to drive home the major selling message and can be reinforced when the same words on screen are voiced, usually by an offscreen narrator.

Structuring the Commercial

Now that you know the language of television, let's focus on the logic of writing the television commercial. The first thing to remember is that in most cases you have a mere thirty seconds to state your case. For this reason, you cannot afford to spend a great deal of time establishing a situation because, by the time you did, the commercial would long be over. Think of the commercial as a thirty-second play or movie. When you waste one second, you have wasted a significant chunk of the entire time available. Or look at it this way: Each second of a national commercial costs thousands of dollars to produce, even more to air. Make sure each second is worth it!

Editing for Continuity

One way to ensure this is to pay attention to how you get from one scene to the next, which involves the process of editing. Editing can accomplish three things: It can condense time, it can extend time, and it can jumble time. To condense time, you might show a man walking toward a house, cut to the man halfway up the walk, then cut to the man on the porch ringing the doorbell. To extend time, you might show a speeding train approaching an object on the tracks, and by cutting to various angles and shots of the train and the object, you actually extend the "real" time it would take for the train to reach the object. To jumble time, you might cut from the present to a flashback of a remembered past event or flash forward to an imagined scene in the future.

The manipulation (especially compression) of real time is a necessity in a television commercial that must squeeze its story into thirty seconds or less. You can accomplish this through three basic types of editing.

Compilation Cutting

In this type of editing, the storytelling is dependent on the narration, usually voiced over the action, and the consecutive shots merely illustrate what is being said. The shots may be somewhat unrelated to each other, may occur in different places, or may consist of a series of people or objects shot in a similar fashion.

Continuity Cutting

This is the primary technique used in dramatic feature movies. The storytelling depends upon matching consecutive scenes without a narrator to explain what is going on. Action flows from one shot to the next. There may even be various angles and cutaways in which the action is not part of the previous shot. For example, a conversation between two people in a room may consist of a 2-shot, several close-ups of each person, another MS of the two, and a cutaway to some action taking place elsewhere that is somehow related to the action within the room.

Crosscutting

Crosscutting combines two or more parallel actions into an alternating pattern. The actions may occur at the same time but in different places, as when we see a farmer driving a tractor, cut to his wife fixing dinner, cut back to the farmer, and cut back again to his wife. The actions may also occur at different times in different places, as in classic commercials for Dial soap where shots of a man or woman in the shower are intercut with shots of the same person at various times during the day. The message, obviously, is that Dial keeps you fresh throughout your day (as if you were in the shower from morning until night). Crosscutting may also be used to suggest details of an action that occurs at one time in one place. In a classic commercial for Clairol, as the announcer says, "The closer he gets, the better you look," we see her running toward him, him running toward her, her running toward him, him running toward her, and so on. Crosscutting may also be used to increase tension, as when we see scenes of a train approaching a crossing crosscut with scenes of a car approaching the same crossing. In a beer commercial, we see shots of a bartender drawing a draft. These shots are then crosscut between shots of a man leaving his office, walking to the bar, sitting at the bar, and, finally, catching the beer after the bartender slides it down the bar to precisely where the man has just sat down.

When to Cut

When you call for a cut, have a good reason. It may be that the product needs to be introduced, or perhaps you need to shift to another location. Try also to use cuts imaginatively. Cut in the middle of the action, rather than prior to or following the action. This "binds" the cut and makes the visual transition seem natural. In a commercial for a stain remover, a woman tosses a dirty tablecloth offscreen right. We cut to a CU of the top of the washing machine and the tablecloth sails in from offscreen left. By placing the cut in the middle of the action, the sequence becomes more interesting.

When writing a television commercial, remember that cuts not only are time-saving devices, but they can also make production go more smoothly. When a cut is introduced, production can be stopped momentarily while the new scene is set up. This makes shooting more controlled, with fewer things that can go wrong in each take.

Avoid the Jump Cut

Another guideline to effective cutting is to steer clear of the jump cut. A jump cut very obviously leaves out a logical part of the action, and in such an awkward way that it distracts viewers. For example, if you show a woman resting her hands on the counter and then cut to a close-up of her pouring milk, it's going to look very bizarre.

To avoid jump cutting, avoid splicing together two actions that don't make sense, unless you're doing it for a special effect. Having people walk into shots from off camera is one way to avoid this awkward situation.

Judge TV Commercials by These Guidelines

1. What is the single central message or idea?

2. What is the function/value of the opening shot with respect to that idea? At what point in time is the viewer involved?

3. To what extent do the pictures, as opposed to the words, tell the story?

4. To what extent do the words reinforce the pictures? Or are they merely redundant?

5. Are interesting, exciting, complicated, beautiful visuals on screen long enough for complete understanding or appreciation? Are dull, static visuals on longer than they should be? Would rearrangement of copy help strike a better balance?

6. Is the story an irrelevant attention-getter, or is the product an integral part of the story?

7. Is the story believable? If not, is the selling message believable within the exaggerated story?

8. Does it all relate to the product concept?

Judge Your TV Commercial Idea by These Guidelines

1. Express the product concept—how you wish the consumer to regard the product and its benefits—in one or two sentences.

2. Turn that concept into a visual that also captures what you want to say about the product.

3. Is this a likely "key visual"—one that sums up the entire message? If not, how will you change it for the better?

4. Write the story of the commercial in simple narrative form.

5. Determine when the product is first introduced. Can you find a more strategic time/place for its introduction?

6. Check identity level for your product/product concept.

7. Check the purpose of the opening shot.

8. Check the purpose of the closing shot.

9. Avoid talky campaigns. Make every word work hard. Let the picture carry the major share of the message.

10. Work to build campaigns, not individual commercials.

11. Add considerations of character, voice, music, sound effects, locations, etc.

Getting the TV Commercial on Paper

To illustrate proper television script and storyboard form, we shall use a commercial for a spot remover called K2R. The concept behind this commercial is that the product can save many people trips to the dry cleaners. (See Figure 10–3). In the script the viewer is told that, while major cleaning problems should be handled by the dry cleaner, there's no reason not to treat minor spots yourself.

1. OPEN ON SLOW ZOOM THROUGH LINE OF WOMEN CUSTOMERS TO DRY CLEANER BEHIND COUNTER OF HIS SHOP. HE IS MIDDLE-AGED, SLIGHTLY BALD, AND CROTCHETY.

The script opens with a long, or establishing, shot to set the scene and then moves quickly using a dolly in through a crowd of customers to the dry cleaner. Although his character is described in the video direction, it might be preferable to write a more comprehensive description in a set of production notes to accompany the script.

2. CUT TO MS DRY CLEANER AND CUSTOMER. HE HOLDS UP A GARMENT OF HERS THAT APPEARS TO NEED DRY CLEANING.

The second direction indicates a transition, a cut. Whenever you call for a new shot, begin a new camera direction, as shown here. This will make it easier for others to follow the script.

3. HE NOW HOLDS UP ANOTHER GARMENT WITH A SPOT ON IT.

The third direction calls for no new camera movement, but does include new action. To correlate this action with the dialogue, it makes sense to break it out into a new direction, as shown.

4. HE REACHES UNDER COUNTER FOR K2R.

Once more, because of new action introduced, we break out this shot into a separate direction.

5. CUT TO CU PRODUCT AS HE REMOVES CAP.

6. CUT TO MS REACTION AS WOMEN CROWD IN TO SEE WHAT IS HAPPENING.

The last two directions indicate cuts. In number 6, the reaction shot of the women's faces adds interest to the commercial. Staring too long at an inanimate product can be dulling to viewers' senses.

7. CUT TO ECU K2R ON THE SPOT AS HE SPRAYS IT.

Here is television's trump card, the demonstration, depicted in extreme close-up so no one will miss it.

8. CUT TO MS REACTION OF WOMEN. THEY ARE MUMBLING AND MOVING ABOUT.

Instead of using a dissolve to indicate the passage of time, this cutaway to a reaction nicely bridges the "five minutes" it takes for the product to work. In such an instance, it's mandatory to let viewers know that the process does take longer than it appears on screen.

9. CUT BACK TO NUMBER 7. K2R IS NOW DRY AND DRY CLEANER BRUSHES IT OFF WITH CAP BRUSH. SUPER LOWER 1/3: FIVE MINUTES LATER

10. DISS TO PRODUCT CU AS HAND REPLACES CAP.

Why the dissolve at this point? Perhaps because it indicates a shift away from the story to its climax. In this shot, we have an unseen announcer voicing a message over the product shot.

11. DISS TO LS DRY CLEANER SHOP AS IN OPENING SHOT. STORE IS NOW EMPTY EXCEPT FOR ONE WOMAN AND THE DRY CLEANER.

The whole point of this commercial is that a customer need not visit the dry cleaner with minor spot problems. It seems logical to end the spot by showing the store emptied of customers who have been convinced by the demonstration that they can do the job themselves.

12. CUT TO CU DRY CLEANER WITH K2R IN HAND. SUPER TITLE: THE HOME DRY CLEANER.

The closing shot includes a good look at the product. The final shot is the one that viewers tend to remember most, which is why the majority of commercials end with the dialogue restating the major selling point as we see the product.

We have purposely omitted the sound portion of the script to point out that pictures must carry the burden of the message in television. Even though you may not know everything that is taking place, you already know that the dry cleaner, by demonstrating the convenience of using K2R, is about to lose some of his business to the new product. Now read the entire commercial as it should be presented in script form (Figure 10–3) and note that the directions for both pictures and sound are clearly indicated in the numbered, double-column format. Note the use of the abbreviation VO to indicate those spoken lines that are read "voice over" or out of camera range. Identifying the VO lines accomplishes two things: It helps performers to understand when their lines are spoken off camera, and also allows the pre- or postrecording of such lines (prior to or after shooting).

K2R SPOT LIFTER
:30 TV (film)
"Dry Cleaner"

1. OPEN ON SLOW ZOOM THROUGH LINE OF WOMEN CUSTOMERS TO DRY CLEANER BEHIND COUNTER OF HIS SHOP. HE IS MIDDLE-AGED, SLIGHTLY BALD, AND CROTCHETY.	DRY CLEANER: These long lines, they can drive a man crazy.
2. CUT TO MS DRY CLEANER AND CUSTOMER. HE HOLDS UP A GARMENT OF HERS THAT APPEARS TO NEED DRY CLEANING.	DRY CLEANER: Now that's a job for a dry cleaner!
3. HE NOW HOLDS UP ANOTHER GARMENT WITH A SPOT ON IT.	DRY CLEANER: But this! Why bring me one little spot to clean?
4. HE REACHES UNDER COUNTER FOR K2R.	DRY CLEANER: Haven't you ever heard of . . .
5. CUT TO CU PRODUCT AS HE REMOVES CAP.	DRY CLEANER (VO): . . . K2R Spot Lifter?
6. CUT TO MS REACTION SHOT AS WOMEN CROWD IN TO SEE WHAT IS HAPPENING.	DRY CLEANER: You spray it on . . .
7. CUT TO ECU K2R ON THE SPOT AS HE SPRAYS IT.	DRY CLEANER (VO): K2R lifts the spot clean out.
8. CUT TO MS REACTION SHOT OF WOMEN. THEY ARE MUMBLING AND MOVING ABOUT.	SFX: OOHS AND AAHS OF APPROVAL.
9. CUT BACK TO NUMBER 7. K2R IS NOW DRY AND DRY CLEANER BRUSHES IT OFF WITH CAP BRUSH.	DRY CLEANER (VO): When it's dry, just brush it away. No spot. No nothing.
SUPER LOWER 1/3: FIVE MINUTES LATER.	

FIGURE 10-3

Television script format.

10. DISS TO PRODUCT CU AS HAND REPLACES CAP.	ANNCR (VO): K2R Spot Lifter from Texize. The home dry cleaner that works anywhere.
11. DISS TO DRY CLEANING SHOP AS IN OPENING. STORE IS NOW EMPTY EXCEPT FOR ONE WOMAN AND THE DRY CLEANER.	ANNCR (VO): . . . And saves you a trip to the cleaners.
12. CUT TO CU DRY CLEANER WITH K2R IN HAND. SUPER TITLE: THE HOME DRY CLEANER.	DRY CLEANER: Hey, where'd everybody go?

FIGURE 10-3 Continued.

The TV Storyboard

Now we take the script a step further to the storyboard stage. It is from this form that most television commercials are presented and produced. A good storyboard contains everything a good script should have and adds pictures. You can see how the "dry cleaner" commercial was transformed from script to storyboard in Figure 10-4. Note that all video directions have been shifted from the left to the upper right of each frame, and that audio is now directly below the video and separated by a few lines of space.

You need not be an accomplished artist to draw storyboard frames, as long as your frames indicate in some manner what you hope to achieve on the screen. As long as your indications are clear, you may use stick figures, trace from comic strips in the daily paper, or draw freehand. However you draw, be true to your directions. Show a close-up filling the frame, draw a long shot to include an entire area. Using storyboard frames will make your ideas easier for others on your team, your client, and the production crew to follow.

Note that in both the script and storyboard, video directions are typed in all capital letters. The directions tell how we get from one scene to the next (CUT TO, DISS TO, and so on), state what type of shot we now see (CUT TO MS, CUT TO LS, DISS TO CU), and describe any action when needed (CUT TO MS WOMAN HOLDING PRODUCT. SHE PUTS IT ON COUNTER).

Indicating Movement

In sketching frames, it helps to indicate zooms, pans, or tilts, as well as the movement of actors and actresses in the commercial. (See Figure 10-5.) You can accomplish this swiftly and simply by using arrows. Four arrows pointing out

Client:		**Commercial #:**	**Job:**
Product:	K2R SPOT LIFTER	**Timing:** 30	**Typed:**
Title:	DRY CLEANER		**Draft #:**

Scene

1. OPEN ON SLOW ZOOM THROUGH LINE OF WOMEN CUSTOMERS TO DRY CLEANER BEHIND COUNTER OF HIS SHOP. HE IS MIDDLE-AGED, SLIGHTLY BALD, AND CROTCHETY.

DRY CLEANER: These long lines, they can drive a man crazy.

2. CUT TO MS DRY CLEANER AND A CUSTOMER. HE HOLDS UP A GARMENT OF HERS THAT APPEARS TO NEED DRY CLEANING.

DRY CLEANER: Now that's a job for a dry cleaner!

3. HE NOW HOLDS UP ANOTHER GARMENT WITH A SPOT ON IT.

DRY CLEANER: But this! Why bring me one little spot to clean?

4. HE REACHES UNDER COUNTER FOR K2R.

DRY CLEANER: Haven't you ever heard of . . .

FIGURE 10-4

Television storyboard format.

Client: | **Commercial #:** | **Job:**
Product: K2R SPOT LIFTER | **Timing:** 30 | **Typed:**
Title: DRY CLEANER | **Draft #:**

Scene

5. CUT TO CU PRODUCT AS HE REMOVES CAP.

DRY CLEANER (VO): . . . K2R Spot Lifter?

6. CUT TO MS REACTION SHOT AS WOMEN CROWD IN TO SEE WHAT IS HAPPENING.

DRY CLEANER: You spray it on . . .

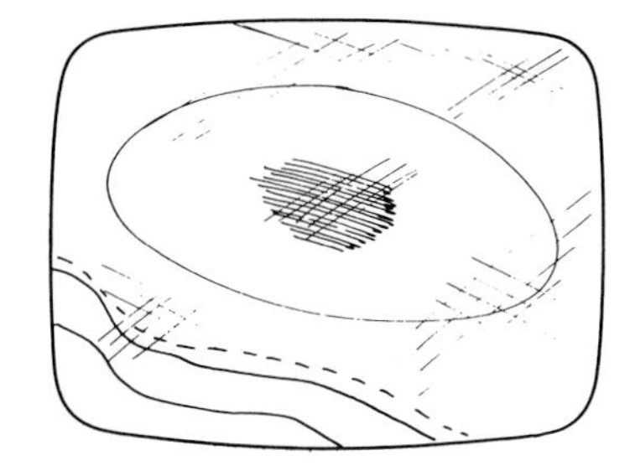

7. CUT TO ECU K2R ON SPOT AS HE SPRAYS IT.

DRY CLEANER (VO): K2R lifts the spot clean out.

8. CUT TO MS REACTION SHOT OF WOMEN. THEY ARE MUMBLING AND MOVING ABOUT.

SFX: OOHS AND AAHS OF APPROVAL.

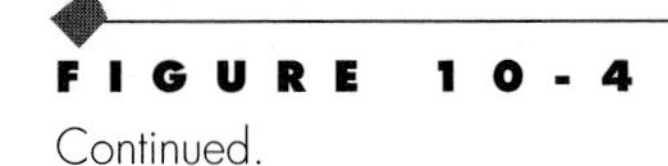

FIGURE 10-4

Continued.

Client: **Commercial #:** **Job:**

Product: K2R SPOT LIFTER **Timing:** 30 **Typed:**

Title: DRY CLEANER **Draft #:**

Scene

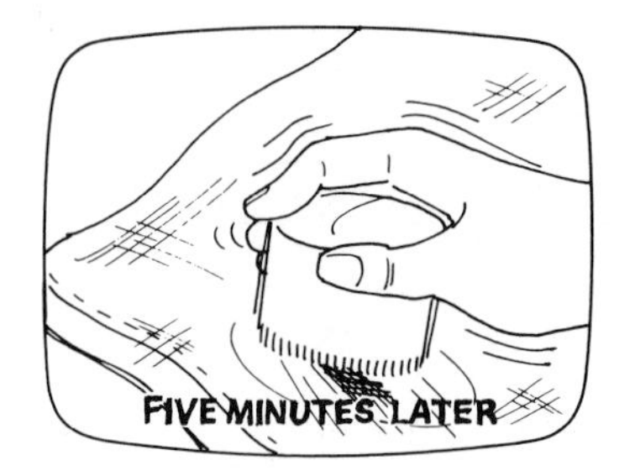

9. CUT BACK TO NUMBER 7. K2R IS NOW DRY AND DRY CLEANER BRUSHES IT OFF WITH CAP BRUSH.

SUPER LOWER 1/3: FIVE MINUTES LATER.

DRY CLEANER (VO): When it's dry, just brush it away. No spot. No nothing.

10. DISS TO PRODUCT CU AS HAND REPLACES CAP.

ANNCR (VO): K2R Spot Lifter from Texize. The home dry cleaner that works anywhere.

11. DISS TO DRY CLEANING SHOP AS IN OPENING. STORE IS NOW EMPTY EXCEPT FOR ONE WOMAN AND THE DRY CLEANER.

ANNCR (VO): . . . And saves you a trip to the cleaners.

12. CUT TO CU DRY CLEANER WITH K2R IN HAND. SUPER TITLE: THE HOME DRY CLEANER.

DRY CLEANER: Hey, where'd everybody go?

FIGURE 10-4

Continued.

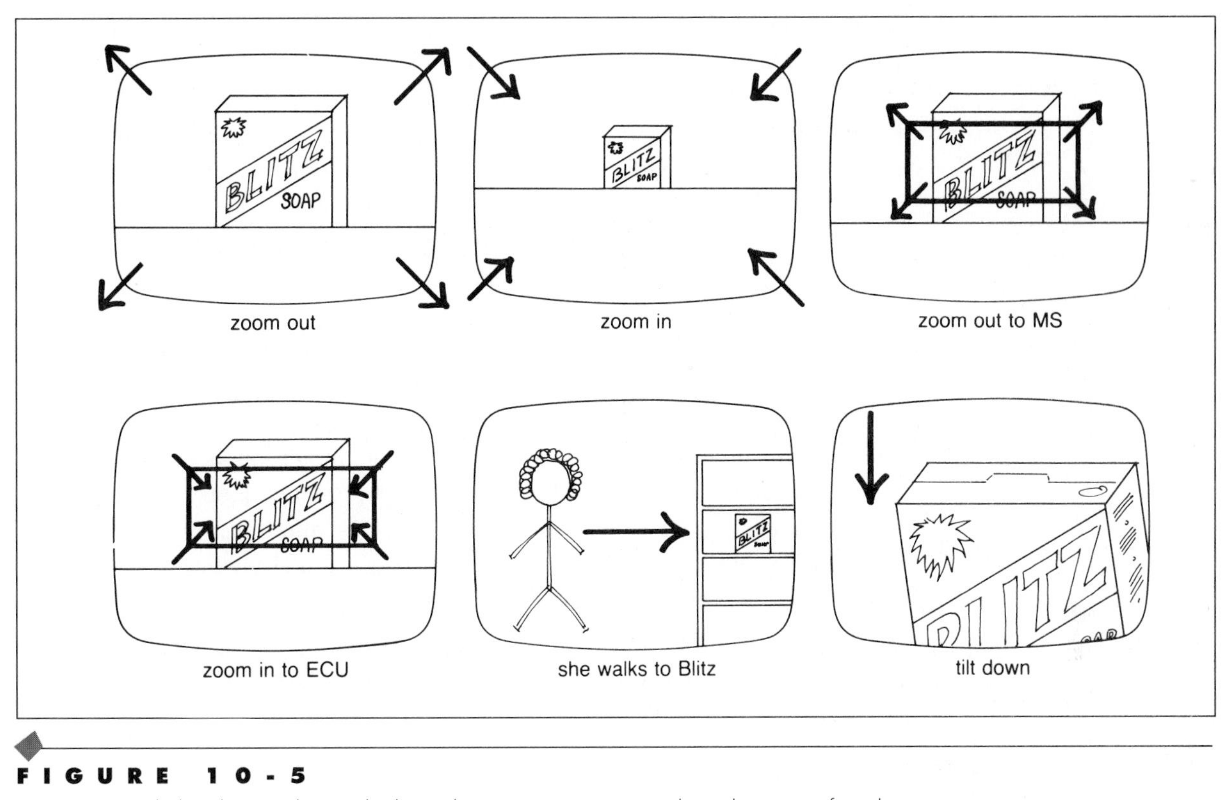

FIGURE 10-5

Use arrows to help others understand what is happening in your storyboard version of a television commercial.

from the corners of the frame indicate a zoom out. Reverse the direction of the arrows for a zoom in. An arrow drawn horizontally across the frame indicates a pan in the direction indicated by the head of the arrow. Similarly, a vertical arrow indicates a tilt up or tilt down.

To save frames you may draw a smaller frame within your larger one to indicate the beginning or end of a zoom movement; then draw your four arrows in the proper directions around this smaller or inner frame. If you want to indicate that someone in the commercial is to walk across the frame, an arrow can accomplish this, too. Use arrows to indicate camera or actor movement. It will help others understand.

TV Production

Once a commercial is approved by the client for production, the agency normally seeks competitive bids from at least three sources. A copy of the storyboard is sent as the basis for the bid, along with production notes which cover all aspects of the commercial not specified by the storyboard. In detail, production notes describe casting preference, wardrobe, sets, special effects needed, specific sizes and packages of the product to be photographed, and other aspects of production. It is a good idea for the agency to discuss the strategy of the campaign with the production house to further clarify the purpose of the commercial.

Once the agency accepts a bid, production begins. Most commercials take a full working day or longer to shoot. Prior to shooting, agency personnel and the commercial director collaborate to: audition actors for parts, agree on locations, and work with crews to locate props, products, and other necessities. After the shoot comes the postproduction work of screening dailies or rushes (all the takes from production), choosing the best takes, and editing them down to the required time frame.

For local commercials, a local television station often serves as a production source. While videotape remains popular for locally produced commercials, many national and regional commercials are still shot on film. Despite major advances in the quality of videotape, many directors prefer film because it can give them more control over the quality of the finished product. Fans of film claim it tends to be kinder to people, products, and settings, affording a richer palette of colors and a softer, upscale texture than videotape. For cosmetics, foods, and automobiles, film seems a natural choice over videotape, but video is closing the quality gap. Already, videographers have created high definition footage which, when projected on a large screen, is virtually indistinguishable from film.

Television Copy Checklist

1. ***Concept:*** The major premise of this commercial is ____________________
____

   ______ a. The concept is stressed primarily through the visual portion of the commercial.

   ______ b. I have chosen the ________________ format because it allows me to express the concept most effectively.

   ______ c. There is entertainment value *linked* to the major premise.

2. ***Video***

   ______ a. The opening shot is designed to get the attention of the viewer.

   ______ b. The opening shot establishes the setting, conceals the setting for good reason, or is otherwise useful in the development of the selling message.

   ______ c. The product is shown or visually expressed early in the commercial.

   ______ d. The initial product shot is a close-up.

   ______ e. Brand identity is maintained by including the package, product, or both in as many shots as possible without making the commercial dull.

_______ f. A key visual is employed to hammer home the main selling point in visual terms (as in the "three temperatures, one detergent" shot used in the Cheer detergent commercial).

_______ g. Shots stay as close to the action as practical, unless it is necessary to establish a locale.

_______ h. The closing shot includes a good product close-up.

_______ i. Super titles, if used, match the audio word for word.

_______ j. Cuts are on the action and do not appear to jump the action forward in an awkward manner.

_______ k. In a musical commercial cuts are timed to the beat of the music when possible.

3. ***Audio***

_______ a. The audio enhances rather than duplicates the picture it accompanies.

_______ b. The audio matches picture to the extent that viewers' attention is not divided between the two.

_______ c. Sufficient mention of the product ensures brand identity beyond visual impressions.

_______ d. The product is mentioned early and again toward the end of the commercial.

_______ e. The main selling point is emphasized at the end of the commercial.

Suggested Activities

1. Watch at least five commercials on television this week and write down the following information about them:

a. Examples of a product close-up when the product is mentioned for the first time.

b. Examples of a final shot that shows the product in close-up.

c. Examples of different kinds of opening devices that gain the attention of the viewer.

d. Examples of a key visual.

2. Practice writing a television commercial by following the method at the beginning of this chapter. Take it through all stages to the storyboard form. Present your storyboard to the class and ask for suggestions. Use the suggestions to revise the commercial.

United Airlines Creates a Meaningful Message for Business Travelers

Bud Watts,
Executive Vice President,
Group Creative Director

Leo Burnett Company, Inc.

In this television commercial, a group of businessmen are getting a pep talk from their supervisor about the way they've been doing business.

"I got a phone call this morning from one of our oldest customers," says the supervisor. "Over twenty years. He fired us. Said he didn't know us anymore. We used to do business face-to-face. Now it's a phone call and a fax and get back to you later. Probably with another phone call or fax."

Then he reveals that he's sending the entire sales force out for face-to-face chats with every customer they have. "But that's over 200 cities," whines one man. Then comes the clincher. The supervisor hands out United Airlines tickets to all and tells his crew that he's going to call personally on the guy who fired them that morning. Although the spot clearly shows the United logo on the ticket envelopes this is one airline commercial that shows no planes, inside or out.

Bud Watts adds: The client said, "Demonstrate United's scope in a manner that will be meaningful to the business traveler."

We said to ourselves, fine. But just telling people United flies to a lot of places won't do the job. We need to cut through. Get people's attention. So, using modern day business methods as the theme, an idea came: the growing popularity of doing business solely electronically and how that can fail you.

There will never be a substitute for a face-to-face with a client or business associate. That's the idea.

Face to face, that's real solid ground—and it worked.

The story starts with a shocker, then empathetically drives home the idea and finishes with a real "Knute Rockne" tug.

The spot was a tremendous success for United. It demonstrated the airline's understanding of business fliers and the realities of business.

UNITED AIRLINES
:60-TV
"SPEECH"

	VIDEO		AUDIO
1	LS BOARDROOM FILLED WITH SALES STAFF. BEN, THE MANAGER, WALKS AMONG THEM.	SFX:	FACTORY SOUNDS UNDER
		BEN:	I got a phone call this morning from one of our oldest customers.
2	CU BEN, GRIMLY TELLING OF DILEMMA. FOLLOW HIM WALKING AMONG STAFF.		He fired us . . . after twenty years.
3	MS BEN WITH GROUP LISTENING.		He fired us. Said he didn't know us anymore. I think I know why.
4	CU BEN STILL PACING THROUGH GROUP.		We used to do business with a handshake. Face to face.
5	WIDE SHOT CONFERENCE TABLE SURROUNDED BY EMPLOYEES.		Now it's a phone call . . . and a fax . . .get back to you later . . . with another fax, probably.
6	CU BEN. WALKS PAST STAFF.		Well, folks, (SIGHS) something's gotta change.
7	WIDE SHOT OF CONFERENCE TABLE SURROUNDED BY EMPLOYEES, THIS TIME FROM BEHIND BEN.	SFX:	MUSIC UNDER THROUGHOUT
			That's why we're going to set out for a little face-to-face chat with every customer we have.
8	MCU SENIOR EXECUTIVE.	SR. EXEC:	But, Ben, that's gotta be over 200 cities.

Courtesy United Airlines.

Here is the television script for the "Speech" commercial. Note how much is communicated in 60 seconds. Where the lines call for "Hackman," read Gene Hackman, the voice over narrator.

	VIDEO	AUDIO
9	MS SECRETARY WALKING IN AND GIVING BEN STACK OF UNITED AIRLINES TICKETS.	BEN: I don't care.
10	SERIES OF CU'S AS BEN CALLS OUT NAMES, HANDING EACH A TICKET. UNITED LOGO VISIBLE ON TICKET FOLDERS.	BEN: Edwards . . . Ryan . . . Nicholas . . . GENE HACKMAN (VO): If you're the kind of business that believes personal service deserves a lot more than lip service, welcome to United. That's the way we've been doing business for over sixty years.
11	CU SALESMAN.	SALESMAN: Ben, where you going?
12	LS OF GROUP AS BEN WALKS OUT TO 'VISIT THAT OLD FRIEND'	BEN: To visit that old friend who fired us this morning.
13	SUPER TITLE: UNITED	HACKMAN (VO): Come fly the friendly skies.

CHAPTER 11

Direct Marketing: Writing to Build Lasting Relationships

Speaking to a group of educators at a Direct Marketing Educational Foundation seminar, Jerry Pickholz, chairman of Ogilvy & Mather Direct Worldwide and one of the most knowledgeable leaders in the field of direct marketing, discussed how the consumer of the '90s has rejected many aspects of the mass marketing approach in favor of a more personalized and intimate one-on-one relationship, a relationship made possible by visionary concepts and modern information technology. Among growing trends in direct marketing, Pickholz cited:

1. Using traditional media to generate new leads, as American Express has done with its television commercials inviting viewers to call 1-800-THE-CARD. Or, as the California division of the American Automobile Association did, using a television commercial to increase AAA membership among female drivers.

2. Using compelling offers to upgrade customers, as the American Association of Retired Persons does by using its membership database to promote related products such as insurance and credit cards.

3. Using high-impact mail to build traffic at the place of business, as Jaguar did when it mailed to a highly selective prospect list and offered an upscale writing pen for visiting the Jaguar dealership.

4. Gathering a list while increasing usage as Miracle Whip did when it invited TV viewers to contribute recipes using Miracle Whip to a newsletter that also featured a photo of the recipe's creator. By including coupons for Miracle Whip and related products in each issue, the marketer was also able to increase consumption and track future sales.

5. Building loyalty, as Ikea furniture stores accomplished by mailing to its "Family" of customers an informative home decorating newsletter, which includes not only a questionnaire to track how the family unit is changing, but also discount coupons to bring its members back into the store.

6. Enhancing value. To convince "tekkies" who influence major software decisions for their companies, Microsoft mailed a 30-minute videotape of Bill Gates, president of Microsoft, in a face-to-face dialogue designed to explain the superiority of Microsoft programs in technical language only this audience could appreciate.[1]

For Emily Soell, vice chairman and chief creative officer of Rapp Collins Worldwide, the winners in direct marketing today are those who recognize that the consumers of the '90s have turned the tables on marketers. Suspicious of claims that formerly promised they could "have it all," Soell maintains that consumers have less faith, not only in advertisers, but in doctors, police, teachers, financial advisors, and even religious leaders.

Soell contends that a savvy direct marketer knows how to change old rules to conform to new consumer values. Instead of showing the product, she says, show the promise. *Allure* magazine found that showing the promise of glamour from its pages was not as powerful to the prospective subscriber as promising that the magazine could help her decide exactly how she could contain her costs for face creams, haircuts, and other, often needlessly overpriced, accoutrements of glamour.

Instead of bribing the prospect, Soell adds, contemporary marketing endeavors to *involve* the prospect. To attract possible convention business, the city of Memphis sent a dogeared package to a select list with a hand-scrawled address and the line, "We found your wallet in Memphis" on the outside. Inside was a real wallet, stuffed with simulated "credit cards" that gave recipients numerous reasons to consider Tennessee's largest city as a convention site. While the claims were compelling, it was the magic of the highly involving package that made the difference.

Rather than simply being personal, Soell also cautions marketers to be relevant. Computer generated statements that read: "New York's best dressed women: Ivana and (your name here)" are laughable by today's standards. A much better way to personalize is Gillette's mailing to young men on their eighteenth birthday, which includes a Sensor razor and a can of Foamy shaving cream, plus a coupon offering a reduced price on the next purchase of Sensor blades.

Finally, Soell says that while "making the sale" may be old fashioned, "building the relationship" by staying in touch with buyers is certainly not, and holds the promise of making many more sales over time.

[1] Courtesy Jerome Pickholz, Ogilvy and Mather Direct.

Direct: The Growth Arena of Advertising

One reason direct marketing is growing is that it has become more difficult than ever for advertisers to find a competitive advantage in today's marketplace. While sales promotion and innovative media buying can provide that competitive edge, direct marketing may be the ultimate way for advertisers to build loyalty among consumers by establishing a meaningful, long-term relationship. The term *relationship marketing* represents this continuous attempt by corporations to develop and maintain a strong bond with their customers, not just for one or two purchases, but forever and always.

Thanks to the computer, advertisers can locate their best prospects with an accuracy never before imagined. And thanks to new media options, they can reach their narrow targets without spending money on excess circulation. Buy fat-free salad dressings and yogurt and the scanner at your grocer's checkout identifies you as a prospect for exercise equipment. Join an airline's frequent flyer plan and your gasoline credit card statement arrives with an offer for luggage. Purchase a new car and receive periodic mail from the manufacturer asking you to complete a satisfaction questionnaire and reminding you it's time to run by the dealer's for servicing. Or purchase a new home and a lawn care service calls to see if it can provide you with its monthly service.

Consider how new technology, by further segmenting media audiences, has made it easier for advertisers to stay in touch with its most important consumers in terms of buying potential. Up to 540 channels may be the norm on the TV of tomorrow. Companies are building their own interactive networks so anything the customer wants to see may be as close as a phone call or the button on a TV set. The role of existing broadcast networks may be taken over by libraries of information owned by businesses, which can relay the data anywhere in the world by satellite, creating a pay-per-use system for entertainment, news, and purchasing. One futurist hints at a time when we may carry electronic newspapers in our pockets for instant news or stock quotes, or any information now found in a newspaper.

The biggest advantage to the consumer is access to a wide array of programs, dial-a-movie, interactive video games, video phone calls to friends, or books from electronic libraries. For advertisers, the proliferation of media and its resulting segmenting of audiences may call for as many as thirty-five versions of the same commercial to be aired on different cable channels.

Marketers around the world are going beyond traditional advertising strategies to influence brand loyalty by capturing names of prospects on databases and using this data to respond to consumer suggestions, answer consumer needs, and use consumer interests as the basis for product promotions.

In France, Nestlé added share points to its baby food sales through relationship marketing that focused on highway rest stop structures where parents could feed and change babies during the peak summer holiday season. Maintaining and updating a database of 220,000 new mothers, Nestlé sent six mailings at key stages of development in the new life, including a Mother's Day mailing that offered a rose for Momma as a gift from Baby.

For its Buitoni pasta brand, Nestlé established a strong relationship with consumers in the UK. First they restored the original Buitoni villa in Italy and then launched an ad campaign, which took the reader through a pasta recipe and invited readers to call for a free recipe booklet (TV commercials did the same). With the respondents' names, Nestlé launched the Casa Buitoni Club, sending members a magazine filled with recipes, articles, and features that drew them into a community of people interested in the mystique of the Italian lifestyle.

To promote its Windows operating system and get owners of its applications software to trade up to new versions, Microsoft has employed a number of relationship tactics, using its own customer databases.[2] About 30 percent of its applications sales are to new customers trading up to new versions, while another 30 percent are to customers buying additional programs. "The customer buys a product—it's great," says Jim Minervino, director of end-user marketing. "Now the relationship begins. It's sort of like a first date. You can just first date a thousand people or you can decide to have a relationship."

Customers in the fast-growing Microsoft database (by 1993, 8.5 million names, gathered from product registration cards that Microsoft asked PC marketers to include in their packages) receive direct mail advertising in the form of a quarterly newsletter with software user tips, product upgrade deals, and information on new products. They are also reached through customer seminars and public relations. Because the various communications are narrowly focused, Microsoft can make the information more relevant to each particular audience.

How Closely Can Relationships Be Built?

To promote a new service, Bell Atlantic mailed customers an envelope that unfolded into a brown paper garbage bag with the headline, "Answering Machine Garbage Bag." On the reverse side were "10 reasons to bag your answering machine and get Answer Call." For its Call Manager package, the company sent customers a letter with a package of Tylenol gelcaps and the headline, "Here's a short-term remedy for life's headaches." On the other side, Bell described its "stress relieving" phone services. In a co-op mailing with Domino's Pizza, Bell sent customers pizza coupons in an envelope also containing glossy stickers of a pizza with messages underneath. Customers were advised to "peel off a slice of pizza and find the service that fits your needs."

While many have viewed database marketing as a short-term promotional vehicle, proponents say its true value is its ability to cement brand loyalty and find the right customers in a way promotions haven't. Studies show that extremely loyal consumers are worth far more in profits because of lower marketing costs,

[2] "In a millisecond, Microsoft boots up marketing database," *Advertising Age*, November 8, 1993.

higher purchase activity, and referrals of friends. This is relationship marketing at its most efficient.

In some categories the best customers are also the best prospects for growth. The AAdvantage frequent flier program is predicated on the notion that 65 percent of American's business comes from just 800,000 customers, or 21 percent of its total.

American Express announced a major foray into database publishing with the development of a hybrid newsletter/catalog/magazine for fashion conscious female cardholders. This is a prime example of finding new ways for its merchants and other marketers to tap into this coveted database. Mailed free to women in eleven major markets (who were identified by researching AmEx's cardholder database as "having a common denominator of a passionate interest in fashion, shopping, and style"), *The Style Report* was offered to five sponsors who could benefit from the controlled circulation mailing of 750,000. Audience, editorial content, and frequency of publication were developed using cardholders' spending patterns and other quantitative and qualitative measures.

More Advertisers Take Advantage of Media Alternatives

Even upscale designers like Calvin Klein are looking at new media alternatives. The first Calvin Klein catalog was intended for an exclusive mailing to Neiman Marcus and Bergdorf Goodman customers, one million shoppers in all, with a cable TV version on a shopping channel as a future possibility. Catalogers are well-positioned for TV shopping because they're clearly oriented to consumers shopping at home. It's just a matter of shifting the medium from print to electronics.

Other established names are also exploring electronic retailing. Saks Fifth Avenue did a trial run of at least four hour-long shows on QVC, hoping to generate $400,000 in sales in an hour.

Little of the present revolution in direct marketing would have been possible without the computer, the credit card, and the 800 phone number. With computers that can capture and assimilate detailed information about businesses and individuals and convert that information into narrowly targeted mailing lists, direct marketing has reached new levels of sophistication.

At the Reuben H. Donnelley computer operation in Lincoln, Nebraska, are the names and addresses from the nation's 2,700 telephone books. Not much to go on—until you start comparing notes with other computers. Census data, for instance, will tell you how many people live at a phone address, with particulars on the value of the home and the family income. Comparing these results with, say, vehicle registrations, you find that some homes have two cars. Maybe Mom works. An RV? Somebody goes camping. Station wagon? Kids. Sports car? A carefree, young-in-heart who may be a spender. Add input from ZIP code data, then inspect, reject, and detect. Since almost everyone buys mailing lists from everyone else, a marketer can detect potential consumers from the magazines they subscribe to. *The New Yorker?* Upscale. *Money* magazine? Strong evidence of loose change. *National Geographic?* Travelers, armchair or actual. If they bought a sleeping bag or fly rod, L. L. Bean and Norm Thompson catalogs won't be far behind.

Once you know your audience well, you can write to them. Richard Thalheimer began his *Sharper Image* catalog by writing clever copy and offering oddball items such as a suit of fifteenth-century armor for $2,450. Gary Comer, a former ad copywriter, started *Lands' End* as a yacht supplier, then transformed it into one of the biggest clothing catalogs. Where but in America could American Express sell 6,000 busts of King Tut through the mail?

Although this discussion will deal primarily with the creative process in writing and designing direct advertising, it's important to point out that there are other areas in direct advertising in which creativity is equally important.

The first is the list. It is an absolute in direct advertising that the list of prospects is the most important element of any campaign. Here's why. The direct advertising message is delivered primarily through the mail, and the cost of outgoing and incoming mail, as well as incoming telephone calls, constitutes the largest single expense of a direct marketing campaign. Because of this high per-contact cost, it is critical to restrict such a campaign to individuals or businesses most likely to respond to the offer.

Nonetheless, the copy is critical. Copywriters estimate they have only four seconds to get a consumer's attention with direct mail. This is why great care is devoted to the design of the envelope, which may be oversized or carry a bold, startling message, or both. It can be laser printed to make a recipient's name look handwritten. Inside the irresistible envelope, many direct mail offers contain the "magic three": a personalized and typewritten letter, a brochure, and a response card. Mailings often include stickers or buttons to involve the consumer.

The letter is a one-on-one message, employing the second person *you* extensively. It's important to devise a salutation that gets as close to the recipient as you can. If you can't call him by name, try such targeted phrases as "Dear Seasoned Traveler," "Dear Music Lover," etc. If a traditional salutation seems out of place, write an introductory sentence and position it so it looks like a salutation.

Interestingly, the traditional four-page letter attracts prospects, who skim rather than read every word. For this reason, subheadings, underlined statements, even ellipses (. . .) seem to draw readers into the story. Because the postscript of the letter is the second most read part (the first is the opening salutation), most letters include the familiar "P.S."

The brochure accompanying the letter is more objectively written. In the third person, it talks in terms of features and benefits. The reply card states the offer in specific terms. It serves as the contract between the buyer and seller and should be short and simple. The offer should be made in inviting terms: "Yes, I want to take advantage of your wonderful travel package. . . ."

Direct advertising is used ideally as one element of a total advertising campaign. Testing has indicated that a direct advertising campaign launched in conjunction with a mass media blitz produces a higher response than an isolated direct campaign. Also, when the direct campaign includes three mailings, varying in copy but not in the offer, that continue over the length of the media schedule, the response will be at least double that of a campaign with only a single mailing.

Advantages of Direct over Other Forms of Advertising

1. ***Ability to pinpoint a select group of prospects.*** Mary Kay Cosmetics, which for years has used personal selling in prospects' homes, used direct mail to get its established buyers to call their May Kay salesperson. The mailing even mentioned the salesperson, as well as the prospect, by name. Those who made the call were promised a free gift. Those who did not respond had their names turned over to the salesperson in the area, who made the initial call with the free gift offer.

2. ***Ability to personalize the message.*** Even though the sales letter is no match for the personal letter, consumers and businesspeople will still respond to a highly personalized sales letter. Successful fund raisers will design letters that acknowledge previous donations before asking for a new contribution. Direct marketers with sophisticated databases will draw on the information about their prospects to personalize letters as much as possible. Take, for example, the letter that begins: "You're one of the special people who chooses his wines as carefully as he chooses his friends," or "Let others read the gossip and personality magazines. For you, a magazine must offer more. That's why we're privileged to introduce you to. . . ."

3. ***Fewer space/time restrictions.*** Print media limit advertising by the parameters of the page, while radio and television commercials are limited by the time available for programming. But with the exception of minor regulations imposed by the U.S. Postal Service, direct response advertising has no space, time, or weight limitations. The creative team can let imaginations run wild, developing multifold self-mailers, odd-shaped boxes, and inserts ranging from fragrances in tear-open packs to actual product samples.

4. ***The message stands out more amidst other media clutter.*** While print and broadcast advertising compete with editorial and programming information and entertainment, the direct advertisement stands alone. If the outer design and copy are successful in getting the recipient to open the package, your message has her complete attention as long as the reader finds it to be of interest.

5. ***Access to a wide range of materials.*** With boxed or three-dimensional mailings, the direct marketer can send product samples. Software manufacturers provide floppy disks with sales messages and visuals about products and services

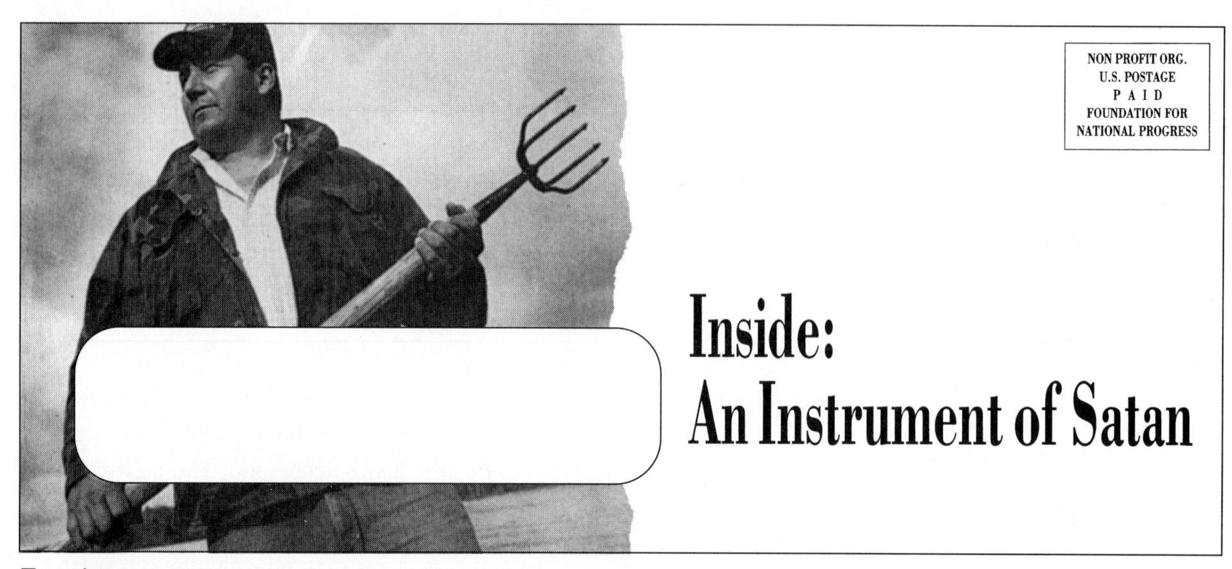

Envelope

Brochure

FIGURE 11-1

Mother Jones, the liberal investigative magazine published in San Francisco, has won the hearts (and subscriptions) of its constituents by admitting exactly what it is: a publication unafraid of big business or big government. Note the provocative envelope (An Instrument of Satan), the brochure (What your mother never told you . . .), and especially the "tell it like it is" letter that contradicts the "satanic image" of the envelope by chronicling the success of the magazine in exposing questionable practices and products. Note especially: (1) the headline at the start of the letter, (2) the opening paragraph which sets the tone and delivers the message instantly, (3) the offer mention on page one, page three, and page four, (4) the "handwritten" signature, and (5) the use of a postscript to repeat the offer. Courtesy *Mother Jones,* copy by Matthew Soyster.

MOTHERJONES

"The Nation's Best Magazine for Investigative Journalism." American Journalism Review

First they dismissed us as flaky and hysterical.
Then they branded us a threat to internal security.
Now they're calling us an instrument of satan.
Find out why. FREE

Dear Reader,

Ever get the queasy feeling you've just read the same six articles over and over again in a half-dozen different magazines?

Wackos in Waco. Yattering with Yeltsin. Soaping up with Schwarzkopf. Hobnobbing with Hillary. Disrobing (yawn) with Demi.

The same torpid insights from the same cast of "experts." The same shallow gossip. The same stale spin.

What's more, you have to wade through 40 glossy ad spreads for floral bed linen, designer perfume and Italian luggage... before you get to one slim nugget of real news.

When you're done, what more do you really know about the world? How will it help you put things in perspective?

No wonder things often look as bleak as a *thirty-something* rerun.

Now -- here's a prescription that will decidedly improve your outlook. Intrigue you. Enlighten you. Empower you. And give a lively new boost to your political IQ.

(In this dramatic year of Washington turnover, it might just make a difference.)

Just fire off the order card in this envelope, and I'll rush you, with my compliments, the latest issue of the all-new MOTHER JONES.

<u>It's yours free</u>. An uncompromising, uncensored, unapologetic journal teeming with the real people, politics and passions that have a daily impact on your world.

Plus some hardheaded tips on how <u>you</u> can make a daily impact for peace, social justice and a safer environment.

It's also a damn good read.

Letter

-2-

MOTHER JONES? Isn't she that feisty old gal who pulled the plug on the lethally defective Ford Pinto?...

Yanked the chain on the corporate criminals who were dumping hazardous junk in the Third World?...

Blew the whistle on federal bureaucrats who twiddled their thumbs while millions of Americans came down with AIDS?

Yep, yep and yep.

Like our namesake, orator and agitator Mary Harris "Mother" Jones, we have a bit of a history. (Including three National Magazine Awards in our first four years.)

Also like the original article, we get results. (In the case of Ford Pinto, a homicide indictment, $20 million in consumer lawsuits and the largest auto recall in history.)

How do we do it? By sponsoring the kind of gritty, time-consuming, often dangerous investigative journalism that the rest of the press just doesn't have the stomach for.

(Or doesn't respect your smarts enough to dig for.)

Result? In an era when corporate megamergers have gobbled up most news sources... tainting what you see, read and hear with fluff, euphemism or outright distortion...

MOTHER JONES remains the unchallenged leader in hard-hitting, between-the-lines, no-holds-barred, nose-to-the-street, no-nonsense news, analysis and consumer advocacy.

The kind you simply won't find in the New York Times, the Wall Street Journal, Esquire, Newsweek or Vanity Fair.

And today we're doing our job with more chutzpah, punch and audacity than ever before.

Just ask our quarter-million avid readers. Or, the media pros polled by the American Journalism Review, who voted us the nation's "Best Magazine for Investigative Journalism."

What do they find in every issue of MOTHER JONES?

<u>In-Depth Exposés</u>. Like the ones that awakened America to the health-threatening Dalkon Shield. Toxic breast implants. The pesticide peril at your breakfast table. The electronics industry's calculated decision to shred the ozone layer.

-3-

Thoughtful Essays. Like our level-headed look at black urban poverty and America's growing trailer-home population. Gays in the military and the crisis in the Balkans. Women in the Men's Movement. Congressional reform.

Practical Advice. Like what to do when job options and principles collide. How to conduct an ecological audit of your home. Protect yourself from skin cancer. Seize back the airwaves. Act up against AIDS. Lead a shareholder revolt.

Also an unabashed point of view. A passion for uncovering government corruption and corporate shenanigans. An aversion to gridlock. A commitment to the little guy.

Needless to say, all this attitude and insight doesn't sit very well with some of the self-appointed legislators of political correctitude and public morality.

Demagogues on the right... who've branded us pro-terrorist, pro-feminist, pro-socialist, pro-hedonist, pro-humanist, pro-communist, pro-gay.

Ideologues on the left... who've squealed when we skewered a few of their sacred cows.

Or the fundamentalist kooks at the Coalition on Revival who denounced our coverage as "a powerful blow by Satan."

Are we going to let this gutter-baiting gall us?... Naaah. You see, the old lady's still got her teeth, and she knows how to bite back.

But she sure could use a few more independent thinkers like you along for the ride. After all, you're the reason we keep raking up the muck.

So -- waste not a second. All you need do is return the enclosed card. Your trial issue comes FREE.

If you like it, I'll round out your year with five more bimonthly issues of MOTHER JONES (6 total) for a full 33% off our regular subscription rate.

Send no payment now, if you like. We'll bill you later.

But -- if you do send payment with your order, I'll sweeten the deal. Extending your subscription by two more issues (that's 8 in all) for the same low price.

-4-

And if at any time you're not thoroughly enthused, engaged and galvanized, simply cancel your subscription. I'll send you a full refund on all unserved issues.

MOTHER JONES. We're not just a mirror of events, but a catalyst. A Molotov cocktail of ideas. A prairie fire of inspiration.

Are we also an instrument of Satan? Well, perhaps not. (The fellow on the envelope is actually a Chippewa spear-fisher named Tom Maulson, one of our 1991 grassroots activist award-winners.)

But we can assure you a devilish good time. While we make things mighty hot for the powers that be.

Can you afford just 23¢ a week to put yourself in the know, and keep America's best investigative machinery humming? ... That depends.

Are you the kind of person who's a little disgruntled with the status quo? Ready for a fresh outlook?

The kind who's willing to read between the lines? See the writing on the wall? Punch a hole in some platitudes?

Are you really? ... Then come on. Take a chance. Fill out the card. Cross the median. Welcome to the other side.

Cheers,

Jeffrey Klein
Editor

P. S. Act now, risk nothing. 33% off the regular subscription rate! And if you don't find MOTHER JONES completely indispensable, cancel at any time for a full refund on all unserved issues.

Pay now, get more. Two extra issues (that's 8 in all) for the same low price!

offered. They know from their databases that every prospect has a computer that will accept their disk.

A commercial real estate developer wanted to interest major U.S. hotel chains in a prime piece of property. One of his selling points was that the property would be developed according to the customized needs of the hotel chain or, in real estate jargon, "built to suit." To make this point, the direct marketing package consisted of a letter, a brochure, and a site map—all attached to an expensive, solid oak suit hanger and mailed in a man's suit box to the presidents of the leading U.S. hotel chains.

Raising the Odds for a Response

Direct advertising differs from other media advertising in that it is driven by one overwhelming consideration: the ability to get an appropriate response from the right audience. This creates an enormous challenge, considering that direct advertising not only must compete with other forms of advertising, but with other direct advertising promotions.

Consider what you receive in the mail daily: bills and personal letters, plus a flurry of mailings asking for your business or seeking a donation from you. If you are typical, you glance quickly at the envelope of a direct advertising piece and decide in a few seconds whether you will open it or not. For business mail, an even greater challenge is to break the barrier of the "censor"—the secretary or administrative assistant who is told to toss out any "junk mail." Some marketers have overcome this hurdle by making their mail as personal looking as possible. A business envelope with the executive's name and address and an absence of frills may have the best chance of reaching the prospect.

In other situations, humor may be the best way to reach the prospect. A mailer to warehouse owners asked: "Is a leaking roof soaking up your profits?" When the mailer was opened, the copy read: "Then use this sponge." Glued to the inside was a freeze-dried sponge that expands when wet. Copy then explained that a more permanent solution might be to have a new roof installed by the company that mailed the brochure. On the advice of its direct marketing agency, the roofing company authorized the preparation of the brochure and agreed to have it mailed only after a heavy downpour. It worked. (See Figure 11-2)

The direct advertising piece can be as effective as a personal sales call, without the high cost of the latter, if certain rules are followed:

1. ***The mailing demonstrates complete and accurate knowledge of the product, service, or organization.*** The seasoned sales representative never makes a call until he or she knows every detail of the product or service being offered. The rep is then prepared to answer specific questions from the prospect. But if you are selling by direct advertising, you can't be there to field

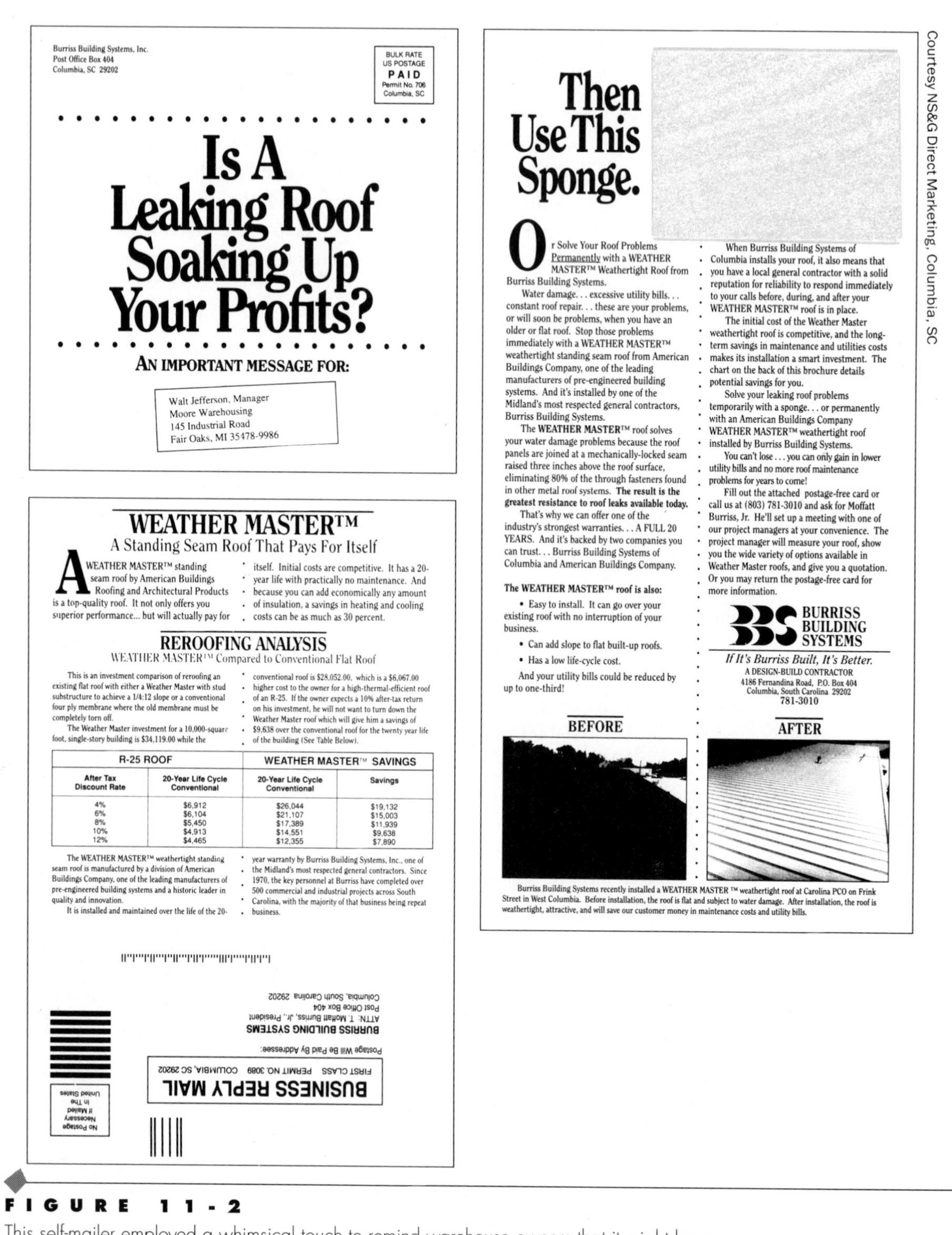

Courtesy NS&G Direct Marketing, Columbia, SC

FIGURE 11-2

This self-mailer employed a whimsical touch to remind warehouse owners that it might be a good time to install a new metal roof, especially since the mailing was prepared in advance and timed to be sent immediately following a heavy downpour. Above average response rates helped launch a new business for the metal building contractor.

questions. That's why it's critical to research your target audience to anticipate any questions and problems and to ensure that the answers are clearly evident in the advertising.

2. ***The mailing describes the product or service with enthusiasm.*** Because it must generate as many responses as possible, direct copy must be written without wasted words or needless digressions. The National Geographic Society, offering a subscription to its *Traveler* magazine, opens its letter:

You be the judge. Enjoy the next issue of NATIONAL GEOGRAPHIC TRAVELER magazine, without obligation, and then . . .

When you become a regular paid subscriber . . . you'll also receive a FREE video of our U.S. national parks!

Line after line, the letter continues with specific benefits of subscribing, ending with a clearly stated set of instructions:

Just drop the attached card in the mail for your free trial issue. Enjoy the stunning photography and entertaining articles. Only then decide if you want the pleasure of continuing as a regular TRAVELER subscriber.

Please send for your free trial issue now. You've got nothing to lose, and so much to experience.

True to form, there is a P.S.: "Don't forget your *free* video with paid subscription!"

The attached reply card states the offer completely:

Yes, please send me a FREE trial issue of TRAVELER. If I like it, I'll pay $17.95 for my annual subscription (making six issues in all) and receive my free national parks video! If I'm not delighted, I'll return the invoice marked "cancel." In either case, the first issue is mine to keep and enjoy!

Lively, specific, convincing. Everything direct advertising not only should be, but must be.

3. ***The mailing must demonstrate an understanding of the prospect's needs and the ability to solve the prospect's problems.*** While formal research can identify needs, a working knowledge of psychology lends insight to those needs. We all have a need for security; we have egos that are fed by the promise of success; we feel pity for human suffering and have doubts about the uncertain future. Such insights can greatly strengthen the appeal of any direct advertising copy. A plant manager may want a computer system to make his operation more cost effective. What he really needs is the security of such a system and ego gratification ("If I make my operation less costly, I'll keep my job and may even earn a promotion.").

4. ***The mailing must emphasize benefits over features.*** As in all advertising, the respondent wants to know, "What's in it for me?" In direct advertising it is essential to get to the benefits early, as this AT&T letter addressed to former

FIGURE 11-3
When I received an envelope in the mail telling me I could type words into the computer and find the word I couldn't remember, I jumped at the chance to purchase this software. Then I realized what a fabulous job Ed Sattizahn of WordStar had done on this direct response piece. Not only the envelope, but the brochure and letter are marvels of persuasion and entertainment. The brochure, for example, includes a quiz, with answers, on ten items many people can't name. If you can't think of the Greek goddess of wisdom, for example, you type in Greek, goddess, and wisdom, and you get Athena. Note in the letter these points especially: (1) the blazing offer in the headline, (2) the inviting opening copy: "I couldn't remember the word, and it was driving me nuts," (3) the bold subheadings throughout the copy, (4) the offer repeated on page 4, (5) the "handwritten" signature, and (6) the postscript with still another mention of the offer. (Figure 11–3 continues on pages 259–263.)

long distance subscribers did. It began with a headline: "Since You Left Us, We're Not the Same." The first paragraph of the letter made the major benefit blatantly clear:

If you left us because of price, we have good news for you. AT&T has changed. And once you see how much, you'll see why it's easy to switch to AT&T.

Act now to get $10 worth of FREE AT&T Long Distance calls!

A benefit, clearly and blatantly stated in the opening lines of the letter.

5. ***The mailing always asks for a response.*** Sounds simple, doesn't it? You would be surprised at the number of businesses that send letters and newsletters regularly and never ask for a response. There are two basic ways to elicit the response. Use a business reply card or envelope, or use a toll-free number. Either way, the benefit to the respondent is that it costs nothing. The recipient is told

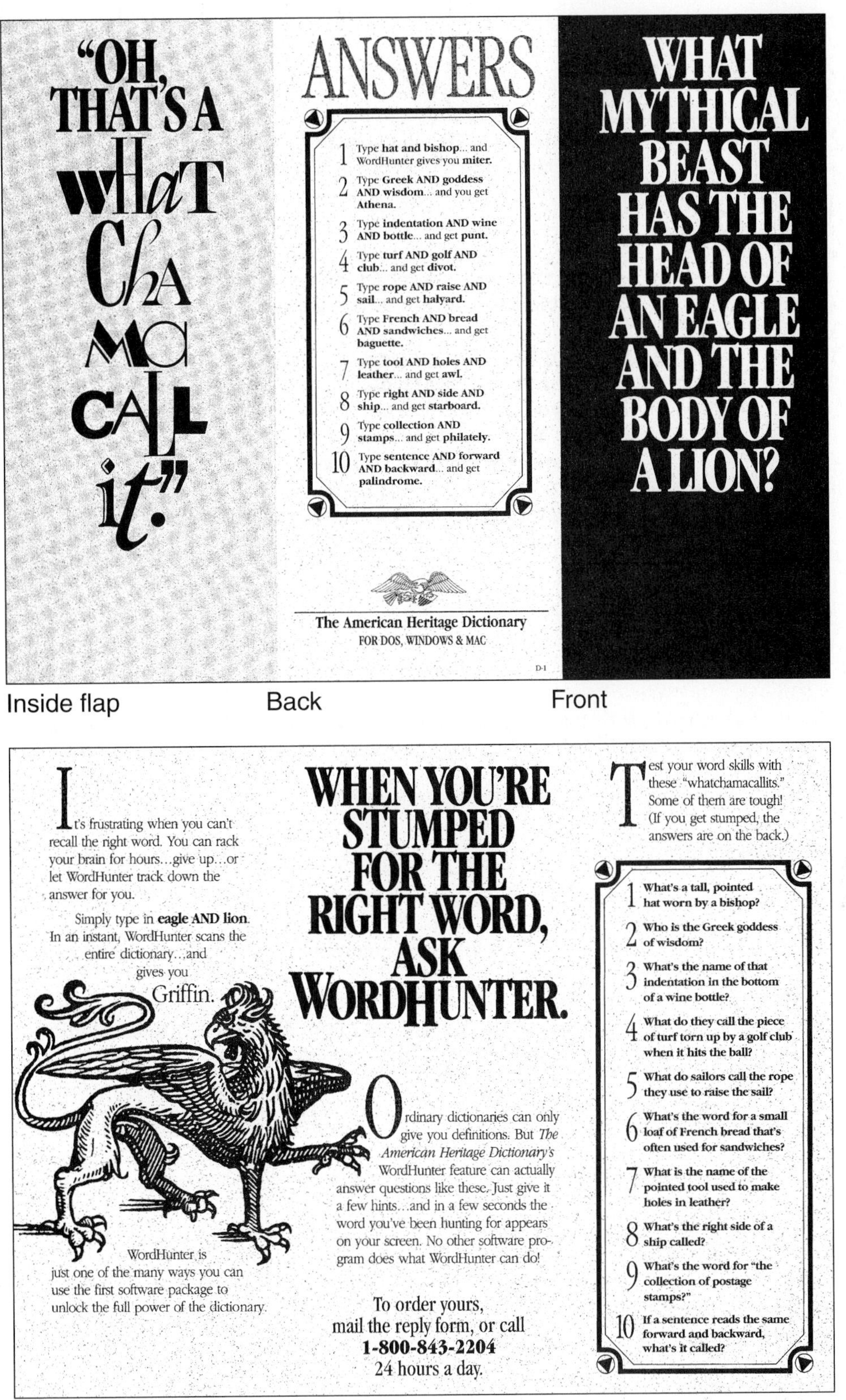

Inside flap | Back | Front

Inside brochure

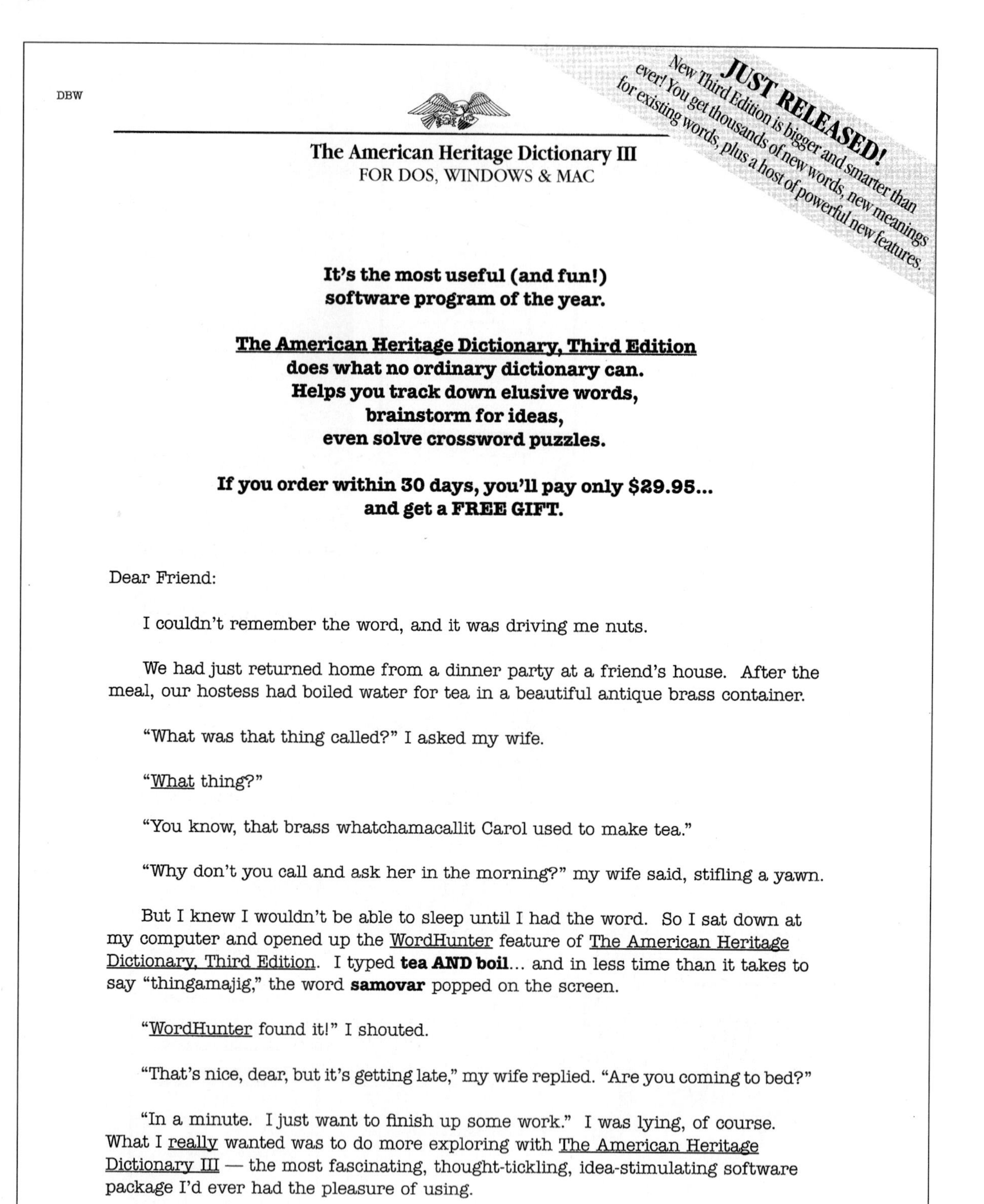

DBW

The American Heritage Dictionary III
FOR DOS, WINDOWS & MAC

JUST RELEASED!
New Third Edition is bigger and smarter than ever! You get thousands of new words, new meanings for existing words, plus a host of powerful new features.

It's the most useful (and fun!) software program of the year.

The American Heritage Dictionary, Third Edition does what no ordinary dictionary can. Helps you track down elusive words, brainstorm for ideas, even solve crossword puzzles.

If you order within 30 days, you'll pay only $29.95... and get a FREE GIFT.

Dear Friend:

I couldn't remember the word, and it was driving me nuts.

We had just returned home from a dinner party at a friend's house. After the meal, our hostess had boiled water for tea in a beautiful antique brass container.

"What was that thing called?" I asked my wife.

"What thing?"

"You know, that brass whatchamacallit Carol used to make tea."

"Why don't you call and ask her in the morning?" my wife said, stifling a yawn.

But I knew I wouldn't be able to sleep until I had the word. So I sat down at my computer and opened up the WordHunter feature of The American Heritage Dictionary, Third Edition. I typed **tea AND boil**... and in less time than it takes to say "thingamajig," the word **samovar** popped on the screen.

"WordHunter found it!" I shouted.

"That's nice, dear, but it's getting late," my wife replied. "Are you coming to bed?"

"In a minute. I just want to finish up some work." I was lying, of course. What I really wanted was to do more exploring with The American Heritage Dictionary III — the most fascinating, thought-tickling, idea-stimulating software package I'd ever had the pleasure of using.

Letter

You've never seen a dictionary like this before!

More than just definitions, more than a thesaurus, more than a spell checker, The American Heritage Dictionary III is a versatile new reference tool that can help you remember words... enhance your creativity... find information... do homework faster... even solve word puzzles.

No other software gives you so much word information, with so many unique ways to use that information. It's the most comprehensive, easiest-to-use dictionary available for your DOS, Windows or Macintosh computer.

End "tip-of-the-tongue" frustration forever!

When the word you want is on the tip of your tongue but you just can't recall it... or you need a specific word but can only think of a vague meaning or related concept... do what I do. Use WordHunter.

Just type in one or more "hints" and WordHunter instantly scans the entire Dictionary, searching for the word (or words) you want.

Let's say you've forgotten the name of a yellow flower. Simply type **yellow AND flowers**. In seconds, WordHunter gives you 54 yellow flowers from which to choose.

Or suppose you're planning a business trip to India and you want to know what the currency is called. Type **India AND currency** and you get **paisa** and **rupee**.

Whether you use it for business, school, personal writing — or simply for your own entertainment — WordHunter can give you fresh ideas and enhance your creativity. And it's available only with The American Heritage Dictionary III.

The full power of the dictionary is at your fingertips.

But WordHunter is just the beginning. You'll also find everything you expect from one of the world's most popular and respected dictionaries. For more than 100,000 words, you get...

* complete definitions
* spelling
* parts of speech
* inflections
* proper usage
* pronunciations
* sample sentences
* hyphenation
* idioms

The program even guides you to the correct entry when you misspell the word you're trying to find.

You also get the complete Roget's II Electronic Thesaurus, with more than half a million synonyms. Now you'll always find the perfect words to keep your writing fresh and vivid. And if you want to check the definition of a synonym you've just found, you can switch quickly from the Thesaurus to the Dictionary.

The liveliest new dictionary in a decade.

The first new edition in ten years, the Third Edition has been completely revised and updated to keep pace with our colorful and ever-changing language.

You get up-to-the-minute definitions for new words like **ergonomics... perestroika... CD-ROM... pixel....nonself... privatize...** and thousands more. Plus, you get new meanings for old words like **rap** (a type of popular music)... and **boot** (to load a software program).

A crossword puzzle-lover's best friend.

Use the Wildcard feature to find words when you don't know all the letters. For example, type **sl??p** and Wildcard gives you **sleep, sloop, slump** and **slurp**. It's the answer to a crossword puzzle-lover's prayers!

Wildcard can even help you compose poetry and jingles. To find words that rhyme, simply type in the letters of the part of the word you want to rhyme, and Wildcard does the rest.

And if you like to play word games, you'll enjoy the Anagram feature, which lets you find the other words hidden in the one you're using. Type **spot,** for example, and Anagram gives you **opts, post, pots, stop** and **tops.**

The dictionary that's always there when you need it.

The American Heritage Dictionary III is so fast and easy to use, you'll never be too busy to use it. The DOS version is a TSR program, which means it resides in your computer's memory until you call it into action. The Windows version can be accessed from the System menu under Windows 3.1. The Macintosh version automatically looks up whatever word you've highlighted.

After you find the word you want, simply paste it into your text. You can even paste in the entire definition. It's never been this easy to polish your writing!

Save more than $30.
Get a money-back guarantee.
And a FREE GIFT!

By ordering direct, you pay only $29.95 — instead of the $59.95 suggested store price.

Use The American Heritage Dictionary III for two full months. See for yourself how easy (and how much fun!) it is to use. See how it helps you find those words you can't remember... write more eloquently... build your word power... stimulate your creativity. If you're not completely delighted, simply return it within 60 days for a full refund, less shipping and handling.

> If you order now, you'll also receive — FREE — Correct Quotes, a handy software library of quotations. You get more than 5,000 quotations on hundreds of topics from the world's greatest writers, politicians, scientists, humorists and philosophers. It's an easy way to add color and impact to your reports, letters, proposals and speeches.

To order, mail or fax the reply card. Or, for faster service, call **1-800-843-2204** 24 hours a day.

Cordially,

Ed Sattizahn

P.S. Correct Quotes is worth $29.95, but it's yours to keep — FREE — even if you decide to return The American Heritage Dictionary III for a full refund, less shipping and handling.

WORDSTAR INTERNATIONAL, INC.
P.O. Box 629000
El Dorado Hills, CA 95762

DOS SYSTEM REQUIREMENTS: IBM or 100% compatible system with 640 Kb RAM; hard disk with 6.5 Mb free space; DOS 3.1 or higher. Works with all character-based applications, including word processors, spreadsheets, databases and E-mail. Runs as a TSR program, so it can be accessed at any time.

WINDOWS SYSTEM REQUIREMENTS: Windows 3.1 or higher; 4 Mb RAM; hard disk with 6.5 Mb free space. Works within all applications, including word processors, spreadsheets, databases and E-mail.

MACINTOSH SYSTEM REQUIREMENTS: Any Macintosh (including Classics, Powerbooks and Quadras) with at least 1 Mb RAM (2 Mb for System 7); hard disk with 5 Mb free space; System 6.0.2 or higher; System 7 compatible; 32-bit clean.

clearly how to respond on every piece in the mailing: in the letter, the brochure, on the order blank or catalog page. Here repetition makes sense because the average direct mail reader skims each piece of the mailing. A significant number of prospects go directly to the response coupon, ignoring the letter and brochure, because they know they will find a short summary of the entire offer there.

Direct Fundraising: Asking for Money with Nothing in Return

Nonprofit organizations such as the March of Dimes and the American Lung Association use direct advertising as their major fundraising tool. In recent years, over $104 billion annually has been raised nationwide for such causes, using creative and aggressive direct mail campaigning. As state and federal funds for nonprofit activities continue to dwindle, more and more charities and cultural groups are turning to direct advertising for support. Competition for consumer donations is fierce and will become more so. Those organizations that cultivate current givers and prove that donations directly benefit their causes will be the winners.

Another factor in the surge of direct pleas for donations is the attempt by organizations involved in advocacy and social change to rid themselves of corporate support and large donors, turning instead to hundreds of thousands of dedicated small donors. Such organizations have discovered that 85 percent of their contributions come from such small donors as a democratic way of funding social change.

Sophisticated campaigns expect to spend heavily to acquire donors, even if the donation fails to cover the expense, because they know the predictability of the payback, or recovery of outlay, is in fundraising solicitations. Accordingly, when a donor is first acquired, the contribution is swiftly and "personally" acknowledged to bring the donor inside the organization. Subsequently, the donor is asked annually to renew the donation, as the organization attempts to increase the amount of the donation each year.

Fundraising solicitations pose other peculiar problems. Remember that a fundraiser asks for money with nothing offered in return. Unless the case for support is made vitally clear, the appeal may fall on deaf ears. Often the benefit to the giver is a sense of helping the needy. In some instances, the giver will respond to support a service, like public television, that she enjoys herself.

Catalogs: Bringing the Retail Store into the Home and Office

Catalog advertising has come a long way wince the early Sears' and Ward's catalogs. Although some tightening is evident in catalog sales, and a number of marginal catalogs have fallen by the wayside, catalog sales have emerged as a major portion of the retail business in the United States.

The successful catalog follows the trend of all successful direct advertising today: target to specific groups of buyers. So today we have:

- Kemp George. Your source for a more beautiful home. This catalog features elegant accessories for the home, from scalloped china sink basins to a free-standing Victorian style mailbox.
- The SelfCare Catalog, with selections for healthful cooking, sun protection, natural skin care, stress control, fitness, massage, and back care.
- John Deere, the catalog for home, lawn, and garden.
- Crate and Barrel, a highly successful marketer of items for the kitchen, bath, and all around the home.
- The Woodworkers' Store, a catalog for do-it-yourselfers.
- Hold Everything, chock-full of organizers for the home.
- Domestications, for linens and dinnerware.
- Lands' End sportswear for the family.
- Gardener's Eden, The Nature Company Catalog, J. Crew, and L. L. Bean sportswear—and hundreds more, each with a particular audience in mind for the types of goods between the cover pages.

To order merchandise, you don't even have to fill out an order form in most cases. You simply dial a toll-free number, place your order, and charge it to a major credit card. Return policies are generally liberal, so the customer need not be concerned about buying sight unseen.

In addition to being persuasive and interesting, catalog copy must anticipate questions and provide all the answers. Prospects who can't examine a knit shirt in person must know it's 100 percent cotton, washable, and comes in sixteen colors and four sizes.

Designing the Direct Mail Piece

Direct mail advertising comes in all shapes and sizes. As long as you observe the U.S. Postal Service restrictions, you can create a design on a huge sheet of paper, and fold it down to a size approved for mailing. Irregular die-cut shapes and cutouts, while more costly, can add visual impact to your mailing and help it stand out from the rest.

Perhaps the most common design for direct mail is the two-fold folder that begins with a standard $8\frac{1}{2} \times 11$ inch sheet of paper folded into equal thirds. Using standard paper size and a standard legal envelope will keep the cost of producing your mailing down.

FIGURE 11-4
This three-dimensional mailing for Kayser-Roth Corporation, Greensboro, N.C., was used to demonstrate the superior quality of a new brand of hosiery. The box was sent to managers of a major drugstore chain and to selected supermarkets.

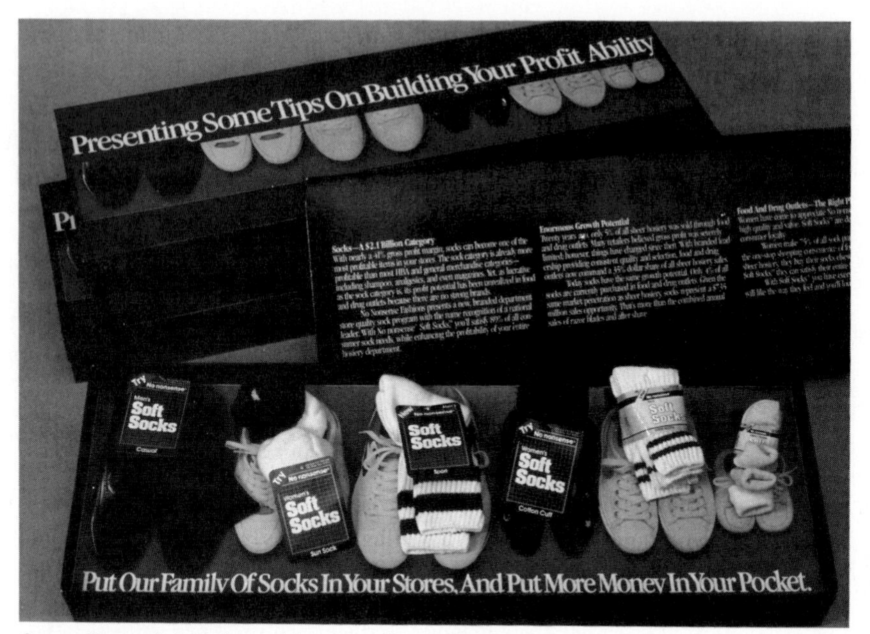

Courtesy Newman Saylor & Gregory Advertising and Kayser-Roth Corporation

To begin creating such a piece, fold a blank piece of standard paper into thirds and roughly pencil in what is to go on each "facing" or panel. In preparing this "dummy," note that when you unfold it, the front panel is on the right, the back panel is in the center, and the inside flap is on the left. When you turn the dummy over, you have the entire inside of the folder.

Now, what goes where?

It's best to begin where the reader will—on the outer envelope. Determine what your "hook" will be first, then continue your copy and visual message in a logical manner, beginning with the front of the brochure. No need for lots of copy on the front; think of it as the title page of a small book. Create another headline that will lure the reader into opening to the first inside spread, which displays the flap on the right side and the inside left panel to the left.

Generally, your reader goes to the next right-hand page—so make the flap work hard for you. You may decide to continue the thought from the front panel to the flap, in the same style and size of type and in the same place on the page. On the left panel, which will also be a part of the inside display, you might want to choose a visual to contrast with the type on the flap. Once the reader unfolds the flap to the three-panel inside, you can continue with details of your message set in text. If your offer includes a coupon, be certain it's an approved size and that it falls on the outer edges of the piece, so that it will be easy to clip.

That leaves the back of the folder, which may carry additional copy and visuals, or may simply feature the brand logo and campaign theme line at the bottom.

Once you work out the design and copy details on the dummy, you're ready to create the final piece. A good suggestion is to prepare the finished layout for each side of the brochure separately, cut them out, and glue them back to back, with a third blank sheet in between to prevent "show through" of any marks from the opposite side. You can also prepare the finished layout on heavy art paper, which will also keep markers from bleeding through to the other side.

Create your envelope copy and design on a regular envelope, place the finished and folded layout inside, and mount the back of the envelope on black matte board or foamcore for presentation, when you can show the envelope and lift out the brochure.

Specialists in writing direct advertising copy claim the key to success is the element of one-to-one human contact. "There's no mystery about the No. 1 social problem in the United States," claims Robert Haydon Jones. "It's loneliness and alienation. Every new research poll confirms this, year after year. In direct marketing, perhaps more than in any other medium, we can take advantage of that reality. . . . The simplest letter gives us the chance for a great platform for dialogue. Someone has written to me. How interesting."

Private Matters? The Other Side of Direct Marketing

While direct marketing represents the ultimate way to establish a relationship with a prospect, its detractors claim that computer technology has caused an invasion of privacy unprecedented in our lifetime. Not only can marketers capture your age, name, and address, but also your buying habits and favorite charities. Every time you pay with a credit card or check, every time you fill out the lifestyle section of a product warranty card or do any number of seemingly innocuous things, you most likely are being added to a number of lists to be sold to advertisers. Your age, weight, and hair color come from driver's license records, your political leanings from your contributions, the due date of your baby from the guest register at the maternity store where you shop. Marketers may know you have a weakness for Haagen-Dazs ice cream or prefer Naturalamb condoms, for every time you pay by check or credit card, the electronic scanner which totals your bill links each purchase to your name. Some fear that even your prescription drugs—birth control pills, tranquilizers, heart remedies, everything—may be the next frontier for list harvesters. As you begin working on your direct response package, it would be well worth your time to consider these issues so that you don't cross ethical boundaries in your quest to create a successful promotion.

Suggested Activities

1. To demonstrate how much you can learn from databases, make three copies of the form below and fill out one of them as if you were the target consumer for a product you are now, or will be, creating advertising for. Give classmates the other copies and have them do the same for their products. Now exchange forms,

read the information, and take turns providing answers to as many of these questions as possible: What products or services might this "person" be a good prospect for? What clues, if any, suggest a basis for the relationship you might build with this person? What sort of offer would appeal to this person? Could this person be reached best through conventional mass media (radio, TV, magazines, newspapers), through out-of-home media (outdoor, transit, point-of-purchase), or through direct response, sales promotion, or a combination of the above? Why? How would you work with the information to begin thinking about an integrated marketing campaign?

Consumer Survey

Where indicated, check all items that apply.

1. Male **Female**

2. Age:_________

3. Marital status:
Married
Divorced/Separated
Widowed
Never Married

4. Occupation
Homemaker
Professional/Technical
Management/Executive
Middle Management
Sales/Marketing
Clerical/Service Worker
Laborer
Retired
Student
Self-Employed
Business Owner
Work from home office

5. Family Income:

____

6. Education
Some high school
Completed high school
Some college
Completed college
Some graduate school
Completed grad school
Vocational school

7. Primary residence
Own a house
Own townhouse/condo
Rent a house
Rent apartment, etc.

8. Interests and activities
Bicycling
Golf
Physical Fitness/Exercise
Running
Snow skiing
Tennis
Camping/hiking
Fishing
Hunting/shooting
Power boating
Sailing
House plants
Grandchildren
Needlework/Knitting
Gardening
Sewing
Crafts automotive work
Electronics
Do-it-yourself
Recreational vehicles
Listen to CDs, etc
Buy pre-recorded videos
Avid book reader
Devotional reading
Health/natural foods
Photography
Home decorating
Attending cultural events

Fashion
Fine art/antiques
Foreign travel
USA travel
Travel for pleasure
Gourmet cooking
Wines
Coin/stamp collecting
Collectibles/collections
Real estate investments
Stock/bond investments
Sweepstakes
Gambling
Science fiction
Wildlife/animal protection
Environmental issues
Dieting/weight control
Science/new technology
Self-improvement
Walking for health
Watching sports on TV
Community activities
Home video games
Motorcycles
Improving health
Home video recording
Career-oriented activities
Current affairs/politics

Courtesy National Demographics & Lifestyles, from whose research this listing was adapted.

2. Begin working on a direct response letter based on the "list" you have selected. Make certain you use all available tactics to get the prospect interested. Also, don't forget the offer. Develop an offer that will make the prospect want to respond. Don't "give away the store" to make the sale, but suggest a premium, special price, limited deal, or some other device that relates to whom you're talking and what your product represents to them. Check how specifically you are targeting the direct response package for your product. Remember, you can target much more narrowly using a good list than you can through typical mass media. That means you can restrict your appeal through direct response to the "ideal prospect."

Now summarize the characteristics of who you're going to be restricting your list to. How will this affect the nature and tone of your copy approach?

Three Examples of the Direct Approach

Cheri Wiles
Copywriter

Washburn Direct Marketing, Charlotte, N.C.

When you must deal with a highly select audience, direct marketing is a natural. In each of the following three situations, it might have been wasteful to employ traditional mass media to accomplish the marketing tasks outlined. In the first case, we were targeting a select group of upscale, environmentally concerned consumers. In the second, our target consisted exclusively of small-business owners and managers. Finally, our third project was directed to banking customers 50 and older who qualified financially for a special banking package. Here's how we used direct marketing to approach each task.

Direct Approach #1: Using Relationship Marketing to Sell a "Replacement" Credit Card for Mellon Bank. To convince an educated, upscale audience to switch credit cards, you have to do more than the ordinary. The answer lay in creating a relationship between the Mellon Bank Visa and MasterCard and the conservation efforts of the World Wildlife Fund. The "sell" became the "cause," as strategy focused on the opportunity to make easy and frequent contributions to WWF by using this special Visa or MasterCard. An important copy point was that there was virtually no risk to the cardholder, since the annual fee was paid for the first year.

Given the age, income, and education of the prospects, we assumed they already were using one or more credit cards. So rather than ask them to apply for yet another card, we chose to position the WWF card as a "replacement" card. We actually said in our letter, "Simply replace the credit card you now use with a WWF MasterCard/Visa. And every time you make a purchase, no matter what the amount, a contribution is donated to WWF conservation efforts. Programs that ensure the survival of thousands of species—from the stately African elephant to the delicate monarch butterfly."

It's a decision customers can feel good about.

Here's how we commanded their attention: First, the package arrived in an oversized outer envelope. Not only was the unusual size more noticeable, it also allowed more design opportunities. A standard $8\frac{1}{2} \times 11$ inch letter, personalized with a return address that showed through the envelope window, was included, with a salutation that included the addressee's last name.

To make it easier to respond, the application also was personalized with the recipient's name and address, and we included a business reply envelope.

Finally, a handsome brochure was designed to complete the sale. This three-panel design measured $5\frac{1}{2}$ inches square when folded.

Envelope front and back

Inside brochure

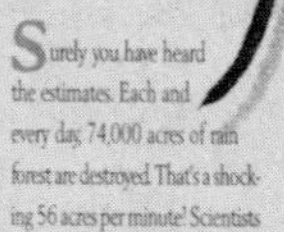

The Bengal tiger is one of only five subspecies of tigers thought to survive in Asia.

Surely you have heard the estimates. Each and every day, 74,000 acres of rain forest are destroyed. That's a shocking 56 acres per minute! Scientists estimate that if we don't act now to save rain forests, they will be gone in the next century.

And deep in the remote jungles of Latin America, the jaguar, one of the largest cats in the Western World, is fighting what may be her very last fight.

The clock is ticking. And now you can help do something to stop it. Every day.

The future of primates depends on the survival of the tropical rain forest.

Simply by using a World Wildlife Fund MasterCard® or VISA®, you take a stand. And your support is tangible. Anytime a WWF credit card is used, WWF benefits.

Your WWF credit card carries all the conveniences you have come to expect from MasterCard and Visa. But as a WWF cardholder, you'll also enjoy other valuable privileges, such as a competitive 17.9% APR, automatic travel and auto rental collision insurance, free additional cards, lost luggage protection, and a complimentary annual review of charges.

And remember, *your card is completely free of an annual fee for the first year.*

Even the North American monarch butterfly is threatened by habitat loss.

Most importantly, every time you use your new card instead of another credit card, you're making a contribution to WWF—at no cost to you.

The time for action is long overdue. The need has never been so critical. The destruction so rampant. The danger so great.

On the other hand, thanks to WWF it's never been easier to take credit for your convictions.

We are counting on your support.

In the past 20 years, the black rhinoceros population has dwindled from 65,000 to less than 4,000.

WWF

World Wildlife Fund

Bill Helms
Washburn Direct Marketing
1123 S Church St.
Charlotte, NC 28203

Dear Mr. Helms:

You undoubtedly receive a number of credit card solicitations every month.

But how many enable you to support the efforts of World Wildlife Fund -- an organization committed to saving life on earth?

More than ordinary credit cards, the World Wildlife Fund MasterCard® and Visa® are a natural way for concerned members like yourself to support WWF, with every purchase, and at no additional cost to you.

Simply replace the credit card you now use with a WWF MasterCard/Visa. And every time you make a purchase, no matter what the amount, a contribution is donated to WWF conservation efforts. Programs that ensure the survival of thousands of species -- from the stately African elephant to the delicate monarch butterfly.

And as a WWF member, you have been pre-approved for this special offering with no annual fee for the first year!* Simply complete and return the enclosed acceptance certificate, to begin taking advantage of all the valuable WWF MasterCard/Visa benefits listed on the reverse side of this letter.

So please don't delay. Take a moment now to complete and return your pre-approved acceptance certificate. The WWF MasterCard/Visa from Mellon Bank - it's just another way to show the world your commitment to saving life on earth.

Sincerely,

Kathryn S. Fuller

Kathryn S. Fuller
President

P.S. Every time you use your WWF MasterCard/Visa, you'll help spread the word about the importance of saving life on earth.

*Pre-Approved status expires March 15, 1991

1250 Twenty-Fourth Street, NW Washington, DC 20037 USA 202/293-4800 Telex: 64505 PANDA
Affiliated with The Conservation Foundation

Personalized letter

THE WWF MASTERCARD® AND VISA® OFFER:

- **No annual fee the first year** - Choose either or both card designs at no additional cost!

- **Competitive 17.9% Annual Percentage Rate.**

- **$500,000 Common Carrier Automatic Travel Accident Insurance** - Use your WWF MasterCard/Visa to buy airline or other common carrier tickets, and you and your family members are protected by $500,000 in travel accident insurance.

- **$3,000 International Auto Rental Collision Insurance** - Charge a rental car on your WWF card (in any country) and you are eligible to receive coverage up to $3,000 for the repair or loss of the car. That can save up to $12 per day!

- **Annual Review of Charges** - A complete record, organized chronologically and detailed by expense category of all your credit card transactions for the prior year, will be sent to you annually.

- **Free Credit Card Protection & Change of Address Service** - This service notifies all your card companies of lost or stolen cards or your change of address with one simple phone call.

- **$1,000 Lost Luggage Protection** - Your WWF Cards help replace items lost while traveling, up to $1,000 in addition to your own insurance coverage.

- **$1,000 in Emergency Cash & Airline Tickets** - These benefits can help arrange for a cash transfer or assist in replacement of lost airline tickets, up to your available credit line.

- **Instant Cash Around the World** - Get cash advances, 24 hours a day from 50,000 MAC® and CIRRUS® automatic teller machines worldwide, and at over 200,000 financial institutions worldwide.

- **Free Personalized Charge Checks** - Your card entitles you to use special "convenience checks" to access your available credit line. They look and work just like personal checks, and you can use them to pay off higher rate credit card balances.

- **Free Additional Cards** - Additional WWF credit cards, with all the special benefits, are free to eligible members of your family or household.

Some card services and features are provided by independent suppliers who assume full responsibility for their programs. Restrictions may apply. Full details supplied upon becoming a cardmember. Travel Accident Insurance is underwritten by the Gresham Group, Inc.

From a marketing angle, we were fortunate to have a well-defined audience with unique values. Hence, we knew the relationship would be a meaningful one. To drive home this relationship, we even used recycled paper for every component of the package, displaying the "recycled paper" symbol on each piece. Coincidentally, the texture and color of this paper gives the package a certain warmth that should appeal to the "naturalist" in the prospect. Although the recipients may not use recycled paper, it certainly is something familiar and meaningful to them.

The copy is clear and direct. We do not hide the fact that this is a credit card solicitation. In fact, the cards are shown on the outer envelope, along with the headline recalling the WWF slogan: Now you can take credit for saving life on earth. The naturalistic style of the color art complements other aspects of the package. Inside, the letter is brief and to the point. Like the letter, the brochure focuses on the cause, providing specific examples of how WWF contributions are used to "save life on earth." Although copy is written from the WWF perspective, it is understated. We did not want to hide specifics about the credit card, such as rate or future annual fees.

This unique positioning allowed us to separate the WWF card solicitation from other credit card solicitations. By exhibiting a sensitivity to the feelings of our target audience, and creating a direct mail package that was both upscale and unique, we dramatically increase both our credibility and the likelihood of response—all within budget restrictions.

Direct Approach #2: A User-Friendly Small Business Mailing for Commonwealth National Bank. Marketing to any business presents a challenge. The average business receives dozens of solicitations weekly—through the mail, in magazines and newspapers, on the telephone, and in personal sales calls. So any marketing attempt to business owners or managers must cut through all the clutter. Just as important, the message must be received by the "right" person and be relevant.

With this in mind, our objectives were to attract sufficient attention so that the package would be noticed, have the package "land" on the right desk, and communicate a relevant message that would generate leads for small business loans. The bank also told us that the ideal package would be one that individual loan officers could personalize and mail individually. Here's how we approached the task.

First, we used the package itself as an attention getter. Instead of a standard #10 business envelope and letter, our package was a box. Few recipients can resist opening a box. To keep our costs down, we chose a small, standard size. We knew that a box has a higher perceived value than a standard, flat mailing, and is likely to remain on the desk longer. We also knew that such packages tended to be circulated to others in the business, and using a box gave us the opportunity to tuck a premium inside.

Top of box

Opened box with seed packet and personal note

To further contain costs, we did not print directly on the box, but used a printed label affixed to the lid. Inside, a specially sized piece of stationery was provided for the loan officer.

We liked the package for several reasons. First, because the contents of the box rattle, we felt the recipient would be curious about opening it. We also liked our choice of words for the label: "Couldn't your business use a little seed money?" We knew that, nine times out of ten, the answer would be "yes." Opening the box, the recipient discovered a packet of watermelon seeds labeled, "Mellon Seeds for Success." Directly below was the personalized note from the Commonwealth National Bank loan officer.

The loan officers followed up each of these mailings with a phone call, making personal appointments whenever possible. We felt that this was one instance where, when the loan officer asked, "Did you get my letter?" the recipients would certainly remember that they did! And to each personal appointment, the loan officer took a special and appropriate gift: a live plant for the customer's office.

Direct Approach #3: Identifying the Vibrant and Active Portion of the Over-50 Market. Valley Bank is based in Arizona, a state with a relatively high percentage of older citizens. In recent years, the over-50 market has become attractive to a number of marketers for several good reasons: they constitute an increasingly large share of the population, are fairly easy to identify, and have considerable disposable income. To meet the needs of this distinct market, the bank offers "Value Partners," a package of attractively priced financial services for customers 50 and older. To increase its market share and customer base in this area, Valley Bank developed an unusual tie-in to Value Partners. Any new Partner customer who responded in time would receive a gift certificate worth a substantial discount for travel.

The creative challenge was to communicate two messages: (1) that this was a valuable bank service, and (2) that this was a highly valuable travel offer. Since this group believes it has all the banking services it needs, a package looking "financial" might be discarded before it was opened. On the other hand, a package looking too "cruise-like" might be mistaken for a travel brochure.

Here's how we solved the challenge. All too often, "seniors" are seen as elderly, grandparent types who lack energy, interests, or abilities. In a sense, nothing could be further from the truth, and our approach indicated our awareness of this market as vibrant and travel-oriented. Because we felt it was important to communicate that this was not your typical bank letter, we established a cruise theme on the outer envelope using tight closeups of portholes, streamers and confetti. Inside, the confetti/cruise motif continues on both the letter and reply device.

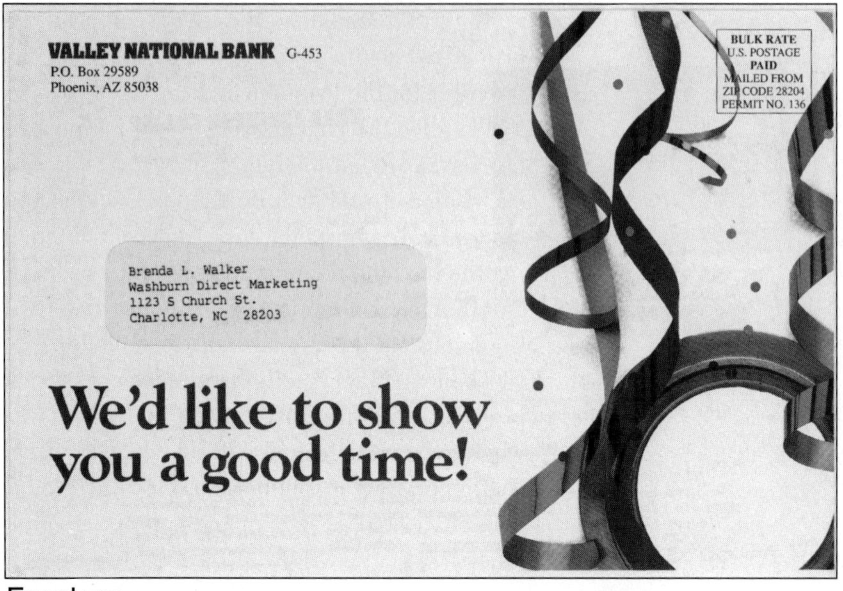

Envelope

To grab the attention of the recipient, we employed an oversized outer envelope. The size and four-color art set the tone for the package as well as for the value of its contents. Inside was one of various personalized letters used to address existing customers or prospects. To make response easy, the application also was personalized with the recipient's name and address. Aware of our market, we made certain that all type was set large enough for easy reading. The upbeat tone of the letter and careful use of underlining and bold type helped pull the reader through the piece.

Because we had to communicate so many copy points, we used a brochure to complete the sell. A four-color approach with an unusual fold reinforced the image of value we were seeking. Opening the first fold, the reader found information about Value Partners. Inside the second fold is information about how the product relates to the offer. The porthole on the front fold serves as a device to pull the reader further into the brochure.

Playing the cruise idea throughout, we constantly reminded the prospect of this unique special offer, even when discussing bank features.

Brochure cover

Inside of brochure

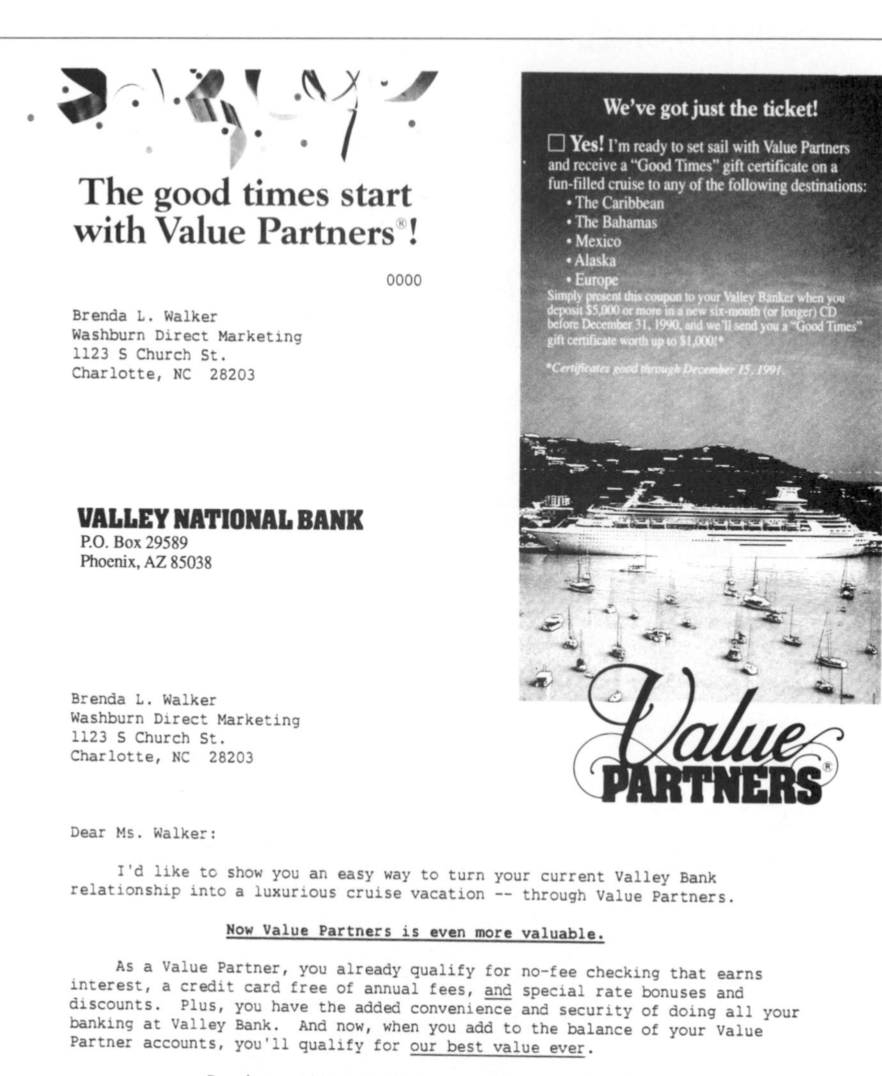

The good times start with Value Partners®!

0000

Brenda L. Walker
Washburn Direct Marketing
1123 S Church St.
Charlotte, NC 28203

We've got just the ticket!

☐ **Yes!** I'm ready to set sail with Value Partners and receive a "Good Times" gift certificate on a fun-filled cruise to any of the following destinations:

- The Caribbean
- The Bahamas
- Mexico
- Alaska
- Europe

Simply present this coupon to your Valley Banker when you deposit $5,000 or more in a new six-month (or longer) CD before December 31, 1990, and we'll send you a "Good Times" gift certificate worth up to $1,000!*

**Certificates good through December 15, 1991.*

VALLEY NATIONAL BANK
P.O. Box 29589
Phoenix, AZ 85038

Brenda L. Walker
Washburn Direct Marketing
1123 S Church St.
Charlotte, NC 28203

Dear Ms. Walker:

I'd like to show you an easy way to turn your current Valley Bank relationship into a luxurious cruise vacation -- through Value Partners.

Now Value Partners is even more valuable.

As a Value Partner, you already qualify for no-fee checking that earns interest, a credit card free of annual fees, and special rate bonuses and discounts. Plus, you have the added convenience and security of doing all your banking at Valley Bank. And now, when you add to the balance of your Value Partner accounts, you'll qualify for our best value ever.

Receive a Gift Certificate valued up to $1,000
toward a Royal Caribbean cruise vacation!

Simply open a new 6-month (or longer) CD with $5,000 or more before December 31, 1990. As always, you'll qualify for bonus rates, plus, you'll get a free "Good Times" gift certificate to be used toward your choice of a number of Royal Caribbean cruises.

These special values are only available through Valley Bank -- the largest bank in Arizona -- and only available to Value Partners like yourself. The exact amount of your gift certificate will depend on the cruise you choose -- from $200 toward the price of a four-night cruise for one, to $1,000 toward the price of a seven-night cruise for two.

Complete details are in the enclosed brochure. If you'd like to see yourself on board a Royal Caribbean cruise ship bound for the Caribbean, the

FOR BANK USE ONLY

Deposit amount $ ____________________

CDA account number ____________________

Term ____________________

Source of funds ☐B of A ☐FIB ☐SECPAC ☐S&L ☐Other

Signed ____________________

Date ____________________

Branch no. ____________________

Return this card to CBS G-453

Bahamas, Mexico, Alaska, or Europe, just be sure to make your deposit before December 31, 1990.

You could set sail as soon as this winter!

Bon voyage!

David J. Renke

David J. Renke
Senior Vice President

P.S. Remember, this valuable offer, a gift certificate worth up to $1,000, sails into the sunset December 31, 1990.

Member FDIC

CHAPTER

12 Writing Retail Advertising

BONNIE DREWNIANY
University of South Carolina

When I was a student, I was very naive. I was convinced that when I graduated, major advertising agencies would come knocking at my door, begging me to create campaigns for international clients such as Coca-Cola and Volkswagen. Guess what? That didn't happen. Instead, I landed a job as a junior copywriter at Bamberger's (now Macy's). What I didn't know at the time was that it was going to turn into a very rewarding career.

After speaking with advertising professors from all over the country, I have learned that my experience was not unique. Many advertising majors work on retail accounts when they graduate from college. In fact, it is very likely that you will create retail ads in the future. Even if you don't work directly for a retailer as I did, chances are you will have retail accounts if you work for a local advertising agency or for the advertising department of a newspaper or radio or television station.

But don't think that you have to be small-time to create retail ads. Many of the advertising greats, including David Ogilvy and Bill Bernbach, worked on retail accounts. Does that surprise you? It shouldn't. Retail advertising is big business. In recent years, retailers spent more on advertising than any other industry.[1]

The size of the advertising budget isn't the only thing that sets retailers apart from other advertisers. Before you learn how to create retail ads, it is important that you understand the many differences between national and retail advertising.

What Makes Retail Advertising Unique?

1. ***Retail ads have a two-fold message.*** When you create an ad for a retailer, you want to get customers interested in the product and you want them to

[1] "Total U.S. Ad Spending by Category and Media," *Advertising Age*, September 29, 1993, p. 8.

buy it at your store. When you create ads for a national brand, you usually aren't concerned with where the customer buys it.

2. ***When you create local advertising, you know your customers.*** They are your neighbors. Your friends. Your family. You know their tastes. Their sense of humor. You know what's on their minds. When you create an ad for a national brand, you deal with demographic and psychographic generalities. It's difficult to get very personal because the ad you create must appeal to someone in New York, as well as to someone in Nebraska.

3. ***Retailers promote competing brands.*** There are times when several competing brands appear in the same retail ad. There are even times when the store's private label is promoted next to national brands. The retail advertiser is challenged to put each brand in a favorable light and to give customers enough information to make intelligent decisions, without offending any of the vendors. This is not always easy. It would be much easier to have one brand to sell, as national advertisers do.

4. ***The message in retail ads is more urgent.*** You want customers to know that to get the best prices and the best selection, they should get to your store today. Not tomorrow. And certainly not a month from now. However, most national ads imply "the next time you go shopping for a particular product, buy our brand."

5. ***In retail, you know the effects of your ad the day it runs.*** Just check a printout of the day's sales and you will know how your ad pulled. The effects of a single ad are much more difficult to measure on a national level because it is part of a long-term multimedia campaign and a variety of outside factors (including retailer support) can influence sales.

6. ***Retail advertising is more volatile.*** Because merchants know how specific ads pulled, they are inclined to make changes in campaigns that aren't drawing in customers. These changes can be made right up to the last moment because newspapers and radio (retail's most widely used media) accept last minute changes. While changes may be necessary, it is important not to overreact. Some of the most powerful national campaigns have been running for decades. If national advertisers reacted as quickly as some retail advertisers, we might not have had the Marlboro man or the Jolly Green Giant today.

7. ***When people read the local paper, they are often in a shopping mood and seek out retail ads.*** They want to know what's on special at the grocery store. They want to know when the White Sale starts at their favorite department store. They want to get ideas for holiday gifts. In a sense, a retail ad is like a news story, while on the national level, ads may be seen as an intrusion by many readers and viewers.

8. ***In retailing, price is an important detail.*** It can be what separates one store from its competition. National brand advertisements don't usually include prices. If they do, it is a "suggested" retail price.

9. ***When you create an ad for a retailer, you have several clients to please.*** Chances are, the retailer is getting co-op funding and that means you have to follow the creative guidelines established by the national vendors. At the same time, you need to create an image for your retailer. It's like doing two ads in one.

10. ***When you create ads for a retailer, you are promoting a broad range of products.*** A retailer may carry everything from high tech to high fashion. Or, a retailer may specialize in a product category and offer a vast variety of brands to suit a range of budgets. Therefore, you need to appeal to a variety of consumer needs, while establishing a consistent image for your store.

How to Create Retail Ads

Creating retail advertising is challenging. You not only have to sell a variety of competing brands, you have to sell your store. You need to convince customers that your store is the place to shop, even though the competitor across the street may be selling the same merchandise at the same prices. You also need to convince customers that the traditional way of shopping is better than buying things in the comfort of their own homes through a television shopping program or catalog.

Before you start to write copy or draw a layout, you should determine why you would shop at your store. Think about it. Carefully. The answers will tell you a lot about your store's personality and that will give your ads direction. To get you started, here are some things you should consider telling your customers:

1. Tell them about your store's employees.
2. Tell them about your location.
3. Tell them about your pricing policy.
4. Tell them about your products.
5. Tell them about your store's history.
6. Tell them where you stand on issues.
7. Tell them the truth.

1. ***Tell them about your store's employees.*** Have you ever stood in line for several minutes, only to be told, "Sorry. This line is closed?" Have you ever waited patiently for a sales clerk to get off a personal phone call? Or have you ever asked a sales clerk a question about a product, only to get a vacant look? Did you leave the store in disgust? Well, you're not alone. According to a 1993 survey sponsored by MasterCard International, 62 percent of shoppers said they'd abandoned a purchase in the last six months because the sales clerks

were too busy to help. On top of that, 60 percent said store employees weren't knowledgeable enough to be of help.

Smart retailers know that good service is key to their survival. After all, it's the face-to-face contact that sets traditional retailing apart from catalog and electronic shopping. Assuming you have the good fortune to work for a retailer who offers good service, you need to tell the story in your advertisements. Simply saying you offer good service is not enough. You need to tell a more convincing story. So do some homework. Read letters from customers. Talk with the sales clerks. The dressing room attendant. The tailor. You'll be surprised what useful stories you learn. For example, the story of a vice president's concern over a seamstress proved that "people really matter at Chappell's" (Figure 12-1).

Don't stop with the obvious people. Look behind the scenes. While your customers may never see the people who buy the merchandise for your store, they certainly see the results of your buyer's efforts. So talk about your buyers. Did an interesting thing happen to them on a buying trip? Were they able to negotiate an extraordinary deal? Did they go to the ends of the earth to find unique merchandise? Then tell their story.

When a freelance art director discovered that her client, Charles W. Jacobsen, traveled on a donkey to find rug weavers who lived in remote parts of the world, she was intrigued. She suspected that other people would be, too, so she created a series of ads featuring a donkey she named "Vincent." It turned out that her instincts were right. The community loved Vincent. Even local radio D.J.s commented on the campaign, giving the store free publicity.

The buying trip doesn't have to be exotic to work. Remember, you're trying to communicate your store's personality. So be yourself. A fashion buying trip to New York can make an interesting story. So can a furniture buying trip to North Carolina. Or a visit to a local craftsman's shop.

2. ***Tell them about your location.*** Things certainly have changed from the days when people went shopping for entertainment and the motto was, "Shop 'til you drop." Today, many customers have abandoned the traditional way of shopping for the convenience and safety of shopping at home. Your job is to convince customers that they should leave the comfort of home and go to your store to shop. Don't just give customers your address, tell them why your location is an advantage. For example, is your store in a convenient spot? Is there plenty of free parking? Is it on a bus route? Is it near another popular store? Tell your customers about these things.

What happens if your store isn't in a convenient location? Then see if you can turn the disadvantage into an advantage. Perhaps your store provides a unique service and needs to be in a special location to get quality workers. Or perhaps it's a matter of economics. Maybe your retailer can offer lower prices because he doesn't pay extra rent for a fancy address.

3. ***Tell them about your store's pricing policy.*** Does your store offer everyday low prices? Value prices? Does it meet or beat the competitors' prices? Or

CHAPPELL'S :60 RADIO

SFX:	SOFT PIANO MUSIC (FADE UNDER).
WOMAN:	I thought I was going to die. Really! I came to work and right away I started feeling bad. The people I work with called an ambulance and they took me to the hospital. All the way I'm saying, "Am I going to die?" When we get there, they put me in the emergency room and I don't believe it. The vice president of the place I've worked for 17 years comes to be with me. Charles Chappell the third. He stayed right there with me until my brother came. Which was a long time. Even the nurses couldn't believe it. Working at Chappell's 17 years, I always hear the advertising about "personally yours" and it's true. I always see the Chappells go out of their way for the customers. I guess you can say it's going to help them too because it's good for business. But then, why did Charles Chappell the third go out of his way for me?
MAN:	This is Charles Chappell, Jr. For over 94 years we've had a very simple customer service policy. People really matter.

Courtesy of Chappell's.

FIGURE 12-1

The story of a vice president's concern over a seamstress proved that "people really matter at Chappell's." By the way, the commercial wasn't the vice president's idea. Nor was it the advertising director's idea. It came from the seamstress. She thought that people would like to hear her story. She was right. It inspired others to tell their personal stories about Chappell's caring employees.

FIGURE 12-2
Isn't it amazing how many times you've said things like this? Smart retailers, like Parisian, know what's on consumers' minds. They know that good service isn't a nicety, but is a requirement for success in the nineties. Parisian's commitment to service has been the key to the chain's rapid growth from five stores in 1980 to thirty stores in 1994.

I WANT A STORE I CAN TRUST TO GIVE ME GOOD DEALS EVERY DAY, NOT JUST ON SALE DAYS. **I don't want to hear, "It's not my department."** If I buy something and then find it cheaper somewhere else, they should give me back the difference. **I'D LIKE HELP WHEN I NEED IT, AND PRIVACY WHEN I DON'T.** *I prefer dealing with salespeople who know a lot about what they're selling.* And if I return something, I don't want to be hassled.

I WANT ALL THIS, BUT I DON'T WANT TO PAY MORE FOR IT.

Courtesy, Parisian.

does it offer such exclusive merchandise that price is no object? Whatever the case, the way you present the prices in your advertising says a lot about your store's personality.

Regardless of your store's pricing policy, you most likely will have to create sale ads for it, whether it is to announce that your everyday low prices have fallen or that your exclusive store is having its annual clearance event. Don't complain. Sale ads don't have to be boring. In fact, they shouldn't be. They should be innovative to break through the clutter. And, most important of all, they should reflect the image of your store.

4. ***Tell them about your products.*** Chances are, you will have hundreds of products to sell for your store. Your challenge will be to become an expert on them all. How can you do this? Examine the products on the selling floor. Ask questions of the buyers and the salespeople. Ask for a demonstration. Visit merchandise shows. Study vendor spec sheets. Analyze national ads. Read articles about products. Pay attention to what your friends and neighbors say. Soon you'll become an expert.

You owe it to your customers to be knowledgeable. Have you ever read vague copy like, "You'll find great savings on a terrific collection of beautiful tops that will brighten your holiday wardrobe"? Remember how frustrated you were? The copy says nothing about the product. Who makes the tops? What styles are on sale? Do they have long sleeves? Short sleeves? Cap sleeves? What about the neckline? What about the fabric? And so on. Chances are, the writer never saw the tops and relied on generic copy to fill the space allotted by the art director. Don't do that. Go to the selling floor to check the merchandise. Phone the buyer. Do anything. But don't cop out.

The way you present the products should say something about your store. You should tell customers about your store's selection of products. Many customers want to shop at a store with a huge variety. As a result, many retailers want their ads to be jammed with merchandise. But don't let your ads get so busy that they are confusing. Try a few layouts. Try combining merchandise categories. Be creative. See how many products can be included on a page without losing the creative integrity.

What do you do if your store doesn't offer a huge selection? Your ad can take several directions. Perhaps your store only stocks the finest merchandise. Or, perhaps your store's small size gives it a friendlier atmosphere. Your layout and copy should tell the story.

The quality of your store's merchandise is another important message to relate to customers. Even the smallest detail can help you tell a big story. For example, a close-up of a jacket's buttons can help you tell customers about fine tailoring. A single strawberry can tell the story about a grocery store's quest for freshness. The way a strand of pearls is hand knotted communicates that a store has beautifully crafted gifts.

Uniqueness is another important message. Does your store carry an exclusive line from a national manufacturer? Does your store carry private labels? What

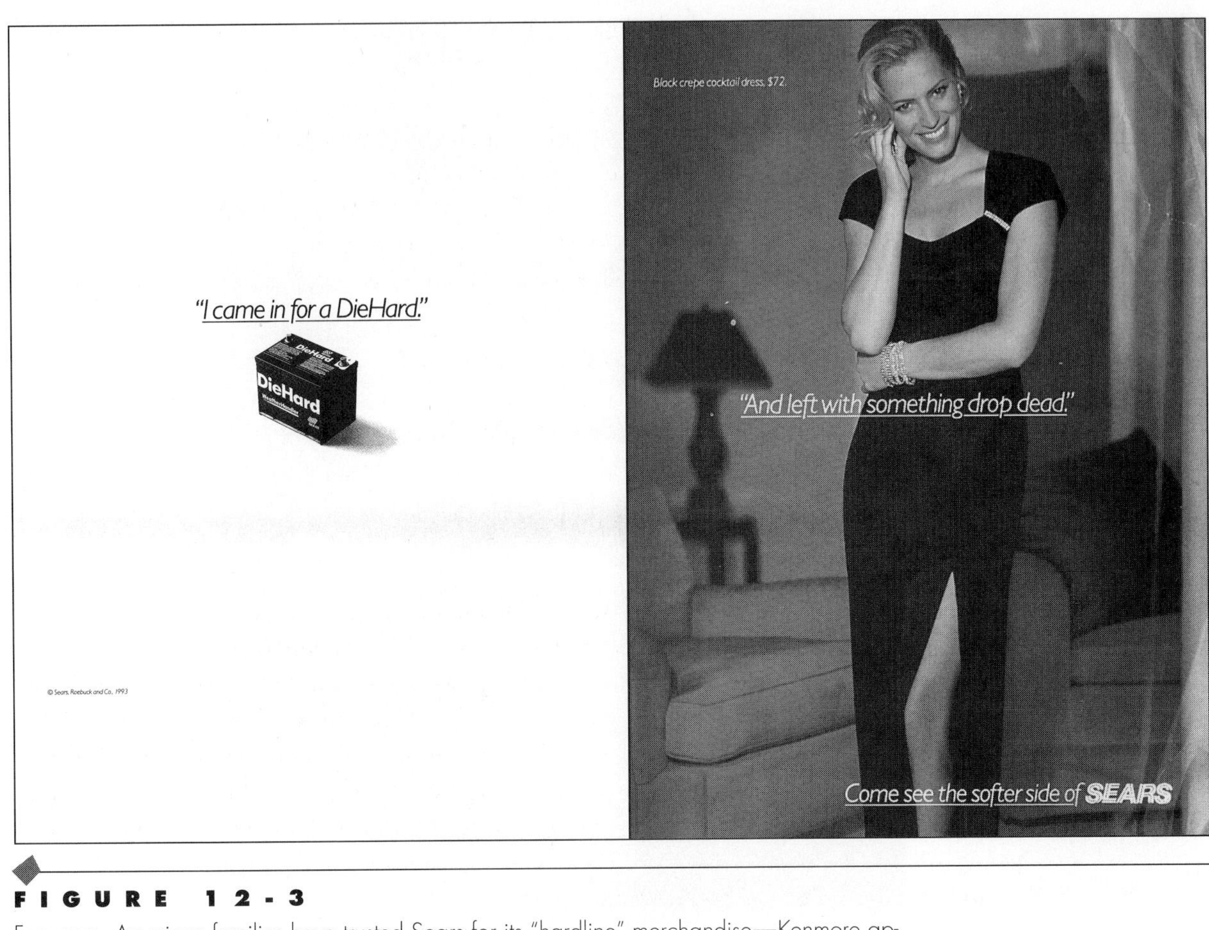

Courtesy Sears Merchandise Group

FIGURE 12-3
For years, American families have trusted Sears for its "hardline" merchandise—Kenmore appliances, Craftsman tools, DieHard batteries, and Easy Living paints. Now, Sears invites its customers to see the "softer side" of its store. "Our campaign was designed to close the perception gap between what our customers expect to find in our stores and what we actually have in our stores in fashionable and affordable apparel," said John H. Costello, senior executive vice president, Sears Merchandise Group.

about special sizes? Get the idea? You want your store to be special. You want to give customers a reason to shop in your store instead of going to the competitor across the street.

5. ***Tell them about your store's history.*** Many people think of their favorite store as they would a friend. They enjoy hearing stories about it, particularly if it makes them look intelligent for choosing the store.

Macy's history saved me one day. I had released a catalog to the printer and on each page a special event (such as a celebrity appearance and contest) was highlighted in a color box. As things turned out, the special events had to be cancelled. This created a major problem because the printer had already completed the color separations. To remove the color boxes would be very costly. To

Courtesy Kroger

FIGURE 12-4 While most grocery store ads are jammed packed with hundreds of price listings and generic clip art, Kroger breaks through the clutter and delivers a powerful message about quality by focusing on one item.

leave them blank would look foolish. Fortunately, tidbits from Macy's history worked perfectly in the special boxes. The fact that Macy's invented the tea bag was placed on a page with kettles. The fact that Macy's introduced the baked Idaho potato was highlighted on the microwave oven page. The fact that colored towels were the brainchild of a Macy's buyer appeared on the domestics page. Macy's history saved the day. It looked like we had planned the whole thing. And it let customers know that creative merchandising has been a long tradition at Macy's.

Even if your store doesn't have a past quite as glorious as Macy's, you still have important stories to tell. For example, has your store been managed by generations of the same family? Does your store's management still hold the same principles that were established years earlier? Maybe there's a story in the fact that you *don't* go by the rules that the founders established.

6. ***Tell them where you stand on issues.*** Remember, your customers are your neighbors and you need to show them that your store is involved in the community. Therefore, your ads should tell customers that you participate in charity functions. They should tell where you stand on issues such as recycling. They should communicate that you care about special groups. By telling customers where you stand on issues, you're establishing important rapport with them.

7. ***Tell them the truth.*** Remember, the ads you create are directed to your friends and neighbors. You can't fool them. If you do, you might lose their trust forever.

One time a colleague of mine was faced with the challenge of selling orange luggage. It was ugly. Plain ugly. What could she do? She could omit the fact that it was orange. After all, she wasn't taking mail and phone orders so she didn't have to mention color at all. And, because the ad was going to run in black and white, no one would know the difference, right? Wrong. Customers would know the minute they came to the store. They would be furious. And the store could lose valued customers. Instead, she wrote something along these lines, "Does your luggage get lost at the airline terminals? We've got the perfect luggage for you!" The luggage sold out because she turned a negative into a selling advantage. And she told the truth.

Telling the truth isn't always easy. In fact, it's often a lot of hard work. Remember, retailers want to get customers into the store that day. They feel the message must have urgency or it will go unnoticed. Your job as a retail copywriter is to be the watchdog. If a merchant tells you that an item is going to be on sale for the "lowest" price, ask for substantiation. The same holds true if you're told that it's the "biggest" sale of the year.

The Better Business Bureau has a code of advertising that all retailers should follow. If you're not familiar with all the rules, call the bureau and ask for a copy. When I was a student, I did an internship with the BBB. Although I wasn't paid, it turned out to be a very valuable experience. One of the things that helped me get my first job was the fact that I understood the guidelines.

One area that seems to confuse many retailers is the difference between the terms *regularly* and *originally.* Actually, it's quite simple. If the item is going to return to its former price at the end of the sale, use the term *regularly* to describe the higher price. If the item is not returning to the higher price, use the term *originally.*

Another area that causes confusion is the term *manufacturer's list price.* Can you use it? Yes. But only if it is the actual selling price currently charged by "representative principal retailers" in your market area.

FIGURE 12-5 You have probably heard the advertising expression, "Sell the sizzle, not the steak." Now, the "quintessential" steakhouse goes one step further by comparing their restaurant to a religious experience. Note the amount of white space and limited copy. What more is there to say after you have used this comparison?

Courtesy, Smith & Wollensky

Still another area that causes confusion is the use of percentage savings. Perhaps you have seen "save up to 50 percent" in an ad. Did you know what it meant? Were you saving 5 percent to 50 percent? 20 percent to 50 percent? or 40 percent to 50 percent? You have the right to know. The BBB requires that you state both the minimum and maximum savings. Additionally, at least 10 percent of all items available should be at the maximum savings (unless local or state law requires otherwise).

Once you know the rules, they are easy to follow. While it may take some effort to learn the rules, your customers deserve it. After all, you want to establish a lasting relationship with them, don't you?

How to Get a Job in Retail Advertising

It's been rough for retailers in recent years. Mergers and a difficult economy raised havoc with this industry. Does this mean that you should avoid retail? Absolutely not! More than ever, the retail industry needs talented people who know how to develop and maintain a creative strategy. They need you.

What should you do to get a job in retail advertising? Here are some suggestions.

1. ***Show some entrepreneurship.*** Let's face it. There's a lot of competition out there. While your classwork is fine to show during an interview, you'll look stronger if you show work that's been printed. One way to get your ads into print is to work for the advertising department of your school's paper. Another way is to knock on some doors and ask merchants (particularly those with student-oriented businesses) if you could create ads for them. Another approach is to study the local paper and identify clients who look like they could use your help. Try redoing their ads. But remember to be tactful.

2. ***Get an internship.*** Once it was an added plus if a student had an internship. Now it's almost a requirement. You'll receive real world experience and you'll get a good recommendation if you do a good job. In fact, you might even land a job at the place you did your internship.

3. ***Show a variety of work in your portfolio.*** Remember, in retailing, you may be expected to write about everything from high tech to high fashion. Try to include some retail ads, too.

4. ***Visit the store before the interview.*** Get to know the type of merchandise that is sold. Know who shops there. Note the pricing strategy. And so on. This added effort will go a long way.

5. ***Study the store's ads and be prepared to comment on them.*** You might want to ask questions about their ads. For example, "I saw your ad for the fashion show in Sunday's paper. How did it go? Did many people attend?" Or, better yet, "I saw your ad for the fashion show and it inspired me to go . . ." They'll love the fact that you showed interest. (But don't lie!)

6. ***Be prepared for the worst-case scenario.*** Remember, things are hectic in retailing. Consider what happened to me during my first interview:

   Bamberger's assistant creative director came to my college to interview a number of students. By the time I got in to see him, he had to leave to catch a plane. But what about me? Couldn't he see my work? He didn't have to say a word; I just knew he wasn't about to miss his plane. But that was okay. I had brought an extra set of my work to leave with him. "No, that won't do," he explained. He didn't want to be responsible for returning it. And, he didn't have time to take down my address. I assured him that it was okay because I had enclosed a self-addressed stamped envelope. That stopped him in his tracks. "You thought of everything, didn't you? That's great." The next day, I got a phone call. They loved my work. The job was mine.

Suggested Activities

1. Create an image ad for your favorite store by describing your own personal experiences with it. Consider creating an image campaign by asking your friends to describe their experiences, too.

2. Find two stores in your town that sell similar merchandise at similar prices. Then determine what makes each store unique. Is it their personnel? The location? The store's history? Once you've determined what makes each store special, create an ad for each of the stores using the same merchandise in each ad.

3. Spend twenty minutes brainstorming about creative "handles" for sale ads. Some examples include Friday the 13th Sale, Leap Year Sale, and Spring Cleanup Sale Days.

4. Remember the story about the orange luggage? Find an item in a local retail store that is just as unappealing and write a newspaper ad and radio spot that point out its advantages—without straying from the truth.

5. Find an item in one of your favorite catalogs and create a retail ad for the same item at the same price. How will you convince customers to leave the comfort of their homes to shop at your store?

CHAPTER 13

Writing to Reach a Minority Market

SHARON S. BROCK
The Ohio State University[1]

Although this chapter addresses the special culture of African-Americans, the author recognizes the substantial importance of the Hispanic, Asian-American, and other ethnic audiences. The U.S. Hispanic market represents at least 24 million people joined by a common language, Spanish, but representing about 20 different nationalities and cultures. It has a buying power of more than $171 billion. By the year 2010, the U.S. Congress Bureau predicts that Hispanics will reach 38 million, close to parity with the African-American community. Already the Standard Directory of Advertising Agencies lists 67 "Hispanic" agencies.

The Asian-American community is smaller, about 9 million people, but affluent, with a buying power greater than $100 billion. It is a challenging group to reach because it is the least monolithic minority market in the country. It does not have a common language or a common culture. In addition, since 1970, the dominant Asian subculture has changed from Japanese (1970s), to Chinese (1980s), to Filipino-Americans (1990s). The Asian Indian and Korean populations now rival the Japanese in size.

I suddenly realized the special challenges of advertising to a minority market the day my copywriting class at Ohio State University solicited Glory Foods for its final copywriting campaign. Glory was an ideal client—a young company

[1] Prof. Brock gives special thanks for this chapter to Howard Buford, UniWorld Group, Inc.; William Sharp, Sharp Advertising; Thomas Burrell and Albert Styles, Burrell Communications Group; Theresa Potter, Glory Foods, Inc.; Bernie Washington, Equinox Advertising; and Georgia Lee Clark, Communications Publishing Group, Inc.

For a more detailed look at advertising to ethnic audiences, see Gail Baker Wood's *Advertising and Marketing to the New Majority: A Case Study Approach* (Wadsworth, 1995).

with a new product line, home office in Columbus, Ohio, with markets opening in other parts of the country, new products still being developed, sales exceeding predictions, and an enthusiastic marketing director with Madison Avenue experience, who was willing to give students a professional creative briefing. And, Glory Foods is a minority-owned company that produces traditional African-American/southern style packaged foods.

An exciting opportunity, I thought. There are almost 3,500 African-Americans on our large campus and a few in the copywriting class, so primary resources would be excellent and convenient. Students could show their stuff with a sensitive, perceptive, hard-hitting campaign that would convince everyone who has a taste for southern style cooking to demand Glory Foods from their grocer (the line was originally shelved in only one large chain's stores; consumer demand moved it to other chains and independent grocers). The well-connected owner of Glory Foods would be impressed by the worldliness and creative insight of Ohio State copywriting students. This was a win-win situation, and my students would love such an experience.

Well, almost.

Glory Foods gave us folders full of descriptive promotional material, including national news clips, about its business. The astute marketing director gave a thorough, perceptive briefing and candidly answered questions about African-American cooking traditions. Then she left.

I noticed a foot-shuffling awkwardness in the classroom and no one was quite looking at the African-American students. They, on the other hand, seemed to huddle with each other. "Let's check Simmons," suggested one student to break the quiet. We didn't check Simmons or MRI or any other books that day. We talked about why it felt awkward to explore a minority segment of the market when we were old hands at dissecting Baby Boomers and Generation X.

Do Minorities Have Different Shopping Habits?

Do American minority segments—Asians, Hispanics, African-Americans, Native Americans (AHAANAs)—shop differently from white European-Americans? Is it necessary to create separate messages for minority audiences? It is important to find out because the buying power of African-Americans in the early 1990s was already at $278 *billion,* equivalent to the ninth largest economy in the world. In a flat economy, manufacturers and restaurateurs have begun targeting minority groups aggressively, and the new generation of copywriters had better know how to reach them.

"If behavior is different, and attitude is different, and interests are different, that certainly translates into different buying habits, different brand preferences, different ways of looking at a particular product category," says Thomas J. Burrell, chairman and founder of Burrell Communications Group (BCG). Burrell heads one of the largest black-owned advertising agencies in the United States. He creates advertising to reach African-American consumers for Coca-Cola,

FIGURE 13-1
General audience agency's ad for long distance telephone service to Jamaica. It didn't work.

We can offer you the world. Unless, of course, you'd rather have your own country.

Now you can get discounts on every call you make to Jamaica with the new AT&T Special Country℠ Plan. Or you can go further than that, with the AT&T Reach Out® World Plan, and save on AT&T calls to Jamaica plus more than 50 other countries and locations during plan hours. Either way, we've got an international calling plan that's just what you're looking for. To find out which one is right for you, call us at 1 800 523-WORLD, Ext. 4375.

INTRODUCING THE PERFECT PLAN TO CALL JAMAICA.

AT&T

These plans may not be combined with each other or with certain other AT&T optional calling plans.
Discounts apply to basic AT&T International Long Distance prices on direct-dialed calls. Other conditions and exclusions also apply. Subject to billing availability. ©1993 AT&T

Courtesy AT&T.

McDonald's, Procter & Gamble, K-Mart, Stroh's Brewery and dozens of other familiar clients. Obviously, those major advertisers believe that minority markets are unique and need separate targeting.

The Standard Directory of Advertising Agencies (the Red Book) lists 24 African-American ad agencies, but minority-directed staffs at most major agencies and small boutiques are not included. The billings of these specialized agencies grow annually, evidence that clients other than Burrell's are seeking minority consumer expertise.

"Politics brings clients to African-American agencies, and the marketplace keeps them here," says Howard Buford, vice president and creative director for UniWorld Group, Inc. in New York. "Clients come to us if a product skews high in the African-American market or if the client has a universal product that needs to work hard in all audiences." He adds that advertising to the African-American market is tough because politicians and consumers routinely evaluate every message. A seemingly simple gaffe can trigger a national boycott. You don't often get this kind of scrutiny of a general audience commercial, he said.

By the year 2000 there will be 33.8 million African-Americans, according to the U.S. Census Bureau. Advertisers will be looking for help to reach all that buying power in a sophisticated, cluttered, and segmented marketplace.

This is an exciting challenge for young copywriters, who can create for themselves a highly marketable niche in a crowded advertising industry. All it takes is the same kind of homework you would give to developing strategies for standard market segments, such as females 18–34 or single-parent males, and some serious listening.

What has made ethnic advertising agencies hotter shops than anytime in their history? Do African-Americans, Hispanic-Americans and Asian-Americans really need a different kind of message to convince them that one bar of soap or one fast food restaurant is better than another? AT&T found that they do.

The general audience agency that handles AT&T's account had created separate advertising for AT&T long-distance telephone service to Jamaica. Many east coast African-Americans are from the island of Jamaica, so encouraging more long-distance phone calls around the time of Jamaica's Independence Day celebration looked like a promising marketing opportunity. AT&T's general agency developed a campaign using a stereotype that most white people have of the West Indies—islands with palm trees and beaches, but long-distance phone use did not increase as a result of this scenic campaign (Figure 13-1, page 297).

AT&T took its problem to UniWorld/New York, the nation's largest multicultural agency, which specializes in advertising to African-Americans and Hispanics. UniWorld used an emotional appeal it knew would work because Jamaicans maintain strong ties to their extended families (not palm trees and beaches). UniWorld also understood that independence was important to these proud people and that Independence Day meant a lot to all Jamaicans, whether they lived in New York or in Jamaica. The new creative used pictures of the children of Jamaica on an interactive puzzle postcard, and the copy on the back celebrated the

FIGURE 13-2
Multicultural agency's ad for long-distance telephone service to Jamaica.

Courtesy AT&T.

island nation's independence (Figure 13-2). This time, the long-distance campaign was measurably successful.

In the new marketplace where minorities have substantial economic and social clout, it's possible to reach minority consumers with a general message, but reaching and selling are separate jobs. You sell when you speak to minorities as viable consumers and are not patronizing or ghettoizing. The marketplace is one of the few places where people care what African-Americans think, and African-Americans are beginning to know their power, Buford explained. You persuade this audience with African-American spokespersons in ideal African-American cultural situations—like a dad tying his small son's tie outside of church, or a group of friends hanging out in an attractive urban social setting.

Targeting the African-American consumer is different from running a general audience ad in an African-American medium or placing a darker face in a crowd. There isn't an African-American "detergent" but there is an empathetic way to talk to minorities who use detergents, or the phone, or fast food restaurants. Students who were working on the Glory Foods campaign discovered that there also is a difference between African-American cooks and their white counterparts. Food is the main ingredient of many African-American celebrations, and family members develop reputations for preparing one kind of food better than anyone else. If Aunt Felecia prepares greens that are memorable, it is a given that she, and no one else in her extended family, will provide that dish for a Kwaanza party or family celebration. This was important information for the students who wanted their messages to make African-American palates salivate at the thought of Glory Foods' products.

What Advertisers Know About African-American Consumers

According to several African-American advertising practitioners, African-Americans pay more attention than whites to the subtleties of advertising messages and they are particularly attentive to advertising that portrays them accurately. African-Americans respond to spokespersons who are warm and attractive rather than to those who are touted as experts. They prefer to see other African-Americans as spokespersons, as long as those persons are regarded as representative of the African-American community. Be careful not to use spokespersons of color who are perceived as "cross-overs." If you're not sure about someone, obtain several opinions from African-American friends.

An important part of the African-American experience is a sense of accomplishment, belonging, and respect in a white-dominated culture. Advertising that includes those qualities is more meaningful to African-American consumers than it is to whites.

African-Americans take advertising messages more literally than whites, so be cautious about wordplay or puns. They notice backgrounds, activity of the models in an ad, messages on building signs. They notice how long a minority person is visible in a commercial and what role is portrayed by African-Americans. Even entrenched characters like Uncle Ben and Aunt Jemima are not much appreciated because of their stereotypical images.

African-Americans want to see an accurate representation of themselves in advertising. They want to see different skin hues, different hair textures and styles, different personalities, and lifestyles. African-Americans do not see one skin color at their family reunions, yet general advertising portrays them with

Courtesy Communications Publishing Group, Inc.

FIGURE 13-3

An example of a magazine that reaches a target audience by celebrating the successes of its frequently unsung middle class.

one hue, which is often lighter for fashion and cosmetic advertising and darker for services or pancake mixes.

African-Americans come in thirty-five different shades and color hues, and just as many hair textures and eye shadings from thin to extra bold, says Georgia Lee Clark, publisher of Communications Publishing Group in Kansas City.

Clark publishes six *Career Focus* magazines for different ethnic groups and is particularly sensitive to the cultural differences of her audiences (Figure 13-3). She attributes much of the success of her magazines to their celebration of successful ethnic people who are not superstars. She features bankers, educators, small business owners, and other African-American, Hispanic, and Asian entrepreneurs. She appeals to the proven ability of minorities to succeed in a white world.

African-Americans tend to have a stronger fashion flair than whites. Colorful high fashion is important to the African-American consumer, and some retailers like J.C. Penney recognize that. Penney's publishes a separate catalog for African-American shoppers that shows more high fashion than its general audience catalogs. It uses deep yellows, fuchsias, and colorful prints which particularly flatter darker skin. Penney's runs full page ads in African-American and Hispanic media. It also advertises generously on Spanish-language broadcast stations.

Education

Middle-class minorities regard education as a means of self-enhancement, as well as a means of group enhancement. This is different from white people who think about education primarily as a means for self-enhancement. This distinction would be important for a copywriter creating a message for a product like home computers—you would target minority parents who want their children to achieve, while general audience copy might appeal to more efficient home management or to the ability to finish office work at home.

Seventy percent of the African-American community is solidly middle-class, but that does not necessarily mean it is formally well-educated, according to Buford. African-Americans achieve success and prominence through sports, entertainment, government, and small businesses, as well as through education.

Language

African-Americans have a cultural lingo that is familiar to them but not to most whites. Should a copywriter use it, or not? The best answer is offered by Buford: "It depends."

Advertising strategies should be clearly targeted and that might call for "right on" language, or not. "Slanguage" appeals to some segments of the minority market, but it turns off many middle-class people. Middle-class African-

Courtesy Heublein, Inc.

FIGURE 13-4
This Christian Brothers outdoor board shows how a sensitive copywriter establishes a link between the product and the targeted consumer.

Americans know slanguage and they use it when appropriate, but probably not in their consumer lives. They may resent an ad that tries to be one of the guys by dropping in some hip terms. It is best to concentrate on being sensitive to minority lifestyles and culture in standard English. All minorities want to be invited to try products. They do not want to be patronized or taken for granted, and they have the economic clout to warrant courting.

Buford describes a headline, "Ritzin' with the Brothers," that UniWorld created for Christian Brothers brandy, targeted to a minority audience (see Figure 13-4). "Ritzin'" is a reference to a posh New York hotel on the edge of Central Park and "putting on the ritz" has been popular in our vernacular for a long time. "Ritzin'" is common among African-Americans to describe dressing up or preparing lavishly for particularly festive occasions. The "inside" word was appropriate for the product and its strategic image, and African-American consumers recognized the message as talking to them. "Brothers" was a clever link between the brand name and how African-Americans often refer to African-American men, whether or not they are related.

Another example is Heublein's Smirnoff vodka campaign, which targeted African-Americans for whom grapefruit juice and vodka is a popular drink. The term "main squeeze" was in the copy, a double entendre which referred to an African-American man's best girl as well as the fruit. Consumers were invited to nominate their "Main Squeeze" as the ideal person for Smirnoff ads. The response was rewarding. As Buford pointed out, however, you have to know the community to know if the language you're using is patronizing or communicating.

Georgia Lee Clark says her magazines "correct" any slanguage that appears in interviews or writing. She said she would extend this courtesy to anyone, minority or not, because people's spoken grammar is always different from what they would like to see in print. She doesn't deny the more expressive, intense, colorful, or self-conscious linguistic style of the African-American culture, but believes that in articles and advertising, people prefer to see the standard forms. This insight was important for the Glory Foods campaign because for some students, their only experience with a group of African-Americans was a pick-up game at the gym or at a concert at one of the campus hangouts. They heard informal slanguage in those settings and would have guessed that this is how to be friendly and empathetic with African-American consumers.

Even deciding when it is correct to say African-American, or black, or person of color is important. "African-American" is used for this book because it is targeted to college students and young copywriters, who prefer that name. For older persons, "black" or "person of color" may be the preferred terms. The National Association for the Advancement of Colored People hasn't changed its name, nor has the United Negro College Fund, so it is important to be sensitive to the group you are writing for.

Music

African-American women do not breakdance across their kitchens, nor do their sons dance on the tables of fast food restaurants. Yet, there is a distinct kind of music that appeals to African-American consumers and some of it cuts across all audiences. Breakdancing in a popular Burger King commercial was created by a black advertising agency. Levi's used a hip theme for its 501 jeans and it caught the attention of African-Americans and whites.

African-Americans are aware of music that's current and they want this interest to be acknowledged. It's the creative team's job also to know what's current in the specific community it is targeting.

Enhancing a commercial with music carries the same caution as language use. African-American people love music as an expression of their heritage and culture. An outsider can easily misunderstand that music and wind up using it in a stereotypical way.

More About the African-American Market

Albert Styles, vice president/research for Burrell Communications Group, describes some of the things BCG learned from data collected through its new partnership with Yankelovich Research. Among them:

- African-Americans have tradition-based values and a strong commitment and loyalty to their families.

- African-Americans are brand loyal, but not blindly so. A different high quality brand can change their minds. African-American consumers look for well-advertised, visible, highly regarded products.

- African-Americans are enthusiastic shoppers. They like the shopping process because it's entertainment and a social time. In contrast, Styles says, instead of shopping till they drop, general audience shoppers have dropped shopping. If they can buy through their TV screen or a catalog, they will do that.

- African-Americans have a high degree of involvement with the media. They use the media, particularly radio, more than the general audience.

Heritage and Culture

Generational differences exist among African-Americans' attitudes, Styles says. His agency categorizes African-Americans for marketing purposes into four age groups, depending on how they participated in the Civil Rights movement:

1. 50+ activists
2. 30–49 achievers
3. 21–29 anticipators
4. 14–20 adaptors

Separating the 14–20-year-olds from 21–29-year-olds is something white advertisers don't do with their three-category breakdown of Generation X, Baby Boomers, and Over 50.

The 14–20 group has a stronger sense of who they are, Styles explains. They confidently call themselves African-American, have their own dress styles, their own music, and they feel "cool." Their expectations for education and jobs are more realistic because they have not experienced what was available in a stronger economy.

The 21–29-year-old "anticipators," on the other hand, look at the 30–49 year-old "achievers" who lived in an economically strong era when racism was the main focus of civil rights incentives. Scholarships were available for blacks who wanted an education and jobs waited for new graduates. What the anticipators find instead are tight budgets that have reduced educational opportunities, which they now must share with other groups. When they do graduate, often there are no jobs. This group is also mixed about whether it wants to be called Afro-Americans, African-Americans, or blacks. As a group, anticipators are angry and less sure about themselves, and Styles says his copywriters create messages for them that are different from copy directed to the less alienated 14–20 year-olds.

William Sharp, chairman and CEO of Sharp Advertising in Atlanta, offers another generational insight of African-American consumers. He says his agency stays keenly aware of three different eras which had a strong impact on the formation of the psychological attitudes of African-Americans.

1. ***The era of slavery.*** African-Americans were the only group of immigrants brought against their will to the United States. They were enslaved, then separated from others by the color of their skin, stripped of their self-esteem, denied equality, and aggressively discriminated against.

2. ***The black power era.*** Influenced by activists such as Stokely Carmichael and Malcolm X and by pacifists such as Dr. Martin Luther King, this period allowed African-Americans to break out of servility and begin to feel empowered. Kinky hair, teased into Afros, and big lips were o.k., even desirable. But most African-Americans in this era held low status jobs and did not have economic clout.

3. ***The present.*** Today, even with no clear leader, African-Americans display a strong link to their heritage. They are proud, loyal, self-made individuals who often extend family ties to nonrelatives. They seek status symbols that show they have something. They look for visible measures—clothes, cars, food—that clearly demonstrate their self-esteem and success.

The children and grandchildren of people from all of these eras are today's consumers, and the heritage and culture of African-Americans make a difference in how they interpret advertising messages. For example, UniWorld vice president and creative director Valerie Graves describes the difference between whites and blacks in the meaning of the headline, "Seal of Friendship," on a bottle of liquor.

African-Americans would read that headline to mean that friends will see that the host has good taste and friends would give the "seal of approval" to the *host's* good taste. A white person, on the other hand, would read the same words and interpret them to mean that friends would be impressed because the host cared enough about *him* to serve the best liquor. This difference is important when you are writing copy to reach and influence specific consumers in a cluttered marketplace.

Burrell also talks about the importance of self-esteem to African-Americans who are establishing themselves in an environment which repressed them for many decades. He points out the preoccupation with cleanliness of many African-Americans who for generations believed their dark skin was dirty. This sensitivity is important when writing effective copy for the hundreds of products that fill the personal and household cleaning products shelves of supermarkets.

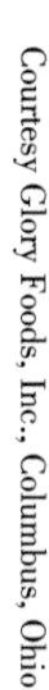

FIGURE 13-5

Glory Foods' sensitively crafted logo tells African-American consumers it understands that no commercially prepared food replaces mama's cooking—but Glory is close.

Burrell also offered a tip for the students who were working on the Glory Foods account. His ancestors, he said, were forced to eat what their white masters didn't want, often the tops of vegetables, left-over crops, undesirable and fatty cuts of meat. African-Americans learned to cook these foods to make them taste good, and those recipes have been passed through generations of African-American women. It takes hours to prepare greens from scratch the way Glory Foods has tried to do in providing a canned product for today's working families who don't have those hours.

The Glory Foods logo, "Just About the Best," is sensitive to the African-American tradition and doesn't presume that anything in a package can beat mama's recipes (see Figure 13-5). But it professes to be a close second. Some white students made a good argument for strengthening the logo so it didn't sound defensive. That probably won't happen unless Glory Foods expands heavily into the white market.

Socioeconomic Realities

Advertisers often perceive African-Americans to be in low-income, female-headed households. While there are more single women as head of households among African-Americans than other ethnic groups, more than half of African-American families are headed by a male/female partnership. Census Department data show that one-third of all black households have middle-class incomes of $35,000 or more, and one in ten families has an income of more than $50,000. African-Americans today are managers, professionals, technicians, and government officials.

African-Americans have a higher discretionary income than most people realize, and they are not hesitant to spend it. Middle-class African-Americans are more like white people than they are like lower socioeconomic African-Americans, in their interests and consumer habits. However, Sharp says that although some middle-class African-Americans do identify with some of the socioeconomic characteristics of their white counterparts, they do not as a group deny their culture or heritage. No matter how affluent or educated African-Americans become, they are conscious of themselves as minorities. African-Americans are aware every day that they are black, while whites don't think about being white, Sharp says. So when African-Americans have convinced themselves that black is beautiful and they are proud of their color, whites who want their business are well advised to be in touch with this strong feeling.

Theodore Pettus, vice president and creative director of Lockhart & Pettus, said it another way. Money and professional respect may exist in the conference room, but "down on the street, I'm just another black guy who can't get a cab."

This strong awareness of being a minority even after one has achieved economic and social status has created yet another market segment, multicultural consumers, people who are ethnically minorities but who have entered the traditional white culture through economic and social status. These people move between cultures, but as Sharp points out, they do not forget their heritage. Smart copywriters don't forget it either.

How to Succeed as a Copywriter in a Diverse Society

- Regard each target market as an exciting opportunity to learn about another culture.
- Be open-minded and talk to a lot of people in your target group.

- Test any copy that you write with members of that group, and keep modifying it until you see an appreciative smile.

- Never forget that your interpretation of the world may not be universal, and others are just as valid.

You will be writing advertising copy in a country that will have no majority in twenty years. Anticipate that and you will be in high demand.

Suggested Activities

1. Choose an ad for a parity product (toothpaste, soap, potato chips) and rewrite the copy to appeal directly to African-American consumers.

2. Clip two ads for the same product, one directed to general consumers and one directed to African-American consumers. Do a content analysis of the ads and tell what assumptions you might make about each group of consumers based on the messages you see.

3. Locate print ads in five categories (cigarettes, liquor, soap, travel, automobiles) for the same product in magazines targeted to African-Americans (*Essence, Ebony*) and targeted to a general audience (*Cosmopolitan, Redbook*). Are the ads identical? If not:

   Comment on differences in visuals and text that appear to reflect different targeted audiences.

   Are the differences *between* African-American and general audience ads greater than the differences *within* African-American targeted magazines and *within* general audience magazines?

4. Are there differences between *categories* in the extent to which print ads are driven by their target audiences? For example, are auto ads clearly targeted to separate ethnic groups in their visuals and messages while soap ads just change the skin color of models handling the product? Account for any differences you find.

5. Some well-known brands have had unchanging themes for decades, e.g., Marlboro, Ivory soap, Jack Daniels bourbon. Are there African-American targeted products whose advertising themes have been similarly constant for more than a decade? Talk to African-American consumers. Look at black-oriented magazines over a period of time. What are the unchanging images/values for selected African-American oriented products? Compare these images/values with the longstanding themes of Marlboro, etc.

CHAPTER 14

Writing to Reach the 50-Plus Market

BONNIE DREWNIANY
University of South Carolina

A few years ago, one of my students created an advertising campaign for toilet tissue. Her target audience? People ages 18 to 34. At first, I thought there must be something unique about the tissue that made it appeal just to younger people. Perhaps it came in neon colors. Perhaps it had Beavis and Butthead quotes printed on it. Or perhaps an electronic music chip played the latest MTV hits when the tissue unrolled. As it turned out, however, the tissue had no age-specific qualities. When I asked why people age 35 and older were not included in the target audience, my student responded, "Gee. I never really thought about them."

While this example may seem a bit extreme, many advertisers make similar mistakes. Like my former student, many advertisers are youth-obsessed and ignore one of the most important segments in America, people age 50 and older.

Why Is the 50-Plus Market So Important?

1. ***This market is 62 million strong.*** Simply put, the 50-plus segment represents 25 percent of the U.S. population. Ignoring one in four Americans doesn't make much sense, does it?

2. ***This market is growing.*** By the year 2000, the 50-plus population is expected to grow by 20 percent, to over 75 million. Reasons for this projected growth include improved health care and the entry of Baby Boomers into this age segment. As Figure 14-1 illustrates, the 18 to 34 age segment is expected to decrease in numbers.

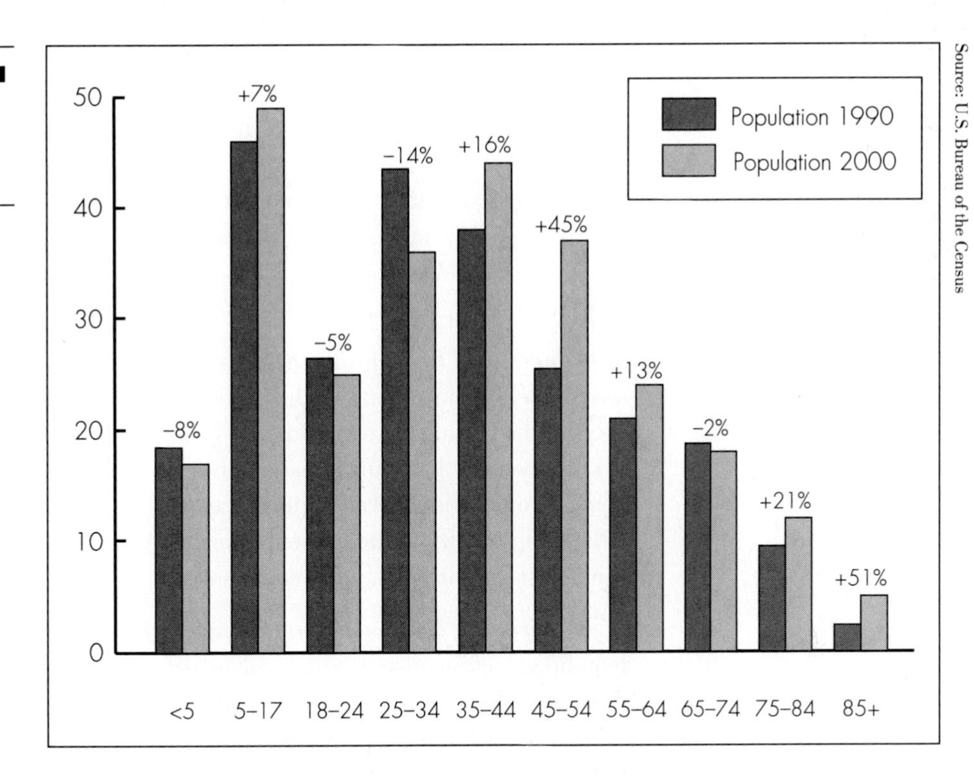

FIGURE 14-1
The shifting marketplace (estimated population in millions).

Source: U.S. Bureau of the Census

3. ***This market has tremendous spending power.*** Those in the 50-plus population hold more than half the discretionary income in the U.S., more than $130 billion. Furthermore, they account for the majority of personal assets—upwards of 80 percent of the money in savings and loans and 70 percent of the net worth of U.S. households.

How Has Advertising Gone Wrong?

1. ***Many advertisers have ignored the 50-plus market.*** Several studies point to the fact that older people are under-represented in advertising. For example, one study found only 5.9 percent of advertisements in seven national magazines contained older people. Another study found only seven percent of television commercials showed older people. These studies noted that when older people are shown, they are usually in background roles. They also pointed out that older women are particularly under-represented which is curious, since as the population ages, women outnumber men.

2. ***Advertisers have insulted this market.*** Unfortunately, many advertisements show elderly people, especially women, as feeble, crotchety, doddering old fools, passing their time away in rocking chairs. A recent commercial shows an older woman munching on chips, oblivious to a runaway steamroller barreling down on

her. A man climbs aboard a wrecking ball to rescue the chips and the woman is plowed into the cement. Another commercial features two dotty sisters. The punchline? One of the sisters is a bit senile and can't remember the name of a restaurant.

While no harm may have been intended by these commercials, the images they project may have a lasting impact. For example, although it has been years since the commercial first aired, people still joke about the line, "I've fallen and I can't get up."

3. ***Advertisers have painted too rosy a picture.*** In their quest to avoid agist stereotypes, some advertisers have gone to the opposite extreme and feature older people who are almost superhuman. While there are some people in their 80s who enjoy skate boarding, most older people don't identify with this portrayal. Some gerontologists warn that this type of advertising is harmful because it causes older people to think there's something wrong with them if they can't do the same things their peers do in commercials.

4. ***Advertisers believe the age-wave is far off in the future.*** In a recent telephone survey of senior-level advertising directors, 99 percent of the respondents said they agreed that the future belongs to those who plan for changes in demographic trends, such as aging. However, half of the respondents felt such trends are too far in the future to be relevant to current marketing and advertising strategies.

Myths About the Older Market

If the 50-plus market is so important, why have so many advertisers failed to reach them properly? How can you learn not to repeat the same mistakes? Perhaps the answers can be found by examining some of the myths and truths about the older market.

Myth #1. All older people are the same and can be targeted with one message. Think about some of the people you know who are 50 and older. Your grandparents. Your older neighbors. Professors. Community leaders. Chances are, these people are quite different from each other. They have different political views. Different senses of humor. Different lifestyles. Like any group, the older population is comprised of people with varied incomes, education, ethnic background, and life experiences. Using one message to reach all these people is about as absurd as saying one message will work for all people age 18 to 49.

Myth #2. Retired people have limited budgets. While younger people are struggling to finance a home and pay off education loans, many older people have paid off their debts and have the advantage of years of savings. As a result, older people can finance major purchases by cashing in stocks, real estate, or

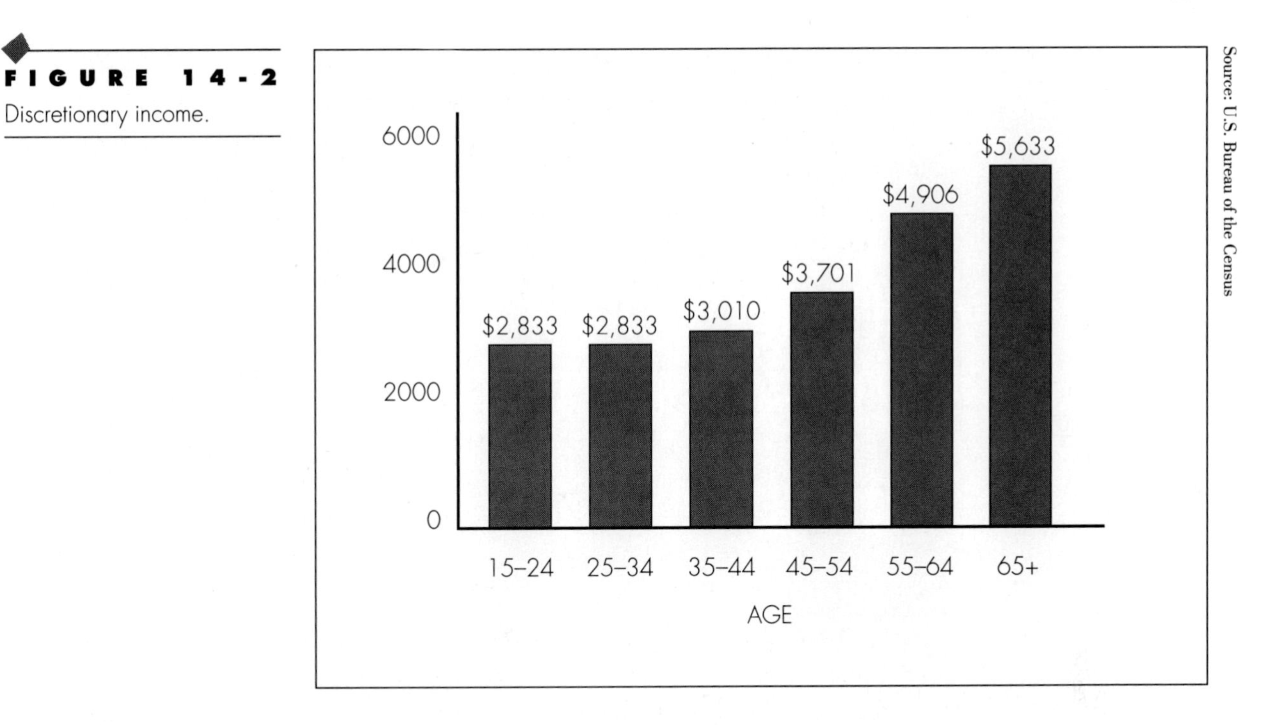

FIGURE 14-2
Discretionary income.

other assets. In fact, of all the ten-year cohorts, the 65 to 74-year-old cohort has the highest percentage of discretionary income (see Figure 14-2).

Myth #3. Older people are brand loyal and won't try new products. According to a recent study, the vast majority of 50-plus consumers say they stay with familiar brands because no one has shown them a reason to change. The majority said they would switch if a new product seemed to be more for "people like me."

Myth #4. Many older people live in nursing homes and don't do their own shopping. Actually, only five percent of people age 65 and older live in institutional settings. Not only do older people do their own shopping, they often shop for others. In fact, the staff of *American Demographics* selected grandparents as one of the twenty-five hottest markets of the 1990s. According to recent statistics, grandparents spend as much as parents for pets, toys, and playground equipment.

Myth #5. Older people buy only practical necessities. The 50-plus population doesn't just splurge on grandchildren. It also splurges on itself. In fact, the 50-plus population purchases:

- 48 percent of all luxury cars
- 37 percent of all spa memberships
- 80 percent of all luxury travel

Courtesy Flex Banking

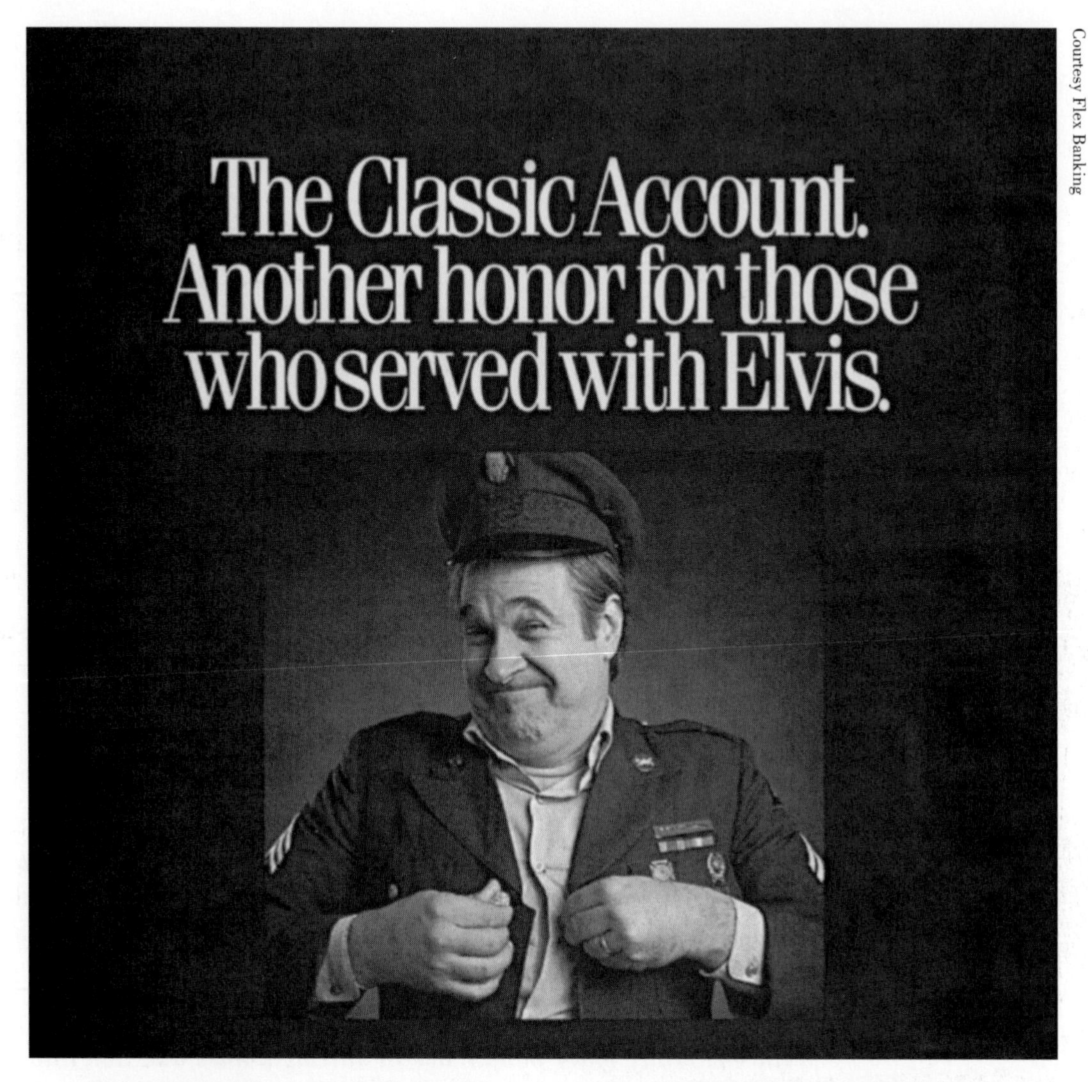

If you're turning 50, you may have buttoned on a uniform about the time Elvis helped to defend us.

Whether you did – or whether it still fits – isn't the point, of course. It's that now South Carolina National has a banking package that fits you very well.

And the only requirement is that you're 50 or older.

If you are, you're eligible for free checking, free checks, free travelers checks and money orders.

Interest on every dollar in your account. Discounts on a safe deposit box. A special Health Care CD. And more.

You can even apply for a special SCN Palmetto VISA® card.

Our Classic Account is the kind of honor most banks won't offer till you turn 55. But we figure it's time someone gave special consideration to the generation that grew up with rock 'n roll.

See your SCN banker. Or call Ann Singer at 1-800-922-5560. (771-3939 in Columbia.)

FIGURE 14-3

The king of rock 'n roll lives in the hearts of many people, particularly those in the 50-plus set. The humorous visual laughs with the audience, not at them. After all, the last time someone saw Elvis, he couldn't fit into his uniform, either.

Myth #6. Older people buy solely on price. After years of shopping, most consumers have learned that value, defined as quality for the money, is what constitutes a good buy. While price is a factor, other issues such as durability, convenience, warranties, return policies, and company integrity are important considerations.

Myth #7. Older people are passive and won't object to ads that poke fun of them. Nearly a third of older respondents in a Georgia State University study indicated they had boycotted a product because of the way advertising portrayed them. If that doesn't persuade you, consider the fact that the 50-plus set will soon include Baby Boomers who were involved in demonstrations, protest movements, and product boycotts. Chances are these people won't take any abuse from advertisers.

Myth #8. Older people are unhappy and therefore aren't positive role models. According to The National Opinion Research Center, people age 65 and over are the happiest age segment. The unhappiest segment? Persons 18 to 24.

Myth #9. Older people are sickly. Admittedly, these folks have more aches and pains than the average college student. However, most are far from what one would call sickly. Because of better medical care, improved diet, and increased exercise, more people are reaching the ages of 65, 75, and older in excellent health.

Myth #10. Older people aren't sexy and we all know sex sells, right? Older people date, fall in love, and become romantically involved just like younger people. In fact, according to a recent study, when older couples fall in love, they experience the same emotional somersaults, sweaty palms, and beating hearts as do younger couples.

Suggestions for Creating the Right Image

1. ***Don't think of them as just one market.*** Rather than rely solely on demographics, consider the powerful role of attitudes. Carol Morgan and Doran Levy, authors of *Segmenting the Mature Market,* for example, looked at how older Americans regard themselves and identified four segments. The first segment, "Upbeat Enjoyers," are the most likely to feel that their best years are now and in the future. Their priorities include looking good and staying active. They feel financially secure, and more likely to return to work after retirement, and don't worry much. On the other hand, the "Insecure" feel that they haven't been successful and their best years are over. They are afraid of not having enough money, shop for value, worry about crime, and are uncomfortable about their appearance. The "Threatened Active" segment has a more positive outlook on life than the "Insecure" segment, but still worries about crime. They are very resistant to change and want to keep living in their own homes, working, and driving

FIGURE 14-4
Have you ever heard your grandparents talk about the good old days when shopping was a pleasure and salespeople knew your name? Well, they would be happy to know that good service doesn't have to be a thing of the past. To see how Parisian tells a similar story to a different audience, see Figure 12-2.

Courtesy Parisian

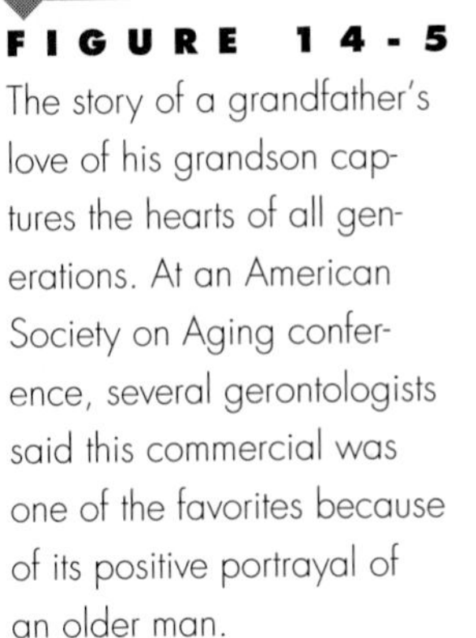

FIGURE 14-5
The story of a grandfather's love of his grandson captures the hearts of all generations. At an American Society on Aging conference, several gerontologists said this commercial was one of the favorites because of its positive portrayal of an older man.

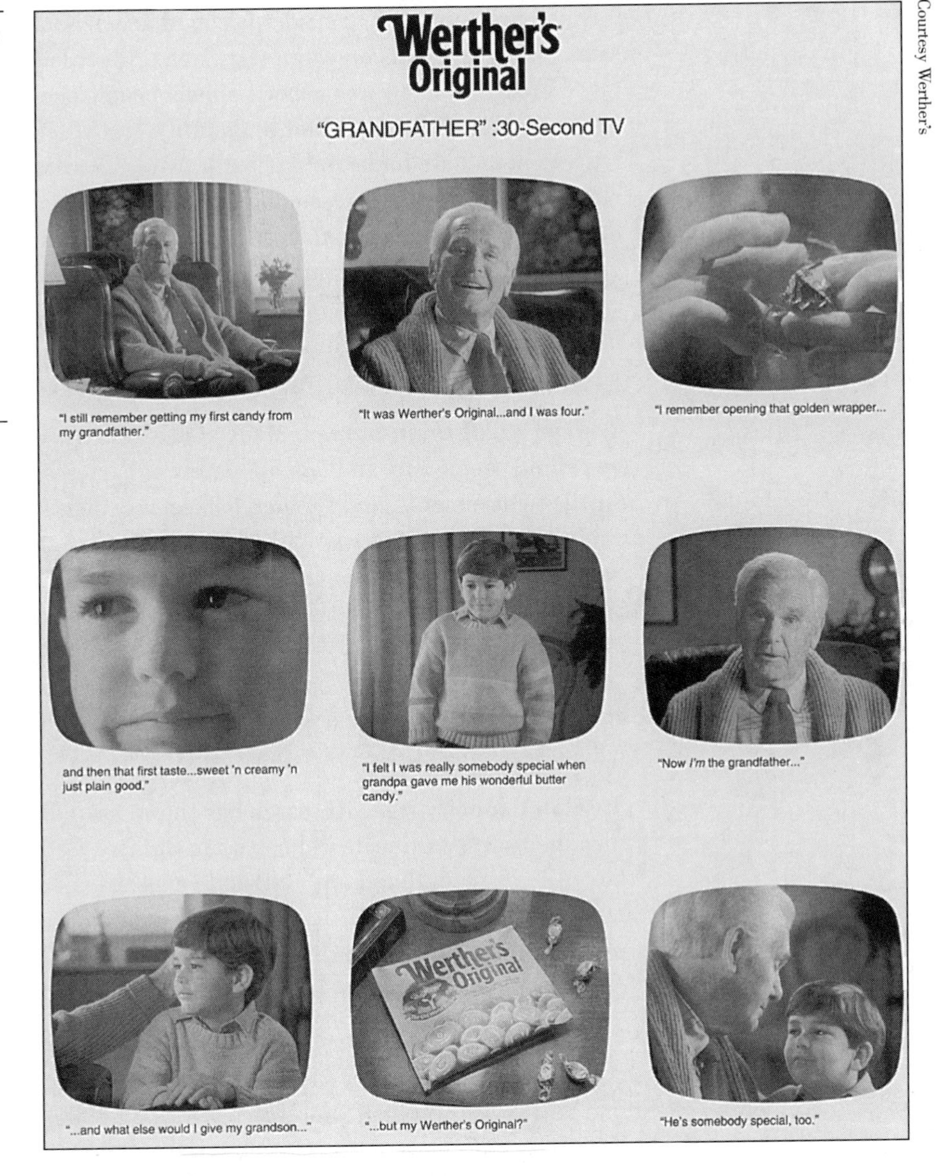

Courtesy Werther's

their cars. They don't worry about looking young. The last segment, the "Financial Positives," are more concerned about looking good. They feel financially secure, successful, and optimistic.

Several advertising agencies have also identified various psychographic segments among the 50-plus market. Grey Advertising, for example, has identified three groups. According to Grey, "Master Consumers" are fit, active, secure, and fulfilled. Half of this group is still working and they look forward to retirement as a time of pleasure. The second group, "Maintainers," are also healthy and financially comfortable, but are not as active as they would like to be. Sixty percent of this group is retired. And finally, "Simplifiers" are interested in streamlining their lives and tend to be light consumers of goods and services. This group offers only modest opportunities for marketers.

Another approach to consider is cohort analysis, the study of people with the same birth years and core values, as Trone Advertising, Inc. has done. According to Trone, there are two cohorts among people age 50 and older, "Traditionalists" and "Transitioners." Now in their 60s and 70s, Traditionalists are enjoying retirement and are in declining health. World War II, Pearl Harbor, the Hindenburg, and the Great Depression influenced Traditionalists' values. As a result, they're patriotic, seek financial security, and have strong work ethics. Transitioners, born in the late 1930s and '40s, have different core values than their older counterparts. The Korean War, McCarthyism, Ed Sullivan, and Marilyn Monroe influenced this group's values. As a result, Transitioners are protective, sentimental, desire choices, mistrust other nations, and are unreceptive to change.

2. ***Don't call them names.*** Many advertisers try to avoid using the word "old" by calling people fifty and older a variety of names including "senior citizens," "mature consumers," and "golden harvest members." However, as John Wrisley wrote in *Midlands Maturity,* "It's okay to substitute the word 'old' for 'mature'. Some of us in our 60s, 70s and beyond will never be mature. Cool it with the 'Senior Citizens' and 'Elders,' too. Do you want us calling you 'Junior Citizens' and 'Youngers'?"

A magazine for older people took years to learn this lesson. It started out as *Harvest Years,* then became *Retirement Living,* and then *50-Plus.* Today, it's called *New Choices.*

3. ***Don't specify age.*** Research has shown most older people feel younger than their birth certificate indicates. As Bernard Baruch said, "To me, old age is fifteen years older than I am." Several years ago, an advertising campaign featured the claim, "the first shampoo created for hair over 40." It bombed. The problem? Younger people refused to buy a product aimed at older people and older people didn't want to be reminded they had older hair.

4. ***Give them facts, not fluff.*** Older people are experienced consumers who aren't impressed by hype. After years of shopping, they're not going to be fooled into buying your product simply because you tell them that it's "new," or "the best." After all, these folks remember product flops, like the Edsel, and they want facts to back up your claims. Give them a compelling reason to try your product and they'll be willing to read long copy or listen to a detailed pitch.

5. ***Tell them the whole story.*** While commercials with fast editing cuts and very little copy may appeal to younger audiences, older audiences prefer a narrative style, with a beginning, a middle, and an end. As Grey Advertising summed it up, this generation is MGM, not MTV.

6. ***Don't remind them of their vulnerability.*** It's a fact of life. Arthritis, high blood pressure, heart problems, and other ailments bother more older people than younger people. However, older people know they have aches and pains without being reminded by you. Rather than dwell on the problems, your advertising should show how your product offers solutions.

FIGURE 14-6
And you thought the pink bunny kept going and going and going! This true story demonstrates that Coleman stoves and their owners are unbelievably tough, regardless of their age. According to Nancy Buell, Director of Advertising for Coleman, "I love the ad because the photo captures L.C. Shaffer's true spirit. He is without doubt a 'what you see is what you get' kind of guy."

Courtesy The Coleman Company, Inc. and Lee Crum, photographer

7. ***Laugh with them, not at them.*** Humor does have a place—if it doesn't rely on insulting stereotypes. To test whether your humor is insulting to older people, consider replacing a younger character for an older character in an advertisement you find funny. For example, remember the commercial that featured a senile woman who couldn't remember the name of a restaurant? Would it be as funny if a young, physically active college student couldn't remember the name? Probably not. What if you replaced the senile woman with a college student who was high on drugs? Would it be a fair portrayal of college students? Of course not.

8. ***Capture their hearts, not their egos.*** At about age 45, people shift from the predominant use of the left side of the brain, which focuses on details and materialism, to greater use of the right side, which focuses on creative, intuitive, and spiritual thoughts, according to G. Richard Ambrosius, a market researcher who studies older consumers. Therefore, to attract older people, show how your product or service supports goals such as altruism and social involvement.

FIGURE 14-7

A sure sign of the times is this USAir ad appearing in *Modern Maturity* and targeted to consumers 62 and older. If older Americans weren't important to advertisers, why do you suppose USAir and the other major airlines would be offering special rates to them?

NOW IS THE TIME TO HAVE THE TIME OF YOUR LIFE.

If you're 62 or older, you can visit the places you've waited years to see with USAir's Golden Opportunities℠ Coupons.

Books of four coupons are just $596. Eight are only $1,032. So now you can travel on USAir or USAir Express within the U.S. and Puerto Rico for as little as $129 one-way. And when you take your grandchildren, ages two to eleven, they can also travel on your coupons.

Just make your reservations fourteen days in advance. Once your ticket has been issued, you're free to change your mind and travel standby any time after that.

And remember, when you take advantage of USAir's Senior Saver Fare, you and a companion always get 10% off any fare.

Contact your travel consultant or call USAir today at 1(800)428-4322. And spend your free time without spending too much.

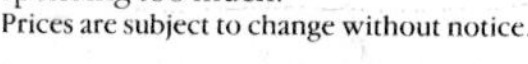

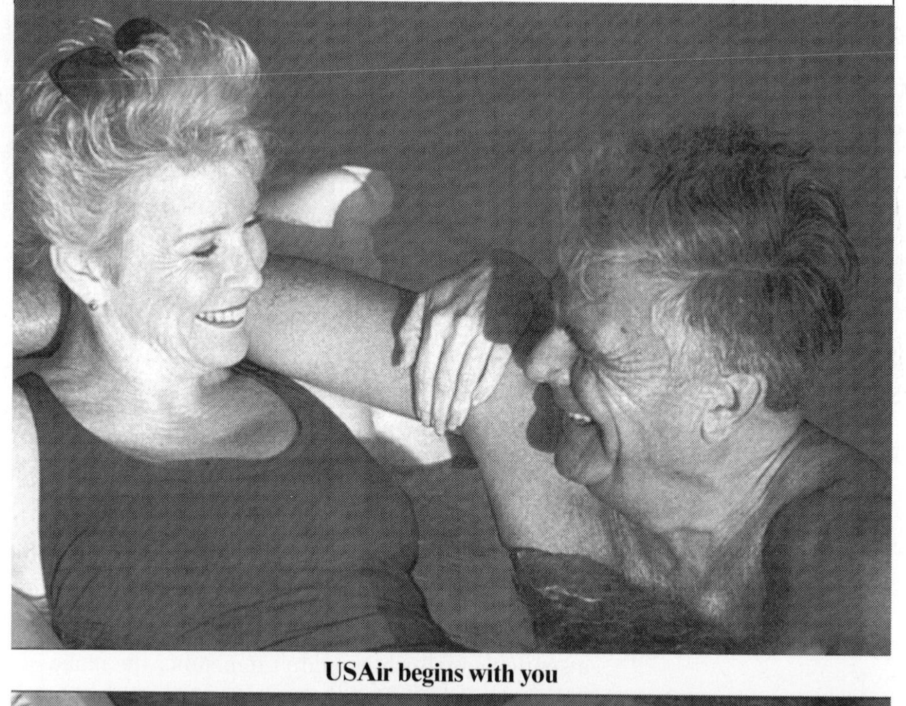

USAir begins with you

Courtesy USAir.

9. ***Cast models who reflect the right physical image.*** Use models who portray an upbeat, positive image, not those who reinforce the negative stereotype of being frail and senile. But don't go to the opposite extreme. While you may be tempted to show a person in his 80s who bungee jumps, most older people won't identify with this. In fact, some gerontologists warn that portraying older people as superhuman can leave older people wondering, "What's wrong with me? Why can't I do these things?"

FIGURE 14-8 Advertising in its own popular monthly *Modern Maturity,* which has the largest circulation of any magazine in the U.S., the AARP group health insurance program wisely suggests that "even if you've never felt better in your life, now is the perfect time to get long term care insurance. Because the younger you are when you enroll, the less it will cost per month." Notice how careful the ad is to steer clear of stereotypical 50+ men and women in the photograph.

You Probably Won't Need Long Term Care Insurance For Years. Which Is Why You Should Get It Now.

HEALTH INSURANCE PLANS DESIGNED TO MEET AARP MEMBERS' NEEDS. CALL US. 1-800-245-1212 OPERATOR #06, MON.-FRI, 9-5 ET.

Even if you've never felt better in your life, now is the perfect time to get long term care insurance. Because the younger you are when you enroll, the less it will cost per month.

And since your premiums are based on the lower rate you pay when you first enroll, those savings will continue for as long as you're covered.

Of course, that's not the only reason to consider a long term care plan from the AARP Group Health Insurance Program, provided by The Prudential. These plans can also help protect you against the ever-growing cost of nursing home care, which can exceed $30,000 a year.*

So even if you don't think you'll need long term care for years, call or send in the attached card today for more information, including benefits, costs, limitations and exclusions.

Because if you'd like to enjoy the peace of mind long term care insurance can offer, as well as the savings, there's no time like the present.

AARP Group Health Insurance Program

AS 166

*American Hospital Association "Economic Trends," Winter, 1991, based on a national average.

Group Policy Nos. G-36000-2-4-10. **The Prudential Insurance Company of America** (licensed in all states) **Fort Washington, PA 19034.** All plans may not be available in your state. AARP's Medicare Supplement plans do not duplicate Medicare's benefits, and unless specifically stated, will only pay for benefits that are Medicare eligible expenses. Long Term Care plans are not available in Kansas or Minnesota. Long Term Care plans are available only to AARP members age 50-79 who meet certain eligibility requirements.

10. ***Cast models who represent the age your audience feels.*** Remember how you identified with the "big" kids when you were younger? Well, the opposite is true as you get older. Most older people see themselves as ten to fifteen years younger than their birth certificates indicate. Therefore, use models who are younger than the actual age of your older target audience.

11. ***Include older people in the ads even when the product isn't targeted exclusively to them.*** Don't just show older people in ads for denture cream, prune juice, and adult diapers. After all, many older people don't even use these products. Instead, include them in your ads for everything they buy, from computer software to diet soft drinks.

12. ***Show them interacting with others.*** Show them with their mates, friends, family, and coworkers. Try to include people of different generations, especially grandchildren. Be sure, however, not to portray them as dependent upon others.

13. ***Show older people as they are, happy with themselves.*** Rather than portray older people as crotchety, show them enjoying life. Playing with their grandchildren. Volunteering their time. Starting new hobbies. And so on.

14. ***Portray aging as a time of learning.*** Now that the kids are grown up and the demands of a career are gone, older people finally have the time to do the things they always wanted to do. Like learning how to play music. Experimenting with photography. Or going back to college to earn a degree. Therefore, don't just show them looking pensively into the sunset, show them setting out to do new things. Advertisements for Fox Hill Village, a retirement community in Massachusetts, used to show smiling retirees on balconies admiring the beautiful landscape. When the community ran a series of ads featuring Ben Franklin, Clara Barton, Noah Webster, and other heroes who became famous during their later years, calls went up 25 percent.

15. ***Offer them a free trial.*** Remember, these folks are more savvy than most consumers. They're willing to experiment with new products, but they don't want to be tricked into buying something that's worthless. Therefore, if possible, offer them a free sample or a coupon. Tell them about your product's warranty. Tell them the story of satisfied users. Tell them about your return policy. But don't tell them any tall tales.

Advertising to 'Tweens (Ages 8 to 14)[1]

Now that you know how to reach grandparents, how do you reach their grandchildren? When *Sports Illustrated for Kids* magazine launched in 1989, the publishers were astounded by the lack of research on children's print advertising. In response to this lack of information, *SI for Kids* Research Division developed a program to study the effectiveness of print advertising among the evergrowing 'tween market. The following guidelines are the result of this research:

1. Use vibrant colors and eye-catching graphics. Kids take notice of ads that are full of action.

2. Copy should be bite-sized. Small chunks of copy are more easily read by children than long copy blocks commonly found in adult advertising.

[1]Citation: Sabino, D. (1993) *Sports Illustrated For Kids*® Research Department *Sports Illustrated for Kids* is a registered trademark of Time, Inc. ©1993. Time Inc. All Rights Reserved.

3. Make sure there is something in your ad for kids of all levels. For example, cool illustrations for younger readers and exciting copy for more accomplished readers.

4. Identify the product and the brand name clearly. Kids want to know which manufacturers are concerned about them.

5. Ads should show relevance to the lives of kids—tell/show what the product has to do with them.

6. Ads should be focused. Tell/show why they should be interested in your product.

7. Tweens/pre-adolescents are self-conscious and compare themselves to each other and adults. When featuring kids in an ad, use kids in the upper end of the age target.

8. Ads should be inviting . . . better yet involving. If an advertiser asks kids to answer a question, they'll take the challenge and as a result spend more time with an ad.

Some Additional Considerations for the 50-Plus Market

As people age, their eyesight, hearing, and memory diminish somewhat. As a result, what may look and sound great to a young art director or writer may not be as appealing to an older person. Therefore, when you create advertisements for older audiences, keep the following things in mind:

1. ***Use larger print.*** Most people become more farsighted with age. Therefore, use a larger type size to enhance readability. Body copy set in 12 point type is generally recommended for older readers.

2. ***Avoid ornate fonts.*** For the clearest image, avoid using ornate fonts and italics. In general, serif type is preferred for body copy.

3. ***Select a format that's reader friendly.*** Smaller blocks of copy, with indented paragraphs, are easier to read. Use a line length of no more than five to six inches.

4. ***Avoid blues, greens, and purples.*** With age, the eye lens yellows and filters out more violet light, making it more difficult to distinguish between blues and greens. On the other hand, reds, oranges, and yellows are easier to distinguish. To understand this phenomenon, you may wish to hold a yellow filter over your designs.

5. ***Choose colors with sharp contrasts.*** With age, less light passes through the eye so there is a need for sharper contrasts. In choosing colors, then, avoid

combining tones and shades of the same color. For example, avoid using red type on a pink background.

6. ***Avoid glare.*** Although metallic type on glossy paper may look elegant to a young art director, it results in a blurry image to older people because it has less contrast.

7. ***Select announcers with deep voices.*** As we age, we lose our ability to hear high-pitched tones. Keep this in mind when selecting music, too.

8. ***Avoid flashing images in television commercials.*** It is more difficult for an older person to see quick moving images because their pupils are smaller and their eye muscles are slower to respond to quick changes in movement. Therefore, when you create a television spot for older audiences, go for gradual transitions from one scene to the next and avoid rapid-fire, unrelated messages.

9. ***Keep your message simple.*** With increasing age, people react more slowly and less accurately to sensory stimulation, so don't clutter your message with unnecessary information.

10. ***Use visual cues to trigger their memory.*** Visual memory declines more slowly than verbal memory, so design your message in a way that gets your older audience to visualize your product. Reinforce your message with point-of-purchase displays.

Suggested Activities

1. Watch two hours of prime-time television and record the way people are portrayed. Are older people shown in any of these commercials? If so, do they portray any negative stereotypes?

2. Create two advertisements for any product. In one advertisement, use a left brain approach. In the other advertisement, use a right brain approach. How are they different? Is one approach more appropriate for older people?

3. Write headlines for the following products: an arthritic pain reliever, a denture adhesive, and an undergarment for adults with bladder control problems.

4. Create an advertisement promoting jeans for older people. How will your advertisement be different if it is targeted to Maintainers? Master Consumers?

5. How would you promote a luxury car to Transitioners? Traditionalists?

6. Write headlines and create visuals to promote a skin moisturizer to the following segments: Upbeat Enjoyers, the Insecure, the Threatened Active, and the Financial Positives.

CHAPTER 15

Writing the Business-to-Business Ad Campaign

JAY SMITH AND JUSTIN C. HUGGINS
Semaphore, Inc., Columbia, S.C.

Historically, business-to-business advertising has been known as "trade advertising," or "industrial advertising." In its earlier incarnations, business-to-business advertising usually consisted of image advertising designed to produce and reinforce awareness of a corporation or its products and services. But with tough economic times and increased competition which peaked in the late 1980s, the focus turned to more aggressive advertising messages for a very important reason—the dramatic rise in the cost of personal sales calls to businesses by commercial and industrial salespeople. The personal sales call (especially "cold calls," where salespeople have little or no assurance that the business will evince interest in their products or services) is now recognized as an inefficient means of prequalifying sales leads, since it often involves a highly paid professional's time and travel expenses.

For more than twenty-two years, the agency we work for has been creating effective advertising for business-to-business clients. We believe that the challenges, opportunities, and rewards of business-to-business advertising are often ignored by students, which makes little sense considering the billions of dollars spent by businesses to advertise their goods or services to others.

Advertisements that appeal to emotion—and the majority of consumer ads employ this tactic—may cause you to wonder why a corporation would spend millions of dollars on an ad that could be refuted with elementary logic. Perhaps that's one reason business-to-business advertising presents a special challenge to those who must deal with it. Although it doesn't usually tug at heart strings or try to influence emotions, neither does it beat a consumer over the head with a hard sell or price points. And rarely in creating business-to-business advertising can you employ the "feeling strategies" you learned in Chapter 4—the brand image, product positioning, resonance, and affective strategies.

Instead, business-to-business advertising relies primarily on reasoning. The ads throughout this chapter use the unique selling proposition strategy. USP is used less today in package goods advertising, where it got its start, but it has become the dominant strategy in economic development advertising, one of the fastest growing segments of business-to-business advertising.

A copywriter and art director working in this area must understand everything from animal health to aircraft and oscillographic recorders and time dominant reflectors so they can speak intelligently with farmers, vets, site selection professionals, construction executives, and aerospace engineers. It takes exceptional creative ideas plus technically accurate details to gain the attention of these professionals. And much as it seems these two things don't go together, they can and they do.

To the general public, as well as to many students of advertising, business-to-business advertising is virtually a secret industry. To a growing number of advertising agencies, large and small, business-to-business advertising has become a major part of their financial and creative success.

As its financial significance became evident in recent years, and traditionally conservative industry leaders allowed their ad agencies to expand their creative approaches, industrial advertising gained favor and credibility, and took the name "business-to-business advertising," which is a more accurate description of the current purpose and approach of such advertising.

Standards for creativity also rose dramatically, largely in response to the increasing cost and clutter of business-to-business advertising, and the insistence by marketing and sales managers that the advertising stand out from the crowd.

"The Other Advertising"

Yet despite its growing use and effectiveness, business-to-business advertising is not what most advertising students will tell you they wish to do once they leave school, for two good reasons:

- Consumer advertising is more visible to them. It is heard and seen on radio and TV, in publications circulated to millions, and on buses and billboards. And because advertising people are like other people (at least in some ways), we like having our work seen and appreciated by others. Because consumer ads are seen or heard or read by millions, while audiences for business-to-business advertising generally are much smaller, consumer ads are assumed to be more important.

- The subject matter for retail advertising is more often related to our personal lives. We can all identify with toothpaste, snack foods, or cars. But the challenge of being creative while marketing less celebrated products such as unfinished textiles, formed meats, industrial sites, and electricity hardly seems exciting or glamorous—at first glance.

The Difference Between Consumer and Industrial Advertising

- In business-to-business advertising, one new sale can mean tens of millions of dollars. Although one good lead, converted to a sale by the sales force, can redefine the corporate success of a company, the goal is still to create a volume of sales.

- The psychology of business-to-business advertising is different from retail advertising. Retail sells products to people for their personal use, often focusing on emotions, ego, and personal benefits. Business-to-business advertising markets products to decision makers who are purchasing for their companies, usually with hard core considerations of bottom line cost, reliability, quality, and profitability.

- You can use technical terms, and you usually have more lead time. Of course, some major opportunities can present themselves quickly.

- The target audiences are more sophisticated and may include CEOs, purchasing and financial managers, and human resources vice presidents. Even the promotional advertising and newsletters that ad agencies themselves use to locate and secure new clients (and new business from existing clients) qualify as business-to-business advertising.

- Because business-to-business media have traditionally been print-dominated, much of the work has involved production of print ads. But in recent years, business-to-business advertising has increasingly utilized a number of the "new" media. The burgeoning cable TV industry and the resultant narrowcasting to very specific audiences has allowed business-to-business to move more into the realm of television.

How to Create Effective Business-to-Business Ads

Business-to-business campaigns generally concentrate heavily on print pieces and publications. But such campaigns may use all of the following: brochures, catalogs and catalog sheets, print ads, corporate identity videos, sales presentation videos, demo computer programs, trade show booths, packaging design, and direct mail campaigns.

The keys to producing effective, creative advertising directed from one business to another are similar to those for other advertising audiences. The few differences are mostly positive; they allow you more latitude in creativity, although they often require more preparation.

1. ***Do your homework.*** Thought you'd be through with homework when you graduate? No such luck. As in all advertising, creativity alone is not enough to produce effective industrial advertising. With business-to-business advertising, research is even more critical. Fortunately, with the generally more focused target markets of business-to-business ads, research is also often easier to accomplish and may well include touring plants and factories and chatting with people on the production lines.

2. ***Talk up to the audience.*** In an era when more and more advertisers are forced to write down to the lowest common denominator, it can be a joy to address a target composed of CEOs, VPs, and other executives and upscale professionals who have survived in competitive industries, and have risen to positions of substantial responsibility. They are generally very knowledgeable, or they would not be in "the target zone." Don't simply show off your vocabulary, but don't underestimate your client's prospective customers either.

3. ***Sell to the committee.*** In the corporate world, few decisions are made by individuals. Because the power structure doesn't encourage impulse buying and requires the approval of several executives—from CEOs, marketing managers, and purchasing officers to engineers, scientists, and salespeople—your ad will be more effective if it responds to all of their concerns about quality, cost, and specifications.

4. ***Know and use the terminology of the industry.*** When working with business-to-business clients, the creative team must master the details of technical and sometimes obscure industrial processes, specifications, and sales environments. This is one place where insider terms, if not overdone, will add to the effectiveness of an ad.

5. ***Use business-to-business psychology.*** Remember that, in business-to-business, the customer's focus is more likely to be on the bottom line. That fact does not preclude a creative approach, but it does usually compound the challenge of selling the product or service. Remember: business-to-business has a different role in that it uses its call to action to generate appointments and calls from customers, not to motivate the customer to enter a retail establishment. This distinction may be lost on creative teams who don't have experience in business-to-business advertising.

6. ***With the growth of the international market for business-to-business goods, be certain ad translations don't change the intent of the original.*** Relying on a play on words, a pun, an idiom, or any other device that might lose its impact in translation can completely destroy the effectiveness of an ad.

7. ***Focus on your key selling idea.*** In most cases, you won't have the space or time to enumerate every advantage of your product, although listing a few key points, or condensing them into one message encompassing several points, will work when executed well. Case in point: the only graphic element in many

economic development ads is a map. Consequently, browsing through economic development/site selection publications is sometimes more like leafing through an atlas than browsing through a series of memorable ads. These advertisers are presumably counting on a clever headline and the customer's desire to improve his/her knowledge of geography to make the sale. Unless informing your prospect of the client's industrial site location is the dominant (or only) factor in your sales pitch, focusing on a distinguishing characteristic of your client's product or service is more likely to get the buyer's attention. In most cases, photographs, illustrations, or copy addressing the benefits of your client's location will more creatively and effectively portray the advantages of the site. And because map use is so pervasive in economic development, your ad will stand out from the clutter of the others.

8. ***Don't be shy, but don't resort to puffery.*** Modesty is no virtue in the world of trade advertising. Get your strong points across, and don't be afraid of using superlatives when appropriate and defensible. Don't fall back on clichés and puffery—use terms such as "state of the art" and "quality" sparingly. Because most of your competitors will likely claim these terms for their products and services, using them and other redundant or meaningless adjectives will merely bore your readers.

9. ***Focus on creating ads that generate a response.*** Very few ads are able to sell the big ticket items in business-to-business ads. Your job is usually to generate calls, encourage the return of response cards, and produce name recognition to help your client's sales force. The decision to make a purchase may rest completely with your reader, but a purchase based solely upon an advertisement—even your best—is a very rare event. (***Note:*** many clients do not adhere to this view. They expect advertising to sell the product and the company, leaving the salespeople to serve as highly paid order takers.)

10. ***Consider media other than print.*** Business-to-business advertising experts are increasingly using video, telemarketing, and other media forms to complete the media mix. If you can reach the market effectively with other media, consider it!

11. ***Solve their problem.*** Remember that when your ad runs in a niche publication, you've got a motivated audience. Readers are interested in the topic because it is their business. Often their reason for reading the publication is to solve a business-related problem.

Suggested Activities

1. Using local resources (the chamber of commerce, the local yellow pages, etc.), identify companies who manufacture products or offer services to other businesses. Contact one company's marketing/advertising manager and ask if

he or she can spend time introducing you to the company and its target markets. Using such discussions, plus any literature he or she might provide, plus some independent library research on the category, write a creative strategy statement and develop advertising for this company.

2. Using Standard Rate and Data business and farm magazine listings, locate several publications that appear to run business-to-business advertising. Call or write the publications and request copies. Study the ads and discuss your reactions to them with others in your class.

3. Create an ad for a product or service offered by one company to make the work of another company's sales force more effective or profitable. For example, you might develop a print ad targeted to the CEO or sales manager which focuses on the benefits to the company of a notebook computer, cellular phone, or pager.

4. Select a consumer product (automobile, video equipment, furniture, etc.). Choose a component part, such as the upholstery cloth or the airbag for the automobile, the electric power cord for the video equipment, or the wood screws or foam cushioning for a sofa, and develop a series of ads that sells the component to the manufacturer of the consumer product. For authenticity, search the library for information on automobile upholstery, airbags, power cords, wood screws, foam cushioning, etc.

The Many Dimensions of Business-to-Business Advertising*

Client: Piedmont Municipal Power Agency
Ad: The Works

Background: The Piedmont Municipal Power Agency (PMPA) is a wholesale supplier of electricity for ten municipal electric utilities in South Carolina. In an effort to get more business, utilities regularly participate in economic development advertising to lure new industries into the utilities' service areas.

Need: Encourage economic development in PMPA service area. Run in such highly targeted publications as *Area Development* and *Site Selection,* as well as general business publications like *Business Week* and *Forbes.*

Strategy: All of the cities that comprise PMPA offer electricity, water, sewer, gas, and other municipal services such as fire protection and trash collection. This "one-stop shopping" is fairly unique, as most electric utilities are usually independent of other services. In selecting a site to locate, an industry has to make sure that everything is favorable. Because PMPA cities provide multiple services, there are fewer entities a prospective industry has to talk to. We thought that the bundled services of a municipality made things easier for an industry. "The Works" was the obvious conclusion. You could get everything with one phone call—the water works, the electric works, etc. The ad ran as a half-page island, so that it could dominate the page. (Semaphore)

* The advertisements in this Creative Spot from Semaphore appear courtesy of its president, Cynthia Gilliam, and represent a portion of a single year's billing for that agency. We are also indebted to Michael Fernandez of Sawyer Riley Compton, Atlanta, for several ads.

Imagine a plain hot dog.

Now imagine having to purchase ketchup from one vendor, mustard from another vendor, onions from a third vendor, and chili from yet another. **Ridiculous?** *You bet it is, but businesses do it all the time with their utilities.*

In northwestern South Carolina, there are ten single source cities offering bundled municipal services, some of the highest quality water in the U.S. and the benefits of a plentiful, reliable source of electricity, with a responsive utility management. Each member city of the Piedmont Municipal Power Agency also offers a ready inventory of industrial buildings and sites.

A reliable work force, an extensive transportation system, state funded worker training programs, and an unparalleled quality of life await you in the ten member cities of PMPA.

the WORKS

Offering Bundled Municipal Services for Your Convenience

To find out more, contact C. Robin Smith, Community Relations and Economic Development Coordinator, PMPA, at (803) 877-9632.

Courtesy Piedmont Municipal Power Agency

Client: Clinton Mills
Ad: Symbols of Excellence and Faces Behind the Quality

Background:

In business since 1896, Clinton is recognized as a leader in the textile field. With its sister companies, Clinton makes a variety of fabrics and cloth materials, and sells directly to furniture, clothing, and automobile manufacturers.

Need:

Ongoing daily ads in *Daily News Record,* the bible of the garment industry. Clinton has run an ad in this daily trade publication every day since the mid-1940s.

Strategy:

The fact that Clinton was already a recognized leader in the production of quality fabric and the name recognition generated by appearing in *DNR* every day for nearly fifty years gave us considerable latitude. We came up with the symbols of excellence ads, a series that would command attention and immediately be comprehended. Each Monday, the symbols would run in color, making the gold star, blue ribbon, and red check mark even more striking. As a follow-up to that campaign, we wanted to push the quality aspect of Clinton's operation. With the symbols of excellence ads, Clinton had promoted a corporate image of quality. The next logical progression was to show the faces behind the quality. Once again, the fact that we could run one day with color played into the strategy. The composite ad with all four Clinton employees ran in color on Monday, followed by black-and-whites throughout the week featuring each individual employee and his or her testimony as to what makes Clinton unique. (Semaphore)

Courtesy CMI Industries, Inc.

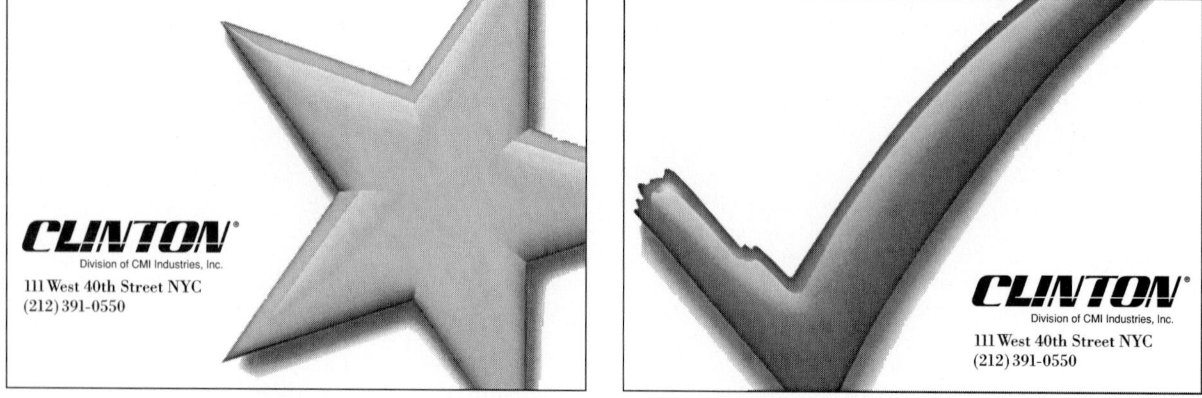

Client: Berkeley Electric Cooperative
Ad: Kevin Crosby

Background: An electric cooperative like Berkeley can be thought of as a power company owned by the people it serves. Unlike investor-owned utility companies who must concentrate on serving their investors, co-ops concentrate solely on serving their members. Part of that service is helping to reduce the bill of each individual customer by educating all of them on energy efficiency. Lowering each member's bill lowers co-op costs and in turn lowers the bill of every other member. Until recently, electric utilities have aimed their educational efforts at residential efficiency. Now, commercial efficiency, or targeting businesses and industries, is receiving more attention.

Need: Show commercial members that the co-op could offer help in improving their financial position. That is great news for a company doing everything to improve its finances in a sluggish economy.

Strategy: Tell commercial members that there is another place they can look to trim expenses. (Semaphore)

The Energy Experts™ at Berkeley Electric Cooperative have a reputation for helping our members, and we know how energy costs can affect your bottom line.

We've helped dozens of companies improve their bottom line. For example, several companies called on us to perform energy audits and make recommendations about how to get the most out of their energy dollars.

In an energy audit, we look for ways to make your energy use more efficient. The recommendations we make can save you money. And, if you qualify for our Commercial *Good Cents*® program for new construction, you'll be saving energy and receive significant cash incentives for meeting the efficiency standards.

We also consider whether there is an alternative rate which would better suit your needs. That alone can save you thousands of dollars in the long run without major adjustments to your operation.

Now, we won't tell you how to run the business, but we're confident that, when you see the numbers, you'll want to make some of the commercial recommendations a part of *your* energy policy.

For information on how the Energy Experts at Berkeley Electric Cooperative can help your bottom line, call Kevin Crosby at 761-8200 or 572-5454.

We Don't Want To Tell You How To Run Your Business, But...

Kevin Crosby
Commercial Marketing Coordinator

BEC BERKELEY ELECTRIC COOPERATIVE

Courtesy Berkeley Electric Cooperative, Inc.

Client: Palmetto Economic Development Corporation
Ad: Exacting Standards and International Children

Background:

The Palmetto Economic Development Corporation (PEDC) is the economic development arm of a system of fifteen electric cooperatives. PEDC attempts to recruit regional, national, and international industries that might have an interest in locating a facility in the Southeast.

Need:

Capitalize on international awareness of the decision by German automaker BMW to locate their first North American manufacturing facility in South Carolina. And, since BMW was just the most recent of several international companies to choose the state, highlight the diversity of the people locating in South Carolina.

Strategy:

"If South Carolina is good enough to meet the high demands of BMW," our logic concluded, "then it's good enough to meet yours, too." The "Exacting Standards" ad was translated into German to run in *Handelsblatt,* the German equivalent of the *Wall Street Journal.* The "International Children" ad was conceived to meet PEDC's second need, to illustrate the diversity of people and industries in the Palmetto state. We wanted an ad that really stood out from the usual fare of economic development advertisements. Using the group of multinational children accomplished just that. In a survey conducted by *Site Selection* magazine, this ad scored highest in readership awareness of any ad in the issue. Because of its success, it was also translated for publication in Japan. The ad effectively conveyed that South Carolina was home to many international corporations, but by using children, it also implied that there was a high quality of life to be found as well. (Semaphore)

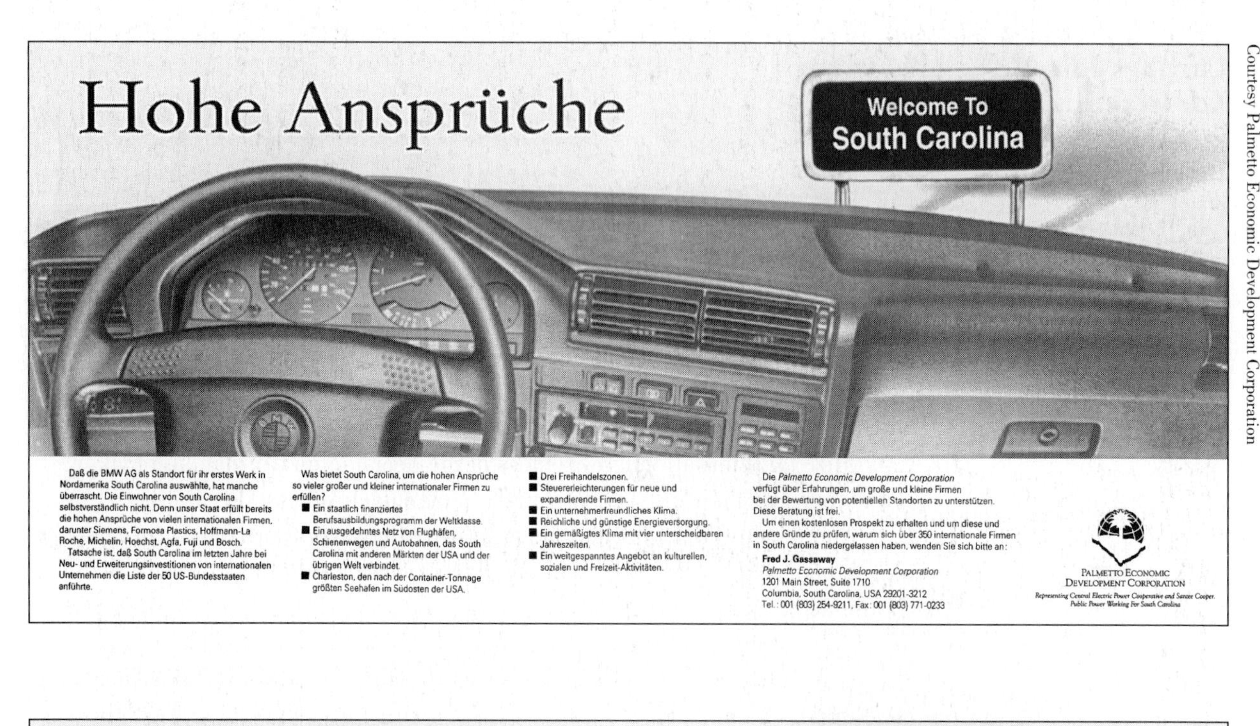

Courtesy Palmetto Economic Development Corporation

Courtesy Palmetto Economic Development Corporation

FROM EVERY POINT OF VIEW

The choice of companies from across the U. S. and around the world, South Carolina provides a nurturing environment for people, productivity and profits.

BMW, Teledyne, Paperboard Industries, Formosa Plastics, Hoffman-La Roche, Michelin, Willamette Industries, SmithKline Beecham, Hitachi, and others have selected South Carolina as their new home.

With world-class training programs, a strong pro-business climate, access to important markets, a superb transportation network and excellent local cooperation, South Carolina is also a wonderful place to raise a family.

Palmetto Economic Development Corporation has the knowledge and experience to confidentially help large and small companies evaluate potential sites at no cost. To find out how South Carolina looks from your point of view and receive a free *Prospectus*, write, call or fax:

Fred J. Gassaway
PALMETTO ECONOMIC DEVELOPMENT CORPORATION
1201 Main Street, Suite 1710
Columbia, South Carolina, USA 29201-3212
Phone (803) 254-9211
Fax (803) 771-0233

PALMETTO ECONOMIC DEVELOPMENT CORPORATION

Representing Central Electric Power Cooperative and Santee Cooper.

Public Power Working For South Carolina.

Client: The National Bank of South Carolina
Ad: Short Hops, Long Hauls

Background:

The National Bank of South Carolina (NBSC) is the largest independent bank headquartered in South Carolina. It is committed to cautious growth in its quest to become the dominant statewide bank.

Need:

Target business owners in order to capitalize on all of the super-regional bank mergers that had occurred over the past two years. Ad to run in the State Chamber of Commerce yearbook, which serves as a reference for businesses.

Strategy:

Position NBSC as big enough and experienced enough to handle the big accounts, yet small enough to care about fostering a good relationship with its smaller banking customers. Target two distinct types of businesses—those needing a bank that could manage all of their financial needs (for the long haul), and those needing a bank less frequently for things like loans (for the short hop). The visual of the 18-wheeler implied a major transportation company or an independent trucker, and the inset illustration of the pickup conveyed that no business is too small for NBSC. (Semaphore)

FOR SHORT HOPS OR LONG HAULS.

Created to meet the needs of South Carolina businesses over 88 years ago, The National Bank of South Carolina continues to work hard for businesses statewide. NBSC provides the fast, flexible, banking service that small to medium sized businesses must have in order to survive and prosper.

Whether you need short term help, or help for the long haul, share some of the challenges and opportunities facing your company with an NBSC business specialist. We offer flexible lines of credit, cash management services, profit sharing programs, and an array of other financial services to assist you and your business.

For short hops. For long hauls. Bring your business banking to NBSC.

Courtesy The National Bank of South Carolina

Client:
Semaphore, Inc.
Ad:
Self-Promotion

Background: Semaphore, Inc., is a mid-size, full-service advertising agency specializing in business-to-business advertising and emphasizing results over awards.

Need: Generally, advertising agencies do not participate in the very practice which they promote. The agency wanted to be recognized by the large number of companies that were certain to increase advertising budgets as the economic environment slowly improved.

Strategy: Create a striking ad that would convey our results-oriented philosophy of advertising. Brief copy explained the illustration and suggested that in addition to producing beautiful work, Semaphore has experience in producing results.

Courtesy Semaphore, Inc.

Client: Eli Lilly and Company, Elanco Animal Health Division
Ads: Series of cattle ads

Background: The Elanco division manufactures and markets animal health products. Advertising is targeted to cattle feedlot managers.

Need: Build awareness and let target audience know that although Rumensin had only recently received FDA approval, product was introduced years ago and has proved its ability to improve feed efficiency in feedlot cattle. Convince prospects that Rumensin delivers improved feed efficiency in cattle and helps prevent digestive disorders caused by coccidiosis, while Tylan, another medication, works to prevent liver abscesses.

Strategy: Use humor to show managers how they can "push" their cattle for higher productivity. Stress that products also cut down on time spent "babying" cattle when ill from coccidiosis. Mention specific benefits. (Sawyer Riley Compton)

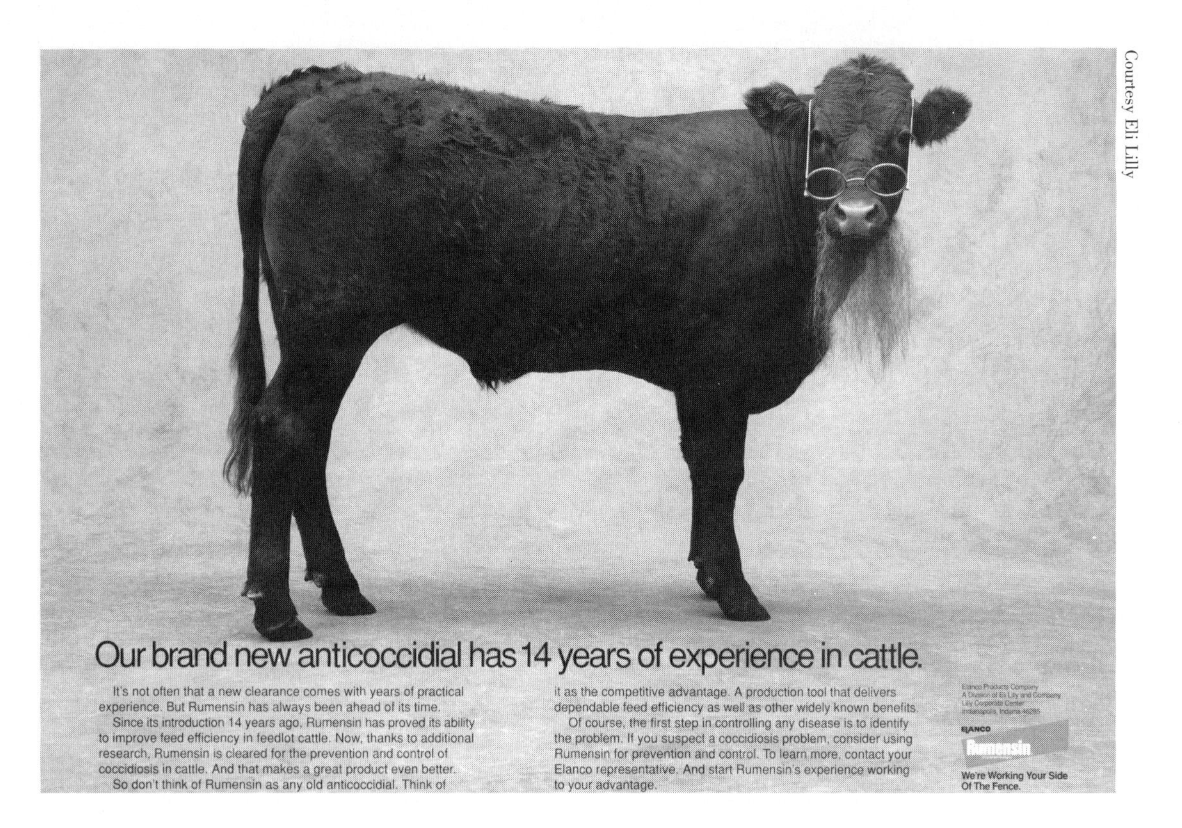

Courtesy Eli Lilly

For a competitive advantage, you don't have to baby your cattle.

Of course you want healthy feedlot cattle that perform efficiently. You practice good feedlot management and take care of your cattle. But having to pamper them costs you time and money. In a competitive environment like the cattle feeding business, you can't afford to waste either one.

That's why so many feedlots have come to rely on Rumensin to keep cattle healthy and productive. Rumensin not only delivers improved feed efficiency, it actually protects against digestive disorders caused by coccidiosis. Coupled with your good feedlot management practices, Rumensin helps cattle perform at their best giving you a real competitive advantage.

Ask your Elanco representative about Rumensin. And let your healthy cattle grow up faster.

ELANCO
Rumensin
We're Working Your Side Of The Fence.

Client: Eli Lilly and Company, Elanco Animal Health Division
Ads: Campaign for Monteban and Maxiban

Need: Introduce two products to growers in the broiler industry without drawing attention or sales from Coban, an existing mainstay product. Sell products as complements to one another.

Strategy: Introduce the products, clearly outlining benefits and how they relate to existing Coban product. Use distinctive visual style to provide continuity and high recall. (Sawyer Riley Compton)

How To Get A Home Run
On A Three-Base Hit.
Warm weather's great. Except for broilers. And the people responsible for them. Because it's hard to hit a home run with your flocks when you're having to compromise your goals to beat the heat.
But now there's Elanco's new three-dimensional approach to cocci control. Not just products. But a whole new program of products you can use to tailor your cocci program to get precisely the results you want. With Coban, Monteban and Maxiban on your team, you've got the players that can work together to help you turn every flock into a home run. No matter what the weather.
Increase your batting average.
If your goal is lower feed costs, try Coban at the plate. Used either in a straight program or in a shuttle, Coban can help control costs with superior feed-conversion ratios.
Or if you prefer to rotate, pinch-hit with new Monteban. Because even in the hottest weather, Monteban gives you the performance you need. With no measurable feed suppression or adjustments in feed formulation! And, as lab tests have shown, Monteban strengthens your game against some of summer's other most common problems, including feathering.
If you're shuttling, you might fill out your line-up with new Maxiban—a synergistic combination of granulated nicarbazin and narasin that offers more effective control than either of its components alone. And since its level of nicarbazin is low, you get the added benefit of far fewer summer side effects.
The beauty of the three-dimensional approach to cocci control is its versatility. Use Coban and Monteban in rotation. Or shuttle either Coban or Monteban with Maxiban. Vary the dosage of each product. The possible combinations are almost endless. Enough to suit your needs—and the weather.
How to find out more.
At Elanco, service is multi-dimensional too. For information on developing your own three-dimensional approach to cocci control, contact your Elanco sales rep or animal science field rep today. Then watch your cocci program hit home.
ELANCO
Making A Habit Of
Making A Difference.

Beat
The
Heat.
This summer, think Monteban. And hold down the heat's effects on your birds while you help them stand up to cocci challenges.
Some anticoccidials add to stress by reducing feed intake. But not Monteban. Maybe that's why 80% of the customers who tried it last year were satisfied. Besides, Monteban tests have shown:
• no reduction in feed intake
• no effect on amino acid utilization
• excellent weight gain and feed efficiency
Stay cool longer.
With Monteban, there's little or no reason to worry about compensatory gain and you'll never have to reformulate. So you can control coccidiosis right up to the end of growout. What's more, Monteban is cleared for use with Flavomycin or Roxarsone plus BMD.
Get your
feet wet now.
At Elanco, the heat is on to produce enough Monteban for everyone who wants to try it. Call your Elanco sales rep or animal science rep today about its availability, or for details on our other anticoccidials. Then kick back and sail through summer.
ELANCO
Monteban
45
ELANCO
Making A Habit Of
Making A Difference.

The Best Method Of Cocci Control Has Been In Development For Over 6,000 Years.
Back around 5400 B.C., when the first domestic chickens appeared, coccidia were right there with them. And nature maintained a healthy balance between the two species. Until modern man upset it by raising birds in confinement.
Since then, with the help of Coban, producers have learned a valuable lesson from history. Used at various levels, Coban permits some cocci to complete their life cycle. This stimulates the birds' immune response. Which means the proper level of Coban allows enough exposure to help confined birds mount their own defenses—and perform their best. Year after year after year.
For details on Coban, contact your Animal Science Field Representative or Elanco Sales Rep. Or see the latest Dimensions video. Before another eon flies by.
ELANCO
Coban 60
ELANCO
Making A Habit Of
Making A Difference.

Introducing The Three-Dimensional Approach To Cocci Control.
For over seventeen years, we've been helping you manage cocci—and you've really taught us a lot. For starters, there's nothing one-dimensional about the broiler industry. In fact, everybody's situation is totally unique.
Our research laboratories have never forgotten this and have continued investing and developing. Now they've complemented Coban with two exciting new anticoccidials—Monteban and Maxiban. Not just new products, but a whole new approach. The three-dimensional approach to cocci control.
Three products, a multitude of possibilities.
The mainstay, of course, is Coban—the standard by which others are measured. For those who like to rotate, now there's also new Monteban. And for those who feel the need to shuttle, there's also new Maxiban to get flocks off to a great start.
To help you build a continuous program, each product offers advantages geared to specific needs. For example, if outstanding performance with superior feed-to-weight ratios is your goal, you might prefer a straight Coban program.
Or if you prefer to rotate, you might try a straight program of Monteban—which even in the heat of summer requires no adjustments in feed formulation. Monteban is also effective against a broad range of coccidia, especially E. acervulina, and doesn't require withdrawal.
And if you're shuttling, try Maxiban—a synergistic combination of granulated nicarbazin and Monteban that offers more effective control than either of its two components alone. An ideal complement to either Coban or Monteban.
You can use Coban and Monteban alone in rotation. Or shuttle either with Maxiban. Vary the dosage of each product. The possible combinations are almost endless. Enough to suit your location, your growing and management techniques and even the demands of your customers.
How to find out more.
At Elanco, service is multi-dimensional too. For information on developing your own three-dimensional approach to cocci control, contact your Elanco sales rep or animal science field rep today. Then watch your cocci program enter the next dimension.
ELANCO
Making A Habit Of
Making A Difference.

Client: Baker Material Handling Corporation
Ads: Campaign for warehouse and distribution fields

Background: This subsidiary of Linde AG of West Germany manufactures and markets electric- and diesel-powered lift trucks for U.S. markets. The campaign targets equipment buyers and decision makers.

Need: Increase awareness, not just of Baker, but also of certain Baker machines for specific applications.

Strategy: Use well-established products and companies to gain credibility and recognition for Baker and specific lift truck models. Use graphic design to gain attention from other ads in warehousing and distribution publications and impart a high quality image. (Sawyer Riley Compton)

Courtesy Baker Materials Handling

WE'VE ELEVATED SOME VERY LOFTY SENTIMENTS.

For generations, Americans have expressed some of their loftiest sentiments with Hallmark cards. And for more than 25 years, millions of them have risen to the occasion on Baker forklifts.

On trucks like the Baker B30TE/S. A nimble little dock truck that loads finished products into trailers at all of Hallmark's manufacturing facilities.

It's not easy to meet the standards of a company like Hallmark. But the BTE/S does it every day. Starting with the combination of maneuverability, comfort and reliability their operation demands.

Thanks to its unique 3-4 wheel design, the BTE/S turns a full 360° within its own radius — even when equipped with Hallmark's slipsheet attachment.

Operators appreciate its low step-up for easy on and off, generous footroom and headroom, two-way adjustable bucket seats, tilt steering and easy-to-reach, logical controls.

And supervisors know they can count on it too. Because every day for more than four years, the BTE/S has lived up to the reliability record of its predecessors — the former generation Baker trucks Hallmark is still using after 26 years!

The BTE/S scores high in other ways too. Like energy efficiency that allows batteries to last up to 12 hours before recharging. And ease of maintenance that comes from placing all components **above** the battery within easy access. And, of course, the local Baker dealer, where Hallmark has received a generation of dependable service and support and a parts inventory that never quits.

Which, after more than a century of service to some of America's greatest companies, is what Baker is really all about. For a free Baker product line brochure and the name of a Baker dealer near you, call us. Baker Material Handling Corporation. At 1-800-627-1700.

Baker
YOU'RE IN GOOD COMPANY.

SOME OF OUR BEST CUSTOMERS ARE COLD FISH.

Fish can be pretty tough customers for a lift truck. Especially when they're frozen. Their environment is brutally cold, and they don't tolerate downtime.

At its national distribution center, where the temperature is a constant −20°F, Mrs. Paul's handles almost 3 million pounds of frozen fish a year. *All* of it on Baker lift trucks. Which makes the cold fish at Mrs. Paul's some of our very best customers.

Mrs. Paul's uses a variety of Baker trucks because of their outstanding durability and dependability in a frozen environment. But one of them has almost revolutionized Mrs. Paul's business. The custom-designed Moto-Truc PAL four-way entry pallet truck. Whereas conventional pallet trucks can load only 18 pallets per trailer, the PAL's unique low-profile fork assembly enables it to load 25. That's a whopping 30% increase in loading productivity!

In fact, the PAL four-way entry truck is an efficiency machine. For speed and productivity, it handles standard 40-by-48-inch pallets from all four sides. For superior clearance over dock boards, it has a lowered fork height of two inches, with six inches of lift. Which means you can use it to load and unload trailers without the help of other types of lift trucks.

And since operator comfort is part of efficiency, the steering handle, attached directly to the drive unit, contains all the controls for travel, lift-lowering and braking. For extra convenience, the travel direction and speed control return to neutral when released. And lifting and lowering are controlled by push button in the control handle.

Add total maintenance and a full parts inventory from the local Baker Dealer—and it's clear why Mrs. Paul's relationship with Baker is no mere fish story.

For the complete story about the PAL four-way entry truck or any other quality Baker lift truck, call us for a free Baker product line brochure and the name of the Baker dealer near you. Baker Material Handling Corporation. At 1-800-627-1700.

YOU'RE IN GOOD COMPANY.

CHAPTER 16

Presenting Your Work and Yourself: Portfolios, Resumes, Job Searches

There's an absolutely wonderful scene in the British film, *Honest, Decent, and True,* a send-up of advertising, in which the copywriter and art director do their best to convince the client that their television commercial for his new brand of lager is just what the brand needs to become a success.

If the comedy weren't so close to home, one could enjoy the laughs more completely. But as in all good satire, this scene has been played, with variations, in nearly every advertising agency or client conference room. It goes something like this:

The writer does an enthusiastic job of presenting the television storyboard, which is handsomely mounted and standing on an easel in full view of those present. These include, in addition to the client, members of the agency (the account executive, the planner or head of research, the media analyst, and, of course, both copywriter and art director who have slaved feverishly for days, even weeks, to come up with this concept.)

The commercial is a bit risky, to say the least. It tells the story of a happy group of voyagers at the bar of a grand cruise ship. Some order embarrassingly complex mixed drinks, while a few are "brave enough" to order what they really want, the client's new lager. Suddenly, there is a loud crash and the ship begins sinking. In the final shot, we see the few survivors in a lifeboat, all of whom are drinking the client's lager. The life preserver carries the name of the ship: *Titanic.*

The client listens in silence and says nothing once the presentation is finished. Mind you, the copywriter has done a wonderful job of acting out the various roles in the script, humming the music, even improvising the sound effects. The client just sits smiling. Soon, the tense silence is broken by the researcher, who explains that this is a spoof, a big joke. The client answers, "Yes, I suppose some people would find this funny. . . . Yes. Well it's just fine. Just fine." There is an audible sigh of relief. Then the client continues.

"There are just a few very small things I'm having problems with. Nothing major, mind you. I wonder about the time frame here. After all, this is a contemporary product and is it appropriate to do it in a period setting? Then, there's the question of whether humor is appropriate to the selling of a lager. I also have a bit of a problem with the use of such an historic disaster to advertise our product."

Silence again. A few clearings of throats. Then the various agency members attempt to brush these "small problems" aside, telling their conservative client that the young singles who are the market for this product don't care about the *Titanic*, that they will just laugh at the disaster and get the message. But it's no use. He just isn't buying. The account executive, sensing this, begins agreeing with the client and assures him that the creative team can fix things up. "Funny," blurts the art director to the account executive, "you thought it was just dandy this morning."

The Presentation Is Half the Battle

Coming up with great ideas is a monumental task, but being able to convince others in the agency and, ultimately, the client to agree with those ideas is no small task, either. When you see great advertising, you can be almost certain that one reason such ideas saw the light of day was due to a client's willingness to take risks (see the case studies for Federal Express and Cover Girl make-up as classic examples of client-agency compatibility and the willingness of both sides to try innovative approaches). The introduction of the phenomenally successful Macintosh computer in 1984, through a television commercial that never once showed the machine, speaks well not only for the agency that conceived the idea, but also for the young entrepreneurs at Apple who had the vision to see the brilliance in the story of a future generation freed from the "ideology" of computers that controlled man instead of having machines that man controlled for his own needs. In simpler terms, this meant that Macintosh would represent a more user-friendly computer than the public had known. But telling it that simply would have obscured the larger message.

Regardless of your client's proclivity for taking risks, you must be prepared to sell the advertising just as thoroughly as you believe the advertising sells the goods.

Generally speaking, presenting the creative portion of an advertising campaign should come after all other aspects have been discussed. These other elements may include a summary of the marketing background for the product or service, a discussion of research the agency has undertaken to help it make strategic decisions, and a proposed media plan which justifies the selection of certain media vehicles and the rejection of others.

Since your marketing summary will have touched on target markets and broad marketing goals, your presentation of creative ideas should be restricted to the communications aspects of your campaign. But where do you begin? In all honesty, you begin weeks or months before the presentation by getting comfortable with your client and making certain she is comfortable with you. Nothing turns off a client more than walking in for a presentation and not having the slightest inkling of what lies ahead. By staying in touch with your client and making her feel as if she is a member of your team, just as you are part of hers, you will put her in a more positive frame of mind to hear you out. This doesn't mean you have to give away your big ideas early, but you should have some agreement on the basic direction of your campaign before the actual presentation. As we said, good clients are risk takers who try not to throw barriers in the way of sound creative judgment. Part of your job is to nurture this attitude with your client long before the date of the presentation. When that date arrives, here is what should usually happen:

Begin with a Brief Recap of the Assignment

You were asked to solve a certain problem. Remind your client of the problem and share with her your creative exploration of the problem. You might even share the many ideas you considered and rejected, which could indicate that you are as concerned about the success of the campaign as your client is, and not merely about selling your ideas to her.

Thoroughly Discuss Your Creative Strategy

You're not talking to the consumer, who shouldn't have to understand the strategy to understand the ads. You're talking to the folks who are going to be paying you for your great efforts. Therefore, you must convince them in a highly logical manner that the ideas you are about to present are the result of sound, logical thinking. So talk about what's going on in the mind of your target audience. Tell what they're saying now. Tell what you would like them to be saying. Tell why your campaign must work hard to stand out from the competition. You might even want to show some competing ads to remind your audience what your competition is doing. Above all, when you get to your strategy, be certain you link it clearly to the original goals of the project. Does it answer the problem? Exactly how and why?

Make a Big Deal About the Theme of Your Campaign

You may be so familiar with the theme by now that you forget that your client may never have seen or heard it before. Introduce the theme importantly. Display it on a board or flash it on a screen. If there is animation or music or sound involved, use them as part of the presentation. If positioning, brand image, or other elements are critical to the campaign, explain how the theme accomplishes the desired effect.

On to the New Ads and Commercials

Now that you've set the stage, you're ready to show how your exciting theme is expressed through the various advertisements and commercials, the sales promotion and collateral pieces, and everything else that is part of your campaign. For television, it's best to have your audio prerecorded and to play it as you flash scenes from the storyboard. For radio, a demonstration version on tape is most effective, and most studios are willing to furnish a "demo" at modest cost if you in turn promise to use them for the final version once the client grants her stamp of approval. When you present print, you'll want to have crisp layouts, appropriately mounted, with headlines and body copy set in type. What about the body copy? Most agree it's best not to read it to your client, but to communicate what it expresses and to invite review at a later time. What you are striving to communicate, obviously, is that all of these ads and commercials are linked by a central theme, which is a result of a well-devised strategy that delivers the intended message to the target audience.

Close with a Summary Statement and Ask for the Order

Remind the client how effective this campaign will be, how thoroughly it satisfies marketing and communications goals, and why it is the best choice for the problem at hand.

Answer Questions Honestly

If you don't know, say you don't know and promise to find out. Avoid direct confrontations, but don't come off as a "yes man" to your client. She doesn't want that. If you disagree with your client's suggestions, explain logically and politely why. Learn to compromise on minor issues and to speak with conviction about those major issues you feel are essential if the spirit and intent of your work are to be maintained. If there is no agreement, the only choice may be to thank the client and go on to another job. Few good agencies will compromise their creative standards to produce what they feel is inferior work. It's a delicate situation at best. Knowing how to handle it demands a thorough understanding of interpersonal communication.

Ron Hoff, who in his long and distinguished career has been associated with Ogilvy & Mather and Foote Cone & Belding, discusses the perils and pitfalls of presenting. Here is what he says:

- "The biggest problem is boring the audience. Sometimes, we even bore ourselves. Seldom do our true identities emerge from our professional selves. Perhaps this is why we're so boring when we make presentations."

- "Visuals, when added to words, will more than double recall of your message. When you get the audience to *participate* in your presentation, recall will zoom to around 90 percent among the people who have actually taken part."

- "The moment of judgment in presentations occurs within the first ninety seconds. That's when audiences decide to tune in or check out. If the presenter talks entirely about himself or herself, the audience disconnects. Or daydreams. Audiences are sitting there asking themselves, 'When is that presenter going to start talking about *me?*' "

Hoff identifies what you should do to prepare for the presentation:

1. ***Know the people on the opposition and know who is your best supporter.*** Address your first words to that person. Then move to someone else you know is favorable. You feel refueled and reinforced at this point, so you can move on to the others. When you reach a seemingly negative person, go back to a friend. Keep warming up the group until it's okay and safe to invade the enemy territory.

2. ***Start with something you feel comfortable with.*** It can be fun, but it must be relevant. Dr. Stephen Zipperblatt of the Pritikin Longevity Center in San Diego opens his workshop with these words: "Man doesn't die . . . he kills himself." And then goes on to tell participants how to live healthier lives. He's off and rolling.

3. ***Appoint a DSW . . . a director of "so what?"*** This person represents the grubby, selfish interests of the audience. Whenever you say something irrelevant, he says, "So what?" and you know you're off course.

4. ***Most agency presentations should start about halfway through.*** That's where most of us stop talking about ourselves and start talking about our clients. Start with the audience's issue of primary concern instead of our issue of concern (get the business). Ask yourself, "How can we help the poor devils?"

Hoff also identifies "what bugs people about presentations," explaining that this is a collection of peeves from people in the advertising business who have suffered through presentations where such comments were heard:

- "You know so much more about this than I do. . . ." The client wants someone who knows more than he does.

- "I'm so nervous. I hope you can't see how much my knees are shaking." True confidence inspirer.

- "I've got my notes so screwed up, I don't know what I'm going to do."

- "We know you're waiting for the creative, so I'll try to fly through the media plan."

Hoff also feels that every presentation should have a burning issue. Too often we fall far short of that. We sort of sputter. He adds that too many presenters act as if they don't know what slide is coming up next and don't know the first thing about eye contact. Many presenters seem to be looking at some distant star. They never connect.

How to Correct the Problems

Eye contact and connecting are extremely important. Keep the lights up. Get near the audience. Reduce the distance between you and them, both geographically and ideologically. People are nervous at the start of a presentation, when the distance is the greatest.

Don't be upset by interruptions. Answer, but never attack. Be professional. If you have drunks or hecklers, continue to be polite. The group will take care of its own. Above all, never lose your temper. This is tantamount to losing the business.

People love to have lists. So give them lists. "Here are six things I really think are important."

How do you overcome nervousness? Tell yourself you're the best and believe it. Relax. Present to yourself in the mirror, and watch yourself and listen to yourself. Better, videotape yourself presenting. Watch it once, a second time with the sound off, a third time with sound only and no picture. Study your nonverbal language on the second viewing. Ask yourself whether you like it and take steps to improve it if you do not. Listen to your voice without watching yourself. Ask whether you like it and what, if anything, needs to be done to make you sound more convincing, such as lowering your presenting voice. Walk. Exercise your jaw just before presenting. Chat with people. Move around. Don't stand still.

It all comes out in the voice—joy, nervousness, anticipation, or boredom. The voice gives your audience its first real clue about you. Yet the voice is most often neglected. Deep voices communicate authority. Anyone can, with practice, present in a deeper voice than his or her normal speaking voice. Spend a day with your voice and play it back at the end of the day. Narrate your day with a microcassette recorder. "It's 9 a.m. and I'm waiting for the bus. I see it coming now. A few people are here, but it's not a busy day. . . ." Then listen to it. Then do it again, and then listen again. Have you found a way to improve the quality of the voice through this exercise?

Most important of all, says Hoff, is to remember that the client isn't always right, but the client is always the client.[1]

Presenting Yourself

Your first interview is in progress, and you're more than a bit apprehensive. You have just shown your portfolio, or "book," to the creative director sitting opposite you. He has made a few pleasant comments but has indicated that you need to work harder at being more original, at taking more risks. He says that it's

[1] The author thanks Mr. Hoff for granting him permission to use these quotes.

easy for him to pull someone back whose work has gone too far but almost impossible to push someone forward whose work lacks the magic touch.

What is this magic touch, and how do you get it into your work? At the beginning of this book, we urged you to take risks when you begin concepting ideas for advertisements and commercials and all but promised that a good teacher would reward those risks with encouragement. The same is true once you begin hunting for your first job as an art director or copywriter.

The Book Is Everything

Students need more than "good" books, they need GREAT books to even be considered by a major agency. This was the consensus of five top creative directors who spoke to a group of advertising educators in a weekend creative symposium. Too many students copy advertising that's already been done by someone else; consequently, their books lack fresh ideas. Above all, individuals seeking their first job need to show they can think and that they can *communicate with symbols.* Agencies reject 2,000 applicants a year because their *letters* are poor. These people never even get an interview. One major agency, for example, hires two to three beginners a year and interviews five every week.

Young people and their books have become so serious, according to agency recruiters. The playfulness just isn't there, and that can hurt. Many aren't aware of the other departments of the agency that are involved in the process of advertising—media, research, account service, etc. Nor are they aware of the layers of approval within and beyond the creative department that their work must be subjected to. Sometimes the good idea is in the book, but it hasn't been developed, or the writing lacks precision, or the design lacks flair. Agencies admire books that break rules instead of complying with them—books that break through the clutter of books in smart, not stupid, ways, just as advertisements must break through the clutter of all the other advertisements.

What are agencies looking for in beginning writers and art directors?

- ***Originality in thinking.*** Granted, that's highly subjective. You don't even get an interview, however, unless your work is special. Furthermore, the work and the person being interviewed have to connect in the mind of the interviewer.

- ***A passion for your work.*** The ability to enthuse about how you came up with the ideas. Being able to bounce back from mistakes.

- ***Enthusiasm for the world.*** More than a fleeting knowledge of music, film, theater, art, current trends in humor. Some travel, especially to other cultures. It's the stuff good ideas come from.

- ***True love for words and design.***

- ***Raw imagination.*** For the book, the ideas don't have to be legal or even feasible. The agency can pull you back. It's much harder to push you further.

- ***Knowledge of research and marketing.*** This means you can converse intelligently about those subjects, but not to the extent that it restrains your creative product.

- ***Bravery to do your dumbest ideas.*** Strike the emotions. Touch people. But don't do too much of a good thing. Too many puns can hurt you. Bad puns can hurt you. Then again, it's subjective.

What Do You Send and to Whom?

Send 5 × 7 inch prints of your book. Send photocopies. Call and find out whom to send them to. If there's a creative services recruiter, send to her. If not, to the creative director. Don't send anything—resume included—to personnel. Send a few samples with your letter, then deliver your whole book in person. Don't include nonadvertising things, such as poetry, news articles, short stories, in your book. Read Maxine Paetro's *How to Put Your Book Together and Get a Job in Advertising*. She's a top creative recruiter in New York.

Resumes should be legible and limited to one page. No errors. You can also do something more creative about yourself as a lead-in to your book. Just remember, it's the book that counts. Be certain you have good print examples to show, especially in smaller markets. The process is to usually send a letter and resume and perhaps several teaser samples of your work. Then call for an appointment within a reasonable period of time.

Students Who Have Made It Recently: How Did They Do It?

A group of recently hired creatives, discussing what they did to get their jobs, drives home the point that seeking a job as a copywriter or art director is different from other job searches. One member of this outgoing group claims he sent no resumes or letters, just came to town with an $800 bank loan and started calling people. He had a great book, by the way. Other suggestions:

Don't put what you see on TV, etc., in your book. Do an entirely visual TV commercial to show you can communicate without words. Show ten to twenty pieces, no more. Go to the store, pick ordinary products off the shelf, and do a great selling job on them. Pick a boring product; pick a product you like. Don't do public service; too many people are showing things like drunk driving. Get an entry-level job in the agency and learn from others. You can learn much on the job. Don't use class work; do your book on your own or after you finish school. Do hard goods and services; a mix is good. Keep changing your book; you will learn as you interview what should be changed. Do four campaigns with two TV and three print each. Demonstrate your conceptual skills; show you can generate hundreds of ideas, even if it's through a collection of concept roughs. These are skills that will count with your employer. It's why he might hire you. Use one professional to guide you to another. At the next interview, say, "so and so told me to get in touch with you." This suggests he wouldn't have sent you if you didn't have some promise—probably true. Get your book together and go hit the market. Scribble ideas on a big sheet of paper to show how you think. Get out and look early, well before graduation.

There is agreement that getting a job in advertising isn't at all like applying for one in anything else. Recruiters won't appear on your campus in droves. Career counselors won't be able to help you much. It's the nature of the beast.

What are the keys to success? Persistence + talent. Professors should grade tougher toward the end of the college program to prepare students for the real world, according to this panel of former students. Students must realize that they must convince creative directors and recruiters that they have done advertising that touches people. In other words, your work must touch the person on the other side of the desk, too!

Agency Creative Directors Tell What Constitutes a Good Book

Although the five creative directors on the panel did not agree entirely, they did agree that students should stay away from campaigns the agency is working on . . . more or less. They agreed that public service advertising was risky . . . but maybe not. They warned students to stay away from inventing new products . . . but suggested this might be a great way to display their originality. You get the picture? Here are some of their comments:

The only rule is that there are no rules. Respect the professional's time. Show no more than fifteen pieces. There is nothing important but ideas. Good design with a poor idea is like putting make-up on a corpse. Think of your book as your very first professional assignment. Make the layouts rough and the ideas fancy.

The abstract qualities of the book are what count. These qualities are brilliance (a characteristic that sets you on fire), a sense of personality, willingness to take risks (it's much easier to pull people back than to push them forward), cleverness and wit, a sense of organization (the campaign effect), a visual sense for writers, a conceptual sense for art directors. Something memorable, so your book isn't forgotten and neither are you. If you think it will improve your book, add a sentence describing the market, what you are trying to do, and how you are motivating the audience. But keep it down to a sentence.

One professional put it this way: Show me good ads that change my perception of the product. Show me a book and a personality that change my opinion of the person I'm interviewing. Show me you have a passion for this business; if you don't care for advertising, you can't do great work. Show me you have a playfulness with the language.

Another creative director says it's important to know how to present yourself as well as your work. Show that you understand the importance of strategy. Talk your work. Tell why you made the decision to do something and then show how you followed through. Organize your work. And write good body copy. It indicates how well you can express yourself in words. Paragraph it for impact. Make certain everything is as clean and neat and professional looking as it can be.

The group agreed that the book must be organized and neat. A spiral book with acetate pages is ideal; it gives you control over your presentation. Or you may choose to place your mounted works in a compact portfolio or briefcase, arranging them in a way that shows off each piece to best advantage. Often, you will have to leave your book; it will have to speak (sell) for itself. You might think about a small leave-behind piece consisting of photocopies of your work, or make copies of your book and have them at several agencies or businesses at the same time.

Your Portfolio or Book

Nothing communicates how well you can create than a sample of your work. Most professionals will want to see somewhere between 10 and 20 samples. These should be mounted on matte board and arranged in a case, or slipped behind protective clear acetate if you are using a portfolio with pages. However you package your work, it's the work that will make the difference. You should include enough samples to prove you can work effectively in print. Print also communicates more quickly in a portfolio than either radio or television. Your layouts don't have to be artistically perfect—unless you're interviewing for a position as an art director—but they must be easy to comprehend and above all must indicate that you have a talent for using words and pictures in unusual combinations. Not every ad you show needs body copy, but you need to have some body copy samples in your book.

Include at least one "campaign," either three print ads in a series, or a print ad-TV commercial-radio commercial in a series. Include radio and television, but make the book mostly print. Television should be storyboarded. Use classroom work only if you're proud of it. If you're not, start all over. Choose boring products at the store and do unusual ads for them. Choose great campaigns and show how you would extend them. Have a mix of package goods, services, and a minimal number of public service ads. Demonstrate that you can handle long copy and short copy. Incorporate several emotions—humor and pathos—but not in the same ad. Invent a new product and show how you would advertise it. Choose a local business that could stand some improvement in its advertising.

Show their ads and show your ads for them. Tell why you did what you did. Make certain every piece is a winner.

The Cover Letter

What is the purpose of the letter? Certainly not to just say, "here's my resume and do you have a job?" The letter is your chance to show the recipient how well you write, how passionate you are about advertising, what sort of potential talent lies waiting to be challenged. Take a moment to write down these things and see if they can be used in a cover letter:

1. Something unusual, unique, or interesting about you from any period in your life.
2. Your interests, hobbies, collections, spare time activities.
3. Pay yourself a compliment. Tell yourself something good about you.
4. Write down a compliment paid to you by friend, family, professor, advisor, employer, anyone.

Which of these has a place in your cover letter? The cover letter is your ad for yourself. Begin by telling why you are writing the letter. Then plunge into your sales pitch, or mention something nice, but not phony, about the company you're writing to.

The main body of the letter should tell the reader why you should get the job.

In closing, say you will provide additional information if required. Don't ask them to call you. Tell them you'll be calling them. Be sincere and forthright. Use plain English and avoid jargon. Personalize your letter by mentioning something about your background or personality to give the employer an insight into your personal side. Don't be flip or too casual. Never write "to whom it may concern."

Let's look at two letters. After reading them, decide which appears to be more persuasive, and why. (See Figures 16-1 and 16-2.)

The Resume

A number of aspiring writers and art directors have impressed agencies with decidedly offbeat resumes. A resume printed on a T-shirt arrives in a Brooks Brothers box. A job applicant dons a sandwich board and parades outside a Manhattan ad agency. A writer named Randy Rensch sends agencies wrenches with the inscription, "When it's a copywriter, it's spelled Rensch." If you're willing to take a 99 percent chance of being totally wrong, you might wish to try an approach like this. Remember, however, that the most important product you will ever sell is yourself.

Roger C. Franklin
Executive Creative Director
McCann-Erickson Worldwide
485 Madison Avenue
New York, NY 10098

Dear Mr. Franklin:

I am writing at the suggestion of Brad Cummings, who is a longtime friend and mentor, and who knows of my desire to enter the world of advertising.

To be perfectly honest, I want to be a copywriter, and I've prepared myself for this difficult task from the time I was about thirteen--devouring advertising on radio, tv, in magazines and newspapers every chance I could get. The walls of my bedroom were literally plastered with my favorite ads. It didn't make Mom happy, but I couldn't resist clipping 'em and hanging 'em.

It's no wonder I pursued a degree in advertising at the University of South Carolina. And while my peers were earning C's and B's, I was getting A's in creative strategy, graphic design, campaigns, and marketing. My professors told me I was one of the best students they had seen in years. I began to believe it.

Now I want you to judge me. I have a portfolio of what I consider to be my best work, and I would be honored if you would grant me a few brief moments to share this with you.

I'm planning to be in New York the week of April 27, and will call you that Monday to see if you can see me sometime during that week.

In the meantime, I'm enclosing my resume and a few samples. Once again, thanks for hearing me out. I'm excited about the prospect of meeting you and having you critique my work.

Cordially,

Victoria Smith

FIGURE 16-1

Cover letter, interesting.

If you decide that this is no time to take a risk and choose to write a more conventional resume, you will have several basic formats from which to choose: the chronological resume, the functional resume, or a combination of the two. No matter which format you choose, be concise. Employers want to know what you did, where, and for how long. Be honest and complete. Be beautiful to look at and read, with no misspellings, no typos, no punctuation or grammar errors.

Personnel Department
McCann-Erickson Worldwide
485 Madison Avenue
New York, NY 10098

Dear Sir or Madam:

This spring I will earn my B.A. in Journalism from the University of South Carolina with a major in advertising and public relations and a cognate in marketing.

I will be seeking a position with an advertising agency in the New York area, preferably as a copywriter, and would like to talk with you about the possibility of employment with McCann-Erickson.

I really enjoy writing copy and have taken two courses in creative strategy with Professor A. Jerome Jewler at Carolina. I have also completed courses in media, campaigns, ad research, ad management, and graphic production. I believe I have much to offer your agency and could make important contributions with my unique ideas and marketing expertise.

By the way, I note in the trade press that you are in trouble with the Nescafe campaign. I have been working up some roughs for Nescafe and would be happy to share them with you, if you're interested.

I look forward to hearing from you.

Sincerely,

Victoria Smith

FIGURE 16-2

Cover letter, dull!

The Chronological Resume

At the top of any resume, put your name, address, phone number. In order of their importance, list the following: education, work experience, and personal information. Should you include a career goal? Some say absolutely, others say never. If you can put your goal in your letter, it shouldn't have to go here. Perhaps it would be helpful to list the position you are seeking, such as "copywriter." Most businesses will want to know at least that much. It confuses companies when you simply say you will take any kind of a job with them.

You should never include such things as number of children or health. Avoid I and me sentences. Start with verbs such as, "improved the service procedures," "supervised ten people," "managed three departments," "created . . . ," "invented . . . ," "designed . . . ," "introduced . . . ," etc. Emphasize your accomplishments, not your duties. For an example, see Figure 16-3.

The Functional Resume

This format can be useful if your job history is not long or neatly categorized. Here you pinpoint what job skills you used in each situation, with less emphasis on the particular job you held. This is very helpful if you want to include community service, other volunteer jobs, student organization work, etc. For an example, see Figure 16-4.

The main body of your resume has three basic sections. Your educational background. Your work experience. Your personal information. Whichever is more important should come first. Reasons for leaving former jobs need not be mentioned. You can explain if asked during the interview. Never blame a former employer. Reasons can be: left for a better opportunity, wanted more pay and more challenging work, etc.

On personal information, include only what you think is relevant. Do not include a photo. Include memberships in associations related to your profession, travel, language fluency. Hobbies and other interests can show employers how you spend your leisure time and reveal a side of you that the rest of your resume cannot show.

References may or may not be included. You may say they are available on request. If references are prominent, and you have their permission, include them. Organize your resume with titles and block sections. Emphasize assets, not liabilities. Omit anything unfavorable. Always tell the truth. Most likely, you will be checked. Use factual, concise language. State facts, not opinions. Use full names, not abbreviations. Be neat. Use standard white paper. Set it on a PC in nice, crisp type.

Some Advice on Job Hunting

John Sweeney of the University of North Carolina offers this sage advice to would-be creatives:[2]

1. ***Decide where you want to live.*** New York agencies want to see strong package goods and print. Smaller markets want to see things like hotels and banks, plus some strong radio and newspaper.

[2] "Step Up Persistence to Get in Agency Door." *Advertising Age,* May 2, 1985. Used by permission.

SALLY STEWART
1234 Highland Avenue
Chicago, Illinois 99906
(345) 678-9012

WORK EXPERIENCE

1974-present	Manager, Junior Bazaar, Woodlands Mall, Woodlands, N.J. Responsible for smooth running of medium-priced boutique directed at the young customer. Plan and buy complete seasonal lines. Run teen board of 55 high school students. Teach modeling course. Coordinate annual fashion show.
1973-1974	Assistant Buyer, Percy's, Perth Amboy, N.J. Purchased upscale lines of ladies' sportswear for well-known retail shop. Worked with manufacturers to provide consumer information on best-selling styles in our market and received national buying award for this project.
EDUCATION	B.S., Cornell University, 1970. School of Human Ecology. Honors.
PERSONAL	Hobbies include classical guitar and piano. Fluent in French and Italian. Amateur actor; work with community theaters in area.

FIGURE 16-3
Chronological resume.

2. ***Write to people, not agencies.*** Use the Standard Directory of Advertising Agencies. Make a list of the agencies you like in your chosen city. Write a personal letter to the senior creative director or the creative manager. Your cover letter should be brief, but involving. In the first paragraph, tell who you are and what you want. In the second paragraph, tell what makes you distinctive. In the third paragraph, tell how you wish to proceed. Finally, say thank you. Give a

SALLY STEWART
1234 Highland Avenue
Chicago, Illinois 99906
(345) 678-9012

MAJOR WORK EXPERIENCE: PROJECT DEVELOPMENT

Researched and originated breakthrough program at university for funding women athletes. Developed grant proposal, set up project, coordinated and administered scholarships. First program of its kind in the country.

Introduced soccer for girls at elementary level in local area. Organized leagues, recruited, coached.

WRITING

Analyzed and reported on university athletics program both for scholarly and popular publications. Contributing editor of Womensports. As undergraduate, first female reporter on sports page. Compiled results of scholarship program.

PUBLIC RELATIONS

Prepared press releases, conducted press conferences. Work with NBC resulted in national coverage of sports program.

ADMINISTRATION

Hired and oversaw staff of three. Managed office within university. Handled annual budget of $250,000.

FUNDRAISING

Developed new sources of alumni and foundation funds for scholarship program.

Organized local merchants in support of girls' soccer team. Developed advertising campaign for program that paid for trip to soccer world championships for girls.

EDUCATION

St. Olaf's College, B.S. Physics, 1982

FIGURE 16-4
Functional resume.

specific time when you will call to ask for an interview. Don't wait for them to call. They won't.

3. ***Invest in a professional portfolio.***

4. ***Avoid creative resumes unless you have a great idea.*** Instead, send a brief cover letter, conservative resume, and three single ads (photocopies).

5. ***Keep audience and strategy statements brief.*** Agencies are looking for original thinking and strong writing skills, not marketing or research potential. Example: Target audience: Mothers with young children. Strategy: Position Crayola crayons as a way for children to develop creativity.

6. ***Less is more.*** It is better to approach ten agencies professionally than a hundred impersonally. It is better to show a small number of samples in an interview. The worst thing that can happen is that the interviewer asks to see more. In other words, you have a second chance.

7. ***Demonstrate the campaign concept.*** Make sure your first campaign is absolutely your best. And close with a flourish. First and last impressions carry weight.

8. ***If you need one, here is a portfolio formula.*** You will adjust your portfolio to meet the need of the interview. But if you want a simple formula: One package goods campaign (toothpaste, deodorant, trash bags, etc.), one hard goods campaign (stereos, cameras, computers, refrigerators, etc.), one food or fashion campaign, one public service or tourism campaign or one new product idea and an introductory campaign for it. At least one campaign should include TV, print, radio, and outdoor—a complete demonstration of the campaign concept. The other four can be less extensive. Also show a range of approaches, if you can. Use music once, demonstration once, testimonials once. Do a range of solutions to a range of products.

9. ***Innovative work is the key.*** Agencies hire new talent to get new thinking. Don't brag. Just write something fresh, new, and exciting that clearly delivers a sales message in a way they've never seen.

10. ***Start with your resume.*** One page, two at the most. It is important to look at your past experiences from the right perspective. One student told that she just worked summers to make money. Further discussion revealed that she earned $6,000 one summer selling dictionaries door-to-door. What a tremendous selling accomplishment! It was expressed appropriately in the resume.

11. ***Primitive art is all right.*** Yes, you can use your dreadful drawings. Work to make them neat and tolerably clear. It is definitely worth the effort to make them decent, even if amateurish. If you want to pay an artist, that's fine. But it isn't mandatory.

12. ***Choose accounts you like, but be forewarned.*** It is easy to write for products you like. You won't always have such freedom in the business. Also, if you try to beat American Express, Coke, and Macintosh you will probably fail. Choose products that are not currently celebrated for their outstanding creative work. Also, don't do work on one of the agency's accounts. You may choose a strategy that was rejected by research.

13. ***Make sure your scripts time.*** The first sign of an amateur is a thirty-second commercial that runs fifty-eight seconds. Learn the proper scripting format. It's an easy way to look professional.

14. ***Include at least two long-copy campaigns.*** Many creative directors are suspicious of beginners. They are afraid of smooth-talking, glitzy TV types who have no fundamental writing skills. Demonstrate your ability to write body copy conclusively. Include at least two long-copy print ads that are substantially different in content. Show your ability to handle at least 300 words per ad.

15. ***Be prepared for subjective interviews.*** And bad interviews. Agencies are very good at weeding out the mediocre but crazy at defining the excellent. Once you are competent, advertising becomes a subjective business. Monitor your feedback. If you get the same comment in many interviews, listen to it. If you get a range of responses to the same ad, welcome to the business. It is subjective.

16. ***Always end by asking for other names.*** Advertising is a small business. Networking is a key way to get in the door. Even if there are no jobs at the current agency, ask for an interview anyway. At the end of an interview, ask for other names to call. A name can get you through a variety of moats, walls, and secretaries.

17. ***Practice persistence.*** One creative director told all beginners there were no jobs available and interviewed only those who called back in spite of the lack of jobs. Agencies can be closed to jobs for months and suddenly be in desperate need of people. You have to get used to it.

Other Options

Since starting with an agency is often the exception rather than the rule, good creative people have discovered other paths. In so doing, they have learned that the advertising agency is by no means the only place for a rewarding career in copy or design.

What are some of these options? Get a job writing or designing for the client instead of the agency. Many manufacturing and service corporations maintain in-house advertising departments that require the services of writers and artists. Or go to work for a retail store in a major market. Many creatives have used Macy's and other great retailers as stepping stones to other advertising positions. Check the printing firms who might need creative assistance for some of their clients. See what creative positions exist within the media: at newspapers, radio and television stations, cable companies, magazines. Don't forget graphic design studios that may service agencies and who might need writers as well as art directors.

Look into the burgeoning fields of direct marketing and business-to-business advertising. Specialized advertising agencies have commandeered much of the business in these areas, as well as in other areas requiring special knowledge, such as medical and pharmaceutical advertising and marketing.

If you're the type of person who has a sense of adventure and the job situation is looking grim, you might try freelancing or setting up your own small agency. Above all, be patient and persistent. If you know you are talented, the right job will come along. Sometimes, it's all a matter of luck and timing, provided you have the skills to succeed.

Suggested Activities

1. Contact an account executive in an advertising agency, a creative director, or the advertising manager of a company, and ask that individual to explain how a particular creative strategy was devised. Make a presentation to your class on your findings.

2. Choose one of the case studies in this book and imagine you are going to have to sell the client on the idea. Make a presentation to the class as if you were selling the campaign to the client. Take comments.

3. Read a book on salesmanship, or interview a speech professor at your school, and prepare a report that identifies the key elements of making a sale. How can you apply these principles to the selling of an advertising idea to a prospective client?

4. Write a resume that you would use if you were about to seek a job in advertising. Try both a functional and a chronological resume. Which works best for you, and why?

5. Write a cover letter to accompany your resume. In preparation, jot down anything unique about yourself that might be used in the letter and carefully evaluate what you have written before making a decision to include your recollections. Remember that a cover letter should communicate something about the kind of person you are as well as express your interest in, and enthusiasm and qualifications for, the position.

6. Try creating a self-promotion in advertising form, just as Ed Chambliss did in the following Creative Spot. How would you use this approach to your advantage?

7. Interview a local advertising professional about the proper way to apply for a job. Assuming you would be applying for a position in copy or design, ask what sort of portfolio you would need to develop and how you should present your work.

Selling the Most Important Product of All: You.

Ed Chambliss
Copywriter

BBDO South,
Atlanta, GA

Last year we received something like 3,000 job inquiries here in the BBDO South creative department. Most of them were from people just like you. People who had just finished a college degree and were looking for their first "real" job in advertising.

And out of all of those, how many fresh-out-of-college people did we hire?

Zero. Zip. Nada. Zilch. None. Niente.

Why? We didn't have any openings. Like any company, an advertising agency has to turn a profit. So it doesn't matter if you have the best portfolio in the world; if they can't afford to hire another person, they probably won't.

Think about it. You have to deal with a world full of advertising agencies, some of which are hiring, most of which are not. And the ones that are hiring today may not be hiring tomorrow. How frustrating.

It's like trying to see the full moon on a cloudy night. You know the moon is up there; it's just hiding. But if you're lucky, a break in the clouds will drift by and give you a quick peek. Call it a window of opportunity.

The same holds true when you're looking for a job in advertising. Out of all the agencies you contact, only one or two of them may be hiring.

And you won't know which ones. That's why it's extremely important to make the best possible first impression with every agency you contact. That way, if they do have their window of opportunity open, they may invite you to climb inside with your portfolio for an interview.

Making a great first impression does not mean sending a standard cover letter and resume to the creative director. Ninety-nine percent of the job inquiries we get in the mail are just plain old and boring letters and resumes. Plain, old, boring cover letters and resumes that the creative director never reads because they're plain, old, and boring.

Come on guys! You're dealing with people who work with ads all day; people whose lives are dedicated to the imaginative, exciting presentation of information. You can't expect a plain cover letter and resume to get noticed in that environment. To them, the first contact you make is an "ad" for yourself. If it's boring, it's going to say you're boring. And it may wind up in the trash along with any chance of your getting a job there.

So how do you get through to a creative person? Do something that communicates who you are in a creative way.

- Send them an ad for yourself. Someone once sent out an ad featuring their picture and the headline, "This is an ad for a product that isn't working."

- Send interesting trinkets that tell your story. A woman I know once sent a goldfish in a bowl to every creative director in town with a tag that read, "There are a lot of fish in the sea, but only one copywriter like me."

Whatever you do, make it totally different—whatever it takes to get noticed, as long as it also communicates something positive about you and your talent. Once you've proved that you can get their attention, you have an excellent opportunity to follow up with a phone call to tell them more about you and what wonderful things you can do for them and for their clients. And more importantly, to set up an appointment so you can show them your portfolio.

That's it! Getting through to the creative director really is that simple! And if you also have a great book, some internships or other advertising experience, and can handle yourself well during the interview, and they're hiring . . . well, you may have yourself a job.

When I completed the advertising major at the College of Journalism & Mass Communications at the University of South Carolina, I threw out every ad in my book that I wasn't totally happy with and filled it up with new ads that I did like. I already had six months of intern experience under my belt from working at Turner Broadcasting Systems and Fahlgren & Swink Advertising. All I had to do was grab someone's attention and hope they were hiring.

To do that, I created EDWEEK, a parody of the advertising trade magazine *ADWEEK.* Looking back, I believe EDWEEK worked for three reasons. First, everyone in advertising reads *ADWEEK* so the creative directors I sent it to knew what the parody was all about.

Second, everyone loves to see their name in print. I capitalized on this by customizing each version of EDWEEK to have each creative director's name as well as the agency's name on the cover.

Third, the title EDWEEK had my name in it. Because of this, the creative directors tended to associate my name with the positive experiences they got out of reading it. All I had to do was call up, introduce myself, and mention that I was the one who sent them EDWEEK, and they knew what I was talking about.

Inside EDWEEK was my resume, listing all the pertinent information on my education and experience. The back cover featured a parody of *Rolling Stone* magazine's "Perception/Reality" campaign that featured me.

EDWEEK was very successful. Of the 15 agencies I sent it to, I won interviews with 11, and at least one offered me a job. So here I am, typing on my Macintosh after hours, one of the lucky ones. I found an open window, climbed in, and sat down.

FOLLOW-UP

For certain jobs, a standard resume and cover letter may be appropriate, but not in the creative department of an agency. Assume you are going to attempt to break through the pile of resumes addressed to the creative director and design a piece that capitalizes on your strengths and particular skills and attributes. Prepare a layout and copy for the piece. And don't borrow Ed's idea of an *EDWEEK* parody. Grab onto an idea that is yours alone.

Vol. I No. 1 SOUTHEAST EDITION June 26, 1989 • INVALUABLE

BBDO/Atlanta Hires Chambliss

Other Atlanta Agencies Mourn Their Loss

By Ed Chambliss

ATLANTA—BBDO/Atlanta made creative history this week when it hired talented Atlanta copywriter Ed Chambliss. Gregg Dearth, executive creative director, announced the decision after meeting with Chambliss and viewing his portfolio.

"What initially got my attention," Dearth said, "was his parody of ADWEEK. It was unique. It caught my eye in a very memorable way."

The parody, received by Dearth early in the summer, featured several cover stories about Chambliss. Inside the four-page publication was an impressive resume detailing (among other things) four years of advertising experience. And, as final reminder, an ad for Chambliss appeared on the back.

Later, Chambliss called and set up an appointment to show Dearth his portfolio. "That was what clinched his sale," Dearth said. "It was an excellent mix of effective print, television, and radio." It was then that Dearth offered Chambliss a job.

Industry analysts are predicting that Chambliss's creative talents will have a "strong positive effect" on BBDO/Atlanta's creative product and its billings.

USC Ad Team Competes in D.C.

By Ed Chambliss

WASHINGTON—Garnett & Black, the University of South Carolina's student-run advertising agency, has placed 7th in the 1989 National Student Advertising Competition.

The team competed against 14 other regional winners by creating a campaign for a new Kellogg cereal. The campaign included the naming of the product, package design, and broadcast and print advertisements, all of which were supervised by Creative Director Ed Chambliss from Atlanta, Georgia.

WHAT'S INSIDE

What a Case Study

While most college students spend their summers eating in greasy fast food joints and trying to bronze their bods, the University of South Carolina's Outstanding Advertising Senior spent his summers preparing himself for more than clogged arteries or skin cancer.

(See page 2)

Experience The Key for Graduates

Atlanta's Hottest New Creative Tells How He Did It

By Ed Chambliss

ATLANTA—After Ed Chambliss, a recent college graduate, was offered a job by BBDO/Atlanta *(see story above)*, EDWEEK asked him a few questions concerning the way he got the job.

"Your book makes or breaks you. But first you have to get the creative director's attention so you can show your book," Chambliss said.

"One attention-getter that I'm proud of is the amount of actual experience I have in advertising. A good college program won't give you a job, just the basic tools you need. It takes experience to know how to use those tools," he said.

Chambliss

In the past four years Chambliss has worked constantly, both at school and during the summer. On the list of recent summer employers are Fahlgren & Swink, Inc., and Turner Broadcasting Systems, both in Atlanta.

"Most people I know hated their summer jobs," added Chambliss. "For them, their jobs were work; mine were fun."

Front page

Perception.
Reality.
COUNTERS I'VE WORKED BEHIND:
McDONALD'S
WENDY'S
BURGER KING
ACCOUNTS I'VE WORKED ON:
Cable News Network
Cellular One
Headline News Network
Kellogg
NAPA Auto Parts
SUDIA
Weyerhaeuser
For at least one advertising college graduate, experience isn't something you get creating burgers to service the drive-thru window. The kind of experience we're talking about involves creating ads to service real clients. And for the past four years, that's what Ed Chambliss has been doing. Getting hands-on experience solving client's problems. So, if you're tired of plain, old, burnt copywriters, try a new, rare one that comes with the works.
Ed Chambliss

Back page

EDWARD WILCOX CHAMBLISS

125 Landsdowne Drive, N.W.
Atlanta, Georgia 30328
404/255-8715

OBJECTIVE An entry-level position as a copywriter in an advertising agency.

EDUCATION **University of South Carolina, Honors College**, Columbia, South Carolina.
Bachelor of Arts—Journalism, cum laude, May 1989.
Major: Advertising/Public Relations, creative advertising concentration. GPA 3.7.

EXPERIENCE **USC American Advertising Federation Student Competition Team.** Columbia, South Carolina.
Creative director of small student-run agency. Produced year-long advertising campaign for a new Kellogg cereal as part of 1989 AAF Student Competition. Placed seventh in national and first in 3rd District regional competition.
December 1988 — June 1989.

Fahlgren & Swink, Inc., Atlanta, Georgia.
Internship with creative department of major Atlanta advertising agency. Concepted ideas, wrote and revised copy, and worked on production of ads and commercials for national and regional accounts. Clients included Cellular One Mobile Phone Service, NAPA Auto Parts, Southeastern United Dairy Industry Association, and Weyerhaeuser Wood Products.
May — August 1988.

Victor Duncan Inc., Atlanta, Georgia.
Worked with the rental of Panavision and Arriflex motion picture camera equipment for movie and commercial shoots. Learned basic maintenance and operation of most standard 16mm and 35mm film cameras, lenses, magazines and support equipment.
May — August 1987.

Turner Broadcasting Systems, Atlanta, Georgia.
Internship with promotion department of Cable News Network and Headline News Network as assistant to the producers. Used 3/4-inch and 1-inch video tape editing equipment. Prepared for and executed various phases of commercial production from conception to pre-production, production and post-production. Produced five spots and assisted on 18 spots.
May — August 1986.

Inside pages

EDWARD WILCOX CHAMBLISS — Page 2

EXPERIENCE (continued)

The Gamecock, Columbia, South Carolina.
Student Supervisor, production staff of University student newspaper. Designed, created and pasted up advertisements for clients. Pasted up camera-ready news copy. Used phototypesetting equipment.
August 1986 — December 1988.

Feature editor, music editor, and weekly columnist. Assigned and wrote stories. Edited and rewrote copy. Wrote humorous weekly column. Used phototypesetting equipment and pasted up copy.
August 1985 — May 1986.

WUSC-FM, Columbia, South Carolina.
Disc jockey at University student radio station. Programmed and played music and public service announcements during weekly three-hour alternative music show. Used mixing board, cart players, turntables, EBS equipment and 3000 watt transmitter. FCC Class 3 license.
February 1986 — May 1987.

The Kroger Company, Atlanta, Georgia.
Courtesy clerk at supermarket.
June — August 1985.

HONORS AND ACTIVITIES

University of South Carolina
USC Advertising Club, Vice President
Outstanding Advertising Senior
Columbia Ad Club scholarship
Paul D. Seabrook journalism scholarship
Dean's scholarship, two years
Rick Temple journalism scholarship
Who's Who in America's Colleges and Universities
Dean's List, all semesters
Omicron Delta Kappa leadership honor society
Alpha Delta Sigma advertising honor society
Kappa Tau Alpha journalism honor society
Gamma Beta Phi scholastic honor society
Carolina Program Union, Cinematic Arts: Publicity and advertising for movies shown in campus theater
Melton Memorial Observatory: Volunteer observer and photographer

Boy Scouts of America
Eagle Scout. Order of the Arrow (service fraternity of honor campers).

REFERENCES — Available on request.

Appendix

Assignments

1. General

Use the following information as the basis for creating ads and commercials for print, radio, television, or other media. In completing these assignments, you may want to do additional research on the following items. In any event, you should know by now that it's important to single out your target audience, consider the competition, and devise a workable strategy before developing your ideas.

The Itty Bitty Book Light by Zelco

Popular for ten years. Clip tiny light to your favorite hard or soft cover book and cool light floods the pages. Optical quality lead crystal bulb. Distortion free. Will not cast shadows that can cause eye fatigue. Will not damage or weigh down your books, like some imitations. Only the book light attaches to your book, not the battery. Folds to store in book or its own travel case. At better stores and bookshops.

Healthy Eggs

The market for egg substitutes is growing. Supermarket sales are up 22 percent and there is more room for growth. Egg Beaters, introduced in 1973, owns nearly half that market ($62 million of $133 million projected to $200 million). Brand leader Egg Beaters is focusing on new uses for its product: when the recipe calls for eggs . . . as opposed to simply cooking eggs. Egg Beaters, like other products, is made with real eggs, but contains no yolk.

Now comes Egg Land's Best Eggs, an actual in-the-shell egg, claiming lower saturated fat because of the diet fed to hens. Also new is Simply Eggs, an all-egg product in a carton, made from real eggs including yolks, with 80 percent of the cholesterol "spun" out of the product. The product is pasteurized for a longer shelf life. Both new products are sold in the refrigerated dairy case as opposed to the freezer case.

The market has exploded in recent years. People want to eat healthier and eggs represent 36 percent of dietary cholesterol for the average consumer. Looks like a great future for healthier egg products. Come up with an advertising idea for either of these two products, targeting people who have already tried the older frozen products.

Device Gets Rid of That Chatty Caller

Got a nuisance phone caller but too embarrassed to end the one-way conversation? An electronic device called Gotta Go can simulate the clicking sound made by the phone company's call waiting service. The gadget is a small white box activated by pushing a button. It can be hooked up to any single line phone. Its inventor came up with the idea after trying to find a polite way to end rambling phone conversations with his rather chatty girlfriend. She was calling every day at his busiest times and just gabbing. One day she actually offered to end the conversation after she heard the click click sound of call waiting and realized he had another call coming through. It struck him that he was very relieved when someone else would call and he'd hear the click, and it wasn't really he who ended the call. Gotta Go sells for $14.95, less than some real call waiting services provided by telephone companies, which usually charge a recurring monthly fee for the service.

Food Labels to Give Scoop in Fat, Fiber

Grocery shoppers are finding new labels on their food packages that give them more information than ever before about what they are eating. Whether they will understand it is another matter. The centerpiece of the new label is a column of numbers under the heading "percent of daily value," a term the label doesn't explain. The idea is to show how much of a day's ideal total of a particular ingredient you're getting. "It's like the recommended daily allowance for vitamins and minerals," said Bruce Silverglade of the Center for Science in the Public Interest, a Washington consumer advocacy group.

For the first time, all food packages, including meats, will have to show how much fat, saturated fat and cholesterol, dietary fiber, and sodium they contain—information deemed vital for consumers interested in reducing their risk of heart disease and cancer.

"For years labels gave consumers the good news about the percentage of vitamins and minerals a food contributes to the amount one should be eating per day," said Silverglade. "But they never really told consumers the bad news about how much fat and cholesterol a food contributes. The new label will do that."

For instance a package of macaroni and cheese would say a half cup serving contains 13 grams of total fat. That's 20 percent of the daily value of 65 grams of fat considered healthy for a 2,000 calorie daily diet. The label does the math and should serve as a useful tool to help consumers select a healthier diet.

Here are some new government definitions for common terms:

FREE: Less than five calories; less than 0.5 grams of sugar; less than 5 milligrams of sodium; less than 0.5 grams of fat; less than 2 milligrams of cholesterol and 2 grams of saturated fat per serving.

LOW: Less than 140 milligrams of sodium; less than 40 calories; 3 grams or less of fat per serving size.

HIGH: Benefits consumer by providing more than 20 percent of daily recommended amount as in high-fiber.

REDUCED or LESS: At least 25 percent less than the original product in sodium, calories, fat, saturated fat, or cholesterol.

LIGHT: If product has more than 50 percent calories from fat, light means at least a 50 percent reduction in fat. If it has less than 50 percent calories from fat, product can be either 50 percent reduced in fat or have one third less calories.

LIGHT IN SODIUM: Reduces sodium of original product by 50 percent.

Your advertising should help the consumer understand the benefits of this labeling system.

Great Guiltless Flavor

Fat is the word among health-conscious Americans, and it's no longer a comment about weight. No, Americans who want to live healthier lives are convinced that reducing fat in the diet is one of the most important things they can do. Enter new kinds of snack foods that promise to satisfy America's need for munching while delivering only tiny amounts of fat.

A popular brand in this small but growing market is Guiltless Gourmet, a company based in Austin, Texas. In 1989 a small group of slightly overweight snack food devotees (as company literature would have it) with expectations as high as their cholesterol counts, scoured grocery shelves for snacks that wouldn't coat their arteries with bad things. No such luck. So they created their own tortilla chips and so was born the family of Guiltless Gourmet no-oil chips, dips, and salsas. Guiltless Gourmet chips are baked, not fried. You taste the full flavor of natural corn. A bag of fried chips can be up to 35 percent oil by weight. But in a 7-ounce bag of Guiltless Gourmet Tortilla Chips you get as many chips as you find in a 10-ounce bag of fat fried chips. These chips are lighter because they have no oil. In a serving of about 22 chips, you'll only get 1.5 grams of fat. Low! Other products include no-fat bean dips, quesos, and salsas.

Electronic Kid Alarm

The old fashioned way to locate your lost youngster is to shout the child's name at a volume that blows out store windows. The new way is to track down your kid electronically. The Child Safety Corporation of Miami markets a child tracking monitor system. The system is a battery-operated transmitter worn with a safety pin by the kid and a receiver carried by the parent. Each system sells for $99.

The device allows parents to log in an alarm range of 30 to 60 feet on the child's transmitter, which he or she wears like a pendant about the size of a silver dollar. If a child wanders further than the preset range, an alarm is triggered on the parent's receiver. The alarm also sounds if the transmitter is switched off or immersed in water.

Mrs. Andrews: Spiritualist, Psychic Reader, Advisor

She will foresee with her eyes. Can help solve all kinds of problems: separations, business, marriages, affairs of the heart. Specializing in tarot card readings, astrology readings, crystal readings. During many years of practice, she has brought together in marriage and reunited more separated people than any other five mediums combined. For many she has located buried treasures, located absent persons, overcome many rivals. Mrs. Andrews does not ask you who you are; she tells you who you are and why you came. She tells you how to be what you want to be. Do you fear disease? Do you give up in despair? Does persistent bad luck follow you? Spells, unnatural conditions, and evil influences of all kinds can be overcome by getting advice and aid from a reliable adviser who bears a reputation for her honesty and integrity. All readings are by appointment only. Look for her name on the sign. Open 7 days a week, 9 a.m. to 10 p.m. Full life reading, past-present-future. Regularly $20. Only $10 with coupon.

How can you write an ad about this service which does not overpromise on results?

A Handy Guide in Paperback

The Toilets of New York by Ken Eichenbaum. A handy guide to the best and the worst public and semi-public relief stations for those with a need to know. Includes walking and trotting maps. Over 100 detailed descriptions of men's and women's toilets all over Manhattan.

Comments: "If you're in the Big Apple with a Small Bladder, you need this book!" "Data on cleanliness, wheelchair access, number of stalls! This book gets four stars!" Funny, but practical. At your bookstore or fax order 414-354-7714.

Pizza Chef Gourmet Pizza

Locally owned and operated. Recipes prepared fresh on premise. Fresh herbs and spices used in sauce and on pizzas. Gourmet salads are tossed using fresh romaine lettuce with homemade salad dressings. Bake their own sub buns and offer pizzas on freshly made whole wheat dough or traditional hand tossed dough. All pizzas available baked or unbaked. All made to order.

Eat in, delivery, or pickup. Beer and wine on premise. Traditional pizza toppings plus "designer pizzas." Garden, Caesar, Antipasto, Southwestern Chicken salads. Set this operation apart from the giants: Pizza Hut, Dominos, etc.

Resorts Sportswear

A new line of exclusive designs on T-shirts and sweatshirts, representing the most popular resorts in the world.

Fifteen beach resorts captured on T-shirts of top-of-the-line Hanes beefy 100 percent cotton in colors plus white and ash: Acapulco, Bahamas, Bimini, Cancun, Hawaii, Jamaica, Key West, Malibu, Nassau, Rio de Janeiro, St. Croix, St. Tropez, San Diego, West Palm Beach, and Venice Beach.

Large and Extra Large, $19.95

Ten luxurious 9-ounce heavyweight 50-50 cotton-polyester blend, long-sleeve sweatshirts in ten original ski resort designs: Aspen, Breckenridge, Gstaad, Innsbruck, Purgatory, St. Moritz, Snowbird, Snowmass, Steamboat Springs, Vail. White or ash only, Large and Extra Large, $31.95.

Available by mail only. Phone 1-800-000-0000 for color catalog or to place order.

Soundmate Personal Safety Device

This small plastic cylinder fits into the palm of the hand. Simply squeeze it and it screams for the owner. Loud and long. Rugged enough to withstand shock. Non-violent design cannot be used against the owner (as in Mace). Can be legally carried on an airplane. Has unique battery tester. Individually coded deactivation—it stops only when you want it to. $129.95. Full 30-day money back guarantee and full 3-year warranty. Call 1-800-882-5778, ext. NY 122 to order.

Every 17 seconds another violent assault occurs. The SoundMate has the power of a unique, piercing 120 decibel "super siren" that oscillates and strobes from 12 outlets.

Phonejak

Turns electrical wall outlet into a phone extension. No installation required. Uses ordinary electrical wiring as telephone circuit. Better sound quality than the best cordless phones. Pay no fees to the phone company; save hundreds of dollars each year. Up to twenty telephone extensions from one number. Works with any phone device, cord or cordless, speaker phones, answering machines, fax machines, computer modems, etc. $79 per system (includes transmitter and moveable receiver/extension device. Additional receiver/extension devices for more phone outlets, $49 each.

The Value of Independent Higher Education

America's private colleges are doing well but have decided to allocate some pooled funds to advertise their advantages and perhaps increase inquiries and enrollments. One region, the Midwest, has combined its efforts through the Midwest Partnership of Independent Colleges (Illinois, Indiana, Michigan, Ohio, and Wisconsin), and will develop a print campaign to attract students.

Print advertising will run in regional editions of national news weeklies, which have agreed to run some of the ads as a public service. Here is some information about the Midwest group of private, or independent, colleges:

They perform an important service to our society, although many of their contributions go unrecognized, perhaps because of the stronger "clout" of major state-funded colleges and universities.

They have an average faculty-student ratio of 14:1. Their enrollments represent all races and income brackets.

The Midwest group enrolls 390,000 students, of which 48,000 are minorities. Eighty percent of students receive some form of financial aid, 20 percent of which comes from the schools' budgets—double that of ten years ago.

They award 30 percent of all bachelor's degrees in the region and 66 percent of their students go on to post-graduate studies.

They contribute an estimated $10 billion and 350,000 jobs each year to their local economies.

Six out of ten Fortune 500 CEOs attended an independent college.

It is clear, therefore, that these colleges are strong contributors to the educational, cultural, and economic well-being of our society.

The Audience: Several choices are appropriate, but for this campaign, you should think in terms of parents of junior and senior high school students in the Midwest region served by this group of colleges. Since financial aid is available, it is important to reach middle and low-middle income families, especially those who might find it difficult to believe they can afford to send children with academic potential to anything but a large state university, where tuition tends to be more affordable and where grants are sometimes available for lower income levels. And since roughly 5 out of 40 students enrolled are minorities, this is an audience that should not be overlooked. Essentially, the message should be written to appeal to whites and minorities who believe in the value of diversity, and who see or can be made to see the value in low faculty-student ratios and other appealing features of these schools which set them apart from competition.

The Competition: This is a broad category which needs to be addressed. People in the target market might consider large state universities, community and technical colleges (lower cost), or you might think of the competition as not going to college at all. Remember that this is an era of inflated costs for everything, and education is no exception. Students from this pool will almost certainly have to finance part of their education, either by working or through grants and scholarships. The general perception is that the smaller and more private the school, the less opportunity for any sort of financial support.

2. New Product

Think up a new product that satisfies certain needs of a particular group of consumers. Use the following guidelines to help you determine what your new product should offer. Then develop an advertising campaign for it.

a. What is the nature of the product? Give uses, description of packaging, approximate selling price, type of store carrying it, sizes available, general shape and appearance.

b. What is its name? What does the name signify?

c. Who is the target audience, in demographic, lifestyle, and relationship terms? Is there a secondary audience?

d. What products will this one replace for this audience? In what ways will it be better than the products they were using before?

e. What is the key selling idea for this product?

3. Campaign

Using one of the products or services in this section, or another product or service you have been assigned, prepare a multimedia creative campaign and present it to the class. It should include, minimally, the following items:

1. A comprehensive creative platform that includes a well-defined strategy.
2. A :60 radio AND a :30 (or another :60) radio script.
4. A :30 TV storyboard
5. A direct response folder with letter and envelope
6. An outdoor board.

Your project may be judged on the following criteria:

1. ***Strategy.*** Is the strategy appropriate for the product, competition, target market?

2. ***Attention.*** Does each message come through loud and clear, whether through the headline, visual, opening shot, or first words of the piece?

3. ***Continuity.*** Do the pieces work as one? Is there an obvious theme running throughout the campaign, with each part contributing to the overall strategic goals?

4. ***Liveliness.*** Does the "passion of creativity" come blazing through each message? Does the writer believe as much in the product as he/she wants the audience to? Is the writing clear, concise, and lively?

Suggested Readings

Agency Book, The. Vol. III. Gavin Brackenridge & Co., Inc. 1988.

Arlen, Michael. *Thirty Seconds.* Penguin Books, 1981.

Baker, Stephen. *Systematic Approach to Advertising Creativity.* McGraw-Hill, 1979.

Baldwin, Huntley. *Creating Effective TV Commercials.* Crain Books, 1982.

Berg, Thomas L. *Mismarketing: Case Histories of Marketing Misfires.* Anchor Books, 1971.

Bureau of the Census, Washington, D.C. 20223. Phone number: 301-763-5820. Ask whatever question you have and it will be referred to the appropriate staff. One staff specifically deals with racial and ethnic statistics. This source can supply information about trends and the makeup of minority populations.

Charmasson, Henri. *The Name Is the Game.* Dow Jones Irwin, 1988.

Cialdini, Robert. *Influence: The New Psychology of Modern Persuasion.* Quill, 1984.

Crompton, Alastair. *The Craft of Copywriting.* Prentice-Hall, 1979.

Fortini-Campbell, Lisa. *Hitting the Sweet Spot.* The Copy Workshop, 1993.

Gill, Bob. *Forget All the Rules about Graphic Design.* Watson-Guptill, 1981.

Goss, Tom. *Print Casebooks 7 (1987–8). The Best in Advertising.* RC Publications, 1988.

Gray, John. *Men Are from Mars, Women Are from Venus.* Harper Collins, 1992.

Harper, Paul. *Working the Territory.* Prentice-Hall, 1985.

Herzbrun, David. *Playing in Traffic on Madison Avenue.* Business One Irwin, 1990.

Keil, John M. *How to Zig in a Zagging World.* Wiley, 1988.

Likeable Advertising. Doner, 1988.

Lyons, John. *Guts: Advertising from the Inside Out.* Amacom, 1987.

Newcomb, John. *The Book of Graphic Problem Solving.* R.P. Bowker, 1984.

O'Toole, John. *The Trouble with Advertising.* Chelsea House, 1981.

Pate, Russ. *Adman.* E-Hart Press, 1988.

Reeves, Rosser. *Reality in Advertising.* Knopf, 1961.

Ries, Al, and Jack Trout. *Positioning: The Battle for Your Mind.* McGraw-Hill, 1986.

Roman, Ken, and Jane Maas. *The New How to Advertise.* St. Martin's Press, 1992.

Schwartz, Tony. *The Responsive Chord.* Anchor Books, 1984.

Settle, Robert, and Pamela Alreck. *Why They Buy: American Consumers Inside and Out.* Wiley, 1986.

Tannen, Deborah. *You Just Don't Understand.* Ballantine Books, 1990.

vonOech, Roger. *A Whack on the Side of the Head.* Warner Books, 1983.

Ward, Dick. *Creative Ad Design and Illustration.* North Light Books, 1988.

Glossary/Index